One Hundred Years
of Kibbutz Life

One Hundred Years of Kibbutz Life

A Century of Crises and Reinvention

Michal Palgi
Shulamit Reinharz

Transaction Publishers
New Brunswick (U.S.A.) and London (U.K.)

Library of Congress Catalog Number: 2011004561
ISBN: 978-1-4128-4229-7
Printed in the United States of America

Library of Congress Cataloging-in-Publication Data

   One hundred years of kibbutz life: a century of crises
and reinvention / Michal Palgi and Shulamit Reinharz, editors.
      p. cm.
   Includes index.
   ISBN 978-1-4128-4229-7
   1. Kibbutzim—History.   2. Kibbutzim in literature—History and
criticism.
   I. Palgi, Michal. II. Reinharz, Shulamit.
   HX742.2.A3O54 2011
   307.77'6095694—dc22

                                                    2011004561

Contents

Preface

The Rise, Fall, and Unexpected Revitalization of the Kibbutz

Michal Palgi and Shulamit Reinharz

Contemporary joke: A reporter visits Israel and wants to get a feel for how things are going. The reporter stops someone on the street and asks, "How would you sum up the current situation?" The pedestrian takes a minute and says, "Good." The reporter is annoyed. "What do you mean by 'good'? That's only one word. Give me at least another word." So, the person turns to him and says, "Not good."

This joke highlights the dilemma one faces when approaching the topic of assessing the kibbutz on its one hundredth anniversary. Is the situation "good" or "not good"? Or both? After examining the most recent social science research and humanistic explorations that address this question, we have concluded that the answer is "the kibbutz has survived and is likely to survive because it is capable of changing dramatically." We call the changed kibbutz "reconstituted." The reader then has a choice—to argue that our notion of the "reconstituted kibbutz" is so far away from the original concept, that it can no longer be called a kibbutz. But to take this approach would defy the recent examinations of kibbutzim by high-ranking government agencies and would contradict the understanding of several hundred thousand people who live in what they call kibbutzim.

Or the reader could agree with us and say that the history of the kibbutz is a history of changes, some motivated from within and some a response to outside pressures. To date, none of these changes—though they are monumental—have led to five essential actions that would compel us to say that the kibbutz is dead: (1) the total disbanding of a majority of current kibbutzim, (2) the departure of a vast majority of kibbutz members from their kibbutzim, (3) the non-arrival of any new members to replenish the places of those who have left, (4) the complete halt in the formation of any new kibbutzim, and (5) the division of all kibbutz property into parts that would be owned by individuals who formerly constituted the kibbutz. If these five criteria are used to determine the life or death of the kibbutz movement, then we must say that the kibbutz *system* is still alive and that the rudimentary factor that determines if an *individual* kibbutz is alive is the presence of an adequate number of members in a given place to sustain the kibbutz in some way. And many seem to be more than just "alive." In a September 2009 article, Dina Kraft wrote:

> Some kibbutzim are struggling for their survival. But more are undergoing a renaissance as they liberalize policies of communalism. With their reputation for high quality of life, kibbutzim are finding more and more younger people are choosing to stay on the kibbutz and newcomers from the city are eager to move in . . . Kibbutz Ma'abarot is . . . flooded with second-generation members who want to return to live here with their spouses and young families. The wave of returnees to Ma'abarot began about a decade ago . . . Kibbutz Mishmar Ha'Sharon has a waiting list of people wanting to move in . . . The kibbutz expects 30 percent growth in the next two years . . . The recovery for the kibbutzim has been striking. Less than 10 years ago, about half of Israel's kibbutzim were considered financially unstable. Today that number is down to about 15.[1]

Social science has a terrible record of prediction. This shortcoming runs across the board: *psychologists* cannot predict whether someone will become violent again after incarceration for a violent crime followed by long-term rehabilitation activities; *sociologists* cannot predict which marriages will last or which societal grumblings will turn into massive social protests; *political scientists* have a poor record of predicting election outcomes and identifying who the candidates might be in an upcoming election; and *economists*, perhaps the worst group of all at predictions, were unable to predict the global economic crisis we just experienced. Ironically, *economics* is the social science most heavily based in quantitative reasoning, and thus it is burdened with the expectation of having the strongest predictive powers. After the fact, of course, social scientists (like everyone else) are very wise and can point out how various trends "inexorably" led to the present. Perhaps this is all for the better. If humankind were able to predict the future, what would the pleasure be in living? If people knew when they would die, how could they live? And if some individuals predicted an unpleasant future with certainty, how would others react? Would they heed the warning, bury their heads in the sand, and reject the message as in the Cassandra myth, or even shoot the messenger?

The editors of this volume are no exception to the general rule concerning social predictions. We, too, *cannot* predict the future. But we *can* point to various trends that produced the present. And we can pinpoint what the issues are around which the future hinges. We can suggest terms to clarify the situation. We face the problem of not being predictors head-on in this volume by posing the key question vis-à-vis the kibbutz: "[I]s the experiment in socialist agrarianism still viable or do we now mean by the term 'kibbutz' an industrial program defined by the capitalist or free market enterprise?"[2]

This book is not a celebratory volume about the flourishing of the kibbutz movement, nor is it a eulogy about the kibbutz demise. Rather it is a collection of voices (psychologists, sociologists, writers, economists, artists, and more) that describe the *unexpected* revitalization of the kibbutz. Looking back at Israeli history, it would have been easy for kibbutz theorists to predict decline as soon as they realized that the Israeli public was *not* flocking to kibbutzim as potential members. Even at its peak of about 7 percent of the population, the kibbutzim were a small-scale jewel rather than the major vehicle for building the country, as the cities were. But what these experts could not predict was that the trajectory was jagged, with ups and downs in terms of kibbutz population size and the relevance of the kibbutz model for the development of Israeli society. Little did anyone suspect that a specific countertrend of reinvention[3] had taken root as early as the first years of the kibbutz, and that this countertrend was strong enough to hold decline at bay.

In 1990, a little over twenty years ago, as the kibbutz movement marked its eightieth anniversary, people raised the same question they are raising today—what does the future hold? One commentator for *The Jewish Post International*, who was also a member of Deganya, wrote: "There will be a continuation of the development of a viable alternative to urbanization to meet the challenges of modern life. [True] There will be continued fostering of the extended family, with aging parents and their adult children and grandchildren living side by side, linked, but independent. [Partially true] There will be an internalized code of behavior that, while it cannot guarantee perfect social justice, it can organize society so that no one is left out. [Not true[4]]"[5]

The combined voices of the contributors to this volume discuss the ideals, hopes, frustrations, disappointments, and reconstruction efforts that brought a few solutions to the fading kibbutz ideals. These solutions are not popular among many kibbutz members, but they demonstrate growth and development of the kibbutz on its one hundredth birthday. They also suggest an answer to the question of why kibbutz-like communities in other countries have disappeared, for the most part. Those societies *did not adapt* in the way the current kibbutz is adapting. According to Yoram Kroll, the average life span of a commune anywhere in the world is seventy years. If this is the case, then the kibbutz movement is truly at a tipping point.[6] The rise of the kibbutz and its "fall" after seventy years of impressive existence have brought about fierce debates and arguments within and outside of the kibbutz. It seems that in the public imagination, the early kibbutz years (i.e., the first four decades) have become a kind of Garden of Eden (when all of us were young) and the later decline is the expulsion (when all of us are all old). This exaggerated image has taken on mythic proportions that make it difficult for people to see what is really going on today. Through the inclusion of a variety of studies, this book hopes to clarify and demystify, rather than justify and fantasize.

When secular Israelis discuss the place of the Jewish religion in Israeli society, they frequently bring up the following widely held attitude: Although they, themselves, do not want to engage in any Jewish ritual practices, they want those who *do* so, to do it in an orthodox fashion. Their words are usually something like this: "I don't want to go to synagogue, but if I *were* to go, it would be to the kind of synagogues my grandfather would go to." It seems to be the same with kibbutzim. Many Israelis do not want to belong to kibbutzim; at the same time, they want the kibbutzim that do exist to have classic characteristics. Many kibbutz members and nonmembers are disappointed at what they consider "the lost ideals." They mourn the present pseudo-kibbutz.[7] A few others have adopted a kind of Darwinian perspective that sees hope in change. Given the large amount of media attention this topic has received,[8] we can surmise that the kibbutz still has a significant place in the Israeli self-concept. In such a situation, research and public policy are all the more useful.

It is easy to understand why so many Israelis care about the future of the kibbutz even if they don't want to join one. After all, the early kibbutzim played an instrumental and elite role in the absorption of Jewish immigrants from all over the world, in the conversion of untilled land for agricultural use, in the creation of a classless society, in the staking of residential outposts and *de facto* borders, and in the training of the

State of Israel's first generation of leaders. In other words, the kibbutz had a major role in shaping the New Jew, the forerunner of the current Israeli. For practical purposes, the debate over whether the "new kibbutz" is "still a kibbutz" was settled recently by the Israeli government who charged the 2002 Public Committee for the Classification of Kibbutzim to define when a kibbutz stops being a kibbutz. According to that report, which is referred to in many chapters of this book, the kibbutz is *changed but exists*.

Until now, kibbutzim have been classified as *identity-based* communities where members bond together to assert a shared ideal. Those who worry about the future of the kibbutz are concerned that the kibbutz will turn into a *geographical* community, i.e., a group of people living in a particular local area with no common ideology or shared culture, and with little meaningful face-to-face contact. Identity-based communities, by contrast, act according to their common ideology, culture, and religion. As is well-known, the entire Western world is concerned that social ties are eroding everywhere as people increasingly become mobile and live in areas of convenience rather than places of meaning. As society loses cohesion on the communal level, we begin to "bowl alone,"[9] we marry late and divorce early, and society actually becomes more dangerous because there are few common restraints that we allow to bind us. The "demise of the kibbutz" conversation is thus a small pebble in this larger pond of despair at growing international anomie.

There are many other reasons that the "kibbutz question" grabs peoples' attention. The kibbutz "dilemma" relates to a wide array of international conversations including the possibility of "green living and green business,"[10] the challenge of ethically managed "international migrant labor,"[11] the conundrum of optimal forms of education,[12] the ineluctable goal of "gender equality," the necessity of "sustainable economies,"[13] the necessity of the comparative desirability of multicultural or unicultural societies,[14] and even the salience of political questions concerning the place of Jews and Arabs in Israel, the Middle East, and the global arena. As Lawrence Joffee wrote in his overview of "100 years of kibbutzim," ". . . Eshbal, the newest kibbutz of all [since 2007] has housed the much-praised Galil Jewish–Arab School, a haven of peace and mutual enrichment for two hundred children of all faiths. Could this be a model for the future?"[15] Here is a new (or an old–new) goal—to create rapprochement between Israeli Arabs and Israeli Jews. At a recent talk in London on a certain aspect of kibbutz life, a member of the audience asked me (SR) how I could have participated in the exploitation and oppression of the Palestinians, by conducting this study.[16] "Surely, the kibbutz members stole the Palestinians' land." For the questioner, this accusation, posed as a statement rather than a question, overrode any other question concerning the kibbutz. For him, the kibbutz was part of a different narrative.

Because the public keeps its eye on the kibbutz in light of all of these frameworks, it is fascinated by trying to determine what the kibbutz augurs for the future. Researchers at the Centre for Innovative & Entrepreneurial Leadership have come up with a four-part developmental schema that can apply to kibbutz history: the vision phase, the actualization phase, the chaos phase, and . . . what is next?[17] *Is it the emergence or the demise phase*? Kibbutz researchers claim that the kibbutz is now at the *emergence* phase, but that its future is enigmatic and uncertain. And since each kibbutz was founded in a different year, even unto the present, each kibbutz (or group of kibbutzim) can be functioning at a different phase in the same chronological year. We, the editors, have reviewed as much literature as we could and concur that the oldest kibbutzim have, indeed, experienced these four stages. We believe the future is one of *increasing experimentations* rather than rigid adherence to structures that no longer serve the needs of the member. We offer this book to those who wish to find out how we reached these conclusions and to join in this conversation.

Notes

1. Dina Kraft, "By Adapting, Kibbutz Movement Finds Success," September 25 (2009). http://jta.org/news/article/2009/09/25/1008166/by-adapting-kibbutz-movement-finds-success.
2. The editors thank Irving Louis Horowitz for this succinct version of the "key question."
3. "The Kibbutz Reinvents Itself" is the cover story of *The Jerusalem Report*, June 21 (2010).
4. On the topic of "no one being left out," see Esti Ahronovitz, "Forgotten Fathers," *Haaretz Magazine*, June 25 (2010): 16–19.
5. Allan E. Shapiro, "Perspective on the Kibbutz at 80," *The Jerusalem Post International*, October 27 (1990): 11, 14.
6. Amiram Cohen, "From Going Concern to Growing Concern," *Haaretz*, February 26 (2010): B7.
7. Leonard Fein, "An Experiment That, for a Time, Did Not Fail," *Forward*, January 5 (2010).
8. Ben Harris, "Once-Failing Kibbutz Pins Hopes for Revival on Conservative Judaism," *JTA*, January 5 (2010).
9. Robert D. Putnam, "Bowling Alone: America's Declining Social Capital," *Journal of Democracy* 1 (1995): 65–78, and *Bowling Alone: The Collapse and Revival of American Community*. New York: Simon & Schuster, 2000.

10. "Israel's Kibbutzim Shift From Red to Green, as They Drift Away from Socialism, the Collectives Are Launching Eco-conscious Businesses," *Newsweek*, Bloomberg. June 24 (2010), and Aviva Lori, "The New Pioneers," *Haaretz Magazine*, October 24 (2008): 8–11.

11. Israel Drori, *Foreign Workers in Israel: Global Perspectives* (SUNY Series in Israeli Studies, Albany, NY: SUNY Press).

12. *Children of the Sun*, film written and directed by Ran Tal, 2007.

13. Larry Derfner, "Kibbutzim Make a Comeback: A Strong Dose of Capitalist Individualism Is Saving the Once Socialist Kibbutz Movement," *The International Jerusalem Post*, September 12–18 (2008): 14–17. And Amiram Cohen, "The Ideology Is Dead. Long Live the Deal," *Haaretz Weekly*, April 17 (2009): A7.

14. "The Kibbutz No Longer Scares Them. The Opposite," *Arnon Lapid*. An entire group of Russian academics joined Kibbutz Dahlia.

15. See Lawrence Joffee, "100 Years of Kibbutzim," *Jewish Quarterly*, July 23 (2010).

16. See Lawrence Joffee, "100 Years of Kibbutzim," *Jewish Quarterly*, July 23 (2010).

17. *Communities "Life Cycle" Matrix*. Centre for Innovative & Entrepreneurial Leadership Version 2.2—2010.

Introduction

The Kibbutz at One Hundred: A Century of Crises and Reinvention

Michal Palgi and Shulamit Reinharz

The Kibbutz and Its Multiple Definitions over Time

The years 1909–2009 mark a century of kibbutz life, a century of achievements, failures, and challenges. Regardless of this mixed record, it is undeniable that the impact of kibbutzim (pl.) on Israeli society has been substantial—kibbutz communities and members were involved in building and defending the country and, subsequently, in developing its economy, culture, and arts according to the kibbutz values. Communes and collectives in other countries have not had a similar impact on their environments; nor have many lasted as long as the kibbutz has, to date. During the hundred years of its existence, the kibbutz as a concept and as a reality underwent many changes, as did the country as a whole both before the establishment of the State of Israel in 1948 and since then. Most significant, perhaps, is that for political, economic, social, and demographic reasons, the kibbutz has slowly moved from the nation's consensual ideal to its romanticized periphery (for more details see Near, 1997). Many articles have been appearing in the Israeli press predicting the demise of the kibbutz as an ideal. Although anyone familiar with kibbutz history knows that in the past, nearly every change in the kibbutz led to doomsday predictions, those who write in this vein today claim that now we *finally* have come to the actual period of its complete demise. The kibbutz, they claim, is an anachronism: although functional in the early years, it is irrelevant today.

The point of this book and its twenty chapters is not to decide the debate as to whether the kibbutz will be viable in the future, but rather to describe a host of changes that have actually occurred and to try to ascertain their meaning. As this introduction will make clear, the kibbutz population has *increased* lately in terms of demography and capital, a point that is frequently overlooked in the debate about kibbutz viability. It turns out that the kibbutz has become a very attractive place for young people who want community life, particularly when that life is stripped of the early austerity measures. Like the founders who tried to establish a particular society grounded in certain principles, so too newcomers to the kibbutz want to establish a new idealistic society with specific social and economic arrangements.

On the other hand, in order for a group of people to remain a kibbutz, it has to vouch for its members' standard of living and to have all its assets owned by the community (see chapter by Ben-Rafael that explains how housing does not have to be collectively owned). Although the contemporary kibbutz may not be what the pioneers idealized, it is a structure that has adapted well to the current reality. In addition, the kibbutz movement is supportive of a whole range of new ventures in communal living (see chapter by Yuval Dror). To summarize our conclusion, the kibbutz is not dead, just different.

In 2009, the Kibbutz Federation counted 267 kibbutzim scattered throughout Israel from the northernmost areas near the Lebanese and Syrian borders to the Red Sea and south near the tourist city of Eilat and east toward the Jordanian border. In fact, until 1967, kibbutzim, as opposed to other types of settlement such as towns, demarcated all the borders of Israel. In this sense they had both military and geographic significance for the country. Most of the kibbutzim were formed by international or Israel-based groups of young people (eighteen to twenty years of age) who had participated in various Zionist youth movements, such as Hashomer Hatzair, Habonim, Dror, Hechalutz Hatzair, Akiva, Gordonia, and Blau Weiss, each with its own particular ideology. Subsequent kibbutz membership came from natural population increase and from new groups tied to youth movements. Today the population size of kibbutzim varies from about thirty to fifteen hundred inhabitants with an average of about four hundred inhabitants. Many communities are top-heavy with older people and an inadequate number of youngsters (see chapter by Yasmin Asaf and Israel Doron for a discussion of aging). Kibbutzim constitute a mere 2.1 percent (120,000) of the current Jewish population in Israel, yet their contribution to the national economy amounts to 40 percent in agriculture, 7 percent in industrial output, 9 percent in industrial export, and 10 percent in tourism (The Economic Unit of the Kibbutz Movement, 2009). On the local scene, therefore, their economy is strong. Kibbutz members and ex-members are overrepresented in Israeli leadership positions in the fields of government, industry, and the military (Near, 1997) among others.

The kibbutz represents a new model of social life, ". . . a comprehensive system in which members live, raise children, work and create, grow old and pass away. In fact, the kibbutz is 'a microcosm of an entire society'" (Golomb and Katz, 1971, p. 7) without courts or police or full-fledged hospitals and some other institutions. In the early days of the founding of kibbutzim until approximately 1950, its members regarded working the land as a central purpose. Ideology was highly significant because the kibbutz was always the "other" society, the alternative that needed to be defined and justified. As kibbutz ideology developed, it drew on Zionist, socialist, and humanist values and integrated them to form a coherent ideology of its own (for a discussion of communes in other contexts, see chapter by Yaacov Oved). The stated goals of kibbutz founders were to *cultivate the land* from its wild condition, *build a Jewish national entity in Israel* (Palestine at the time), and *create a just society*. The introductory section of "Kibbutz Regulations" (The Kibbutz By-Laws) states: "The kibbutz is a free association of people for purposes of settlement, absorption of new immigrants, maintaining a cooperative society based on community ownership of property, self-sufficiency in labor, equality and cooperation in all areas of production, consumption and education" (http://www.kibbutz.org.il/mishpatit/takanon-t/980101. takanon-t.htm [Hebrew]). A key component of this definition is the word "free." People are *free* to leave the kibbutz, although not all people are free to become members—they have to prove their ability to live a collective life style. Similarly, "The kibbutz considers itself an inseparable part of the Hebrew workers' movement in Israel, which aspires to establish the Jewish people concentrating in Israel as a working society built on foundations of social cooperation" (http://www.kibbutz.org.il/mishpatit/ takanon-t/980101.takanon-t.htm [Hebrew]).

Thus the main values upon which the kibbutz was based begin with *equality* among members as well as among kibbutzim (i.e., all kibbutz members receive goods from the community according to their needs and contribute to it according to their ability). From this idea stemmed some other important practices such as giving equal value to *all types of work* and providing mutual financial guarantees and help *within* the kibbutz and *between* kibbutz communities. The kibbutz movement as a whole aimed to attain a standard of living that was equal in all kibbutzim. Thus economically strong kibbutzim helped weaker ones via taxes they paid to the kibbutz movement. A second important value concerned decision-making. Kibbutzim opted to govern themselves with *direct* (rather than representational) *democracy* as well as rotation of officeholders both in kibbutz society and in the economic units. A third basic value was *self-labor*, which was rooted in Zionist ideology and the socialist ideal of not exploiting cheap paid labor, particularly Jews from development towns and Arab labor at first but increasingly foreign labor. That meant that members had to tend to the needs of the community and the economy by themselves. In practice, the principle of self-labor was applied to a greater extent in education and less so in production (see chapter by Marjorie Strom).

Nevertheless, differences in the ideals among the various kibbutzim led them to separate and organize into different kibbutz movements. Thus in 1927, less than two decades since the founding of the earliest long-lasting kibbutz, Deganya, two kibbutz movements (i.e., associations) were formed. Hakibbutz Hameuchad believed in establishing big kibbutzim, open to absorbing newcomers. These kibbutzim intended to develop an economy based on a variety of production branches, not solely on agriculture. Hakibbutz Hameuchad kibbutzim aimed to serve the needs of the country and to exercise autonomy in handling their social and cultural life, as well as their work and economy. This organization became the biggest kibbutz movement until a schism in 1951 spun off an additional movement—Ichud Hakvutzot Vehakibbutzim. The root of the schism was political: the kibbutzim in the new movement or off shoot adhered to the Labor Party (Mapai), while the others adhered to a more Socialist Party (Mapam). After thirty years, the two movements reunited. The second kibbutz movement formed in 1927 was Hakibbutz Haartzi. This movement required ideological and political unity among kibbutz members and adhered to the most leftist political orientation of all the movements. In 1929, a third kibbutz movement was formed—Chever Hakvutzot—based on the principles of Deganya, particularly the goal of maintaining small, intimate kibbutzim. In 1951, Chever Hakvutzot joined Ichud Hakvutzot. In 1935, the Religious Kibbutz Movement, which formed seventeen religious kibbutzim, was established. In 1999, Kibbutz Artzi joined the other secular kibbutz movement to form the United Kibbutz Movement.

The Kibbutz Economy:
From Agriculture to Industry and Tourism

As is true of economies throughout the world, the Israeli economy at the beginning of the twentieth century was based primarily on agriculture. But unlike the United States, for example, that experienced rapid industrialization, kibbutzim did not institutionalize industrialization across the board until the 1960s. Industrial innovation provoked many debates about the way industry should be organized in line with kibbutz values and the kibbutz way of life (see chapter by Menachem Topel). Ultimately, kibbutz members developed a pattern of industrial organization that differed from that operating in society at large. This unusual organizational structure drew on kibbutz values, social structure, and culture. Industrialization was introduced into the kibbutz economy within this ideological framework.

Kibbutz industry began around the time of World War II, when 13.7 percent of production workers in kibbutzim worked in industry (Rosner and Palgi, 1977). At that time, industrial plants developed from small workshops that were designed to repair tractors and pipe systems. These workshops met a real need on the kibbutz and produced a skilled workforce. However, in the 1960s, a major rise in the *rate* of industrialization occurred: of the 320 kibbutz industrial plants operating in 1981, only 34 percent were established before 1960 (Association of Kibbutz Industry, 1982). In the 1960s, changes in economic and demographic conditions hampered agricultural development and provided the impetus for industrial growth. At the time, the main reasons for the economic turn to industrialization included a mix of surpluses, shortages, policies, demography, and self-actualization needs. Specifically:

1. The market was saturated with agricultural products.
2. A shortage of land and water obviated an increase in agricultural production, and the government-imposed production quota of various crops was insufficient to support the members of various kibbutzim. At the same time, the kibbutz population was growing at a rate of 2–3 percent per year.
3. Israeli government policy supported industrialization, particularly in border settlements. Kibbutzim comprised a large proportion of border settlements, making them eligible for government benefits (long-term loans and grants) for the advancement of industrialization.
4. Older kibbutz members, unfit for physical work in agriculture, were seeking alternative places of work (Reinharz, 2011).
5. Kibbutz members with technological abilities (especially the young) were seeking work in which they could employ these abilities (Palgi, 1998).

In recent years, the kibbutzim have developed a tourism industry that includes hotels and/or bed-and-breakfast facilities, craft shops, museums, galleries, and other tourist services (see chapter by Amit-Cohen). These sites are located throughout the country and include central booking and other conveniences.

Crises in the Kibbutz Economy

The transformations in Israeli society, together with the economic crisis in the mid-1980s, led kibbutz communities to introduce changes that eroded their basic values (see chapter by Alon Pauker). At the same time, the weakening collective ideology of the younger generations and newcomers to the kibbutz made the kibbutz more amenable to change (see chapter by Eliezer Ben-Rafael and Menachem Topel). Taken as a whole, these changes represent an erosion of the barrier between society at large and the "other" society of the kibbutz. New internal regulations in five areas served to lower the barrier between the kibbutz and the surrounding society:

1. Kibbutz societies legitimated *paid hired labor* in both production and education, thus forfeiting the value of self-labor.
2. Kibbutz societies *opened the children's houses to non-kibbutz children*, thus *diluting* one of the most important channels for passing on kibbutz values to the next generation.
3. Kibbutz societies legitimated and encouraged members to *work outside the kibbutz* in order to increase the cash flow.
4. Kibbutz societies *partnered with non-kibbutz investors* in kibbutz enterprises, that is, investors with a different set of values.
5. Kibbutz societies *rented kibbutz apartments* to nonmembers and *built residential neighborhoods adjacent to the kibbutz*, neighborhoods that do not follow the kibbutz way of life (see chapters by Zeev Greenberg and by Igal Charney and Michal Palgi). As a result, as hoped, the permanent kibbutz population started to grow once again because members stayed and newcomers joined.

Another extraordinary change concerned internal governance—specifically, the transition from direct to representative democracy. The main kibbutz body that functions on the basis of direct democracy is the general assembly of all members (similar to a weekly town hall meeting in other contexts). Nowadays, this general assembly typically meets less frequently than in the past and has been partially replaced by a council of elected members and boards of directors.

Within this whole array of changes, the innovation that has provoked the most vehement discussions among kibbutz members, officeholders, and the general public is the privatization of aspects of kibbutz life (Hecht, 2006; Reinharz, 2011). Although it seems new, the process of privatization in the kibbutz actually started in the 1950s, soon after the establishment of the State of Israel. At the time, a slow shift occurred from the social value of allocating consumption services (e.g., laundry, education, food, housing) according to needs, on the one hand, to the economically oriented principle of allocating the same amount of money to each member so that he or she could buy these services as they saw fit. In kibbutz jargon, this shift is an example of privatization. An issue that garnered public attention and incited much tension within kibbutzim came at the end of the 1990s, when some communities went beyond allotting funds for personal consumption and started to privatize members' earnings, that is, people henceforth would be rewarded differentially for the amount and type of work they did. By 2010, about two-thirds of the kibbutzim engaged in significant privatizing actions, legitimizing this fundamental change by labeling themselves "differential" or "new" kibbutzim, the other third being the "collective" type or traditional. A few kibbutzim even transferred ownership of houses to their members and some are now considering the division of kibbutz property to members (see chapter by Alon Gan). One can label this extraordinary change as signifying the demise of the kibbutz idea or, alternatively, as yet another set of changes in its hundred-year-old history.

Reinventing the Kibbutz

Ironically, at the same time as some kibbutzim were veering far from their core definitions, a few social groups "on the outside" were *taking on* key kibbutz attributes. Criticism of the kibbutz from within and from the outside, as well as a search for an alternative collective way of life, inspired new initiatives that tried to preserve the basic values of the kibbutz. These new entities were *urban kibbutzim* formed by groups of young singles or young families who believed that a kibbutz should address external problems in Israeli society rather than be focused only on itself (see chapter by Yuval Dror). Specifically, new kibbutzim should be established in which members could live within the communities they served. These new kibbutzim would focus not on production, but rather on developing social and educational activities in depressed areas. In 1979, Kibbutz Reshit was formed in Jerusalem, locating itself in an impoverished area with high crime and drug abuse rates. Following this model, in 1987, Kibbutz Migvan was established in Sderot and Kibbutz Tamuz in Bet-Shemesh. In 1992, Kibbutz Beit Israel took root in Jerusalem. Several additional communal groups have formed since the 1990s. Each of these communities is small, with a combined membership of fifteen hundred to two thousand individuals who earn their livelihood mainly from educational community activities paid for by the government or various nonprofit organizations. This extremely interesting phenomenon suggests that the original kibbutz idea is still potent in Israeli society, and that if the kibbutzim themselves deviate sufficiently from the key ideas, new groups will form to take up the old banner.

Evolving Family Patterns

The much discussed structure of family life in the early days of the kibbutz movement included the (heterosexual) parent couple residing in a small apartment, and their children living and sleeping in small houses designed for each age-group, beginning with infancy. This structure is widely criticized today as "unnatural" or "damaging to the children," and hard on parents, though in the early years of kibbutz life, *collective child rearing*, as this arrangement was called, was thought to answer the needs of the kibbutz and to adhere well to modern psychological principles (see chapter by Eldad Kedem and Gilad Padva). With the absorption of newcomers who had not been raised to accept collective child rearing and with the growth in the size of individual kibbutzim, the communities became less homogeneous and sometimes difficult for individuals to adapt to on this intimate level. In this new situation, people found "emotional refuge" in the family in lieu of the "kibbutz" (see chapter by Hadas Doron).

At the same time, in the 1950s–1960s, the importance of kibbutzim for the attainment of national goals began to diminish. Kibbutzim turned inward and members concentrated more on developing themselves as people. This shift further aided the change in the centrality of the family and was matched by an increasingly sharp gender division of labor in kibbutz occupations. The kibbutz increasingly became a family-oriented rather than a nation-oriented society. Many of the alterations that took place at the end of the 1980s and throughout the 1990s affected the role of the family and gender equality. For example, women, more so than men, pushed for a change in the sleeping arrangement of the children, and, as a result, in the 1970s and 1980s, many kibbutzim abandoned the children's collective sleeping arrangements. Children started sleeping in their parents' apartments rather than in the kibbutz children's houses (Shepher, 1967; Palgi, 1991). By the end of the twentieth century, nearly all the kibbutzim changed their educational (i.e., dormitory) system and the family came to dominate kibbutz life. This sea change transferred more chores from the public domain to the private home, from communal to family responsibility. Examples of these transfers include the closing of the communal dining room and communal laundry services. Research shows that from the women's point of view, these transformations led to a greater investment of work hours in the private sector and in the family house (Palgi, 1994, 2002), a change women desired.

What happened to women during these processes? To answer this question, we have to recognize that although strikingly imperfect, the kibbutz did promote a version of gender equality (see chapter by Sylvie Fogiel-Bijaoui). Most women belonged to the kibbutz workforce (although the range of jobs for kibbutz women was limited because of their obligation to work in childcare, at least periodically). Their personal economic situation was equal to that of men, in terms of the individual budgetary allowances they received, pension plans entitlement, general insurance, and occupational security. The socioeconomic situation of a single female parent was similar to that of a single male parent. Neither faced any danger of poverty or inability to support her or his dependents. Participation in the governing bodies of the kibbutz was open to all members (Palgi, 2003) regardless of gender.

The current transformation of kibbutz society has had mixed effects on women. Opening the outside job market to the kibbutz has expanded the variety of women's occupations, has allowed women to penetrate new occupations, and has enabled women to achieve more in professional and economic fields. In turn, these achievements improve their social status. However, this trend also exposes women to the social discrimination, increased gender inequality, and increased inequality among women that exists in the larger Israeli society. The abolition of extensive branches of communal services such as the dining room and laundry has erected new stumbling blocks for career-oriented women. As the kibbutz loses its unique characteristics, women lose the advantages that the old kibbutz bestowed upon them: economic equality, equivalent social security, and legal equality. The status of women in the kibbutz is nearing the status of women in Israeli society with its advantages and drawbacks (Palgi, 2003).

Cultural and Educational Activities

Kibbutz festivals and cultural activities were well known to the larger public and attracted many visitors who spent their vacation in the kibbutz. Some of these activities formed the cornerstones of Israeli culture. In 1937, the first art museum was opened in Kibbutz Ein Harod, and forty museums and galleries have been opened in kibbutzim since then. In 1939, the kibbutz movement inaugurated two publishing houses (Sifriat Hapoalim and Hakibbutz Hameuchad). Merged in 1999, these presses publish Israeli literature, children's books, poetry, encyclopedias, and books on philosophy (see chapters by Shula Keshet and Iris Milner). Two teachers' colleges have been opened, the first in 1940 (Seminar Hakibbutzim) and the second in 1950 (Oranim), initially for kibbutz educators and later for all students. Kibbutz youth have organized and led many of the Israeli youth movements. The kibbutz movement has its own choir (since 1957), orchestra (since 1970), theatre (since 1964), and dance group (since 1964); all of them perform in Israel and abroad. The contribution of kibbutz members to Israeli folk dancing was enhanced by the inauguration of the yearly folk dance convention in Kibbutz Dalia in 1944. Kibbutz writers (e.g., Amos Oz), poets (e.g., Nathan Yonatan), composers (e.g., David Zehavi, Michael Wolpe), musicians (e.g., Galilah Ribner), and painters and sculptors (e.g., Shmulik Katz) are well known (see chapter by Ranen Omer-Sherman). In recognition of the flourishing of the arts in kibbutzim, this volume includes a discussion of the arts to illustrate changes in the kibbutz over the past hundred years.

Future of the Kibbutz

The history of kibbutzim shows that they are moving from a welfare society to a market society. Members are more independent economically from one another; there are new forms of membership for their adult children, "a member with economic independence" (full participation in kibbutz life but economic independence with no rights over kibbutz property); mutual aid in the kibbutz is more limited; and trends in privatizing property are evident. Given all these transformations, the question arises as to the future of kibbutzim. The answer depends on the vision of its members, and on the local and global economic and political processes that will affect strategic decisions the kibbutzim will have to make. Will they be able to find a new meaning and mission (see chapter by Amia Lieblich)? Are they going to require candidates for membership to agree with the new meaning and mission? Are they going to limit the nonmember population so that kibbutz members remain the majority? Will they be able to attract entrepreneurs to develop new ventures within the kibbutzim in accordance with their new meaning and mission (see chapter by Michael Livni)? Are they going to keep the community small and maintain a rural ecological environment? Will they wither or be socially resilient (see chapter by Avraham Pavin)? Will they be able to unite and formulate a common action program for impacting on the surrounding society or are they going to be merged into neighboring towns (as some government officials have initiated)? These are only a few issues that will determine whether the kibbutzim will develop their own unique social economy by updating their communal, social, and economic way of life or whether they will become ordinary gated neighborhoods or suburban residential communities.

The aim of this volume is to look at all the issues discussed in this introduction in greater depth. We believe that the work of people doing research in a variety of disciplines can help us understand what Martin Buber claimed to be an "experiment that did not fail" (Buber, 1949). These original chapters written by leading scholars and practitioners of the kibbutz encompass many (but not all) facets of kibbutz life. As editors, we sought to identify fresh topics that both document and disentangle the complexities of kibbutz life. As the kibbutz enters its second century, it is important to take a step back to examine how contemporary changes might lead to its ultimate demise or, as Charles Darwin might have said, whether social groups such as kibbutzim are *invigorated by changes* that lead to their adaptation and survival.

Bibliography

Association of Kibbutz Industry. *The Yearly Review of Kibbutz Industry.* Tel-Aviv: Association of Kibbutz Industry, 1982.

Buber, Martin. *Paths in Utopia.* Translated by R. F. C. Hull. London: Routledge & Kegan Paul, 1949.

Golomb, Naphtali and Daniel Katz. *The Kibbutz As a Social System.* Tel-Aviv: Sifriyat Hapoalim, 1971 [Hebrew].

Hecht, Esther. "Privatizing Pots and Pans." *Hadassah Magazine* (May 2006): 8–11.

Near, Henry. *The Kibbutz Movement—A History, Vol. 1: Origins and Growth, 1909–1939.* Oxford: Oxford University Press, 1992.

———. *The Kibbutz Movement—A History, Vol. 2: Crisis and Achievement, 1939–1995.* Oxford: Oxford University Press, 1997.

Palgi, Michal. "Motherhood in the Kibbutz." In *Calling the Equality Bluff—Women in Israel,* edited by Barbara Swirsky and Marilyn Safir. New York: Pergamon Press, 1991.

———. "Women in the Changing Kibbutz Economy." *Economic and Industrial Democracy* 15 (1994): 15–73.

———. "Organization in Kibbutz Industry." In *Crisis in the Israeli Kibbutz—Meeting the Challenge of Changing Times,* edited by U. Leviatan, H. Oliver, and J. Quarter. Westport: Praeger, 1998.

———. "Emanzipierte Frauen in einer gerechten Gesellschaft? Die Frauenfrage im Kibbutz (Emancipated Women in a Just Society? The Women's Matter in the Kibbutz)." *Psychosozial* 25 (2002): 75–87.

———. "Gender Equality in the Kibbutz—From Ideology to Reality." In *Jewish Feminism in Israel,* edited by Kalpana Misra and Melanie Rich, 106–32. Brandeis: Brandeis University Press, 2003.

Reinharz, Shulamit. *Observing the Observer: Understanding Our Selves in Field Research.* New York: Oxford University Press, 2011.

Rosner, Menachem and Michal Palgi. "Ideology and Organization in Kibbutz Industry." *The Economic Quarterly* 96/7 (1977) [Hebrew].

Shepher, Joseph. *The Effect of the System of Children's Sleeping Arrangements on the Social Structure of the Kibbutz*. Tel-Aviv: Union of Kevutzot and Kibbutzim, 1967 [Hebrew].

The Economic Unit of the Kibbutz Movement. *The Yearly Report of the Economic Unit of the Kibbutz Movement*. Tel-Aviv: The United Kibbutz Movement, 2009.

Part I

The Unfolding History of the Contemporary Kibbutz

Introduction to Part I

Michal Palgi and Shulamit Reinharz

In this, the first of the book's three parts, we present the work of scholars who have studied the *status of the kibbutz in Israeli society*. We focus on the decline of communal ideology and the link of that decline to changes in the kibbutz way of life, such as the kind of people chosen for leadership roles within the kibbutz. This part concludes with a look at changes surrounding the *individual in contemporary kibbutzim*.

Alon Pauker's historical analysis of the roots of the changing status of the kibbutz in Israeli society points to the role of kibbutz leadership. According to Pauker, *kibbutz leadership did not manage to find an alternative role for the kibbutz after Israel gained independence*. The leadership's failure to adapt to the new situation by finding new goals spurred a double reaction. First, the status of the kibbutz in Israeli society diminished, and second, the kibbutz became very vulnerable, leaving it open to nearly total collapse during the economic crisis of the 1980s. *Alon Gan* delves further into kibbutz development by analyzing the overt slogans as well as the covert aspirations evident since the 1960s. He describes five indicators of the process of ideological change from extreme collectivism to blatant individualism. Both Pauker and Gan maintain that the changed ideology was at the root of privatization in the kibbutz. The economic crisis only exposed and enhanced it. In other words, they adopt the Weberian rather than the Marxist model of change, with ideology driving the economy rather than the reverse.

Throughout the history of the kibbutz, "the female member problem" has persisted unresolved.[1] Despite promoting gender equality in many domains, the kibbutz system is thought to have failed in the project of creating gender equality in the division of labor and the division of power.[2] Men have always controlled the economic functions, and women

15

controlled the services offered in the kibbutz. Because of the persistence of gender inequality, at the end of the 1960s, the Kibbutz Artzi movement held a special convention to find ways to improve the status of women kibbutz members. Their recommendations enabled women to participate more fully in public life in part by allocating one working hour a day for household chores, thus operating under the assumption that household tasks were the responsibility of women. The contradictions inherent in these decisions and the general social and political atmosphere at the time did not improve gender equality. But the faulty suggestions did bring the topic to the forefront, leading to the secular kibbutz movement's formation of a department for the advancement of women in the 1980s. *Sylvie Fogiel-Bijaoui* analyzes the formation and activities of the department, its ups and downs, as well as its cooptation by the kibbutz movement and the reasons for its weakness today. The underrepresentation of women in key positions in the individual kibbutz and in the kibbutz movement, and the continuous threat to shut the unit down, are blemishes on its activities. Nevertheless, Bijaoui maintains that the department will not be eliminated.

Gender inequality also appears in the chapter by Menachem Topel, which deals with changing kibbutz elites. He shows that changes in the kibbutz supported the formation of new social relations including distinctive elites. Topel's chapter examines these new elites composed mainly of technocrats and people with advanced degrees. He points out that at the beginning stage of the kibbutz when values of equality were predominant, the elite consisted of people who had good standing among kibbutz members and had valuable social capital, that is, connections within and outside the kibbutz. Moreover, the technocratic kibbutz elite included many nonmember managers. The change in the characteristics and structure of the elite occurred as a result of the emergence of more individualistic values. According to Topel, the change in the nature of the elite was another impediment to women. *Avraham Pavin's* chapter looks into this issue. He maintains that during times of crisis a high level of pro-social behavior, such as volunteerism, mutual assistance, the desire to cooperate, the motivation to help one another, and to work together for the good of the whole, is essential. When there is a debate about kibbutz values, polarizing factors between members emerge, reducing the community's social resilience. Accordingly, the more radical the changes in the kibbutz, the more its resilience declines. Current sociological theory suggests that social resilience is required for safety and survival in response to threat.

Kibbutz social resilience reflects the level of its social capital. One facet of social capital is the quality of the relationships between its members. The changes in the kibbutzim that were obvious at the end of the last century were opposed by the older generation and advocated by their children or grandchildren. The children of the founders are considered to be "the young elderly" in kibbutz society. The way the "young elderly" managed the changes in the kibbutz determined its social resilience. Through in-depth interviews, *Yasmin Asaf and Israel Doron* tried to understand how these people perceive their position. The researchers found that the "young elderly" wanted to cut loose from the protective umbrella of the kibbutz. They believed in their *own ability* and in the strength of their *own families* to help them in their old age. Many of the young elderly have key positions in the kibbutz and feel that they are in control of their lives. Their multiple roles in the changing kibbutz include caring for their elderly parents and helping their adult children raise the grandchildren.

Do the new economic and social pressures caused by the changes affect family stability? In her comparative study, *Hadas Doron* tries to answer this question by asking kibbutz families and moshav families about their marital relations. She found that the level of spousal interdependence is affected by the organizational and economic arrangements prevailing in their community. In the kibbutz, each individual has personal rights regardless of gender and marital status. Each person receives from the kibbutz personal services that are usually provided by the family. Therefore, spousal interdependence is low and so is the cost of separation or divorce.

This part concludes with a chapter in which psychologist Amia Lieblich identifies three *developmental stages* of a large kibbutz that symbolizes many other kibbutzim. Using in-depth interviews and regular returns to this kibbutz over the years, she shows how the kibbutz changed from an ideologically driven community to a "regular" village. From a psychological perspective, however, the kibbutz remains a home that its members cathect emotionally. Her chapter describes the kibbutz at its peak period, its slow descent from the peak, and its new slow ascent. Her chapter suggests that we understand the kibbutz anew as a home rather than as previously appropriate as a way or a place.

Notes

1. See Shulamit Reinharz, "Toward a Model of Female Political Action: The Case of Manya Shohat, Founder of the First Kibbutz," *Women's Studies International*

Forum 7, no. 4 (1984): 275–87, for a discussion of how an early founder predicted that gender equality would not be forthcoming in kibbutzim.

2. Eyal Kafkafi, "The Psycho-Intellectual Aspect of Gender Inequality in Israel's Labor Movement," *Israel Studies* 4, no. 1 (1999): 188–211.

1

The Early Roots of a Later Crisis—The Kibbutz Crisis of the 1980s and Its Roots at the Time of the Establishment of the State of Israel[1]

Alon Pauker

> *With the establishment of the state, like a hovering curse realized at last, the mental petit bourgeois returned and landed upon us. The revolution ended, so we thought, and the age of normalcy has come. And normalcy is of course the ethos of the bourgeoisie.*
> —*Amos Oz,* Under this Blazing Light, *Tel-Aviv, 1979, p. 130*

About a generation ago, in the 1980s, after seventy years of kibbutz history, the kibbutz movement suffered its greatest crisis. Crises always accompanied the kibbutz, perhaps because of its great aspirations. It aspired to be the avant-garde of the national rebirth of the Jewish people. Therefore a permanent pioneering tension became part of the kibbutz. Simultaneously, the kibbutz aspired to be an exemplary society and hence condemned itself to the permanent restlessness, characteristic of someone who seeks perfection in an imperfect reality. This restlessness was expressed in objective and subjective crises. Leaders as well as rank-and-file members sensed that the kibbutz had not fulfilled its goals. And indeed, the first kvutzot[2] experienced a crisis about whether they would be able to survive. This question became more acute in the 1920s when the Zionist establishment defined the moshav[3] (in contrast to the kibbutz) as the preferred form of settlement (Near, 1997, p. 314). Later, in times of relative material well-being and peace, the kibbutz experienced another crisis—members left in great numbers, tempted by the lure of the city.

Later the kibbutz experienced a severe crisis with the establishment of the State of Israel. That crisis is the focus of this chapter.[4]

Yet the crisis in the 1980s was different from those that preceded it in both duration and depth. As for duration, the kibbutz is beginning to recover only now. As for depth, this last crisis has led to the abandonment of the classical framework of equality and collectivity and exchanging it with something looser. Some kibbutzim seem to have renounced *all* the features that distinguished them from their surroundings. This crisis of the 1980s is usually explained by two overt phenomena: an unprecedented economic crisis and the rise of the Likud Party to power in 1977, signifying the transformation of the state leadership's social and economic ideology, leaving the kibbutz to confront its hardships for the first time without the backing of a sympathetic government.[5] Serious as they were, I contend that these overt factors were insufficient in causing the crises and required an additional covert source—which I define as the crisis of the self-image of the kibbutz in the transition from the Yishuv to statehood.

Kibbutz ideology that was formed during the Yishuv period perceived the kibbutz as both an exemplary collective society and a voluntary pioneering instrument for fulfilling Zionism's goals. The tempestuous pre-state days compelled the kibbutz to concentrate on its pioneering mission. With the establishment of the state, kibbutz leadership on the whole aspired to continue this trend. A representative example can be found in the words of Ya'akov Hazan, a prominent kibbutz movement leader, who wrote the following in March 1949 in preparation for a conference of his movement, Hakibbutz Haartzi[6]:

> Even after the establishment of the State of Israel, Zionism remains a movement lacking an obligatory, organizational framework. The State of Israel is a huge implementation lever. It can trigger and prod the process of awakening the Jewish Diaspora but it cannot turn it into a constructive creative force. This demands socialist, national, ideological and mental motivations that are beyond its jurisdiction . . . the pioneering flame can be ignited these days . . . only if the vision of national rebirth converges with . . . a grand socialist vision . . . *And only a pioneering movement*, which builds its life upon foundations of bold, socialist revolution, *can carry out this historic mission*, meaning *a pioneering movement with the kibbutz movement at its center*.[7]

Given this understanding, the kibbutz should stand at the forefront because it is a pioneering body willing to enlist people to fulfill Zionist goals and because its collective revolutionary way of life is the best for leading the national rebirth. Yet with the establishment of the state, these ideas among kibbutz leadership were inappropriate both for the status of the kibbutz in the state and for the mood of rank-and-file kibbutz members.

With the establishment of the state, the kibbutz soon realized that, contrary to its leaders' presumptions, it was no longer perceived as the spearhead pioneer of significant current endeavors. Therefore it was no longer entitled to the enormous prestige it had gained for pioneering during the pre-state era.

Transformation of the kibbutz's public status stemmed from the atmosphere created by Ben-Gurion, who sought to place the state and its institutions in the center, by canceling the unique status of secondary bodies including the kibbutz. Ben-Gurion named his approach *mamlachtiyut* (etatism). Furthermore, the tasks that the young state confronted were mighty indeed and, unlike the issues faced by the Yishuv, could not have been implemented by a relatively small body such as the kibbutz. The main challenge immediately following the formation of the state was absorbing mass immigration. Enormous unprecedented waves of immigration doubled Israel's population within four years. The kibbutzim did not remain indifferent to this tidal wave. They were, in fact, the most significant factor in the veteran Yishuv to absorb immigrants into its ranks. The kibbutz was nearly unique in enabling immigrants to be integrated on the same premises as veterans with whom they lived side by side. In the cities, by contrast, immigrants were housed in separate neighborhoods. This separation policy also applied to the many newcomers who joined the Moshavim Movement. These families were not integrated into existing settlements but were settled in moshavim of their own.

Despite this distinction, the kibbutz did not absorb immigrants to such an extent that it could be considered the spearhead of absorption or even a major player. The kibbutz was unable to have that role for reasons of scale. At the establishment of the state in 1948, it numbered about fifty thousand inhabitants and therefore could not absorb seven hundred thousand newcomers who arrived between 1948 and 1952. In addition, unlike during the period of the Yishuv, only few newcomers considered the kibbutz way of life as culturally and ideologically suitable for them. Therefore, although the kibbutzim represented more than 7 percent of the Jewish population in 1948, within a decade it was less than 4 percent (almost eighty thousand kibbutz inhabitants in comparison to a Jewish population of over two million people). That is to say that even though the kibbutz population increased by more than 50 percent during the first decade of independence, the ratio of the kibbutz to the general population decreased by half.

And issues that arose with mass immigration also arose in settling the land: the sheer size of the absorption challenge necessitated a settlement task that had to be speedier, larger, and more complex than that was true before the establishment of the state. A form of settlement as complex and unusual as the kibbutz could not be the core of such a settlement endeavor. And this is without taking into account the aversion of most newcomers to the kibbutz way of life. Hence, although in the first two years of independence the rate of settling new kibbutzim was higher than ever (75 kibbutzim were added to the existing 155 kibbutzim in two years), it was still not extensive enough for the kibbutz to be at the forefront of settlement. Indeed, the number of moshavim built in the first two years of independence (approximately 150) was twice the number of new kibbutzim. The vast majority of new moshavim were specifically built for new immigrants.

At the same time, in the two years after the founding of the state, vast numbers of kibbutz members (approximately 10 percent) left the kibbutzim, among them key members. These people saw their future in the newly created apparatus of the state with its broad range of opportunities. Therefore, because of the difficulties in recruiting a significant number of newcomers, the kibbutz movements were forced to direct their attention and their limited human resources toward the survival efforts of those kibbutzim that suffered massive departures. Thus, the capacity of the kibbutz movements to establish new kibbutzim and become a significant factor in immigrant integration diminished. Accordingly, the trend of inferiority of the kibbutz compared to the moshav increased. From 1951 till the end of 1958, fewer than five kibbutzim were settled annually with only a marginal involvement of newcomers, compared with the fourfold rate of settled moshavim at the same period, most of them settled by immigrants.[8]

Parallel to absorbing mass immigration and settling the land, the core agenda items of the young state, it was necessary to construct a governmental, military, and bureaucratic apparatus. This task was of an entirely different scope from the voluntary apparatus the Yishuv had constructed. In these matters, too, the kibbutz could not maintain its pre-state prominence.

As a result, although the kibbutz had been a pioneer in carrying out the missions of the Yishuv, it could no longer do so after the establishment of the state. It still played a prominent part in the army, in settlement, and in various national missions. Newer studies showed that even those young newcomers who lived on kibbutzim for short periods during the 1950s had an easier integration process into Israeli society than did youngsters who had not live on kibbutzim (Ovnat, 1983). The kibbutz also continued to be the most prominent icon of the Zionist revolution and a central showcase of Israeli society. Yet despite this symbolism, its unique status of the Yishuv days was lost.

Kibbutz leadership were frustrated that the kibbutz was being pushed away from the central endeavors of the period. Thus, for instance, just before the end of the war of independence, in a meeting of "Chever Hakvutzot" to discuss the relation between the kibbutz and the state, Shmuel Gavish, an education functionary of that movement said, "We are going through such a great period in the life of the people and the country—at such speed—that we fail to catch up altogether." Years passed and Yitzhak Tabenkin, leader of "Hakibbutz Hameu'had," expressed frustration that the kibbutz had only a minimal impact on pioneering, "It is bad that we do not take part in running the affairs of the state, the army, the settlements; it is bad we do so little for absorption; it is bad we do not contribute properly to the growth of the immigrant person." The picture did not change in the ensuing years, and thus, in 1957, Arie Avinary said the following at a "Hakibbutz Hameu'had" writers' convention:

> great positive endeavors were carried out with enormous efforts and we were not included. And the kibbutz—for nearly eight years—is witnessing this mighty spectacle, and its hands are tied—not guiding and directing, operating and promoting.[9]

The ideology supported the necessity of kibbutz pioneering, yet in reality the kibbutz was becoming irrelevant to the central issues of the times. The leadership saw this as danger both to Israeli society and to the kibbutz. The danger to Israeli society was clear—it was not evolving as it should. The danger to the kibbutz stemmed from its ideological and practical ties with society outside—with the unfortunate result that the kibbutz's lack of influence meant that society was influencing the kibbutz.[10]

As we have noted, the kibbutz status in the Israeli society weakened after the establishment of the state. Influenced by this trend, members of the kibbutz concentrated more upon the kibbutz as a home. The state of affairs in their kibbutz home, however, was far from encouraging. Members frequently expressed frustration with kibbutz system whose reality did not correlate with the ideological image that presented the kibbutz as exemplary.

This frustration inundated every possible outlet of expression in the kibbutz movement: movement conventions, movement periodicals, kibbutzim journals, and other more covert means of expression such as personal letters. One of the most telling letters was written anonymously over a few months by a woman kibbutz member of the "Hakibbutz Hameu'had" movement and sent to Yitzhak Tabenkin in December 1951.[11] Assuming that her views represented the majority of kibbutz members, her letter expressed profound uneasiness about the dissonance between vision and practice. She maintained that the day-to-day running of kibbutz affairs offers only minimal breathing space for the individual:

> A person has no opportunity to shed tears, to consummate his love, to create his art, without fearing a stranger's eye. I am concerned that even sex life on the kibbutz is criminally restricted; it is limited and narrowed and does not fulfill all its potential joy and glory, since a person is in a constant fear of being observed, of being heard . . .

These words should be understood within the context of the early fifties when in many kibbutzim, members lived in wooden shacks or tents and ate from tin plates in the dining hall. Only a few members in the oldest kibbutzim were privileged to live in a "veteran residence' of thirty square meters that spared its residents the use of the distant public shower-room.[12] According to the writer, despite the rise in the standard of living, people feel that their rudimentary needs are not being met. This attitude causes the rise of materialistic values in the kibbutz, since a person is preoccupied to obsession by his unfulfilled basic needs. This is all the more the case now when members do no longer want to give up their standard of living for a pioneering kibbutz life. Their frustration increases when they feel that kibbutz life does, indeed, demand such payment. ". . . the rise of materialism also stems from members feeling shackled when facing the opportunities allegedly given to their counterparts in town."[13]

As a result:

> It is true that every member knows in his heart how superior his way of life is, but in his day-to-day existence he flounders in the mud, and this causes him pain. . . . He bows his head, and the light which he himself creates passes over him, and his eyes are blind to it. There are many who cannot leave the kibbutz because they are deeply aware of its greatness, but who cannot live in it because *we have not yet learnt* how to make life possible.[14]

It means that the vision of kibbutz life is beautiful, but many members maintain that reality did not live up to the ideal. The vast dichotomy between the vision and the daily life raised doubts among members: ". . . Within the Kvutza a shining light falls on the roots of our life, yet shadows are cast on our daily existence, its pettiness . . . in our daily life there is but little light. Are those shadows necessary? Are those shadows innate to commune life?"[15]

The difficulties in pioneering bothered the leadership, while the members were preoccupied with the unsatisfactory standard of living and organizational operations on their home kibbutz. Despite these differences in emphasis, both members and leaders agreed shortly following the birth of the state that "the situation is not good and there is a crisis. The whole kibbutz movement is taken over by a sense of inferiority."[16] The actual crisis worsened and undermined people's faith in the kibbutz. The kibbutznik's sense of pride turned into a sense of unworthiness. Since all agreed there was a problem, the kibbutz sought ways out of the crisis, assuming that the way to cope must be suited to the causes of the frustration. According to this rule, there was a gap between the kibbutz movement leadership and the widespread attitude of rank-and-file members about how to resolve the crisis.

With the establishment of the state, the kibbutz movements' leadership strove to preserve the kibbutz ideology from the Yishuv period, and since they were more concerned about the kibbutz's weakening pioneering spirit than its difficulties as a way of life, they hoped that by "returning to its former pioneering glory," the status and image of the kibbutz would be rehabilitated. That is to say, parallel to expressing frustration over the kibbutz's lack of impact in the realm of pioneering, they insisted that it should not give up on this matter. This approach was expressed by Meir Ya'ari, the leader of the "Hakibbutz Haartzi" movement. Ya'ari's followers demanded that he and his coleaders call for a convention to deal with the kibbutz' internal social issues so as to improve the kibbutz as a home. His reply was "To work twice as hard—that is the remedy—and fight every self-indulgence and public weariness . . . *We shall not look for new ways*; we shall restore this way[17] and make it suitable to this period."[18] Yaari's words were radical but characteristic of kibbutz leadership who hoped that pioneering determination, together with preserving the old systems and ideas, would restore the kibbutz to the lead, despite the difficulties incurred by the establishment of the state. The leadership was aware that the pioneering motivation among the members had diminished. How, then, could members be convinced to invest even more in pioneering tasks? Yitzhak Tabenkin, the "Hakibbutz

Hameu'had" leader, addressed that issue in an article in his movement periodical *Mebefnim*, 1952:

> The kibbutz is under a heavy siege; *it needs to restore its ideological resistance* . . . ideological strengthening will bring with it a sense of value, understanding of the project, pride. This sense of meekness in comparison with the outside is a disease; it exhausts our energy.[19]

That is to say, the road is not to be altered even if walking on it is hard for the members. Members' difficulty is a weakness that should be dealt with by ideological reinforcement. And though Tabenkin was more adamant than others, generally speaking, kibbutz leadership accepted the method of ideological reinforcement. That was a reason all kibbutz movements founded ideological institutes during the 1950s. In these institutions, kibbutz members engaged in ideological activities and planned ideological seminars in the kibbutzim themselves. "Hakibbutz Haartzi" founded Givat Haviva; "Hakibbutz Hameu'had" founded Efal and the permanent seminar at Ein Harod; "Ichud Hakvutzot VeHakibbutzim" (a continuation movement of "Chever Hakvutzot," established in 1951, following the split in Hakibbutz Hameu'had) founded Beit Berrel, and by the end of the first decade of independence, the religious kibbutz movement (Hakibbutz Hadati) established a permanent seminar center on Kibbutz Sde Eliyhu.

In accordance with this approach, movement leaders did not embrace or adopt ideas others raised. They did not update the pioneering way so that the kibbutz would better function in the new era.

Defining leadership as "more of the same" meant not changing anything, but rather reinforcing the will of the members. And so the leadership's response to members' expressions of frustration about their kibbutz as a home was usually in the spirit of Kadish Luz—a prominent leader of "Chever Hakvutzot," and later of the "Ichud Hakvutzot Vehakibbutzim," —in the first conference his movement held after the birth of the state:

> If a comfortable life becomes our main objective, we shall reject it. We must solve some problems in order to free ourselves of the dissatisfaction involved in a lack of feeling of home, for this dissatisfaction suppresses our sense of mission. But if we make the improvement in our standard of living our central aim, this can only be a temporary stop. Only if we enhance the Kvutza and movement's awareness, renew its spirit, its joy of creativity—will life of the collective, experiences of sharing—shine in our eyes and eyes of others once more. Only then will Israeli youth find us attractive again. It is not the attraction of a high standard of living which will bring them to us, but the attraction of our exalted human, national, and socialist mission.[20]

This means it is wrong to position the improvement of "the kibbutz as a home" in the epicenter. It is not the main issue. Covertly, what is articulated here is a much-discussed tension between changes in the kibbutz lifestyle and the pioneering endeavor of the kibbutz. Therefore, the leaders maintained that discontent with the kibbutz as well as pioneering listlessness should be dealt with by strengthening the members' belief that it was right, proper, and important to preserve the kibbutz way of life. Accordingly, the movements took only few guiding actions to update the kibbutz way of life so it would better answer the members' wishes.

As a result, the kibbutz leadership actually took "the kibbutz as a home" for granted and implemented no changes. The changes that did occur on kibbutzim during the 1950s (and later on) stemmed from local initiatives. At the conventions, the leaders tried to curb changes by passing decisions. But on the whole, the kibbutz public refused to abide by those decisions, and therefore, in a recurring pattern, the movements' establishment had to confirm, ex post facto, changes in the kibbutz way of life that they previously had attempted to prevent. Burning issues on the kibbutz movement agenda were dealt with in this way during the fifties and later. That included issues such as providing personal budgets for clothing and shoes instead of a uniform supply of items by the kibbutz, offering matriculation examinations in kibbutz schools, and creating sleeping accommodation of children in their parents' homes instead of in the common children houses, and more.

Kibbutz members, by contrast, repeatedly maintained that:

> the kibbutz does not exist solely for the sake of developing the land and settling it; it is not only a home for the whole people, but should be the *best home* for every worker . . . if only it were so, that could be used as the best propaganda for bringing the masses to us.[21]

The contrast between these words and those of Luz is marked. The lure of the kibbutz itself, and not its task of renewed missionary zeal preached by the leadership, could demonstrate the superiority of the kibbutz's unique way of life. Accordingly, members and activists demanded that leaders understand that the kibbutz home could not be taken for granted. All movements had demands such as this one raised by Yeshaihu Wienberg in the Nir David convention of "Hakibbutz Haartzi" (June 1949):

> We must demand from Meir [Ya'ari] concern for the development of the kibbutz unit, for it has been neglected . . . we have created a huge reserve of human capacity, but for years we have been using up this reserve, and not adding to it . . . [the solution is]

for the leaders of the movement to appraise the life of the kibbutz community with the same seismographic sensitivity, and the investment of the same creative intellectual effort, as that with which they appraise our political life today. For years our most eminent comrades have not dealt with the social problems of the kibbutz movement, and from that point of view we must bring about a fundamental change.[22]

Many others raised similar demands. They maintained that the leadership and the kibbutz system in general should cease focusing on the pioneering mission but instead nurture the kibbutz as a home. Meir Ya'ari's response to this demand is a testimony to how deep the contrast was between the leadership and its members. His response was "to work twice as hard," meaning carrying on as is, though it takes extra determination and exertion.

The members were not convinced and, as mentioned before, proceeded to initiate changes themselves. They also rejected the concern that changes would negatively affect kibbutz values and its image as a task-oriented society:

I am *unwilling* to trust the social ideology of the founders of the first kvutza on all its components, as suitable for our times and as obliging us today. I am *unwilling* to view the dynamic development of the kvutza as a deviation from the straight and narrow, a neglect of values.[23]

The members doubted that the leadership's approach of ideological nurturing would solve the problem. As the anonymous woman member wrote to Yitzhak Tabenkin, leader of Hakibbutz Hameu'had,

The answer [to the crisis] might be thus: Lets reawaken afresh the idea in the hearts of the kibbutz' public: seminars . . . information . . . and it follows that the members . . . will become better, more moral . . . yet . . . this suggestion . . . we have never proven it was ever carried out . . . [Therefore] as long as we declare that the commune is a suitable and worthwhile way of life for the masses, we should gather, explore and formulate a form of life that would prevent moral ugliness, even before we manage to educate the whole public and before we overcome its habits and concepts—the fruit of an utterly strange and weird mentality.[24]

The outcome, therefore, was that with the establishment of the state, two fundamental differences were growing between members and their leadership concerning the right way to restore the stature of the kibbutz. The first difference was that, contrary to the leadership, members saw *the kibbutz as a home and not its pioneering function* to be the key issue for restoration. Second, members maintained that *changes were a required process*, as opposed to the leadership that was determined to preserve the kibbutz way of life from the days of the Yishuv with minimal changes.

The kibbutz leadership refused to accept the diminished status of kibbutz pioneering and thus focused on ways to restore it. Beyond the fact that this perception was delusional, it prevented the leadership from seeking and formulating a relevant *modus operandi* for the kibbutz in the new era. As a result, the kibbutz's public status diminished, with no noticeable strategy by its leaders to reinstate its prominence in Israeli society. Similarly, the kibbutz leadership did not accept members' demand to focus on nurturing the kibbutz way of life and turning it into a satisfactory home for its members. The leadership was concerned, instead, that changes in the kibbutz lifestyle would affect its pioneering purpose. The result was that rank-and-file members led the changes in the kibbutz without the guidance of leadership. This caused difficulties, since a unique lifestyle such as a kibbutz is not a simple task to uphold, even more so when the kibbutz must operate in a new reality. And on those very days of crisis, instead of leading, the leadership found themselves dragging behind reality, rather than shaping it.

Thus the kibbutz did not regain its Yishuv-era glory, nor did it create compensation for its members in shape of the kibbutz as a satisfying home for its members, nor did it present an exemplary model for its surrounding. This lack of success weakened the faith in "the home and the way" of many kibbutz members and created a crisis across the kibbutz movements. This sense of crisis was repressed during the economic prosperity of the 1960s to the 1980s. But a generation ago, when the economic crisis of the 1980s struck, the unresolved identity crisis of the kibbutz was exposed in full and threatened to destroy the kibbutz. The structure, values, and way of the kibbutz that thrived during the unique period of the Yishuv were not successfully redesigned to face the new reality of an independent state. Therefore, ever since 1985, when the kibbutz faced an economic crisis coupled with a political crisis caused by absence of a sympathetic government, it did not demonstrate the self-confidence or relevance that would mitigate this crisis.[25] It seems, therefore, that the roots of the identity crisis of the kibbutz, originating in its infertile encounter with the state, are as important in understanding its enormous last crisis as its obvious and well-known causes. Furthermore, those covert roots alone can explain the powerless response of the kibbutz to the explicit causes of its recent crisis.

Notes

1.   This chapter was written with the assistance of "Yad-Ya'ari"—Hashomer Hatzair Institute for Research and Documentation in Giva'at Haviva. It is partly based on my essay published in Chalamish, Aviva and Zameret, Zvi (eds.) *The Kibbutz—The*

first Hundred Years (Jerusalem: Yad Itzhak Ben Zvi, 2010) [Hebrew]. Thanks to my colleague and friend, Prof. Eli Tzur, for his helpful remarks on this chapter.

2. In the formative years "kvutza" was an accepted term for a kibbutz.
3. A moshav is an agricultural settlement with limited features of collectivity and mutual support.
4. For details of the series of kibbutz crises since its origins till the crisis of the 1980s, see Near (1997, pp. 314–16).
5. See Rosolio (1999, especially pp. 11–12, 243–45, 250–51).
6. There were four kibbutz movement at that time: "Hakibbutz Haartzi," "Hakibbutz Hadati" (the religious kibbutz movement), "Hakibbutz Hameu'had," and "Chever Hakvutzot." In 1952, Chever Hakvutzot united with the split group from Hakibbutz Hameu'had and renamed "Ichud Hakvutzot Vehakibbutzim" (shortly, Haichud). For details about the movements, see Near (1992, pp. 150–57, 191–92).
7. Yaakov Hazan, "The Kibbutz Movement in Light of Policy Changes," March 1949 (A preliminary circular before the Nir David convention of "Hakibbutz Haartzi"), CAHH 5-20.6(1), pp. 5–6 (my emphasis). For writings in the same vein from other kibbutz movements, see Tabenkin (1950, p. 519); Una (1957, p. 304).
8. For data about departures, see Near (1997, pp. 173, 362–64); Pauker (2005, pp. 22–23). The data are approximate since a small number of newly founded settlements changed their nature or disintegrated within a few years. For details about the massive departures and the effort to survive, see Canary (1990, p. 194); Near (1997, p. 180).
9. Shmuel Gavish speaking at a members' meeting, discussing issues of the kvutza and the state, February 20, 1949, G.A. 2/3/ p.7; Tabenkin (1952, p. 414); Arie Avinary, words at Hakibbutz Hameu'had writers' convention, Ramat Hakovesh, July 5–6, 1957, quoted in *Mebefnim* 20, no. 1–2, p. 61.
10. For representative examples, see Levy Greenblat, speech at the twenty-ninth convention of "Hakibbutz Haartzi" (Tiberias 1950), quoted at *Yediot Hakibbutz Haartzi*, August 1950, p. 85; Chaim, H. "A Call to Lift a Load" (an excerpt from a speech in ideological convention of "Hakibbutz Hameu'had" in Efal) *Bakibbutz* 5, no. 11 (December 9, 1953), pp. 2–3; Efraim Risner, speech in a meeting of "Aichud" central committee in Biet Berel, June 8, 1956 (Ichud archive/protocols/Center meetings/3/3, third meeting, p. 57).
11. K.M.A./15/Yitzhak Tabenkin/11/13/45.
12. Barkay (1980, p. 119); Near (1997, pp. 177–78).
13. K.M.A./15/Yetzhak Tabenkin/11/13/45, pp. 2, 4.
14. Ibid., p. 4 (my emphasis). For details in the same vein, from a previous year, see "the member in his mundane life sees mostly the negative, the shadows in our life, and is not capable of seeing the great light of joy of creation, and his consciousness is totally unaware of the many achievements and positive aspects" (Gran, 1950, p. 3).
15. Levy (1952, p. 5).
16. Yaakov Hazan, words at a debate in "Hakibbutz Haartzi" executive committee on the issue of young kibbutzim, C.A.H.H.5–10.5(15), March 19, 1951, p. 8.
17. That is, the kibbutz pioneering way in the Yishuv period.
18. Meir Ya'ari's summation speech in the twenty-eighth convention? of "Hakibbutz Haartzi" (Nir David, June 1949), C.A.H.H.5–20.6(1), pp. 9–10 (my emphasis).
19. Tabenkin (1952, pp. 414–15) (my emphasis).
20. Kadish Luz, speech at the fourth conference of Chever Hakvutzot, September 1949 quoted in *Niv Hakvutza* April 1950, p. 40.
21. Rosner (1951, p. 4).

22. Yeshaihu Wienberg's speech in the twenty-eighth convention of "Hakibbutz Haartzi" (Nir David, June 1949), printed in "Yediot Hakibbutz Haartzi," September 1949, p. 62.
23. Words of Akiva Skidle in a debate in "Aichud" Central Secretariat meeting, on the issue of "Social Committee—Its Trend and Activity," published in *Igeret Lahaverim*, 78–79 (May 14, 1953), p. 4 (my emphasis).
24. K.M.A./15/Yetzhak Tabenkin/11/13/45, p. 1.
25. For the discrepancy between the hesitant kibbutz reaction to the crisis and the mighty impact of that crisis, see Rosolio (1999, pp. 146, 238–39). For the improvement of the economic condition of the kibbutz from the 1960s onward, see Barkay (1980, pp. 139–62).

Bibliography

Barkay, C. *Development of the Kibbutz Economy*. Jerusalem: The Morris Falk Institute for Economic Research in Israel, 1980 [Hebrew].
Canary, B. "The Kibbutz Movement in Transition from the Yishuv to the State." In *Transition from "Yishuv" to State, 1947–1949: Continuity and Change*, edited by V. Pilowsky, 187–97. Haifa: Hertzel Institute, 1990 [Hebrew].
Gran, A. "Our Status in Economy and Society." *Givaat Hayiem Magazine* 404 (1950): 3 [Hebrew].
Levy, N. "Does It Have to Be?" *Igeret Lahaverim* A', no. 31 (1952): 5 [Hebrew].
Near, H. *The Kibbutz Movement: A History*. Vol. 1. London: Oxford University Press, 1992.
———. *The Kibbutz Movement: A History*. Vol. 2. London and Portland, OR: The Litman Library, 1997.
Ovnat, A. "The Influence of Kibbutz Education on Youth of Middle East (Oriental) Origins." Ph.D. thesis, Bar-Ilan University, 1983 [Hebrew].
Oz, A. *Under This Blazing Light*, 130. Tel Aviv: Keter, 1979 [Hebrew].
Pauker, A. "The Self-Image of the Different Kibbutz Movements? vis-à-vis the State of Israel, 1948–1958: A Comparative Analysis." Ph.D. thesis, Tel Aviv University, 2005 [Hebrew].
Rosner, H. "Following a Social Debate." *Na'an Journal* 1286 (1951): 4 [Hebrew].
Rosolio, D. *The System and the Crisis: Crisis, Recovery Plans and Changes in the Kibbutz Movement*. Tel Aviv: Am-Oved, 1999 [Hebrew].
Tabenkin, Y. "Examining the Foundations." *Mebefnim* 14, no. 4 (1950): 517–30 [Hebrew].
———. "From Siege to Living Space." *Mebefnim* 15, no. 3–4 (1952): 405–14 [Hebrew].
Una, M. "The Village as Crystallizing Traditional Experience." In *A True Partnership*, edited by M. Una, 304–09. Tel Aviv: Moreshet, 1957 [Hebrew].

Archives

C.A.H.H.: Central Archives of Hashomer Hatzair, Yad-Ya'ari—Givat-Haviva.
K.M.A.: Hakibbutz Hameu'had Archive, Yad-Tabenkin, Efal.
G.A.: Gordonia Archive, Hulda.

2

From "We" to "Me": The Ideological Roots of the Privatization of the Kibbutz

Alon Gan

There is evidence of increasing fundamental changes taking place in the kibbutz way of life, a tendency labeled "kibbutz privatization." The process began with the privatization of various components of the shared expenditure, including payment for electricity, food, and laundry; continued with a tendency to assign financial reward for overtime work; and reached the stage of differential pay and private ownership of kibbutz apartments by its members. Today, over two-thirds of kibbutzim in Israel no longer adhere to the traditional collective model, and in most of them, the members receive differential financial remuneration for their work.[1]

In public discourse, the gradual privatizing is generally considered to be the consequence of the acute economic crisis, affecting the kibbutz movement in the wake of the Israeli government's 1985 economic program for the stabilization of the country's economy. The financial crisis (leading to the arrangements of debts with the state and the banks, amounting to seven billion NIS) and the economic crisis created a tremendous shake-up, obliging the kibbutzim to reshuffle its "rules of the game" (Weber, 1992, pp. 12–30). The economic crisis was undoubtedly an essential factor in the evolving of privatization; however, the main argument in this chapter asserts that in order to understand the sources of dissatisfaction leading to the tendency to privatize, we must go back some thirty years—to the 1960s. The aim of this chapter is to attempt to identify the ideological roots that prepared the ground for the radical changes we are witnessing today.

The 1960s were the years during which the gap between the overt verbalization and slogans on the one hand and the covert aspirations of the members on the other hand was growing. Those were the years during which the founding leaders of the kibbutz movement were struggling to preserve a way of life that was losing its vitality (Gan, 2006, pp. 343–72). During the 1960s, the kibbutz agenda shifted:

1. From the kibbutz as a meaningful way of life to the kibbutz as a home.
2. From "exclamation marks" to "question marks."
3. From ideological discourse to psychological parlance.
4. From "we" to "me."
5. From the collective to the self-realization ethos.

A fundamental organizational change does not emerge in a vacuum; it develops slowly and is internalized gradually. This chapter investigates the various underlying phenomena that initiated the process of privatization and of the resulting dismantling of the kibbutz.

From the Kibbutz as a Meaningful Way of Life to the Kibbutz As a Home

> *I am here because it's home, not because of any ideology.* (Minutes of the general assembly in Kibbutz Naan, *1961*)

A gradual change has occurred in the factors influencing the members' identification with the kibbutz. In the past it was mainly ideological—identification with the kibbutz way of life as a unique ethos, proposing an alternative to the maladies of the capitalist system. For the second generation, born in the kibbutz, it was above all "home." The sense of belonging and identification with it was natural, not requiring any ideological justifications. After the Six-Day War, many discussions (talk culture) were held with the young people in the kibbutz movement. From these talks, it became clear that these young people perceived the kibbutz as a "home" not as "commitment to an idea."[2]

- Dinah (Marom Hagolan): ". . . We feel that we want to live in a kibbutz, because it suits us . . . not at all because of any ideals and not in the least because it's a just way of life, but because it suits us." (Tzur et al., 1969, p. 74)
- Dinah (Tirat Tzvi): "I am here mainly because it's my home." (Tzur et al., 1969, p. 107)
- Achi (Giv'at Brenner): "I can't deny that I live here because I feel I am attached to this place, to the natural and human landscape. . . . I don't think I live here because the kibbutz is a way of life that conveys a distinct message to the Jewish people and to the world at large." (Tzur et al., 1969, p. 145)

A comprehensive survey carried out at the end of the 1960s among the second generation established this point of view statistically. When the young people were asked what was the main factor involved in their attachment to the kibbutz, only 18 percent mentioned its ideological underpinning. Some of them mentioned factors such as the landscape, their family, their work. However, the item "I live here as a matter of habit" received the highest percentage (44 percent). The researchers summed up the findings on this subject in the following way:

> The kibbutz is at a stage of becoming a routine way of life; conscious affinity with certain values has been replaced by the impact of routine . . . almost a half of the second generation did not point to any explicit factor attaching them to the kibbutz, and they maintain that they live in it as a matter of habit. (Rosner et al., 1978, p. 536. See details of the findings on the Table p. 537)

We cannot ignore the fact that the main source of affinity with the kibbutz at that time was the sense of it being home. If so, we should not be surprised that thirty years later, striving for fundamental changes in the kibbutz way of life did not receive overwhelming opposition on ideological grounds.

From "Exclamation Marks" to "Question Marks"

> We were never permitted to have doubts, to err. . . .
> It's as though I am someone who lost something
> and wants to know what it is. . . . It's a void, and I
> loathe the attempts to fill it with meaningless slo-
> gans and declare "It's full! Full!" . . . I don't know
> how to silence the questions within me crying out to
> be given expression. (Shdemot 35, 1970, p. 42)[3]

One of the phenomena characterizing a generation of revolutionaries is the fervent desire to impart to the next generation "the legacy of the revolution" and the aspiration to see that generation committed to and implementing the aims of the original revolution. This desire led the first generation to burden the next one with the demand to follow in the earlier path. Some among the second generation were living under the burden of constant tension between their desire to fulfill their parents' expectations and their awareness that they were forgoing their distinct individuality.

An article published in 1965 created turmoil in kibbutz discourse. It was written by Omri Lulav, born in Affikim, entitled *And You! But We . . . ?*

> *Your generation is punctuated by exclamation marks, ours by question marks.* That is why we are so preoccupied by ourselves. Introverted, and for that reason also a little shortsighted: Lacking in a feeling for the collective—the movement, social class;

and *our answers are halting*, replete with commas and three-dot pauses of implicit deliberation. . . . They do not end in exclamation marks. . . . The right to focus on dilemmas and end up in the grip of "a crisis," the right to fail and even to err—that is a fundamental right that will enable us to live without miserably imitating others, to imprint a personal mark on our lives. [The emphases are mine.] (Lulav, 1965, p. 9)

The book *The Seventh Day* was published two years after the publication of Lulav's article. Its editors took pains to shape it in such a way that the silences and the halting speech would reflect the prominent presence of "absentees." "Against frameworks and in favor of dilemmas"—that is how Shlomit Toib (Tene), one of the editors of *The Seventh Day*, defined one of the explicit aims of the book (Dalmatzki, 1967). The Six-Day War was an existential experience that imprinted itself deeply in the soldiers' minds. Their search for ways to express what they experienced during the war highlighted the difference between the language of exclamations marks and that of question marks. There was a feeling that the exclamation marks of the parents' generation were not appropriate for all the dilemmas and searching that intensified in the wake of the war. During the many interviews with the editors of the book, the soldiers admitted that the experience of the war "generated a mode of expression that rejected the stock of clichés, the 'isms', the movement's and the kibbutz terminology, burdening and even to a great extent shackling us" (Toib, 1968). The wider the gap between the world of slogans and of reality, the more they felt the increasing disparity between the glow of the bombastic language and the gray everyday reality, and the sharper was their criticism of the convictions of the parents' generation: "We are the skeptical, doubting generation," protested the poet Ali Alon. "All that is left to us are contradictions and disintegrated dogma. What is left for us to believe in? We did believe once, but we were deceived—now we no longer comply. They won't be able to deceive us again" (*A Year After the War*, 1968, p. 7).

The transition from "exclamation marks" to "question marks" reflects the gradual fading of the relevance of kibbutz ideology. A considerable number of the members of the second generation felt that their parents' world of values and slogans was losing its vitality and had gradually become irrelevant to them. Yehiel Hazak expressed this feeling very well:

The ideology no longer serves those who hold on to it. . . . From the moment that it no longer permeates our psyche, a void appears in kibbutz life, and any void carries a price. . . . I dare say that this togetherness, with its moral and cultural content, is by now devoid of the power of the ideology and this void has to be confronted on a daily basis. (Hazak, 1969, pp. 104–06)

This quotation illustrates my assertion that many years before the start of the dismantling of the mechanisms and regulations underpinning the collective way of life, the process of ideology erosion that had sustained it had begun. In other words, the structural changes that occurred in the 1990s cannot be explained without highlighting the gradual waning of the relevance of that ideology.

From Ideological to Psychological Parlance

> The ideology was the glue, now it has evaporated.
> The next stage is alienation. (A Year After the War,
> p. 93)

The sense of a void and of the infiltration of the end of ideology into the kibbutz precincts generated a tendency to perceive the ideology as the root of all evil and to search in other pastures for spiritual empowerment. In the 1960s, we witnessed an attempt to switch from ideological parlance to a psychological perspective.

Starting in the 1960s, the *Shdemot* group[4] sought to revive Martin Buber's dialogical philosophy and the intimate talks in Upper Bitania of the Hashomer Hatzair pioneers. From the mid-1960s, kibbutz movement educators became exposed to the psychological tenets of Abraham Maslow and Carl Rogers. Rachel Manor (from Mishmar Haemek) studied social work in the USA and returned to Israel, having learned basic techniques of group dynamics and interpersonal communication. In a series of articles and interviews, she deplored the flawed interpersonal culture in the kibbutz movement. She wrote about "the fear of spontaneous expression of opinions and its repression"; that "we impede the expression of feelings"; and that "kibbutz society is in danger of conservative introversion, of exerting pressure leading to conformism, instead of enabling an open-minded atmosphere furthering 'the spreading of wings' and fostering personal initiative, spontaneity and creativity" (Manor, 1968b, pp. 99–103). To counteract these tendencies, she proposed intimate discussion groups, group dynamics, and workshops using the Training Group Method—as a way of confronting this situation.

A lively discussion was carried on in *Shdemot* about these approaches in a section named "group work and personal relationships in the kibbutz" (Tanenbaum, 1970, pp. 81–92). The section contained articles such as "From the World of a T Group" and "Behavioral Sciences and Their Implementation in Everyday Life." Bob Tenenbaum and Art Shadlin, American professors who came to Israel to teach techniques of interpersonal communication, introduced into kibbutz lexis concepts such as long-term planning, organizational procedures, feedback, the process of decision-making, and organizational reconstruction. It would take almost twenty years before these concepts would be internalized in the organizational language of the kibbutz movement (Tanenbaum, 1970, pp. 81–92).

Alongside these workshops, many kibbutzim began to adopt the method of intimate home discussion groups. The kibbutz assembly was perceived as a formal and rigid framework, impeding a true, frank dialogue among the members. The idea to hold such small group discussions was intended to overcome the limitations of the general assembly and enable personal expression and intimate discussion among all the members. Starting in the mid-1960s, many reports began to appear in the kibbutz papers about small discussion groups on various topics. The main feature the reports shared was the sense that finally "hearts opened up," "the barriers came down." The frank and spontaneous discourse that the members had yearned for made them feel elated.[5]

The ensuing combination between the dialogic philosophy of Martin Buber and the humanistic psychology of Maslow and Rogers gradually shifted kibbutz discourse from an ideological to a psychological perspective. The "talk culture" that sprang up after the Six-Day War, the intimate group discussions, and preoccupation with techniques of group dynamics gradually assumed a prominent role in kibbutz life. A comprehensive scrutiny of the various means of expression prevalent in the kibbutz movement shows that, starting in the mid-1960s, a new language developed. Articles and speeches of the time display great differences between the two languages. Ideology appears rigid, while the psychological stance is lenient; the former is demanding, the latter is flexible; the former is unequivocal, the latter is hesitant; the former is judgmental, the latter is tolerant; the former looks down from above, the latter speaks at eye level; the former worships rationality, while the latter is responsive to the display of emotions. The tone, body language, and words project a different atmosphere. The penetration of a new language into the kibbutz mitigated the harshness of ideological opposition to the process of privatization that developed twenty years later.

From "We" to "Me"

> *Everything begins with the individual and depends*
> *on the individual. (Landauer, 1963, p. 83)*

The kibbutz movement preserved the collectivist ethos as its formative and guiding principle (Shapira, 1977, pp. 25–33). While opposition to this ethos was already in the air in Israel, the kibbutz movement fought against this "destructive" tendency. The principles of the collectivist ethos were laid down by the pioneer generation. The 1948 generation made its own contribution by adopting "the culture of we," consolidated as the Palmah soldiers (an acronym for the assault companies, the crack military force of the 1940s) gathered around the bonfire. The kibbutz made the collective tasks a top priority and demanded that the members comply—that they sacrifice their private desires and aspirations to the needs and demands of the society (Almog, 1997, pp. 351–82). From the early sixties on, however, we can discern a growing tendency to divert the emphasis from "we" to "me." Avraham Shapira, the editor of *Shdemot* and prominent among those who wished to move in this new direction, wrote: "Even partial liberation from the influence of the collective is a precondition for choosing an independent path, the only means enabling experiences that would help each person to become 'me'" (Peretz, 1964, p. 105). The journal *Shdemot* was among the main change agents in the gradual process of the dismantling of the collectivist ethos in the kibbutz movement. Shapira opened up the journal to any assertion striving to undermine the kibbutz collectivist ethos and to impede individuation. The journal's pages were interlaced with quotations derived from the writings of thinkers such as A. D. Gordon, Buber, Landauer, Krishnamurti, Tagore, and many others; Shapira enlisted them all in the task of placing the individual in center stage, a person that strives for self-realization, refusing to be swallowed up and effaced by the collective herd.

> That's how it is, we are afraid of each other; public opinion dictates the course of our lives too predominantly, it reduces them to awful routine. And what does this lead to? Anything a little original, with a smattering of true individual expression, is prohibited! We act according to the kibbutz conventions, to what is acceptable in this country, in the world. . . . The main aim is to behave like everyone else, speak like everyone else, sing and dance like everyone else, dress like everyone else. (Yehiel, 1962, p. 153)

The right to assert one's individuality, the wish to resist the "herd culture," and the need to behave "like everyone else" became a central motif among the second generation. If in the past it was clear to everyone that the desirable order of priorities in the kibbutz is that the individual places himself/herself at the disposal of the community, in those days the discourse changed diametrically: Instead of asking what the individual should sacrifice for the sake of the community, the question arose as to what the community can do for the benefit of the individual's development. Many young people in the kibbutz movement were in the vanguard, in calling for a new kind of relationship between the individual and the society. These youngsters sought a change of direction from "what will they say" and "like everyone else" as a force that paralyzes and inhibits the individual to a society that legitimizes variation and seeks to empower the individual living within it.

From the Collective to the Self-Fulfillment Ethos

> *Self-realization without any concern for the common goal leads to lack of responsibility and of consideration for the needs of the community. In the USA the yearning for self-realization brought about the setting up of Hippie communes by young people living according to their momentary whims, without any commitments whatsoever. Are we on the way to turning the kibbutz into a hippie commune?[6]*
> *(Yosefial, 1970, p. 7)*

The most significant expression of the transition from "we" to "me" was proposing self-realization as an alternative to the collective ethos. *Shdemot* was also one of the prominent agents of the internalization of this process. As in the process of transition from ideology to psychology, the notion of self-realization was also consolidated via the fruitful encounter between two different streams. The idea developed, on the one hand, from the philosophy of Gordon and Buber; on the other hand, it was promoted by the psychological school of Maslow and Erich Fromm, mediated and interpreted by Rachel Manor. She exposed *Shdemot* readers to the ideas of self-realization, emphasizing its relevance to kibbutz reality:

> Every healthy person aspires to self-realization. . . . When he still has far to go in this direction, he lives in a state of self-deception, escaping from himself. . . . It is the role of the environment to enable him to realize all his potential—not that of the environment. (Manor, 1968a, pp. 59–60)

As the notion of self-realization began to take root in kibbutz discourse, the journals of the kibbutz movement and "the talking" that took place after the Six-Day War became replete with demands to recognize each individual's need for self-realization within the framework of kibbutz society.

Benko Adar beautifully expressed this new idea:

> Until now the kibbutz was perceived mainly as a tool, and so was the individual—as a soldier on the line, called upon to sacrifice, serve certain aims, give up for the sake of. . . . That is the way of all great revolutions at their inception. . . . Gradually a new

perception takes hold, emphasizing the kibbutz as an aim in itself, as a framework—not as a fighting unit committed to the execution of missions of national importance. This leads to a change in the attitude to the individual. The person becomes an aim, an end in itself. The individual, his happiness, joy. . . . Today our task—that of the younger generation—is to build on the foundations laid down by the generation of the first settlers, a society enabling each person to assert himself, realize himself, to fulfill the potential of his personality. A society of happy people, not people sacrificing themselves "on the altar." Not "kibbutz" as a group of people living for the sake of the kibbutz itself, but kibbutz as the people living in it, its aim being the people themselves. (*A Year After the War*, p. 70)

The implementation of the principle of self-realization was channeled into four domains: temporary leave, travel abroad, higher education, and choice of occupation. Young people in kibbutzim began to hold discussions, forge sets of rules, and create tracks enabling them to realize their aspirations in these four areas.

The social committee of Kibbutz Beit Hashita, for example, held a discussion entitled "Requests for leave from work—an urgent need for our youngsters?" in view of the fact that "we are flooded by requests for long leave." These requests reflected a yearning to see the world, to wander, and to become acquainted with other ways of life. In the wake of these requests, most kibbutzim forged a set of rules regarding travel abroad. An expression of this desire can be found in the book *Among the Young*. The singer Meir Ariel, who participated in a discussion in his kibbutz, Mishmarot, said:

I'd like "to kill" three years in Jamaica among the bananas . . . I know how people live there, and I won't get married until after I've trudged round the world, because I must first see all kinds of things. (*Among the Young*, p. 23)

A young member of Ein Hashofet continued the same line of thought:

I think there must be some kind of procedure enabling people—in particular young people—to wander and develop their personality to the full. (*Among the Young*, p. 167)

The struggle for the right to self-realization in the sphere of education—higher studies—took longer than the others that started in the early sixties and lasted until the mid-1980s when the notion of "functional studies"[7] was finally abandoned with the initiation of the young members' track, enabling every youngster to choose the course of studies he/she was interested in. At the beginning of the 1960s, to aspire to academic studies was considered "a bourgeois's sin," a dangerous tendency, a characteristic of the "culture of certificates" of the capitalist world. One of the basic tenets of the kibbutz movement was the adoption of Borochov's idea of the need to turn the pyramid upside down. Aspiring to white-collar academic studies was perceived as a real threat to the "revolutionary" emphasis on maximum productivity, a dangerous reaction, reminiscent of the characteristics of the Diasporic Jew that the pioneers wished to counteract.

In the 1960s, members of the second generation wanted to turn the pyramid back again:

> *Our fathers revolted against studies and various intellectual pursuits and embraced manual labor; now society in this country in general, and we in particular, should and must revolt once more.* Not to mince words, I think we are about to return to those occupations that the first generation deliberately avoided. . . . I expect that within ten years, over 50% of the members will work outside the kibbutz. There will be people with higher education, working in their professions. [The emphasis is mine.] (Zartal, 1969, pp. 13–14)[8]

A young member of Neot Mordechai also maintained that it was the right time to change direction:

> Among the first generation, professors became peasants; this is not appropriate for the younger generation. I am wondering how peasants can turn into professors, how one can be a little less a man of action. (*Hashomer Hatzair Archives*, 1968, p. 4)

This is how the demand for recognition of the desire to study—not only to meet the needs of the kibbutz but also according to personal inclinations—started to gain momentum. At the conference of the young members of the Ichud Movement, held during the Succot of 1971, the following decision was made: "The kibbutz is obliged to find the course of studies appropriate to the ability and inclinations of the member" ("Summary of the Conference," 1971, pp. 10–11).

It was only natural that after the taboo on the subject of higher education had been lifted, the next sacred cow would be discussed—the kind of occupation. The above-mentioned conference also dealt at length with the need to expand the variety of occupations matching the members' inclinations. When someone voiced the inevitable question "So who will be left to work in the cowshed?" one of the young ones dared to respond in this "heretical" way:

> If no one wants to work in the cowshed, there won't be a cowshed; the cowshed exists for me—not I for the cowshed. Who said that there must be a cowshed in the kibbutz? (Winkler, 1970)

Yaron Rochli from Rosh Hanikra, one of the organizers of the conference, was clarified the young people's attitude in a more elegant way:

> Until now it was customary to adapt the wishes of the people to the needs of the kibbutz, and they were dominant. This was usually accepted without opposition. But now the younger generation is promoting a new approach, calling for changes in the kibbutz structure that would provide more opportunities for the realization of a greater variety of aspirations in the occupational domain. (Dagan, 1970)

These statements are the first signs of a major change in attitude. Researchers pointed out that "the second generation's professional aspirations did not meet the needs of the kibbutz occupational structure at the time of their research" (*The Second Generation*, p. 352). From this time onward, the kibbutz movement was embroiled in an ongoing struggle between two diametrically opposed approaches: one approach sought to subordinate the members' aspirations to the occupational needs of the kibbutz and the other sought to adapt the occupational structure to the members' professional aspirations. Just as in the educational domain, it was only in the mid-1980s that the balance between the two approaches began to tilt toward the latter approach.

Thus the concept "self-realization" became popular. Many people interpreted it in a simplistic way, different from the original intention of the *Shdemot* group, and used it as an ideological cover for personal demands, such as for leave and studies. In 1970, the bulletin *This Week in Kibbutz Artzi* carried out a poll regarding the main events that had taken place in 1969. One of the respondents described aptly the way the idea of self-realization was taking shape: "The process of seeking 'self-realization' is taking the usual course—turning into a demand—and the response is also spreading" (*This Week in Kibbutz Haartzi*, 1969).

The seed sown by the *Shdemot* group in the pastures of the kibbutz movement at the beginning of the 1960s grew into a sturdy tree, spreading its branches in all directions. The slogan of self-realization rapidly turned into a mantra, seeking to legitimize any material demand, and the more, the better. Even though that was not the intention of the *Shdemot* group, their contribution to placing the individual with his/her aspirations at the center of the kibbutz's attention cannot be ignored. The idea of self-realization created an upheaval in kibbutz perceptions and discourse, diverting the focus from the individual as a means to the realization of the aims of society to society as a means to the realization of the individual's potential.

Conclusions

The processes described above focused on developments within the kibbutz movement. Obviously we cannot ignore their wider context, such as processes occurring in Israeli society as a whole or Western society generally. We cannot explain what was happening in the kibbutz movement without pointing out the debacle of ideologies, the disappointment and awakening by the Western and Israeli left wing from their belief in the USSR as representing "the forces of tomorrow," the growth of "the new left" in the wake of student revolts, and processes of privatization occurring in the world and in Israel in particular. These factors undoubtedly affected the kibbutz way of life, and the five components, dealt with in this chapter, were to a great extent inspired by "the spirit of the times" (in Hegel's words), the second half of the twentieth century, worldwide and in Israeli society.

The kibbutz movement of the beginning of the twenty-first century is different from that in the 1960s. Many people deplore the process of the "dismantling of the kibbutz" and lament the fading of the most challenging alternative to the capitalist way of life. Others perceive in the change processes a precondition for the survival of an organization that wishes to adapt to changes. However, both those who deplore the situation and those who praise it cannot deny that the changes of the 1990s stemmed from the transition from "we" to "me."

Notes

1. Today the kibbutzim are usually grouped according to three categories:

    1. Collective kibbutzim—based on the traditional model, i.e., with no connection between the member's work and his/her budget.
    2. "Combined budget" arrangements—where a certain percentage of income from work constitutes a component of the member's budget.
    3. Differential pay—where the members receive all the income from work and sometimes also from other sources (except for the deduction of taxes).

    According to the 2005 survey, more than two-thirds of the kibbutzim no longer keep to the traditional collective model (Pavin, 2005, p. 66). For more than ten years, The Institute for Research of the Kibbutz has been carrying out surveys of public opinion in kibbutzim, examining the attitude of the members to the privatization and change processes. Almost on all the parameters examined in the context of these changes, there is a growing tendency of support for privatization and changes. For instance, in 1989 only 45 percent of TAKAM kibbutzim and 31 percent of Kibbutz Haartzi kibbutzim supported financial remuneration for hours of overtime work, while in 2001, 73 percent of TAKAM kibbutzim and 62 percent of Kibbutz Haartzi kibbutzim did so (Palgi and Sharir, 2001, pp. 41–59).

2. At the end of the 1960s and the beginning of the 1970s, the concept "talks" became widespread in the kibbutz movement. It was introduced by the book *The Seventh*

Day (in Hebrew *Soldiers Talk*), after the Six-Day War (*The Seventh Day*, 1970). Its success led to what was called "talk culture." Talk became the main means by which the problems related to the kibbutz way of life and the intergenerational relationships were confronted. Many of these talks were later recorded and printed in the kibbutz journals or separately, for instance, *A Year After the War*, 1968, and *Among the Young*, 1969.

3. This chapter appeared without a title and unsigned in *Together*—a bulletin of the young of the Kibbutz Hameuhad, September 1966. It aroused a plethora of reactions in the newspaper. Two years later the article again appeared in *Together*, this time under the title "No, don't give me all the answers, they are less important than the questions!" *Together*, November 1968, p. 11. The article was published again for the third time in *Shdemot* 35, fall 1970, p. 42.

4. The journal *Shdemot* was first published in 1960. It became one of the main platforms used by some of the second generation of the kibbutz movement to challenge the reality in which they lived and examine the degree of relevance of a considerable part of the ideas on which they had been brought up. The *Shdemot* arena is above all that of Avraham Shapira (Kibbutz Yizrael), the journal's founder and editor, who made it into a sensitive seismograph, well able to sense the stress and the sources of the unease, and point to ways of coping with them. With sensitiveness and humility, Shapira succeeded in turning *Shdemot* into a prolific environment, giving voice to young, sensitive people, seeking a channel for spiritual growth. The journal generated "the *Shdemot* group," comprising young people from the three kibbutz movements (Hakibbutz Haartzi, Haihud, and Hameuhad). This group edited the book *The Seventh Day* and later created "talk culture" in the kibbutz movement (see note 2).

5. For reports about intimate group discussions, see e.g., *Shdemot* 16, January 1965, p. 34; *Shdemot* 17, April 1965, p. 43; *Naan Bulletin*, November 25, 1966; *Ein Ha-horesh Bulletin*, May 6, 1966; *Letter to the Members*, August 13, 1969; and *Letter to the Members*, May 27, 1970.

6. These are the words of Senta Yoseftal, who was the secretary of the Ihud Movement.

7. The concept "functional studies" expressed the perception that members could undertake only studies matching the needs of the kibbutz, not their own aspirations.

8. It is worth mentioning that Adam Zertal was at that time "community economic administrator" of Kibbutz Ein Shemer and today he is a professor of archeology at Haifa University.

Bibliography

Dagan, D. "Struggle for Independence by the Young Members of the Ihud Movement." *Maariv* 10 (1970): 23 [Hebrew].

Dalmatzki, B. "The Story of One War and of Battles Within." *Hotam* (1967) [Hebrew].

Gan, A. "Social Changes in the Kibbutz Movement in the 1960s." *Iunim Bitkumat Israel: Studies in Zionism* 16 (2006): 343–72 [Hebrew].

Hazak, Y. "Shattered Tablets in the Kibbutz Yard." *Shdemot* 29 (1969): 104–06 [Hebrew].

Lulav, O. "And You! But We …?" *Shdemot* 17 (1965): 9 [Hebrew].

Manor, R. "Encounter between the Individual and Society and Mutual Understanding." *Hedim* 88 (1968a): 59–60 [Hebrew].

————. "Therapeutic-Educational Activity and Its Implementation in the Society's Life Experience." *Shdemot* 29 (1968b): 99–103 [Hebrew].

Almog, O. *The Sabra—A Portrait*, 351–82. Tel Aviv: Am Oved, 1997 [Hebrew].

Palgi, M. and S. Sharir. *Survey of Public Opinion in Kibbutzim in the Year 2001*. Haifa: The Institute for Research of the Kibbutz, Haifa University, 2001 [Hebrew].

Pavin, A. *The Kibbutz Movement, Information and Numbers*. Tel Aviv: Yad Tabenkin, 2005 [Hebrew].

Peretz, L. "Should the Spirit of the Jewish Städtel Predominate in Israel and in the Jewish World?" *Shdemot* 15 (1964): 105 [Hebrew].

Rosner, M., Y. Ben-David, A. Avnat, N. Cohen, and A. Levitan. *The Second Generation—The Kibbutz between Continuation and Change*. Tel Aviv: Sifriat Poalim, 1978 [Hebrew].

Shapira, Avraham, ed. *The Seventh Day: Soldiers' Talk About the Six-Day War*. Translated by Henry Near. London: Steimatzky's Agency & André Deutsch, 1970.

Shapira, Y. *Democracy in Israel*, 25–33. Ramat Gan: Masada, 1977 [Hebrew].

Tanenbaum, B. "The Behavioral Sciences and Their Implementation in Kibbutz Life." *Shdemot* 37 (1970): 81–92 [Hebrew].

Toib, S. "About the Talks and Beyond." *This Week in Kibbutz Haartzi* (1968) [Hebrew].

Tzur, M., Y. Ben-Aharon, and A. Grossman, eds. *Among the Young: Talking in Groups in the Kibbutz Movement*. Tel Aviv: Am Oved, 1969.

Weber, U. *To Reconstruct Itself: The Kibbutz Confronts Its Future*. Tel Aviv: Kibbutz Meuhad, 1992 [Hebrew].

Winkler, Y. "Shattering the Tablets, Summary of the Conference of Young Members of the Ihud Movement." *Haaretz* 12.4 (1970) [Hebrew].

Yehiel, N. "From Where Will the Calamity Descend Upon Us?" *Shdemot* 5–6 (1962): 153 [Hebrew].

Yoseftal, S. *Archives of the Ihud*, File 3/398 (1970): 7 [Hebrew].

Zartal, A. "Our Future in the Kibbutz—A Kibbutz Discussion for the Young, Hefer Valley." *Shdemot* 33 (1969): 13–14.

Local Kibbutz Publications and Archives

A Year After the War—Discussions by the Younger Generation. Ein Shemer, 1968.

Together. Tel Aviv: Kibbutz Hameuhad, 1966, 1968.

"No, Don't Give Me All the Answers, They Are Less Important Than the Questions!" *Shdemot* 35 (1970): 42.

Naan Bulletin, November 25, 1966.

Ein Hahoresh Bulletin, May 6, 1966.

Letter to the Members, August 13, 1969.

Letter to the Members, May 27, 1970.

Minutes of the General Assembly in Kibbutz Naan, February 24, 1961. (Kibbutz Naan Archive, Hebrew)

Mouthpiece of the Kvutzah 20, no. 1–2 (1971).

Landauer, G. *Shdemot* 11–12 (1963): 83.

Hashomer Hatzair Archives 11.5, no. 5 (1968): 4. Tel Aviv.

"Summary of the Conference of Young Members of the Ihud Movement." *Ichud Movement Archives*, File 3/398/398/3 (1971): 10–11.

This Week in Kibbutz Haartzi. (1969). Peace is as far as the moon from the earth, questionnaire on the occasion of the start of 1970 (9.12).

3

The Changing Composition of Kibbutz Elites

Menachem Topel

Kibbutz elites (people who exert exceptional influence on decision-making) have always aroused interest, owing to the "classless" kibbutz's principle of equality. While the issue of kibbutz stratification has been studied extensively, the dramatic changes through which the kibbutz is currently passing make it imperative to analyze the relationship between these changes and the composition of the dominant elite in the new conditions.

The initial assertion regarding Kibbutz stratification was made by Rosenfeld (1951), who found that the founders of the kibbutz who were active in countrywide organizations constituted an aristocracy enjoying prestige and influence. They also tended to block the trend toward liberalization on the part of the rank and file. Taking issue with this analysis, Talmon-Garber (1970) maintained that kibbutzim were run in a democratic manner but confirmed the existence of informal leaders who, in her opinion, represented the public. Other scholars have emphasized different aspects of kibbutz stratification (Fedida, 1972; Yuchtman-Yaar, 1972; Shapira, 1978/9; Ben-Rafael, 1986; Topel, 1992). The network of connections among kibbutz functionaries together with their loyalty to the movement and its leadership developed into personal power resources. The local elite became part of the kibbutz elite and then the national elite (Avrahami, 1992). Later, people with formal education as professional managers—the technocrats—made their way into the elite.

Historical Background to the Growth of a Kibbutz Elite

Early in the life of most kibbutzim, central activists within the founding core established ties with the movement leadership, the authorities, and kibbutz institutions—vital elements in the economic and social life of the kibbutz—and transformed these relationships into political resources to be utilized in relationships within their community. Their connections, as well as their activities as representatives of kibbutz ideology, placed them at the center of local political life over a prolonged period, unlike the formal occupants of roles, who were subjected to frequent turnover. In this way, the informal political structure of the kibbutz took shape (Topel, 1992). The leaders furthermore held the key to the personal advancement of their fellows, which depended upon ratification on the part of the kibbutz leaders passed through various roles within the kibbutz, activity in kibbutz organizations, and acquisition of higher education in fields required by the kibbutz (Fedida, 1972; Ben-Rafael, 1986).

These personal resources underwent devaluation following the changes that occurred after the establishment of the state. The resources that accrued to the kibbutz from the connections of the leader now formally allocated independently of the leader. The community's livelihood depended on the kibbutz's economic branches and regional economic activity rather than upon its connections within the movement. The kibbutz economy became stronger and the standard of living rose. Population growth resulted from natural internal increase rather than from youth groups directed by the movement leadership (Meron, 1987). Those active in the kibbutz economy became heads of large branches within the kibbutz, managers of industry, and representatives of the kibbutz in umbrella organizations. Under these conditions, the "economists" gained power at the expense of "social leaders," as the kibbutz became increasingly dependent on self-generated income, particularly industrialization (see Kressel, 1974).

The "economists" were not concerned with issues of equality or democratic participation, but they remained loyal to the kibbutz norms of task achievement, ascetic lifestyle, and allocation of resources to production. Together with other elites, they safeguarded the "kibbutz rules of the game." This elite grew out of positions in industrial enterprises and in the economic institutions of the movement, the region and the sector. The image of these "economic people" was one of devoted, hardworking individuals who, even though they had not engaged in physical labor for many years, continued to conform to the accepted norms.

Emergence of a Technocracy

The proliferation of managerial roles in the various sectors is associated with separatist processes within the kibbutz system in the economic and social spheres (Etzioni, 1980). Demographic and economic growth, an improved standard of living, and processes of differentiation and industrialization all contributed to the rise of professional experts in agriculture and education, of industrial managers, and of people versed in matters of economy and information who acceded to organizational roles. At the same time, mechanisms were developed to prevent the empowerment of those in managerial positions. These included periodic replacement, differentiation between management and expertise, appointment of public committees, decentralization of authority, and the sovereignty of the general assembly.

As a result, some of the experts and managers found their advancement blocked and left the kibbutz. Others established themselves in the semiautonomous industrial plants or in the powerful regional industries, which became the foci of a technocratic spirit (Shapira, 1978/9). On the other hand, an opposing "ideological" spirit characterized the managers of the kibbutz economy, the leaders in the national movements, and the "social" leadership within the kibbutzim. These different emphases masked the power struggle between the movement and the regional industrial plants (Rosolio, 1975; Rayman, 1981; Fogiel-Bijaoui, 1994).

Influenced by the high status of the "new class," kibbutz members increasingly favored a path of study at academic institutions. For the most part, they took the economics track at the Rehovot Agriculture Faculty or the advanced course in economics at the Ruppin College. The kibbutz movement amended its own vocational courses to include study programs in management (Helman, 1987, pp. 1037–38). These study tracks became more prolonged, expensive, and professionally oriented.

All of these processes strengthened the economic and managerial leadership within the kibbutz economy. The growing power of the independent economic branches of the individual kibbutz and its industrial plants generated a sense of dependence on the part of kibbutz members on the experts in charge of them (Warhurst, 1994, p. 217). The new professional managers and their expert consultants at staff level became less dependent on the local political systems since their positions as essential experts were assured and they were not confined by the conventional work scheduling. The demand for professional managers grew steadily, owing to the development of auxiliary systems and staff positions. These were complex systems developed by the professional managers, such as pricing, computerization, information, entrepreneurship, location of industries, and expansion of activity in the area and within the movement. Management was transformed from leadership to an occupation

(Lanir, 1992). The managerial stratum became institutionalized as an irreversible phenomenon (Helman, 1987).

The former brand of "traditional economists" was unable to contend with the younger generation of professionals with formal academic degrees, and most were removed from their posts. A few completed their studies, became more professional, and generally remained in the system in staff positions. By contrast, present-day technocrats grew out of academic management studies. The authority of these new managers is recognized on the strength of their expertise rather than of their past or their connections. Their image is one of businessmen. The change in the characteristics of the economic elite did not affect the personal, nonmaterial benefits, status symbols, or rewards attached to the roles, such as inherent work interest, control of promotion tracks, free use of a vehicle, social esteem, trips abroad, and connections with external bodies (Topel, 1992). Generally, up to five members in each kibbutz were located at the central economic core, with heads of branches, senior management in industrial and tourist enterprises, and the managers of the large production branches or the larger service units occupying the second echelon. Their numbers vary according to the size of the kibbutz and its plants, from five to twenty and more. The group is mainly of men, kibbutz veterans, spouses of kibbutz veterans, and relative newcomers who joined the kibbutz in search of an improved quality of life.

The Influence of the Crisis on Composition of the Elite

The latter half of the 1970s witnessed a rapid deterioration in the environment's attitude toward the kibbutz, despite the generally pervasive sense of power and success (see Meron, 1987; Weber, 1992): the political parties associated with the kibbutz movements were removed from power. The individualistic atmosphere encouraged youngsters to leave the kibbutz and reduced the number of new arrivals; the rise in living standards in Israeli society encouraged a similar rise in the kibbutzim, not necessarily linked to their economic ability.

The economic crisis of 1985 severely affected most kibbutzim and the status of the kibbutz movements, their economic organizations, and the regional industrial plants. In these circumstances, dependence on the kibbutz's professional experts increased. The experts increasingly made the decisions themselves and accepted the formal and, at times, the actual supervision of political or social leaders, only to a limited extent. The status of other leaders dwindled considerably, and they generally took on the role of critics (or annoyances, in the view of the managers).

The inability of the movement's functionaries to obtain government aid reduced their importance as a track for personal advancement. In parallel, a greater variety of advancement opportunities became available to kibbutz members in areas uncontrolled by the elite, both within governmental bodies and public organizations and in commercial companies, academia, or the cultural sphere. The social capital of members of the political elite diminished rapidly, leaving the traditional leadership bereft of actual influence. The attempts by these leaders to utilize their former status were occasionally pathetic. The erstwhile "economists"—those whose status was based on their experience and loyalty to the movement and its tasks—also declined in stature.

An additional aspect of change in the kibbutz that had direct implications for the composition of the elite was the lowering of the surrounding fence around it (Ben-Rafael and Topel, 2004). This refers to the integration of the individual or commercial subunit into the economic and social surroundings and to the entrance of outsiders into the kibbutz. The kibbutz factory and even the community itself now constitute additional places of work available to technocrats in the open market. And they have indeed seized the opportunity: kibbutz management is full of people from the outside who function as managers of industry and businesses, salaried directors, community managers, human resources managers, educational managers, organizational consultants, and so forth. This constantly expanding echelon constitutes an integral part of the kibbutz elite.

Technocrats as a Dominant Elite

The place of the political elites that mediated between the kibbutzim and outside society was now appropriated by the technocrat managers, who previously had been merely part of the elite or had acted as technical assistants to the political leadership. Thanks to their position and education they became the liaison functionaries with the significant financial systems such as banks and the economic government ministries. Internally, they offered intelligent management of the crisis. The focus was on the results of the crisis, rather than these technocrats' involvement in generating the crisis, an assertion made by members of competing elites (Pavin, 1992).

My research into change in the kibbutz led to the conclusion that technocrats play a dominant role in contemporary kibbutz society (To-pel, 2005). Their power enables them to initiate change in the society's organizational patterns and to establish a differential reward system. Modification of the organizational system in turn further empowers the technocrats. They behave as a "rebel elite" even though (and perhaps because) they already constitute an established elite and play an important part in the running of the kibbutz. Moreover, even in robust kibbutzim that have remained unaffected by the crisis or those in the collective stream, the elite is likewise composed of economic, financial, and managerial experts, as in the majority of the kibbutz system.

Given such circumstances, it is unsurprising that many of the former political or "general" leaders appear as the hard core of traditionalists and representatives of the "deprived." This explains the difficulties experienced by "general" leaders in finding new power bases within the current political context and the general atmosphere in the kibbutz and the country. As mentioned above, some make an effort to preserve the legitimacy associated with former power bases. Others hesitantly participate in the ongoing process.

My aforementioned study found that the kibbutz technocratic elite displays the classic technocratic characteristics and principles outlined in the literature: they are not centralistic, but rather construct a decentralized and highly autonomous system, which they control by means of computerized systems and managerial reports. They operate pragmatically in the open market, free of any movement-based, ideological, social, or political commitments. They clearly favor advancement according to qualifications and achievements, and rewards based on performance. Their "significant others" are their colleagues in the general technocratic systems, rather than their fellow kibbutz members. They do not operate as part of a group characterized by solidarity, but as individuals who empower themselves and their image.

The disappearance of the old-style, centralistic "economists" and the demand for efficient professional management of the decentralized sectors contributed to the formation of sector-based elites. The general managers and their staff naturally determine the budgetary framework, investment directions, operational principles, the organizational and economic structure, and the measure of integration of activity of the units with external systems. The technocratic elite does not altogether replace other elites, but there has been a significant change in the relationships between them. The general elite, which formerly employed the experts in its service, is now appointed by the technocratic elite, supported by it and dependent on it. It is given a say only when it suits the technocratic elite.

Given these conditions, the technocratic elite does not behave in a way that is generally expected of a dominant elite, namely, as a protector of the existing social structure that assures its advantages as an elite. In the past, change stemmed from the efforts of the "rank and file" who sought personal freedom in the face of the elite. In this case, the elite consistently supports proposals for change (Ben-Rafael and Gajst, 1993, pp. 181 and 211). This phenomenon stems, as noted, from a sense of frustration and deprivation on the part of an elite within an egalitarian society, limited in its ability to exploit its advantages while required to make a greater effort than others.

On the National Movement Level

The movement's national-level organizations underwent a parallel change. In the past, the central elite was mobilized from above, in both senses: kibbutz activists were inducted into the movement's various bodies and associated organizations by the movement elite and were likewise promoted within the elite, as a function of their connections with the national political leadership to which the movement was connected and this elite's internal procedures.

The change that occurred in the method of choosing the movement secretary, from "mobilization" to election by the movement's membership, expresses the waning power of the political leadership, which was thus prevented from determining the composition of the kibbutz elite. It is nevertheless clear that candidates are "mobilized" by various elite groupings, as is the case in the public sphere. And at this stage, there is no doubting the power of the technocrats belonging to the more cohesive systems, such as the powerful regional structures.

Even after the crisis, the movements sought to continue regular operation, but were obliged to curtail their operation because the kibbutzim were unwilling to grant them sufficient budgets or to allow them to maintain their role in determining internal matters within the kibbutzim. Certain departments ceased to function. The continued existence of other departments was made conditional on their ability to finance themselves by commercializing their services. Leaders no longer emerged from local kibbutz activity but rather were educated experts. Economists and business managers, lawyers, and accountants carried far greater weight in decision-making. Such activity no longer constitutes a springboard for general leadership since it is confined to a circumscribed professional realm. Thus, at the movement level, a transition has occurred from a charismatic to professional leadership (Rosolio, 1995, abstract).

As part of the process of decentralization, various roles were transferred from the movement to the regional institutions as a result of the movement's economic hardships and the ability of the regional councils to provide these services within the framework of their operational budget. This move served only to weaken the movements further and empower the regional elite (Avrahami, 1993; Fogiel-Bijaoui, 1994; Degani, 2006). Their weakened position naturally affects the stature of the kibbutz representatives among the political elite and their ability to deal with the government machinery.

Elite as Social Category or Consolidated Group?

Neither the growing power of the technocrats nor the proliferation of the pragmatic rational paradigm is sufficient to form a cohesive elite. Its present heterogeneous composition in fact detracts from its ability to coalesce. Today's community elite includes managers and external consultants drawn from different backgrounds. Similarly, many kibbutz members who enjoy prestige within their kibbutz attain this stature thanks to their standing outside the kibbutz system.

A factor that impedes consolidation among the technocrats is the brake on development and even a waning of influence of the regional enterprises in the wake of the economic crisis. Moreover, the public remains sensitive to the consolidation of a "class" elite within an egalitarian society. On the contrary, those seeking to preserve the traditional kibbutz warn members of the danger of class stratification. Thus, technocrats take great care not to create the impression of an elitist grouping, in contrast to the classic elitist model that seeks to establish its standing by emphasizing its image as an elite.

According to our research findings, the technocrats constitute a social stratum rather than a consolidated elite. They are people with similar education who engage in neighboring fields of activity and share common interests and thought patterns, all of which are reflected in their activity. Among them, a communication network is emerging on an inter-kibbutz, interorganizational, or interregional basis. But for now these are as yet informal, unstable networks, not connected with one another and by no means institutionalized.

The changes in the kibbutz are associated with changes in the running of the country and in global society in general. Israeli society may now be termed a "technocratic democracy" with an unconsolidated elite, decentralized organization, and hegemonic thought.

Summary

In the latter half of the previous century, the kibbutz underwent a gradual process of change of elites, associated with the greater importance of educational and professional assets at the expense of political connections. This process gathered momentum following the crisis of the 1970s and reached public awareness during the first half of the 1980s. The crisis made more people recognize the significant resources required to gain stature in the kibbutz elite at the local and national levels. Political connections suddenly shed their values, and the vacuum was filled by the technocratic elite. These individuals were recruited or volunteered to take command on the basis of skills. It became their job to point the way toward a new solution.

The technocratic elite found itself in a new situation in which the leadership and ideology of the Kibbutz movement were losing their legitimacy. The technological elite has learned that to succeed it must "play politics"—to quote Keren (1996)—and take into consideration the wishes of rank-and-file kibbutz members. It thus willingly adopts the demand for liberalism at the personal level, without relinquishing control over organizational and economic assets. These circumstances work in its favor, in terms of both public support for its actions and advantages on the personal level. The continued existence of the cooperative association is a condition for continuing the management of shared assets, which is the technocrats' source of power.

It should be noted that the new elite comprises individuals both from within and outside the kibbutz, whereas the previous elite included kibbutz members only. Not only consultants and technical experts, but also managers of the kibbutz's general institutions and its particular sectors are employed as an integral part of management. These are people who exert tremendous influence on decision-making in the kibbutz.

The overwhelming dominance of men within the group of technocrats raises the question of gender equality in a society that proclaims itself to be egalitarian. Much has been written on gender disparity in the kibbutz, but at a time when women obtain higher education in greater numbers than men, this question warrants attention. The influence of technocratization on gender disparity is complex: physical labor has been reduced, and there are now greater opportunities to work from home. Formal education has expanded, and there is greater awareness of gender disparity. These developments have generated the potential for massive inclusion of women in elite track positions, certainly with regard to the technocratic elite. In reality, however, only a few women have reached managerial roles, and gender disparity has not declined significantly (Topel, 2009). This phenomenon may be explained by the abolition of middle-management positions that constituted a clear advancement track for women. Gender-based socialization reduces women's chances of reaching senior technical levels. An example is an ideology that espouses male "rationalism" as opposed to female "emotionalism."

It is too early to determine if gender disparity will diminish given the expansion of education among women, a greater variety of occupations available within the kibbutz, development of gender awareness, and the attempt to shape a new type of community imbued with kibbutz values.

Bibliography

Avrahami, E. *From Center to Periphery: The Kibbutz within the Political System*. Ramat Efal: Yad Tabenkin, 1992 [Hebrew with English abstract].

———. *The Functioning of the United Kibbutz Movement: Dilemmas and Directions of Change*. Ramat Efal: Yad Tabenkin, 1993 [Hebrew with English abstract].

Ben-Rafael, E. *Progress versus Equality: Stratification and Change in the Kibbutz*. Tel Aviv: Ramot, 1986 [Hebrew].

Ben-Rafael, E. and I. Gajst. *Perceptions of Change in the Kibbutz*. Ramat Efal: Yad Tabenkin, 1993 [Hebrew with English abstract].

Ben-Rafael, E. and M. Topel. "The Kibbutz's Transformation: Who Leads It and Where?" In *Jews in Israel: Contemporary Social and Cultural Patterns*, edited by Chaim Waxman and Uzi Rebhun, 151–73. Waltham, NY and Lebanon, NH: Brandeis University Press and University Press of New England, 2004.

Degani, O. "The Regional Council as an Alternative Supporting System for the Changing Kibbutz." *Horizons in Geography* 66 (2006): 134–53 [Hebrew with English abstract].

Etzioni, A. *The Organizational Structure of the Kibbutz*. New York: Arno, 1980.

Fedida, M. *The Dynamics of Career Patterns in a Kibbutz*. MA thesis. Tel Aviv University, Tel Aviv, 1972 [Hebrew with English abstract].

Fogiel-Bijaoui, S. *The Emergence of Regionalism in the Kibbutz Movement*. Ramat Efal: Yad Tabenkin, 1994 [Hebrew with English abstract].

Helman, A. "Development of 'Professional Managers' in the Kibbutzim." *Economic Quarterly* 131 (1987): 1031–39 [Hebrew with a short English abstract].

Keren, M. *Technocrats versus Populism: Peres Government 1984–1986*. Tel Aviv: Ramot, 1996 [Hebrew].

Kressel, G. *"From Each According to His Ability . . ."*: *Stratification versus Equality in a Kibbutz*. Tel Aviv: Chericover, 1974 [Hebrew].

Lanir, J. *Leadership, Participation and Communication in the Kibbutz*. Ramat Efal: Yad Tabenkin, 1992 [Hebrew with English abstract].

Meron, S. *Kibbutz as a Communal Household*. Ramat Efal: Yad Tabenkin, 1987.

Pavin, A. *The Emergence of a "Collective Awareness" of the Kibbutz Crisis*. Ramat Efal: Yad Tabenkin, 1992 [Hebrew with English abstract].

Rayman, P. *The Community and Nation Building*. Princeton: Princeton University Press, 1981.

Rosenfeld, E. "Social Stratification in a Classless Society." *American Sociological Review* 16 (1951): 766–74.

Rosolio, D. *The Regional Structure in the Kibbutz Movement: Sociological Perspectives*. Jerusalem: Van Leer Institute, 1975 [Hebrew with English abstract].

———. *Factors in the Crisis and the Changes in the Kibbutz System: An Analysis of the Kibbutz System*. Tel Aviv: Golda Meir Institute, 1995 [Hebrew with English abstract].

Shapira, R. "Autonomy of the 'Technostructure': A Case Study of a Regional Inter-Kibbutz Organization." *The Kibbutz Interdisciplinary Research Review* 6–7 (1978/9): 276–302 [Hebrew with English abstract].

Shepher, I. *The Kibbutz: An Anthropological Study*. Norwood, PA: Norwood Editions, 1984.

Talmon-Garber, Y. *The Kibbutz: Sociological Studies*. Jerusalem: The Hebrew University, Magnes Press, 1970 [Hebrew].

Topel, M. *Organization, Power, and Leadership in the Kibbutz Community*. Tel Aviv: The Open University, 1992 [Hebrew].

———. *The New Managers: The Kibbutz Changes Its Way*. Sde Boker: Ben Gurion University of the Negev Press and Yad Tabenkin, 2005 [Hebrew with English abstract].

———. "Kibbutz Transformation, Technocracy and Gender." In *Old Dreams, New Horizons: Kibbutz Women Revisited*, edited by S. Fogel-Bijaoui, 129–46. Tel Aviv: Hakibbutz Hameujad & Yad Tabenkin, 2009.

Warhurst, C. *The Nature and Transformation of Communal Socialism: A Case Study of Kibbutz Industry*. Ph.D. Department of Organisation Studies, University of Central Lancashire, 1994.

Weber, O. *Renewal: The Kibbutz Facing Its Future*. Tel Aviv: Kibbutz Hameuchad, 1992 [Hebrew].

Yuchtman-Yaar, E. "Reward Distribution and Work-Role Attractiveness in the Kibbutz." *American Sociological Review* 37 (1972): 581–95.

4

Crisis, Social Capital, and Community Resilience

Avraham Pavin

In the second half of the 1980s, the kibbutz movement suffered economic and morale difficulties that gave its members a feeling of failure and fragmentation. Government measures of 1985 meant to curb galloping inflation brought about a crisis severe enough to pose a threat to the very existence of several kibbutzim. As a result, the kibbutz movement in general, and each kibbutz in particular, has engaged in a ferment of change over the past two decades. All the kibbutzim were affected, and no one doubted that changes had to be made. Discussions took place about the nature of the crisis, its origins and the reasons behind it, and, principally, solutions that could be implemented. Those who *supported* change claimed that the structure of the kibbutz had to be adapted to its surroundings. Adaptive changes would improve the quality of life in the kibbutz and make it more convenient and attractive for the members, particularly for the young people in the kibbutz, and would make it possible to survive and even prosper in its relations with the outside world. Those who *opposed* the changes maintained that the suggested modifications, in particular those connected with granting differential rewards, struck at the heart of the kibbutz, destroying its special nature and making it similar to "non-kibbutz" society.

Public controversy contained much talk about the "classical" or "traditional" kibbutz. But the kibbutz that would undergo changes was the kibbutz of the 1980s, not that of the early twentieth century, the kibbutz at the time of the establishment of the State of Israel, or the ideal kibbutz that may never have existed. Changes are not a new phenomenon. Kibbutzim have changed continuously: A small, close-knit group of young people became a multigenerational population numbering hundreds;

an economy based on arable crops became an economy based on modern agriculture and industry; spontaneous decisions made by the whole community gave way to a complex hierarchical structure; and an antifamilial ethos transformed into a society based on a multifunctional family with a central role in kibbutz life. Changes in the kibbutz began to be made from the beginning of its existence. In effect, every problem that had to be solved constituted a moment of decision and sometimes a moment of change in the nature and character of the kibbutz.

Some of the changes, such as the transition of children's sleeping to family quarters, were adopted after years of spirited discussion. Others were adopted when people deviated from the rules, and, in effect, gave approval ex post facto to forms of behavior that diverged from the norm. When several of the decisions that changed the nature of the kibbutz—particularly its economic system—were approved, people did not believe that they could affect the kibbutz's essence. The present wave of changes differs from those of the past in its strength, its nature, and the attitude of the kibbutz public. In the past, discussions focused on concrete suggestions. Now, in the shadow of the economic crisis, kibbutz members have to consider the claim that the kibbutz must change more fundamentally in order to survive.

Despite considerable evolution in the socioeconomic structure and accepted values over the years, the institutional arrangements of the kibbutz changed very little until the eruption of "the crisis." The economic crisis served as a stimulus for change in many respects, including the following:

1. The need to find solutions for economic distress and the problems that it entails
2. The need to deal with decreased budgets that revealed and exacerbated hidden contradictions between parts of the population that had accumulated over the years as a result of unplanned changes
3. The weakening of the kibbutz revealed and strengthened desires that had been repressed or obstructed

Changes in circumstances, and crises in particular, often constitute an opportunity to improve the status of sectors whose strength has grown over the years. They call existing social arrangements into question.

The controversy over change is a struggle over the character of the kibbutz. But the public discussion of the crisis is couched in terms of assigning responsibility and searching for ways to overcome it. An analysis of the "discourse of change" in the kibbutz shows that participants use concepts that connect factors held responsible with the desirable or necessary changes required, in their view, to extricate the kibbutz from the current situation. These constitute keywords or codes in the struggle over the social structuring of kibbutz reality. Apart from a small minority of kibbutz members who opposed any change, and those who maintained that what was required was a return to the pristine kibbutz principles, most members agreed on the need for change in the kibbutz system. It is possible to distinguish several approaches among those who initiated changes:

1. The *pragmatic* approach maintains that an *adaptation of kibbutz practices to today's conditions* is required. This approach assumes that the causes of the crisis are primarily external to the kibbutz (changes in the world market, government policy to restrain inflation, etc.). The kibbutz is "not guilty," and *there is no need for changes*, apart from those required to lighten the hardships resulting from the crisis. According to this view, the focus should be on solutions that will enable the kibbutz and its members to cope with day-to-day problems. It takes a positive view of a broad variety of changes that have, in fact, spread quickly and are part of day-to-day reality in most kibbutzim. Nonetheless, according to this approach, the central principles of cooperation and equality are still valid.

2. The *managerial* approach blames the crisis on *decision-making procedures*. Adherents point to the authority of the general meeting (sichat kibbutz) and the involvement of the members as obstacles to the prompt, "professional" decisions required in the modern market, particularly in times of crisis. This approach demands change in the *structure of the kibbutz*: from democratic management to the creation of administrative institutions with no direct public supervision. This change in the social framework represents a movement from participatory democracy to an authoritarian structure, expressed in institutions such as a board of management and profit centers, among others.

3. The third approach is *ideological* and more extreme. It claims that *the system has failed* and that the crisis stems from the kibbutz's failure to adapt itself to the changes in its surroundings, particularly individualistic values and competition, accepted in the world and in Israeli society. This approach holds the kibbutz members responsible for the crisis—they do not work hard enough and act wastefully in matters of consumption—and looks for ways to change their behavior. Therefore, it calls for *a significant change in the principles of the kibbutz* and demands that the individual be made responsible for the family's livelihood. On the other hand, this approach also claims that the change in the members' needs should be taken into account, primarily "the autonomy of the individual." This phrase means that the individual should be freed from "excessive dependence" on the kibbutz framework. This frequently heard demand and discussion of changes in particular justify changes in the kibbutz system. Ideological advocates want to change various arrangements in order to influence members' behavior.

They aim to change the principles on which the kibbutz system is based and to create a different social system. In general, they wish "to live like everyone else" and to enable the increase in economic differentials between the members. This approach reflects a readiness to abandon "kibbutzism", but not the kibbutz settlement—in other words, to preserve the living place and abandon the ideological commitment to equality, cooperation, and social solidarity (Pavin, 1995, 1999).

The first implemented changes were meant to cope with the hardships stemming from the economic crisis and to moderate, at least in part, the distress caused by budgetary limitations. These changes spread quickly and, in fact, now constitute part of everyday life in most kibbutzim:

1. "Privatization" of food and other consumer products
2. Opening of the kibbutz to the outside world (for instance, outsourcing educational services, guesthouses as well as apartment rental)
3. Payment for overtime and extension of the possibility of members' working outside the kibbutz

These changes had social implications that led to the demand—and readiness—to make more radical changes. Privatizing food was one of a broad group of decisions that transferred budgets and consumption to the authority of the individual or, more exactly, to the family. The expression "privatization" is, in fact, an umbrella term for a number of completely different phenomena:

1. The transfer of spheres of activity (and budgets) to the family and the reduction of the whole community's responsibility for individual needs.
2. Freeing the individual from dependence on institutions and individuals who dole out resources.
3. In apparent contradiction to the former point, privatization is also a mechanism for public control by market forces.
4. Change in the distribution of rewards between different groups and strata in the kibbutz. Distribution reflects the personal budget rather than need (usually, distribution according to the average of the total expenditure in a given sphere creates an advantage for those who do not consume a particular product).

These changes facilitated the creation of economic differentials among members in three ways:

1. Accumulation of resources and their exchange for money (privatization of food).
2. Legitimization of private property and resources from outside the kibbutz (for instance, the purchase of automobiles).
3. Creation of differentials according to the ability to work (payment for overtime) and, eventually, according to skill, training, or function.

In addition, opening the kibbutz gates to outsiders expresses the understanding that social solidarity has been reduced and is less important to members today than in the past. This phenomenon increased members' contacts with the surrounding culture. Permission to own private automobiles and to pay for additions to one's house stems either from the fact that the members are tired of efforts to enforce the prohibition on private property or from a reduction in the importance attributed to equality as a principle of the kibbutz.

Following these, many changes in the administrative structure of the kibbutz were instituted.

1. Decentralization (the creation of centers of profit or responsibility).
2. Exclusion of economic administration from public discourse (the transfer of authority to boards of management).
3. Replacement of direct participation in collective decision-making to a representative council. Thus, the internal political system became more centralized and free from public control over its decision-making.

Continuing the process of change, a number of kibbutzim abandoned the principle of equality and the traditional methods of supplying member and family needs. Most of these changes concerned the system of recompense and altered the accepted arrangements in the kibbutz way of life. The methods vary, but in general two fundamental models of change can be discerned:

1. The *combined budget,* which includes an equalizing component based on the family situation; a component based on the wages earned by the member; and a component of seniority, which expresses his/her part in the common property, that is, the income that the member created by his/her (equal) work in the past. This model creates moderate differentials between the members.
2. The establishment of *differential wages,* on the strength of the members' work and functions, as in the external market. This model enables the creation of considerable economic differentials between the managers and practitioners of a trade in great demand on the one hand and the pensioners and unskilled workers on the other. Unskilled pensioners are particularly badly hit. This system is supplemented by a system of welfare known as a "safety net" that assures a minimum livelihood to all.

These changes have spread quickly and have far-reaching social consequences.

Some kibbutzim had not yet recovered from the effects of the economic crisis of the 1980s when the present global crisis erupted. Every kibbutz faced the question of whether it has the inner strength needed to overcome the crisis, that is to say whether the community is capable of mobilizing its members for the good of the community and to their mutual advantage. In other words, what is the community's social resilience? "Social resilience" is part of a broader concept, "community resilience," which embraces all the resources at the disposal of a community. This term refers to the ability of groups or communities to cope with pressures or disruptions that arise from social, political, or environmental changes. Community resilience includes the following:

1. *Resistance*: the ability of the system to prevent disturbances from becoming injurious—a sort of fortified wall that may result from actions taken to warn against danger, to guard against it, or to prepare appropriate reactions.
2. *Endurance*: the system's ability to suffer damage and not lose the ability to function.
3. *Mitigation*: the ability to restrict the damage by suitable preparations.
4. *Recovery*: the system's ability to recover from damage if and when it is inflicted, and for the necessary time (Adger, 1999, 2000, 2003; Tobin, 1999; Carpenter et al., 2001; Holling, 2001; Kimhi and Shamai, 2004; Rose, 2004).

The ability of a community or society to cope with crises depends to a great extent on its ability to act collectively. At a time of crisis, the reaction of the individuals who belong to an institution may be influential and may determine whether the situation will improve or deteriorate. The willingness of individuals to act over and above what is required of them by the law (in a state), by custom (in a community), or by their position (in an organization) is of particular importance. The individual can work toward a *collective* solution (improvement of the state of the institution and/or its individual members by bringing it back to its previous normal or successful state) toward an *individual* solution so that, despite the grave state of the organization, the individual can "manage" and continue to obtain important resources (including actions liable to worsen the state of other sections of the population) or, in an extreme case, can *leave* the framework.

The question arises as to how these types of behavior are adopted. Collective behavior is the fundamental problem of every social organization. In the kibbutz, however, this problem is exacerbated because cooperative action in the daily functioning of the community, especially in times of crisis, is central. Recently, the perception increased that the economic and social development of a society or region depends on factors far beyond the narrow definition of "economic factors." It appears that, apart from physical and human capital, societies are distinguished by the quality of relationships among its citizens and their readiness to cooperate with each other. These relationships, known as "social capital," facilitate the social and economic development of the community. "Social capital is related to the characteristics of the community, such as trust, social norms and networks, which can improve the efficiency of the society by facilitating coordination of the activities of its members" (Putnam, 1993, p. 167).

Like other kinds of capital, social capital is productive and useful, and makes it possible to accomplish aims that otherwise could not be realized. It is a resource in every respect (Coleman, 1988, 1990) although it differs from other types of capital. In most cases, the social capital increases the efficiency and degree of activation of other types of capital and influences the ways in which they are created:

1. Trust in the fulfillment of contracts reduces the cost of transactions.
2. A positive attitude toward others increases the consideration of the individual for the results of his activity on their behalf.
3. A positive attitude to the community leads to preference of public products.
4. In a friendly atmosphere, cooperative activity becomes a "profit" rather than a "price." When people can be sure that their trust in others will not be exploited to their disadvantage, the possibility of cooperation, the basis of social resilience, is heightened.

Studies of social capital have focused on the individual or on the society. At the micro level, social capital is a resource or group of resources available to the individual as a result of his/her mutual relationships with other individuals, that is, being part of a social network (Bourdieu, 1986). At the macro level, social capital is related to the characteristics of the community, such as its accepted norms and trust between individuals. An intermediate level may also exist characterized by its ability to afford support to its members.

The special characteristic of social capital, on the community level, makes it possible to resolve the apparent conflict between the good of the individual and the good of society. In contrast with the usual types of capital such as private possessions, social capital aims to create both public goods and more just distribution of private goods in such a way that the general welfare is enhanced. Hence, social capital can increase the efficiency of the community in attaining common objectives while facilitating cooperation between individuals for the attainment of a society that is "better" for all. Although "social relationships" are a component of all definitions of social capital, the meaning of "relationships" differs among levels of analysis. At the micro level, relationships define the connections *between* two individuals that broaden into a social network built on a great number of dyadic connections. At the intermediate level, relationships are defined by the connections between individuals *within* the group and usually relate to solidarity, team spirit, or esprit de corps. At the level of the community or the society, relationships are the special positive attitude *toward* generalized others (including those with whom he/she has no personal connection) or toward the community as an overall entity.

Social capital can influence the state of a community and its resilience in various ways:

1. Promoting the transmission of relevant knowledge.
2. Increasing the probability of normative behavior.
3. Exercising informal social control.

The state of the society, or the degree of its "communityness," is the product of behavior derived from the level of social capital in the community. The social capital of the community turns a collection of individuals competing or struggling with each other to a network of co-operating citizens. The community's success in coping with its problems is a function of the discovery of solutions accepted by the majority of the public because they take account of the interests of all. The existence of social capital in a community brings about a change in the identity of individuals, by emphasizing its collective aspect, emphasizing "we" rather than "I," and thereby creating complete or partial preference for the public good. Societies characterized by a high degree of social capital are outstanding in pro-social behavior such as volunteering, mutual aid, and voluntary cooperation. In communities with a high level of social capital, the probability that, in stressful situations, individuals will be prepared to help each other and to act together for the good of the community is greater than in those societies with low social capital.

From the point of view of social capital, kibbutzim are a special group. Apart from their members' agreement to live together according to the socialist principles of equality, cooperation, and mutual aid, social arrangements also render them a total community containing social groups, families, and economic and social organizations. In the past, the power of the kibbutz movement to influence political and economic trends, its prestige in Israeli society and its position in the labor movement, and its components (party, Histadrut) did not stem from the *economic* power of the kibbutzim or their numbers in population, but rather from their mobilization to achieve national aims and their members' readiness to make personal sacrifices. The strength of the social capital that the kibbutz had in its early days enabled its members to take on national objectives far beyond their proportion in the population and to maintain an egalitarian way of life that provided its members with a high quality of life despite their low standard of living and poverty.

The direct encounter between people—in convenient conditions and with "friendliness" between the partners—depends on the creation and preservation of social capital. Meeting with the whole kibbutz population (and not only with one's friends) broadens the scope of the community for the individual and increases his/her readiness to practice pro-social behavior. These conditions existed in the early days of the kibbutz. But the time when members spend almost the entire day together as a group is long gone, and the conditions of encounter have changed beyond recognition. The history of the development of the kibbutzim is the history of the depletion of the community's reserves of social capital.

Despite the ideology and egalitarian arrangements of the kibbutz, inequalities arose among members, which have only increased over the years. These inequalities are not great in comparison with those outside the kibbutz, but kibbutz members are aware that some of them are "more equal" than others. The administrative arrangements that characterized the political system of the kibbutz for many years prevented the accumulation of power in the hands of a small group of people and enabled members to participate in the democratic management of kibbutz affairs. Changes in the kibbutz gradually led to the formation of hierarchies and increased the social distance between members and between subgroups of the population. These processes diminished the social capital of the community. In addition to the general trends common to all the kibbutzim, each community had its own special historical circumstances: the founding group's character, the geographic location of the kibbutz, the type of industry the kibbutz developed and its place in the kibbutz economy, past decisions, and more. Each separate factor influences the levels of social capital and community resilience.

Today, with a world economic crisis threatening many kibbutzim severely, the question arises as to how recent changes have influenced the kibbutzim's present level of social capital. In a 2003 study, we tried to estimate the reserve of internal strength in twenty-nine kibbutzim with which they could withstand the problems with which the community has to contend (Pavin, 2008). The findings demonstrate a relationship between the extent of the change and the perception of the quality of life in the kibbutz. We identify four types of kibbutzim: (1) communal kibbutz communities that didn't make meaningful changes, (2) communal + privatization of important areas, (3) combined budget, and (4) "safety net" (differential wages) (Table 4.1).

The more the kibbutz has preserved its principles and arrangement for ensuring equality, the more members define their kibbutz as a good place to live in (a pleasant environment that supplies the need of the individual and his family); the more they feel at home in their kibbutz (have a feeling of belonging); and the more they are satisfied with their life in the kibbutz (satisfies their needs and desires).

The influence of changes is expressed in the profile of the kibbutz members' readiness to engage in coping behavior according to the type of kibbutz. Table 4.2 shows the average of the replies of members to the question, "To what extent are you ready to do the following things in order to improve the state of your kibbutz?" The questions distinguish between individual acts and the relationship to other kibbutz members. Comparison of the replies in different types of kibbutzim shows that the more radical the changes, the less the social resilience of the community.

In every dimension of social resilience, the more radical the change in the kibbutz, the more the level falls.

This decline is marked particularly in kibbutzim that have adopted differential wages. Nonetheless, change is not the only factor that influences the social resilience of the community. The "social condition"

Table 4.1   Life perception in Kibbutz communities according to the type of kibbutz (averages—scale from 1 = low to 5 = high)

	Kibbutz as a good place to live in	Degree of feeling at home	Satisfaction with life in the kibbutz
Communal kibbutz	3.89	3.93	3.52
Communal + privatization	3.65	3.70	3.31
"Combined budget"	3.49	3.60	3.25
"Safety net"	3.43	3.49	3.24
General average	3.61	3.67	3.33
Standard deviation	0.94	1.17	1.01
Significance of differences[a]	0.000	0.000	0.000

[a] Significant difference between averages of replies in at least one characteristic.

Table 4.2 Readiness for coping behavior, according to the type of kibbutz (averages)

	Readiness for personal sacrifices	Readiness to contribute	Readiness to volunteer	Readiness to take other people's interests into account	Readiness to cooperate with every member	Readiness to help every member
Communal kibbutz	3.77	4.04	3.77	4.00	3.48	3.62
Communal + privatization	3.60	3.91	3.62	3.93	3.29	3.45
"Combined budget"	3.51	3.80	3.52	3.95	3.26	3.34
"Safety net"	3.30	3.56	3.22	3.74	3.07	3.20
General average	3.53	3.81	3.52	3.89	3.26	3.39
Standard deviation	0.96	0.92	1.13	0.86	1.10	1.12
Significance of differences[a]	0.000	0.000	0.000	0.002	0.001	0.000

[a] Significant difference between averages of replies in at least one characteristic.

of the community (the degree of solidarity or social capital) *before* the changes began is highly significant. The *process* of change is also important: whether it was belligerent or conciliatory, or whether it was seen as fair or exploitative. *How* the change is brought about is no less important than *what* is changed. Pro-social behavior on the part of "others" contributes to the creation of positive attitudes toward them and toward the community in general. Hence, support for a policy that cushions shocks and enhances the welfare of all initiates a *virtuous circle* leading to an increase in the community's reserve of social capital. On the other hand, egoistic and antisocial behavior of groups in the community, or policies that lead to competitive or even belligerent behavior, may well create a *vicious circle* leading to depletion of social capital.

Summary

In the second half of the 1980s, Israel underwent an economic crisis that affected kibbutzim so severely that their very existence was threatened. The economic difficulties provoked extreme social reactions that amounted to a struggle about the nature of the kibbutz and the direction in which it should go in the future. All could see the necessity for change. The bitterest controversy centered on the causes of the crisis and on the best way to solve the problems it raised. This controversy revealed the existence of different conceptions of the nature of the kibbutz and divided the kibbutz movement at the level of the individual kibbutz and of the movement alike. In some kibbutzim, the change—or the controversy it engendered—undermined the basis of minimal agreement needed to continue the normal functioning of the system. In the kibbutzim in which radical changes were instituted, new arrangements changed relationships between members, and between members and the community. This situation led to a decline in the social capital on which the resilience of the community is based.

A community's social resilience includes its ability to act collectively when coping with difficulties. This ability is derived from the level of its social capital, which in turn depends on the quality of the relationships between the members. Social capital is an important resource that makes it possible to exploit effectively other resources at the community's disposal. The profile of members' willingness to engage in coping behavior illustrated the influence of the decline in social capital. Our research shows that in all the dimensions of social resilience, the more radical the changes in the kibbutz, the more its resilience declines. This decline is most marked in the kibbutzim that have instituted differential wages.

Today, when some kibbutzim still have not recovered from the economic crisis of the 1980s, the global crisis poses a serious threat to the whole State of Israel. In a situation of crisis, the central questions are the following: "What is the social resilience of the society?" Can it mobilize its members for the good of all in order to face its difficulties efficiently and correctly? The challenge for the kibbutz movement as a whole and for each kibbutz individually is to stop the erosion of social capital and mobilize inner strength needed to surmount the new crisis.

Bibliography

Adger, W. N. "Social Vulnerability to Climate Change and Extremes in Coastal Vietnam." *World Development* 27, no. 2 (1999): 249–69.

———. "Social and Ecological Resilience: Are They Related?" *Progress in Human Geography* 24, no. 3 (2000): 347–64.

———. "Social Capital, Collective Action, and Adaptation to Climate Change." *Economic Geography* 79 (2003): 4.

Bourdieu, P. "The Forms of Capital." In *Handbook of Theory and Research for the Sociology of Education*, edited by J. G. Richardson. New York: Greenwood Press, 1986.

Carpenter, S., B. Walker, J. M. Anderies, and N. Abel. "From Metaphor to Measurement: Resilience of What to What." *Ecosystems* 4 (2001): 765–81.

Coleman, J. S. "Social Capital in the Creation of Human Capital." *American Journal of Sociology* 94, supplement (1988): S95–120.

———. *Foundations of Social Theory*. Cambridge, MA and London: Harvard University Press, 1990.

Holling, C. S. "Understanding the Complexity of Economic, Ecological, and Social Systems." *Ecosystems* 4 (2001): 390–405.

Kimhi, S. and M. Shamai. "Community Resilience and the Impact of Stress: Adult Response to Israel's Withdrawal from Lebanon." *Journal of Community Psychology* 32, no. 4 (2004): 439–51.

Pavin, A. *Internal Forces to Deal with the Crisis*. Ramat Ef'al: Yad Tabenkin, 1995 [in Hebrew].

———. *The Struggle over the Character of the Kibbutz*. Haifa: The Institute for Research of the Kibbutz and the Cooperative Idea, Haifa University, 1999 [in Hebrew].

———. *Community Resilience: Social Capital in the Kibbutz*. Ramat Ef'al: Yad Tabenkin, 2008 [in Hebrew].

Putnam, R. D. *Making Democracy Work*. Princeton, NJ: Princeton University Press, 1993.

Rose, A. "Defining and Measuring Economic Resilience to Disasters." *Disasters Prevention and Management* 13, no. 4 (2004): 307–14.

Tobin, G. A. "Sustainability and Community Resilience: The Holy Grail of Hazards Planning?" *Environmental Hazards* 1, no. 1 (1999): 13–25.

5

Co-optation and Change:
The Women's Sections of the Kibbutz

Sylvie Fogiel-Bijaoui[1]

Introduction

The purpose of this preliminary study is to shed light on the institutional role and unique accomplishments of two bodies that appeared on the kibbutz scene, beginning in the 1980s, with the aim of promoting gender equality. They are the Section for Gender Equality (hereafter, the Section), which was active from the start of the 1980s until the early 1990s, and the Department for the Advancement of Women (hereafter, the Department), which was founded in 2000 when the Kibbutz Movement (TAKATZ) was formed. The Department is still functioning today.

Our theoretical foundation rests on the concept of co-optation, as posited by Philip Selznick (1949) and developed by other researchers.[2] As described by Selznick, co-optation is a procedural process that enables an organization's leadership to bring representatives of potentially destabilizing groups into its loci of power, thereby—somewhat paradoxically—maintaining, and even augmenting, its strength. Co-optation is a form of "win-win" situation. On the one hand, it confers legitimacy on the opposing groups and, as a consequence, allows them to gain representation and function as part of the organization (even if for a limited time frame and still subject to the organization's control) until the leadership is able to dismantle them. And on the other hand, co-optation strengthens the formal leadership, whether the organization is democratic or not, by enabling it to appear open to the public's wishes and hence to gain added legitimacy. On the operational level, co-optation bolsters the leadership by neutralizing the groups that threaten to undermine it, since their representatives are brought into the centers of power only on a small scale, thus preventing them from wielding any real influence.

The present work is based as well on the literature in the field since Selznick's classic study (e.g., Couto, 1988; Garbaye, 2005; Body-Gendrot et al., 2008). These works highlight the fact that co-optation is not a static process but a dynamic one that can take on different meanings over the course of time. Consequently, there can certainly be situations in which groups that have been co-opted vanish from the organizational landscape. Yet there also can be circumstances where these same groups survive, flourish, and even exert influence.

In the first section of this chapter, we focus on the process of co-optation at the time of the Section's founding and during its years of activity until its closure in 1992. The second section relates to the dynamics of this process. It is our thesis that the co-optation processes that took place in the 1980s and the early 2000s, which enabled representatives of kibbutz feminists to gain entry into the formal leadership of the kibbutz movement as a whole, took on distinct meanings over the years. As a result of co-optation, the Section was neutralized and faded from the scene; by contrast, the Department continues to exist, despite opposition, and may even become stronger in the future under certain circumstances.

We will also be arguing that despite all the predictions to the contrary, the kibbutz movement and its institutions remain a central and important body representing the kibbutzim before the state authorities. In addition, they supply the kibbutzim and their members with a range of services. As Ben-Rafael and Topel (2009, p. 77) argue, the movement is still a "real factor in the cognitive map and action space of kibbutz members." Thus, from the standpoint of supporters of feminism in the kibbutz, the movement and its institutions are still a fitting setting for the advancement of gender equality.

Our study is based on the professional literature on the subject and on various documents issued by the different kibbutz movements, along with in-depth interviews conducted by Eli Avrahami in late 2007 with two kibbutz members who played a role in founding these bodies and were in turn called to lead them: Vivian Silver, the first coordinator of the Section; and Smadar Sinai, who has served since 2004 as chair of the Department.

The Section for Gender Equality: Co-optation or Cultural Change from the Top Down

The Section was established as part of a gradual, and not necessarily planned, process. In response to gender inequality on the kibbutz,[3] the Section attempted to ensure that women would be represented in the kibbutz institutions by reviving the so-called one-third law (allocating one-third of the seats on elected bodies to women). The purpose of this law, the product of an initiative by women members of Kibbutz Ein Harod in the 1920s, was to enhance women's representation on the kibbutzim and in the movement. The governing council of Hakibbutz Hameuchad, with the active support of Tabenkin, passed the "one-third law" in 1930 and, subsequently, the council of Hakibbutz Haartzi passed the law in 1945 when it also decided to establish a women's division. Over the years, the "one-third law" became the cornerstone of all kibbutz legislation, though it was not always applied in practice, to say the least (Fogiel-Bijaoui, 1992; Palgi, 1998). Several years after Vivian Silver immigrated to Israel from the United States in the early 1970s and while she was the Mazkira of Kibbutz Gezer, she attempted to revive the one-third law. She recalls the wide-ranging opposition she encountered:

> I tried to pass this resolution before the merging (of Hakibbutz Hameuchad and Ichud Hakvutzot Vehakibbutzim).[4] . . . I felt so alone in the fight at the time. We lost. We were unsuccessful in passing the one-third resolution. And when I brought it to meetings of the movement, there was a lot of scorn there too.

The scholarly literature defines a 30 percent representation rate as the "critical mass" that turns the representatives of any group into a source of significant power and influence in a given system (Fogiel-Bijaoui, 2010). To guarantee such a level of representation for women was apparently seen as too far-reaching a change, almost tantamount to a "takeover from within." In light of these results, Silver turned to the kibbutz leadership with a request to establish an organizational framework as part of the movement's institutions. In February 1982 the United Kibbutz Movement's Social Committee initiated a meeting to discuss setting up a special section for gender equality. This meeting took place after such a section had been founded in Hakibbutz Haartzi (thanks to the involvement of the sociologist, Menachem Rosner) and after a course on the topic was organized at Givat Haviva in October 1981 by Gila Adar. These developments led to the establishment of the Section for Gender Equality in 1982, with Gila Adar and Vivian Silver recruited as part of their work in the movement (Silver, 1984, p. 147).

The leadership's consent to establish the Section may have reflected a "new awareness" of gender inequality in the kibbutz. But that still leaves the question of why it agreed to the move, or to put it bluntly, what was in it for the kibbutz leadership? The primary explanation is tied to the rise of second-wave feminism in Israel in the early 1970s, which saw the shattering of the myth of gender equality. The gendered structure of Israeli society, including the kibbutz, was now exposed. Given this new reality, the leadership feared a blow to the kibbutz's standing, in particular following the political upset of 1977, when its status suffered a steep decline (Ben-Rafael and Topel, 2009). In fact, it was not only gender inequality, but the lack of a policy to reduce its scope as well, that threatened to undermine the status of the kibbutz. Silver's words are as follows:

> They accepted me on the kibbutz secretariat, because it didn't seem right to them that there were no women members. They wanted to show, to prove that there were women. . . . I also managed to convince them to allocate resources for this [activity]. . . . The establishment wasn't opposed.

Other factors were also relevant to leadership support. One was the fact that some women members already were part of the leadership echelon in kibbutzim (as stated, Silver herself was the secretary of the kibbutz). Hence, leadership believed it could rely on their loyalty to the movement. Moreover, the feminists were few in number and lacked external organizational support, meaning that the extent of their influence was judged to be limited in the extreme. Ultimately from an organizational perspective, women activists were "alone at the top," so to speak, with the Section's budget supplied by the movement—an ideal situation that ensured oversight and control of the Section and required a much smaller concession than pledging one-third representation for women.

The Section operated until 1992 in conjunction with the institutions of TAKAM and Hakibbutz Haartzi. Male and female activists joined in the endeavor, in a professional capacity or on a volunteer basis. The Section's *modus operandi* reflected a desire to generate gender imbalance awareness through actions from the top-down coupled with grass—roots activities (seminars, conferences, and workshops). In addition, courses— offered by the Section—were held, with some success, to train women for administrative and political positions. To promote gender equality in the Kibbutz, the Section also cooperated with feminist organizations, primarily "second wave" organizations, such as the Israel Women's Network (founded in 1984 by Alice Shalvi). Overall, the close ties between the Section and women in academe were readily apparent, as was the manner in which grassroots and academia fed one other, in the best feminist tradition (Silver, 1984, pp. 147–49; Palgi, 1998, 2003).

At the same time, there were signs of an ambivalent attitude on the part of the establishment, which in practice did not support the expansion of the Section's activities, and, along with most kibbutz members, continued to see it as superfluous and ineffective (Palgi, 2003, pp. 87–88). For this reason, the Section remained modest in scope and did not become a force to be reckoned with.

The economic crisis that began in 1985, which struck kibbutz society, leading to the "great neoliberal transformation" of the kibbutz, compounded the situation. The fight for economic survival, individually and collectively, became everyone's priority, and the issue of gender equality was not deemed worthy of systemic treatment (Palgi, 2003; Fogiel-Bijaoui, 2009). The Section's organizational weakness along with the onslaught of socioeconomic changes allowed the kibbutz establishment to suspend transferring monies to the Section as part of budget cuts, without arousing a significant reaction. As a result, the Section was shut down, and, for several years, feminist voices in the kibbutz were silenced.

Department for the Advancement of Women: Co-optation or Social Change from the Bottom Up?

At first glance, the atmosphere at the time of the Department's founding was different from that which surrounded the establishment of the Section. For one, the Department was organized amid a more "feminist" climate. In the 1980s and even more so in the 1990s, Israel had experienced an intensified process of cultural change making the notion of gender equality and the creation of bodies to promote this goal, more normative (Herzog, 2006; Fogiel-Bijaoui, 2010). In addition, the Department for Promotion of the Status of Women (which became the Department for the Advancement of Women when Sinai assumed the post years later) did not have to create awareness of gender inequality in the kibbutz—at times amid insults and ridicule—since the Section had already paved the way. Likewise, the women members who spearheaded the demand to establish the Department had become (even more) prominent in Israeli society in the intervening years. They were primarily—but not only—members of Hakibbutz Haartzi who were active in the Meretz political party. Outstanding among them was Anat Ma'or, at the time one of the most active Knesset members, who made a real contribution to feminist change. And finally, unlike the Section, the Department enjoyed formal status from its inception, since it was established as part of the October 2000 process of uniting the kibbutz divisions, when the Kibbutz Movement (TAKATZ) was formed. At the time of the merger, it was even stipulated that the Department would be located in the movement's headquarters and that its chair would be a member of the secretariat. Further, representatives of movement's institutions pledged to aim for at least 40 percent representation for women (Kibbutz Movement, 2000).

Upon the founding of the Department, Rosi Wagschall of Kibbutz Metzer (Hakibbutz Haartzi) was invited to serve as its chair. In this post, she relied on what was sometimes referred to as the Women's Forum—one of the informal women's networks that had been operating since the time of the Section—and which she convened once a month for consultations. During her tenure, kibbutz members founded the so-called Glass Ceiling Group with the aim of promoting gender equality by "shattering the glass ceiling" in the kibbutz, that is, fighting against the covert discrimination against women that serves as an invisible barrier to achieving equal status (Wagschall, 2002).

But it is my contention that the kibbutz establishment did not alter its basic approach, but rather continued to see the Department as a framework that would keep the gender issue in check—and perhaps neutralize it. This conservative tendency is evident in the leadership's refusal to implement the recommendations of the Glass Ceiling Group Report—a rebuff accompanied by Wagschall's leaving her post as chair of the Department in favor of someone perceived as less militant.

A further expression of this approach was the establishment in 2002 of the Ben-Rafael Commission, which focused on two issues: the formal classification of kibbutzim under the Cooperative Societies Regulations and the "allocation of apartments," that is, the transfer of possession of kibbutz-owned housing to individual kibbutz members. The Commission also addressed issues such as differential wages on kibbutzim, with its recommendations becoming statutory regulations entered into the Israeli legal code. However, although movement leaders, public figures, and academicians from various fields participated in the Commission, not one female kibbutz member, not to mention a representative of the Department, was selected (Ben-Rafael and Topel, 2009, pp. 1–82).

This noninclusive approach persisted with the accession of Smadar Sinai of Kibbutz Ein Gev (Hakibbutz Hameuchad), a woman with a wealth of organizational experience, in addition to her academic area of expertise in the gendered history of the kibbutz. Sinai placed less importance on the Glass Ceiling Group Report and its recommendations, in favor of working with the Women's Council (formerly the Women's Forum)—the advisory body that had served her predecessor. Sinai revived an organizational pattern/strategy practiced mainly (but not only) during the time of the Section, that is, active cooperation with other feminist bodies:

> I see my role as representing the women of the kibbutz movement in every possible body to which I've gained entry. So I'm invited to meetings of the Knesset's Committee on the Status of Women. I focus on topics that, in my opinion, are also relevant to kibbutz members, and bring the kibbutz perspective.

In addition, Sinai has stepped up regional cooperation, primarily with advisors on the status of women in the local and regional authorities:

> I work with them . . . some more, of course, and some a little less, with all the advisors in the local authorities that encompass kibbutzim. . . . I can talk about the Upper Galilee and the Jezreel Valley and the Jordan Valley and Eshkol and the Sharon plain, etc.

As with her predecessors, the bulk of Sinai's efforts are devoted to developing feminist consciousness and empowering women, primarily in the personal and economic spheres. She promotes these goals through seminars, gatherings, conferences, training courses, and the like. Sinai sees a breakthrough in the appointment on each kibbutz of a person responsible for preventing sexual harassment.

None of this, however, has altered the attitude of the establishment toward the Department. Among other things, this stance is expressed in the Department's static nature. For example, the Women's Council, as an advisory body, did not receive formal status. Similarly, the "prevention of sexual harassment" post on each kibbutz remains a voluntary position without remuneration. Furthermore, the office of department chair was cut by 40 percent as of January 1, 2007, by recommendation of the Commission to Monitor the Department for the Advancement of Women, established by the movement in 2006. The Commission also recommended the following: "In future (upon completion of the present term of office), consideration should be given to making this post an additional, part-time function of one of the active male or female members of the movement, if he/she is found suitable" (Kibbutz Movement, 2009). In other words, on the Commission's recommendation, the Department stands to become a "function" of one of the male/female kibbutz member, en route to its eventual dismantling. This recommendation reflects the traditional academic approach that constructs co-optation as an organizational process that enables the leadership of a given body to take control over groups that challenge it—until the latter ultimately vanish from the organizational arena.

A "dynamic" reading of the co-optation process, however, leads to a different conclusion. As a consequence of cultural and political changes, groups that have undergone a process of co-optation can amass legitimacy and authority, making it difficult to eliminate them from the organizational landscape. One of the political–cultural changes that has gained momentum in Israel in recent years is the perception—for which feminists have worked long and hard—that state institutions must advance gender equality by means of "state feminism." Accordingly, in the kibbutz community, where there is long-standing gender inequality, the closure of the Department is liable to distance the kibbutz move- ment from the normative mainstream. This may explain the following statement by the Monitoring Commission: "The gender equality vision of the Department is consensual and relevant." In other words, a subject that was downplayed for decades has since become acceptable, leading the Monitoring Commission to recommend "only" its downsizing and not its actual closure—for the time being.

Moreover, in recent years, Sinai has placed on the Department's agenda such major feminist concerns as paid employment and vio- lence against women. In this context, she exposed problematic issues and worked to establish mutual support networks, from the Authority for the Advancement of the Status of Women in the Prime Minister's Office to various entities in Israel's civil society that can mobilize and influence public opinion, in the event this is needed. Moreover, working relationships and collaborative ties have developed with various bod- ies at the regional level, in particular with those regional councils that have kibbutzim in their jurisdiction. Since regional councils have long been an influential local factor (Ben-Rafael and Topel, 2009), regional cooperation appears to be a significant anchor that stabilizes the status of the Department.

At the same time, additional steps could be taken to bolster the De- partment, among them the issue of ensuring 40 percent (and why not 50 percent?) representation for women—one of the articles in the founding charter of the Kibbutz Movement (TAKATZ)—along with a demand to accord official legal status to the Women's Council. Interactive dialogue with rank-and-file members should be initiated and promoted through the Department's Web site. In this global era, the Internet has become a key political instrument (Kahn and Kellner, 2004; Dominelli,

2006, pp. 101–34). It is therefore vital to advance gender dialogue "from the bottom up," so as to increase the influence of kibbutz members on the policies of the Department. Conversely, this dialogue space is essential to the Department, in order to create feminist awareness and mobilize kibbutz members.

Summary and Conclusions

In this work, a theoretical discussion of the concept of co-optation is the starting point for examining the institutional role of two groups established to advance the cause of gender equality on the kibbutz: the Section for Gender Equality and the Department for the Advancement of Women. Despite the noticeable weakness of the Department today, co-optation theory suggests that it will not be erased from the organizational–political landscape of the kibbutz because cultural changes in Israeli society since the 1970s have intensified and legitimized the call for gender equality and their associated supportive frameworks. State feminism has contributed to these changes.

Similarly, the process of "democratizing the kibbutz democracy" needs to be accelerated, in particular by demanding guaranteed representation for women and promoting an Internet dialogue space. If women kibbutz members reorganize to demand guaranteed representation, they will be contributing both to kibbutz democracy and to Israel's entire civil polity because women's representation in elected institutions of the state is lower than the global average. Despite the fact that guaranteed representation (quotas) has proven itself the world over (Fogiel-Bijaoui, 2010), there has been no systematic public discussion of this topic in Israel. Thus, if and when the political activity of women kibbutz members becomes more organized, it will enhance the "democratization of kibbutz democracy," spur the same process in the larger society, and contribute to the democratization of Israeli democracy as a whole.

Notes

1. I wish to thank my dear friend Eli Avrahami, who contributed so much to the development, writing, and editing of this chapter. His instructive comments helped me in time and again to clarify my thoughts. For this, I am deeply grateful.
2. The literature relates to both formal and informal co-optation. In this study, we focus on formal processes of co-optation.
3. On the subject of inequality in the kibbutz during that period, see Tiger and Shepher (1975), Palgi et al. (1983), Fogiel-Bijaoui (1992), and Lieblich (2002).
4. The United Kibbutz Movement (known by the Hebrew acronym TAKAM) was established in 1981 as a result of this union.

Bibliography

Ben-Rafael, E. and M. Topel, eds. *The Kibbutz on Paths Apart.* Jerusalem: Mossad Bialik and Ramat Efal: Yad Tabenkin, 2009 [in Hebrew].

Body-Gendrot, S., J. Carré, and R. Garbaye, eds. *A City of One's Own: Blurring the Boundaries between Public and Private in Historical and Comparative Perspective.* Farnham-Surrey: Ashgate, 2008.

Couto, R. A. "TVA's Old and New Grassroots: A Reexamination of Cooptation." *Administration and Society* 19, no. 4 (1988): 453–78.

Dominelli, L. *Women and Community Action.* Bristol, UK: Policy Press, 2006.

Fogiel-Bijaoui, S. "Women in the Kibbutz: Members or Mothers?" In *Kibbutz Society: Change and Continuity*, Unit 7, edited by E. Ben-Rafael and E. Ya'ar. Tel Aviv: Open University, 1992 [in Hebrew].

———. "Introduction, Kibbutz and Gender: The Neo-liberal Challenge." In *Old Dreams, New Horizons: Kibbutz Women Revisited*, edited by S. Fogiel-Bijaoui, 7–25. Ramat Efal: Yad Tabenkin, 2009 [in Hebrew].

———. *Democracy and Feminism: Gender, Citizenship, and Human Rights.* Raanana: Open University, 2011 [in Hebrew].

Garbaye, R. *Getting into Local Power: The Politics of Ethnic Minorities in British and French Cities.* Oxford: Blackwell, 2005.

Herzog, H. "Between the Lawn and the Gravel Path." *Tarbut Demokratit* 10 (2006): 191–214 [in Hebrew].

Kahn, R. and D. Kellner. "New Media and Internet Activism: From the 'Battle of Seattle' to Blogging." *New Media and Society* 6, no. 1 (2004): 87–95.

Kibbutz Movement. *Protocol of First Committee, Founding Conference, Kvutzat Kinneret.* Ramat Efal: Yad Tabenkin Archive, 2000, section 1–4, file 3 [in Hebrew].

———. *Summary of Findings of Commission to Monitor the Department for the Advancement of Women in the Kibbutz Movement.* Tel Aviv: Headquarters and Manpower, Kibbutz Movement, 2009 [in Hebrew].

Lieblich, A. "Women and the Changing Israeli Kibbutz: A Preliminary Three-stage Theory." In *Women's Time: New Studies from Israel*, edited by Hannah Naveh. *Special Issue: Journal of Israeli History* 21, no. 2 (2002): 63–84.

Palgi, M. "Women in the Kibbutz." In *Kibbutz Lexicon*, edited by Eli Avrahami. Ramat Efal: Yad Tabenkin, 1998 [in Hebrew]. http://www.kibbutz.org.il/orchim/3-IshaBakibutz.htm.

———. "Gender Equality in the Kibbutz: From Ideology to Reality." In *Jewish Feminism in Israel: Some Contemporary Perspectives*, edited by M. Kalpana and M. S. Rich, 76–95. Hanover and London: Brandeis University Press of New England, 2003.

———. "Occupational Status of Women in the Kibbutz in an Era of Change." In *Old Dreams, New Horizons: Kibbutz Women Revisited*, edited by S. Fogiel-Bijaoui, 147–61. Ramat Efal: Yad Tabenkin, 2009 [in Hebrew].

Palgi, M., J. Blasi, M. Rosner, and M. Safir, eds. *Sexual Equality: The Israeli Kibbutz Tests the Theories.* Norwood, PA: Norwood Edition, 1983.

Selznick, Philip. *TVA and the Grass Roots: A Study of Politics and Organization.* Berkeley, CA: University of California Press, 1949.

Silver, V., ed. *Male and Female Created He Them: Problems of Sexual Equality in the Kibbutz.* Ramat Efal: Yad Tabenkin, 1984 [in Hebrew].

Tiger, L. and J. Shepher. *Women in the Kibbutz.* New York: Harcourt, Brace and Jovanovich, 1975.

Wagschall, R. *Breaking the "Glass Ceiling": Recommendations for Implementation.* Kibbutz Movement, Department for the Advancement of Women (internal document) 2002 [in Hebrew].

6

The Meaning of Aging among Mature Kibbutz Members

Yasmin Asaf and Israel Doron

Introduction

In recent decades, we have witnessed the swift aging of the human population; fertility and birthrates are shrinking and, simultaneously, the average life expectancy is increasing. Because people are living longer, the older population represents a significant percentage of the population, requiring a unique approach to their various needs (Marin and Zaidi, 2007). Alongside the "elderly," there has been an increase in awareness of the importance of the "middle-aged" sector, also known as "midlife," "adults," or the "pre-aged," who are between fifty-five and sixty-five, and are "in line" for the world of the aged. They too have specific characteristics as well as needs and demands. With the aging of human society, this group is also becoming important (Neugarten, 1996).

In this respect, the kibbutz movement is not different from Israeli society or from the rest of the world. The kibbutz movement's population is also aging quickly and its population of aged is growing both relatively and in absolute numbers (Leviatan, 1999). Alongside this demographic process, for the past two decades, the kibbutz society has found itself in a deep socio-ideological crisis covering all aspects of life. In order to pull themselves out of this situation, kibbutzim have begun to undergo processes of structural change, including privatization of services and consumer products, a separation of the economic–business organization from the social one, and the establishment of a direct connection between the work and the remuneration of a member (also known as "differential salary") (Harel, 1993; Rosner and Getz, 1996).

Despite the fact that the kibbutz movement has been dealing with these changes for years now, little attention was been given to the impact of these changes on the status of adults on the cusp of old age, those who are between fifty-five and sixty-five years old. This age-group has its own particular characteristics within the shifting kibbutz. They are located at a complicated crossroads in life, just prior to the formal entry into the "third age." They spent their lives as members of kibbutzim upon whose ethics they were raised and educated, and now they are expected to support and even initiate changes that dictate a completely different way of life. Furthermore, many of them do not possess the formal education or professional skills demanded by the market in the twenty-first century and thus find themselves faced with a foggy, uncertain old age. The purpose of this study was to comprehend how kibbutz members on the verge of old age saw the impact of these changes on their personal process of aging.

Literature Review

As mentioned above, the rise in a population's aging results from a drop in birthrates and an increase in life expectancy. Before the twentieth century, average life expectancy did not exceed fifty, whereas now, the expectancy in most Western countries is approximately eighty, depending on gender and the society. Over the past two hundred years, there has been a clear decrease in birthrates, from more than four children to fewer than two children per woman in certain Western countries (Friedlander et al., 1990; Noam and Sikron, 1990). The result of these processes has been that the elderly represented close to 7 percent of the global population since the early 2000s. This trend is expected to continue. The UN projects that by 2025 the elderly will represent close to 11 percent and, in 2050, 25 percent of the world population (Habib and Brodsky, 2000; Doron and Linchitz, 2002; Brodsky and Davis, 2003).

The rate of aging in Israeli society is a little lower than that of other developed countries, but Israel too has undergone a transformation from a relatively young society (fewer than 4 percent elderly in 1948) to an aging one (nearly 10 percent in 2008). Given that the fertility rate in Israel is still relatively high (at least among some sectors), the rate of aging in Israeli society is lower than that of other Western countries. Immigration plays a role in the makeup of Israeli society, unlike in some other countries where only the natural demographic processes of birth and death are significant (Brodsky and Davis, 2003).

Increased understanding of the characteristics of the older population has produced the need for understanding its heterogeneity or age-based split. It becomes imperative to examine the needs of each age subgroup, to decide an appropriate welfare policy, and to design the relevant services (Brodsky and Davis, 2003). Over the years, researchers have given labels to various subgroups within the aging population and have attempted to define them in different ways. For example, Be'er and Factor (1990) established a dichotomy between the "young elderly" (sixty-five to seventy-four), and the aged (seventy-five and older). Bar-Tur and Prager (1996/7) raised the age bar and label the sixty-five- to seventy-nine-year-olds "young elderly" and those aged eighty and older, the "old elderly." Orchan and Goldemberg (1994) used the term "adult" for those aged fifty-six to sixty-five. Baruch and Brooks-Gunn (1984) used definitions such as middle-life, middle-adulthood, or middle-age for younger people aged forty-five to sixty-five years. Doron and Linchitz (2002) referred to those aged seventy-five and older as "the older old," and other age differentiations also exist.

Neugarten (1996) made one of the better known divisions of older age-groups. She presents a separation between "young elderly" aged fifty-five to seventy-five and the "old elderly," a division we adopted for this study. Neugarten distinguished among groups using the criteria of retirement from the workforce, which she sees as a central characteristic of the "young elderly." The "young elderly are involved in smaller households but they care for 'old elderly' parents, support their children financially, and help to raise grandchildren, as well as function within community and social frameworks. These people generally are physically healthy, economically stable, aware of their surroundings, and still have around 30 years to live" (Neugarten, 1996). Their search for self has emerged following the decrease in their formal commitments. Members of this age stratum experience the "empty nest" as grown children leave home for an independent life. As a result, they reorganize their relationships with partners who have also been affected by the changes (Orchan and Goldemberg, 1994). This study will focus on this group of "young elderly" people in the kibbutzim.

The desire to create a just and equal society that would provide an alternative to capitalist society is part of the kibbutz idea. In such an ideal society, people would be expected to contribute according to their abilities, and at the same time, they would receive according to their individual needs. Kibbutzim emphasize such values as equality, cooperation, social solidarity, help, and responsibility for one another

(*The Kibbutz Regulations*, 1973). Collective ownership of property and production through the democratic administration of all life systems, and the implementation of personal and collective responsibility, was also important foundational ideas (Avrahami, 1998).

In recent years, many have claimed that the kibbutz movement is in a deep crisis that has touched all aspects of life and was expressed in the quick changes in lifestyle and internal organization within the kibbutzim. These phenomena have shaken members' confidence regarding both the future of the community and their own personal futures (Pavin, 1992)—the result of many socioeconomic factors and the crisis began in the 1980s and impacted the structure, values, and social life of the kibbutzim. Salem (2003) has summarized these changes in two central elements:

1. A move from a society that emphasizes the centrality of the community to one that reveres, by contrast, the family and the individual.
2. A shift from a lifestyle that emphasizes the independence of the individual's income from work and the meeting of his needs to a new system that posits a direct link between the individual's contribution and meeting of his/her needs, in the form of monetary compensation.

"Utopia" is the expression researchers used to describe the way in which kibbutz society cared for its old people. In the kibbutz, older people could find a response for their most pressing social, physical, and emotional needs (Gal, 1995). Carmel et al. (1996) noted the importance of social cohesion for determining the level of life satisfaction on the part of kibbutz elderly. Nechushtan (1997) pointed out that in the past retirement from work rarely occurred in kibbutzim, contributing to a longer and more productive old age. Since work represented the highest value in the original vision of the kibbutz, it was an ideal community in which to age. The kibbutz promised social security, a community framework, and meaningful citizenship that permitted continuing productivity and participation and in a manner that adapted itself to disability and illness.

While old age was "ensured," the weight of implementing the promise fell on the younger elderly. Thus, for example, a dozen kibbutzim studied in 1992 presented a picture of the characteristics and positions of the members aged forty-five to sixty-five. Interest in this age-group arose with the understanding that they assume the major financial and public roles in the kibbutz. Many of them were at a stage of soul-searching and uncertainty because of the changes in kibbutz society. Their confidence concerning the kibbutz and the processes it is undergoing was their faith concerning aging within this structure. They expressed feelings of frustration and failure concerning their lives' work. They grew up within a clear, stable system of values, and as the research shows, both they and these values are now at a crossroads (Orchan and Goldemberg, 1994).

Rosner et al. (1999) also noted the sensitivity of the forty- to sixty-year-olds (nearly overlapping with the Orchan and Goldemberg age-group) to changes in the kibbutzim. The research subjects expressed concern about the current state of their kibbutz, as they considered the difficulties they were likely to encounter if they tried to begin life out-side the kibbutz at this stage of their lives. People aged fifty and older carry a heavy burden in the kibbutzim: they lead the kibbutz, yet they are concerned of their personal futures. They are charged with carry-ing out the changes required by the changing reality, yet many of them were born into the community and deeply appreciate and respect their parents' lifework (Rosental, 1998). Relatively little attention has been given to this age-group and the meaning it gives to its place and role in the kibbutzim. This study attempted to fill this empirical gap and un-cover the meaning they give to aging and social place in the changing kibbutz movement.

Methods

This qualitative, phenomenological study describes and clarifies the human experience in the context of the event the researcher seeks to examine. The approach focuses on comprehension of the significance of various events as expressed by people who underwent these events (Shkedi, 2003). Data were gathered through in-depth interviews with the subjects who lived the events personally. We asked them to address issues from their personal point of view. The method of analysis of the interviews was based on qualitative research principles, in order to identify the common themes among the subjects. The purpose was to locate shared threads, unifying significances and consolidating links among them, despite the fact that each interview stands alone and all that was exposed in them represents a world unto itself (Bruner, 1985; Patton, 1990).

Sampling

The research used a "purposeful" convenience sample. We selected the informants who fitted the sampling criterion, that is, Kibbutz mem-bers between the ages fifty-five to sixty-five. The subjects underwent an experience with the phenomenon and were able to share their personal experience, emotions, and meanings (Mason, 1996). The researchers turned to subjects living in kibbutzim in the northern part of Israel and with whom they were acquainted (Beit-Marom, 1986). Fifteen "young elderly" subjects aged fifty-five to sixty-five were interviewed, and an effort was made to maintain as similar numbers of male and female subjects as possible—eight women and seven men were interviewed.

Process

We interviewed all of the participants using semi-structured in-depth interviews. The process of telling one's personal story allowed participants to reflect upon the experience they were living and to give it meaning, which they may not have been conscious of previously (Mason, 1996; Flick, 1998). At the end of each interview, the subjects were asked to fill in a short questionnaire with personal details to help us document and construct the conclusions. All interviews were recorded and later transcribed and printed. A thematic analysis was used to analyze the transcribed interviews. This approach referred to words, expressions, and descriptions chosen by the informants during the interview. These choices reflected their feelings, opinions, and beliefs with regard to the subject and thus made it possible to learn about the human experience that they were undergoing. The thematic analysis focused on what the interviewees said, and the manner and order in which they said it (Shkedi, 2003).

Findings

Thematic analysis of the interviews produced three central themes, integrated in three "journeys in time." These revolve around three central axes: personal, familial, and the kibbutz.

First Theme: Aging as a Personal Journey in Time

> *Shlomit:* All through the years my father used to say, "I don't have time." Now I feel that I don't have time. Before I didn't really understand what he was saying . . . ok, I went with him, but now I understand. So for me the strongest experience for me now is that I don't have time . . .

The first theme reflects a personal internal struggle by the interviewees with the process of their aging. This is a journey in time in which the "young elderly" locate themselves within the continuum between nostalgia for eternal youth and visions of losses and solitude. This is a journey to and from old age, which includes coping with opposing expressions of acceptance and denial. Aging is exposed as a confusing and paradox-laden stage.

"We are Younger"—On the Road to Far-Off Aging

From the point of view of various generations, aging appears very differently. Despite the fact that this is an expected, normative developmental stage, the "young elderly" identify themselves as young, relative to the members of the founding generation when these were the same age. The "comparison" to the generation preceding them allows the "young elderly" to create a "differential" between themselves and the real "elderly":

> *Interviewer:* How would you define aging today, in your opinion? What does it mean?
>
> *Chaim:* First of all, I think that there is a very big difference between today's older people and those of our parents' generation . . . The kibbutz founders, once they reached about forty, began to act like old people, maintaining all sorts of privileges. There were sometimes ridiculous arguments about who was first on the boat, who was first off the boat, and that should be the person with the most privileges, but they began to act old when they were younger than I am now . . . It seems to me that people of my age today are much younger in spirit than our parents were . . . I think that we are more in tune with the needs of the younger generation than the veterans were regarding our needs.

While Chaim describes the narrow internal world of the founders, Shoshana expresses her view of the difference in aging for the two generations from another perspective—openness and exposure to the outside world.

> *Interviewer:* What is the difference in your aging and maturing and your parents' experience?
>
> *Shoshana:* . . . I could say that unlike my parent's age-group, we are much younger. We are much more assimilated into the world and want to change, unlike them. With them it was the opposite, and they closed themselves off in their own world and hung on with all their might so that it would not change. We always look for something else that will enrich us . . . we open up to the world outside and accept things from it.

In Shoshana's opinion, the ability to receive from and assimilate into the outside world is proof of the fact that she is not old. According to her description, the founding generation was closed, conservative, and disconnected, and needed the familiar kibbutz setting in order to preserve it. This stability allowed them to construct an entire life, as well as to create an old age within which they felt secure. The journey she describes is external—it is held up against the conservative old age of the founders' generation. She sees a successful old age as the one that maintains continuous and dynamic dialogue with the outside world.

"Setting the Tone"—Journey to a Meaningful Present

A gap exists between external time, chronological age, and internal time. From the interviews, it emerges that the "young elderly" feel young and full of energy. At the same time, surrounding society expects them to diminish roles—retire their work, reduce physical activity, and take grandparenting duties. One way to bridge these gaps is by locating their roles within the various spheres of life. Thus they blur the paradoxes exposed by external and internal aging.

> *Yitzchak:* Most of us are really very busy with our work, and the change also meant that a lot more emphasis has been placed on this idea of earning a living and of using work to the fullest, financially. But even beyond that, so this is an age, you could say, at the peak of one's career, when people have, in a certain sense, finished their training and they are professionals and they have experience and they still have a lot of ability . . . They are also the ones with the social and political positions—the fifty-year-olds among us. Most of the positions are in the hands of this age-group, and the groups following us are much smaller, number-wise. But some of them are also beginning to get into the experience of being grandparents, which is something . . . something new.

Reality demands that the "young elderly" maximize their earning potential, carry out central roles within the internal network, and expose themselves to the significant role of grandparenthood. Their journey is within a present rich with activity. It seems as if there is not enough time to consider aging.

"I am a Working Man at Heart"—Work as Deceptive in the Dimension of Time

"The work ethic" is an important concept in the kibbutz movement. The founding generation believed that members ought to work until their last day, and some of the "mature ones" hold a similar belief. Work is both a right and a duty, and it defines a person's experience. Leaving the workforce often signifies a move to old age. It is no accident that most of the participants did not plan to quit the workforce:

> *Interviewer:* What part does natural retirement play in aging, according to your view of things?
>
> *Shoshana:* I am not at all concerned about that. Not at all. I see myself working more, I hope, ten more years, I hope, until they toss me out (*laughs*) . . . I'm not one of those people who dreams of a retirement in a café. Not at all. I think that there's time for that as well, and for culture and for all of the things I've dreamed of doing at one time. At heart, I am a working person . . .

Work is a defining factor in the lives of the "young elderly," as well as a personal trait. They do not refer to old age as a relaxed, comfortable stage in life and seem even to express a certain disdain for those to do so.

"It Has Not Hit Me Yet"—and Old Age Is Not Knocking at the Door

The multiple roles of the "young elderly" have led some of them to say that "we are not old." When the expression "old age" was mentioned in interviews, it bothered the interviewees, and they had difficulty locating it in their own lives. Many of them were insulted by the term and asked us to use other expressions, such as "maturing."

> *Yael:* First of all, we are not even talking about old age. We feel very young. Really. We are now the leading group in the kibbutz, naturally. Our children are learning and setting up families and moving to new homes and just starting out professionally, and our group is the one that is dominant, financially speaking.

The "young elderly" feel young because their age-group is at the center of social and financial action on the kibbutz.

Second Theme: Aging as an Intergenerational Family Process

> *Shaul:* So today on our kibbutz, it is possible to live . . . how can I put it? People leave the kibbutz and forget to abandon it, it's possible. What does that mean? They leave the kibbutz; in other words, they don't participate in anything, live within four walls . . . they call this the process of familialization—within the family . . . a bit-by-bit process of familialization; it's part of an ongoing, uninitiated process where someone . . . people slowly withdraw into their families . . .

In its beginnings, the kibbutz was composed of homogeneous groups of young people whose goals and purposes were similar. From a small, unified, intimate community, kibbutzim have become large, multigenerational communities that are complex and heterogeneous. The "young elderly" play a central role in the family journey. Often they are expected to decide how to invest their own and the kibbutz's limited resources, whether in the care of their aging parents, in helping children and grandchildren, or perhaps in the changing kibbutz itself. Furthermore, they must find their place anew, as private citizens and as members of a particular generation, according to the current reality.

"Turning into a Normal Society"—Completing the Circle of Life

Fifty-five- to sixty-five-year-olds navigate the tension between caring for aging parents and worrying about children and grandchildren.

Their parents, the kibbutz founders, came to Israel in their youth, leaving behind their families in Europe. The kibbutz became their family unit, their refuge, and their center of belonging. These people did not have the good fortune to see their own parents aging and at the same time were not exposed to the care, worry, and pain inherent in watching a parent age. Their children, the "mature" generation, were raised by the kibbutz veterans within a complete and well-defined framework that took parenting roles away from the biological parents. The children of the "mature ones" were raised, and are still located, in a kibbutz that no longer adheres to the classic model. In the new system, parental authority has been returned to the biological parents. These young people were able to enjoy the active presence of grandmothers and grandfathers in their lives, unlike the "young elderly" as young adults. Interviewees describe how the kibbutz is now becoming a normal society in which the circle of life is completed.

> *Chaim:* One point that maybe we have not discussed but which is a problem on kibbutzim is that the older people whom I accused of deciding they were old before their time, they never got to live with old parents. Because they left Europe at a very young age and their parents, most of them, died in the Holocaust.
>
> I am from a completely different generation . . . and it seems to me that the kibbutz is becoming a much more normal society in that the generation of sons, who are seventy and younger, are able to watch their parents age. Therefore I think that your generation (the interviewer's), for my children's generation, it will be even more natural to live with aging. I think that the kibbutz veterans had a hard time at first and that it took them quite a while until they set up nursing homes . . . I think that your generation, that they will be able to see two generations aging on kibbutz. I think that they . . . will know better how to deal with it.

An Intergenerational Hierarchy on the Family Journey

The "young elderly" are located between aging parents and their own adult children. They are examining their resources and how they wish to distribute them between their own needs and those of other generations. More than once, the "mature one" is forced to "choose" sides in the nuclear or extended family. Working from the point of view that there is a need for a living, dynamic community, some prefer to the next generation.

> *Avraham:* I don't think that sixty-year-old people should tell thirty-year-olds how to live. Therefore, I do not get involved in the process.
>
> *Interviewer:* But you are only sixty.
>
> *Avraham:* That's right, and I hope it's not the end of the road for me, but still, if I look back at how I saw life at twenty or thirty or forty, I wouldn't have wanted people at the peak of their professional careers to lecture me about processes or

anything. I think it was quite justified that that's how I felt then, and I think it's still justified today.

Yitzchak has a slightly different perspective:

Yitzchak: We didn't do something to suit our children; we did what suited us. If we had wanted to do something to suit our children, we should have made a more drastic change, which would have been difficult for the older populations. Look, we're in between our parents and our children, so we went with something in the middle, which is not so terrible for one, but is not attractive enough for the other.

The participants in this study view themselves at the center of their familial life, surrounded by both their children and their parents, while at the same time keeping control over the nature of the kibbutz. The "young elderly" on the kibbutz are in the process of constructing a community that fits their needs, while taking into account the needs of other generations.

Whose Kibbutz Is This?—A Journey through Intergenerational Conflict

The intergenerational family is divided into various interest groups, moving forward on a common path. This is a complex journey of divisions: parents against their children, suspicious adults against those younger than them, women against men, and so forth. Both open and hidden arguments occur within the self-renewing, intimate kibbutz community. One way in which the "young elderly" stake their place is through standing strong on their rights. They have a strong need to protect those rights in an era of change and intergenerational tension:

Shoshana: We will go along with the change. All of our age-group will go along with it, because we all understand that there is no other way, but we have to watch out for our rights so that we don't end up "bald" from all of this, since we really are at the peak of our work years.
Interviewer: You said you needed to protect your rights—is there a feeling that your age-group is threatened?
Shoshana: Yes, yes. There is a feeling. Absolutely. The young people today will fight well for their rights . . . I mean the thirty- to forty-five-year-olds who will definitely look out for their own interests and are doing it as we speak.

Third Theme—Aging as a Community Journey within a Changing Reality

Ya'akov: Look, I'll tell you something; those who are planning and dreaming and are nostalgic for the kibbutz that once was . . . which was very, very special and beautiful, that has stayed with them; no one can take it away from them. The kibbutz as it was before, with all of the special, lovely things we had when we were children and then young people and they even more than that, it is still ours, and no one can take it away, even if they change it ten times . . . I'm not scared of changes. I remember when they introduced the first electric kettle into the kibbutz and there were people who said, "It's the end of the kibbutz. The kibbutz is finished," and then they introduced the first television and the first refrigerator and they said the same thing. I don't think this will be the end of the kibbutz, but it will be a different way of life; the community will live differently. We have to learn to live with that.

The third journey underway in the kibbutz is that of the "young elderly" as part of the collective journey of the kibbutz as a community. All members are walking this path together, toward a renewed version of the collective. This theme deals with the concerns connected to the change in the collective, the end of a stage of life, and a moment before the implementation of the new reality. Here a personal, and also a collective, self-examination is underway.

Kibbutz—A Choice?

All of the "young elderly" participants addressed the matter of their choice to live on kibbutz. These issues become even more pointed today, given their age and the fact that the option of leaving the kibbutz has become less relevant at their age. Still, most of the interviewed "young elderly" play with the idea in their own minds. The possibility is examined in hindsight: Was life on the kibbutz in fact an active choice, and if so, was it the right one? Were there times when the "young elderly" reconsidered their original choice of life on kibbutz? And today, given what they know, do they see this personal and collective choices differently? As in the example of Amos, many young elderly resolve the "choice" question in an interesting way:

> *Amos:* I can't say it was really a choice, but I am very happy with the life I've had. For many years I thought I was choosing, but it was not really a choice. It was a matter of rolling with, running, like a stick; they can describe the stick to you, and you run with the task. I don't know who made it; it doesn't matter, but you roll with it. I think everyone lives this way, but whatever. We thought we were choosing and I chose. Fine. Today I realize it was not really a choice. I never really questioned this, so it was never really a decision . . .

"To Speak of the Disgust"—Money as Inhibiting the Journey

One element that points to the new wind blowing on the kibbutzim is the open discussion of salaries, money, and financial affairs. Members of the collective kibbutz avoided talking about these issues altogether. The principle of equality meant that everyone in the community was equal and their budgets would be the same. Thus, a person with a central role and collective responsibility received a monthly stipend equal to the lowest of workers. Today, with the discussions of privatization and change, new ideas have been placed on the Kibbutz agenda, including differential salary scale, setting individual financial value to each position, maximization of earning power, and a wage comparison to those earned in the free market. It is now understood that the standard of living on kibbutz is not always in sync with a worker's salary. Today, kibbutz members understand that they need to earn a living from their work.

> *Chana:* When I found a new job, I spoke to the human resources manager and said, "I'm giving you all the possible options; tell me what's the best in terms of salary," though I have to admit that as a member of *Hashomer Hatza'ir* and a kibbutz member, it was considered (not today but in my time) that to speak about money was to speak about something disgusting, sort of as a joke. But we don't speak about money, because we don't . . . Money is not a subject we discuss, and suddenly it seemed strange to me that suddenly I'm like this, asking who and what earns more, but . . . I learned to speak about it respectfully . . .

"Kibbutz Is Not the Right Thing"—Reality Forced by Change

Despite the difficulties, the rich and respectable history, and the pain inherent in bidding farewell to an entire world, many of the "young elderly" relate to the kibbutz as if to a personality whose very existence is incorrect. In their words, continuing to manage the community in the present manner is not legitimate. Some say this painfully, but firmly. From a historical point of view, this lifestyle did not stand the test of time and cannot survive forever.

> *Avraham:* If you ask me if I would live this experiment a second time? I don't know. Today I don't know. All in all the feeling is that . . . that this way failed because it isn't surviving. It did not outlast the survival test . . . These systems broke down, if not before, then in the third generation. This means that despite the fact that in my eyes this is really a beautiful thing, it's not the right thing, because it did not last.
> *Interviewer:* And is that the only test?
> *Avraham:* There is no stronger test, is there?
> *Interviewer:* You say, "It's not the right thing."
> *Avraham:* That's right. Exactly. It is not the right thing. This does not mean it's not beautiful and it doesn't mean it's not the just thing, and it doesn't mean that sort of thing; it only means that this is not the right thing because it did not last.

The next interviewee also expresses an understanding of the need for change, but in her opinion, it is a matter of being or abandoning.

> *Dvora:* In my view, a community that does not change becomes *Mea Shearim* [a kind of a ghetto], it's a community that dies, that fossilizes. This is why even if these changes are not easy and need to be learned, it still means that there is vitality, that there is life, that we're not going off uncontrolled, that every step we check whether

I should have taken that step a year ago or the previous step or it doesn't matter, or I want to change the angle, or change the shoe I'm moving ahead in or change the rhythm or I don't know what, or to change something. I think, it means that there is . . . there is awareness, there is need, there is power to change, there is a desire to change, there are people who want to, and if the kibbutz has not changed over the course of three generations now, then there is some sort of clinical death here.

The need for change in kibbutz society is equated with the need for life. Without examination and change, the community will cease to exist. Avraham relates to the processes of change as a taking apart of the system, while Dvora prefers to see things as a chance to develop and create. In her opinion, the desire of the members to renew and breathe life into the place has saved the kibbutz from clinical death. Designing the place according to the needs relevant to the current reality is the source of its life. The kibbutz is not falling apart, dying, or ceasing. The opposite is true. This change is reviving the community and breathing air and hope into it. Without considering the collective existence and the common consideration of principles, the kibbutz would fossilize and die. The fact that the members dare to make changes in the community is what permits its eternal survival.

Discussion

The purpose of this study was to describe, analyze, and deepen the understanding of significances ascribed to old age and aging by the "younger elderly" in kibbutzim undergoing changes. These men and women, aged fifty-five to sixty-five, are at the center of the research as well as at the center of the storm taking place on kibbutzim. Although there is a feeling of extended family on kibbutz, it is not, in fact, a family. On the classic kibbutz, into which the "young elderly" were born, there were clear signs of an intimate family. These elements crumbled and lost their importance over the years, and today there is a clear difference between the "kibbutz"—the overall, central framework—and the "family"—a close and safeguarded unit. Still, one may still find "family" elements within the broader kibbutz system and there are family functions for which the kibbutz is responsible. The "young elderly" on kibbutz today are not interested in maintaining the community ties that bind, and most feel strangled by them. The need to distance the individual and their nuclear family from the community organizations came up in many of the interviews. It seems as though the "younger elderly" are uninterested in the protective umbrella of the kibbutz and believe in their own ability and in the strength of their families to help them in their old age.

Intergenerational relations on kibbutz were also examined in this study: the "young elderly" describe themselves as the central axis upon which the kibbutz and family systems revolve. They hold key positions on kibbutz, are expected to care for their elderly parents, and help their adult children raise the grandchildren. By doing so, they allow the next generation free time to develop professionally and personally. The study subjects are the driving force and the guardians of the circles of belonging. The "young elderly" display a responsibility and deep duty toward their families and the extended kibbutz framework.

Agreeing with the change is also tied to family. As may be seen in the interviews, the kibbutz founders tend to accept the change as long as the "younger elderly" in their family are in favor of it. "The socialization of change" is how one of the interviewees refers to it. In other words, the desire to change trickles down through the family generations, as long as the "young elderly" indicate an interest and desire. Moreover, the social location of the young elderly as the axis of kibbutz and family life does not allow them to retire or disconnect. They appear to have a decisive influence upon the design of the kibbutz and the unfolding of family life. The involvement of the young elderly in kibbutz and family life emphasizes the fact that they do not see themselves as "old." It is as if the kibbutz reality does not allow them to age. They therefore do not seek this label for themselves.

Most of them have central positions in their communities and are among the leaders of the change. It is likely that for these people, creating the change means regaining control in an uncertain reality. In this way, they are able to strengthen their self-worth and emotional well-being. These people are not merely reacting to what is happening around them; they are taking a part in creating it. It is clear that despite the difficulty in bringing agreed changes to the kibbutz, involvement in its processes is a sign of the individual's emotional and physical health, and may be the key to positive and successful aging.

This study arose from insecurity with regard to the ability of young elderly people on kibbutz to handle the dramatic changes occurring there. This age-group of fifty-five- to sixty-five-year-olds is central within many kibbutzim that are trying to find their way. These people are divided between working and retiring, between aging and renewal. As this research revealed, this age-group acts as a central axis in the circles to which they belong. They have been forced to redesign their parents' lives' work, after they themselves were educated by the classic kibbutz system. They are expected, even today, to retain responsibility for managing the kibbutz so that their children will be able to establish their families and careers. The "young elderly" view themselves as the past, present, and future of the kibbutz society and have been central in creating each of these periods: The past—as being the living and existing string to the "old, traditional" Kibbutz with all its communal principles and values, the present—as discussed through this chapter, filling the roll of the "young elderly," and the future—as those who keep the kibbutz community alive, creative, and significant in a changing reality.

Within this kibbutz complexity, some people find old age peeking into their lives. Despite the researchers' mistaken assumption that the meeting with this group would expose scared, confused people, in fact brave people appeared: mature men and women who long for change in the kibbutz lifestyle and are interested and prepared for it. They are not fearful of the challenges. With courage and a certain measure of personal, community, and family responsibility, the young elderly head out on their path toward the creation of a new community, the construction of which will respond to all the needs of all the members.

Bibliography

Aldous, J. "Family Development and the Life Course: Two Perspectives on Family Change." *Journal of Marriage and the Family* 52 (1990): 571–83.

Atchley, R. C. "A Continuity Theory of Normal Aging." *The Gerontologist* 29 (1989): 183–90.

Austin, C. D. and M. B. Loeb. "Why Age Is Relevant in Social Policy and Practice." In *Age or Need?* edited by B. L. Neugarten, 263–88. London: Sage Publications Ltd., 1982. Avrahami, E. (Ed.). *Kibbutz Lexicon*. Efal: Yad Tabenkin, 1998.

Baltes, P. B. "The Many Faces of Human Aging. Toward a Psychological Culture of Old Age." *Psychological Medicine* 21 (1991): 837–54.

Baltes, P. B. and M. M. Baltes. "Psychological Perspectives on Successful Aging: The Model of Selective Optimism with Compensation." In *Successful Aging, Perspectives from the Behavioural Sciences*, edited by P. B. Baltes and M. M. Baltes, 1–34. Cambridge, England: Cambridge University Press, 1990.

Baruch, G. and J. Brooks-Gunn, eds. *Women in Middle Life*. New York: Plenum Press, 1984.

Bar-Tur, L. and A. Prager. "The Elderly—What Does He Have in Life? The Meaning of Life in Late Old Age." *Gerontology* 76 (1996/7): 37–47 [in Hebrew].

Be'er, S. and H. Factor. "The Demographic Development of the Elderly Population in Israel 1988–2000." *Gerontology* (1) (1990): 3–22 [in Hebrew].

Beit-Marom, R. *Research Methods in the Social Sciences*. Tel Aviv: Open University Press, 1986 [in Hebrew].

Bengston, V. L. and D. J. Mangen. "Family Intergenerational Solidarity Revised: Suggestions for Future Management." In *Measurement of Intergenerational Relations*, edited by D. J. Mangen, V. L. Bengeston, and P. H. Landry, Jr., 222–38. Beverly Hills: Sage, 1988.

Bengston, V. L. and R. E. L. Roberts. "Intergenerational Solidarity and Aging Families: An Example of Formal Theory Construction." *Journal of Marriage and the Family* 53 (1991): 856–70.

Birren, J. E., G. M. Kenyon, J. E. Ruth, J. J. F. Schroots, and T. Svensson, eds. *Aging and Biography: Explorations in Adult Development*, 131–48. New York: Springer, 1996.

Brodsky, J. and M. Davis. "The Demographics and Epidemiology of the Elderly." In *Aging and the Elderly in Israel*, edited by A. Rozin, 289–342. Jerusalem: Eshel, 2003 [in Hebrew].

Bruner, J. "Narrative and Paradigmatic Modes of Thought." In *Learning and Teaching the Ways of Knowing*, edited by E. Eisner, 97–115. Chicago: NSSE, 1985.

Carmel, S., A. Lapidot, A. Motran, and G. Shemi. "Predicting Subjective Health Status among Elderly in Kibbutz and in Cities." *Society and Welfare* 16, no. 3 (1996): 361–80 [in Hebrew].

Cumming, E. and W. E. Henry. *Growing Old, the Process of Disengagement*. New York: Basic Books, 1961.

Doron, I. and G. Linchitz. "Labor and Aging Is Israel: The Law and Employees Caring for Their Older Family Members." *Labor, Society and Law* 9 (2002): 197–227 [in Hebrew].

Flick, U. *An Introduction to Qualitative Research*. London: Sage Publications, 1998.

Friedlander, D., E. Ben-Moshe, J. Schellekens, and C. Feldman. *Processes of Demographic Change and Aging in Israeli Localities: Implication for Welfare Policy.* Jerusalem: The Jerusalem Institute, 1990 [in Hebrew].

Gal, J. "Kibbutz Pensions—The Evolution of a Social Problem." *Social Security* 44 (1995): 77–95 [in Hebrew].

Habib, J. and J. Brodsky. "Changes in the Perception of Old Age and Preparing of an Aging World." *Gerontology* 27, no. 1 (2000): 45–54 [in Hebrew].

Harel, I. *The New Kibbutz*. Jerusalem: Keter, 1993 [in Hebrew].

Kahana, E. and B. Kahana. "Conceptual and Empirical Advances in Understanding Aging Well through Proactive Adaptation." In *Adulthood and Aging: Research on Continuities and Discontinuities*, edited by V. L. Bengtson, 18–40. New York: Springer, 1996.

Karp, D. A. "A Decade of Reminders: Changing Age Consciousness between Fifty and Sixty Years Old." *The Gerontologist* 28, no. 6 (1988): 727–38.

Lawton, M. P. "Environmental Proactivity and Affect in Older People." In *The Social Psychology of Aging. Newbury Park*, edited by S. Spacapan and S. Oskamp, 135–63. Thousand Oaks, CA: Sage, 1982.

Leviatan, U. "Successful Aging: The Kibbutz Experience." *Journal of Aging and Judaism* 4 (1989): 71–92.

———. "Contribution of Social Arrangements to the Attainment of Successful Aging—The Experience of the Israeli Kibbutz." *Journal of Gerontology* 54B (1999): 205–13.

Lincoln, Y. S. and E. G. Guba. "Paradigmatic Controversies, Contradictions and Emerging Confluences." In *Handbook of Qualitative Research*, edited by N. K. Denzin and S. L. Lincoln, 2nd ed., 163–88. London: Sage Publications, 2000.

Maddox, G. L. "Disengagement Theory: A Critical Evaluation." *The Gerontologist* 4 (1964): 80–83.

Marin B, and A. Zaidi (Eds). *Mainstreaming Ageing Indicators to Monitor Sustainable Progress and Policies*. Aldershot; Brookfield, USA; Singapore; Sydney: Ashgate.

Mason, J. *Qualitative Researching*. London: Sage Publications, 1996.

McAdams, D. P. "Narrating the Self in Adulthood." In *Aging and Biography: Explorations in Adult Development*, edited by J. E. Birren, G. M. Kenyon, J. E. Ruth, J. J. F. Schroots, and T. Svensson. New York: Springer, 1996.

Nechushtan, G. "Aging in the Kibbutz—A Time Perspective." *Gerontology* 77 (1997): 44–55 [in Hebrew].

Neugarten, B. L. "The Awareness of Middle Age." In *Middle Age and Aging: A Reader in Social Psychology*, edited by B. L. Neugarten, 93–98. Chicago: University of Chicago Press, 1968.

Neugarten, B. L. and N. Datan. "The Subjective Experience of Middle Age." In *The Life Cycle: Readings in Human Development*, edited by L. Steinberg, 273–83. New York: Columbia University Press, 1981.

Neugarten, D. A., ed. *The Meanings of Age—Selected Papers of Bernice L. Neugarten*. Chicago: University of Chicago Press, 1996.

Noam, G. and M. Sikron. *Socio-Demographic Change among the Elderly in Israel: 1961–1983*. Jerusalem: Eshel, 1990 [in Hebrew].

Orchan, E. and H. Goldemberg. *In the Middle of Life—The Study of Kibbutz Members in the Ages 45–65*. Haifa: The Institute for Research of the Kibbutz, the University of Haifa, 1994 [in Hebrew].

Palmore, E. "Ageism in Gerontological Language." *The Gerontologist* 40, no. 6 (2000): 645.

Patton, M. Q. *Qualitative Evaluation and Research Methods*. 2nd ed. London: Sage Publications, 1990.

Pavin, A. *Is the Kibbutz a Home, a Way of Life, or a Business?* Haifa: The Institute for Research of the Kibbutz, the University of Haifa, 1992 [in Hebrew].

Rosental, R. "The Cracks That Became a Break-Down." *Panim—Journal on Culture, Society and Education* 4 (1998): 57–63 [in Hebrew].

Rosner, M., D. Peleg, H. Goldenberg, and I. Glick. *Social Security in the Kibbutz*. No. 165. Haifa: The Institute for Research of the Kibbutz, The University of Haifa, 1999 [in Hebrew].

Rosner, M. and S. Getz. *The Kibbutzim in Times of Change*. Tel Aviv: The Kibbutz Hameuchad, 1996 [in Hebrew].

Salem, H. *The Differences in Health and Welfare Status between Members (Age 55 and Above) of Kibbutzim That Were Privatized and Those That Kept Communal Setting*. Masters thesis. Department of Gerontology, University of Haifa, 2003 [in Hebrew].

Shkedi, A. *Words That Touch: Theory and Practice in Qualitative Research*. Tel Aviv: Ramot, 2003 [in Hebrew].

Silverstone, B. "Older People of Tomorrow: A Psychosocial Profile." *The Gerontologist* 36, no. 1 (1996): 27–32.

The Kibbutz Regulations. Tel-Aviv: The National Kibbutz Movement, 1973.

Vaillant, G. E. *The Wisdom of the Ego*. Cambridge, MA: Harvard University Press, 1993.

Whitton, L. S. "Finding the Elder Voice in Social Legislation." In *Aging: Culture, Health, and Social Change*, edited by D. N. Weissub, D. C. Thomasma, and G. F. Tomossy, 101–17. Dordrecht: Kluwer Academic Publishers, 2001.

Woodruff, D. S. and J. E. Bierren. *Aging—Scientific Perspectives and Social Issues*. 2nd ed. Monterey, CA: Brooks/Cole Publishing Company, 1983.

7

Varying Spousal Relations in the Kibbutz and the Moshav

Hadas Doron

Research on marital relations is rich and diverse as is research on the community and its importance to the individual. By contrast, research on family–community interaction is fairly meager.

The theoretical basis for hypotheses regarding the relationship between community structure and the family is inspired by Lewin's field theory (Lewin, 1951), as well as exchange theory (Blau, 1964; Homans, 1974; Bagarozzi, 1993; Sabatelli and Shehan, 1993), and finally by the communitarian approach (Bott, 1971; Etzioni, 1993).

The main mechanism explaining the community–family relationship, according to Bott (1971), is social control. When resources (e.g., economic, social) are provided to each spouse directly by the community, spousal interdependence is reduced. The present study picks up where Bott left off and expands on her work by comparing two types of communities: one in which social support is given directly to the individual (the Israeli kibbutz) and the other in which it is generated in the family (the Israeli moshav).

Holman (1981) and others have proposed mediating variables (e.g., allocation of roles, balance of power) to elaborate the relationships between individuals and groups. We follow this approach but emphasize one mediating variable: spousal interdependence, its strength and symmetry (the latter term relating to which spouse is more dependent on the other). We suggest that this variable impacts both the spousal equality and the marital stability.

A comparative analysis of marriage patterns in two unique, long-standing, and close-knit communities in Israel—the kibbutz (collective rural settlement) and the moshav (cooperative smallholders' rural settlement)—was conducted.

These two settlement types have many features in common. Both are based on small communities. Both began as Gemeinschaft-type groups of young pioneers (Talmon-Garber, 1970). Over time, both evolved into communities including several generations. Both became established and stipulated in their bylaws, the rights, and obligations of individuals and families. Both were founded on the basis of an ideology in which the fundamental principles are Jewish nationalism, hard labor (as a value and not just as an instrumentality), preference for primary occupations (agriculture and crafts), material equality, cooperation, and communal democracy.

Despite their numerous similarities, the kibbutz and the moshav differ, for our purposes, with respect to spousal interdependence. On kibbutzim, interdependence is minimal because each spouse's social and economic needs are directly provided by the community, and each spouse is a member of the community in his or her own right. By contrast, on moshavim there is much interdependence because the two spouses are jointly responsible for supporting their family and cultivating their farm. This joint responsibility is reflected in the fact that it is the family as a single unit that votes in the local elections.

To sharpen the comparison, we chose localities with a similar demographic, cultural, and environmental background so that the difference in spousal interdependence remains as one of the very few outstanding disparities. In this study, the kibbutz serves as a "laboratory" for the examination of some postindustrial family issues. We have an opportunity to observe family relations when each spouse's income and welfare are independent of the goodwill and capabilities of his mate. Therefore, the significance of the study extends beyond the investigated communities studied and is relevant to the relationship between spousal interdependence and marital stability in modern urban settings.

Theoretical Background

Spousal Interdependence

Interdependence between marital partners is impacted by intrapersonal, interpersonal, and communal–social factors. Professional and research literature offers numerous definitions of the term "dependence," most of them on a continuum with extreme situations at either pole. Lewin (1951) coined the term "interdependence" as the primary variable aimed at describing the relations between independent parts comprising a system and von Bertalanffy (1975) adapted this notion to family therapy.

Exchange theory, based on concepts introduced by Blau (1964), Homans (1974), and Sabatelli and Shehan (1993), maintains that marital relations, their main features and success, are impacted more by the spousal exchange system functioning at present than by the partners' personality traits shaped in the past. According to social exchange theory, interdependence between marital partners is based on the benefits embodied in the present marriage compared to its alternatives.

Levinger (1999) asserts that in a satisfying marital relationship, each of the spouses receives the best return in comparison with being alone or with someone else. He found that the stronger the interdependence, the greater the stability of the relationship. Studies conducted by Veroff (1999), Swim and Sura (1999), and Crawford et al. (2002) demonstrated the relationship between mutual dependence and various marital qualities: commitment, stability, and satisfaction. Scanzoni (2001) attributed the proliferation of alternative marital patterns to the lack of spousal interdependence.

In traditional societies, communal, economic, and legal control created commitment of the individual to his/her marriage, leading to marital stability. In contemporary Western society, by comparison, the stabilizing effects of external control are diminished. Modern couplehood is based primarily on personal investment, emotional bond, and mutual satisfaction. A certain tension exists however between these foundations of modern couplehood and marital stability. Relationships based on subjective emotions are more likely to change over a lifetime than are relationships stemming from interdependence. Levinger (1999), as well as Mintz and Kellogg (1988), claim that one of the factors undermining family stability is the displacement of the communal ethic by modern individualism. We turn now to a consideration of how spousal interdependence finds expression in each of the two community types studied.

Spousal Interdependence on the Kibbutz

The kibbutz community is composed of individuals and families. Marriage is not a precondition for membership in the community. The shift from singlehood to marriage, while certainly having a significant emotional transition in the individual's life, does not change one's formal status in the community. Daily routine, housing conditions, work requirements, and voting rights are retained. For the same reasons, the dissolution of a marriage has little impact on the individual's formal status. Separation does not diminish one's rights as a full-fledged member of the kibbutz.

On kibbutzim, alternative arrangements that parallel the familial functions (such as a communal dining room, communal children's home, and laundry) are available. These arrangements weaken the spouses' interdependence and leave individuals free to maneuver between the family setting and the public–community domain. These community-based arrangements persisted even when, over time, the kibbutz family regained many of the functions associated with non-kibbutz family life. As Ben-Rafael and Weitman (1984) argue, "We can see . . . that the broadening of family activity did not always eliminate previous collective patterns; a duplication of patterns regarding the same function sometimes develops, making individual choice possible." Adopting Nye's classification of family roles (Nye, 1979), we conclude that the main spheres of spousal interdependence on the kibbutz are emotional and sexual, as against economic or educational; in the latter, spousal interdependence is relatively low.

Spousal Interdependence in the Moshav

Marriage in the moshav constitutes a prerequisite for joining the community. It is required even in the case of a son who wishes to inherit his parents' farm. Being married signifies both the intention and the capability to become a part of the moshav community. The family is autonomous in performing its various functions, and the community does not provide structural alternatives. Many women in the moshav are fully or partially employed on the family farm, and the family's livelihood may be entirely dependent on the joint success of both spouses operating as a team (Applebaum and Margulies, 1979).

Marriage dissolution in the moshav affects various aspects of life: the economic dimension constitutes a weighty impediment since it is legally impossible to divide the farm and the property. The farm may be transferred to another family member or returned to the moshav, but bequeathing it to the next generation is rarely an option. Relations between the couple and the extended family (usually the wife's relations with her in-laws) are eroded. The husband often moves back to his parents' home, and members of his family of origin resume intensive interaction while the wife is isolated. Thus the full impact of the wife's dependence on her husband in the moshav emerges when a marriage dissolves. A common saying among family therapists is that "it is almost impossible to divorce in the moshav." The centrality of marriage and the family's low dependence on the community lead to greater spousal interdependence in the moshav. This dependence is asymmetrical as the woman is more dependent on her husband than vice versa.

Marital Stability

As stated previously, stability increases as spouses' options outside marriage decrease. Rusbult (1983) and Rusbult and van Lango (1996) have found that an increase in high-quality alternatives reduces commitment to the existing marriage and increases the likelihood of separation.

Marital stability is generally measured by the divorce rate in a particular population (Raley and Bumpass, 2003). However, Booth et al. (1983) and others (Johnson et al., 1986; Heaton and Albrecht, 1991) related marital stability to the couple's assessment of their chances to separate. This definition pertains to perceived marital instability, which, similar to employment insecurity, reflects confidence concerning the viability of the relationship.

The Israel Central Bureau of Statistics data indicate that divorce rates in the kibbutz population have been consistently higher than that in the moshav and similar to rates in the overall (Jewish) population. Although not always so, in the 1970s and the beginning of the 1980s, the kibbutz divorce rate even exceeded that of the general population. For example, the average divorce rates in 1978 were 0.5 percent in the general population, 1.45 percent in the kibbutz, and 1.2 percent in the moshav, and in 1988, the average rates were 3.85, 3.7, and 2.2 percent respectively.

Marital Quality

There is some disagreement about the theoretical and operational definitions of the term "marital quality." The operational definitions range from almost poetic concepts such as "happiness" to pragmatic ones such as "mutual adjustment" (Spanier and Lewis, 1980; Trost, 1985; Crane et al., 1990). Despite this vagueness, the term "marital quality" is frequent in studies on marriage and the family (Johnson et al., 1986).

This study employs the multidimensional ENRICH scale (Fowers and Olson, 1993) based on a model that combines theoretical considerations with an empirical perspective and is widely applied in clinical work. The scale measures marital quality for the couple as well as the individual partners.

Spousal Equality and Marital Stability

Numerous studies have examined the relationship between spousal equality and marital quality. Rachlin and Hansen (1985) did not find a significant difference in marital satisfaction between egalitarian and non-egalitarian marriages. Aida and Falbo (1991) on the other hand found that couples with an egalitarian marriage reported a higher level of marital satisfaction compared to those in non-egalitarian marriages.

In a study that examined marital satisfaction among "traditional" and "egalitarian" married couples, Altrocchi (1988) found that the latter reported enhanced communication and an awareness of the need to invest in the relationship. However, he found no significant difference between the two marital patterns. Rubin (1983) found that couples with a higher marital satisfaction level also reported egalitarian power relations. This finding was supported by a comprehensive study conducted by Shapira-Berman (1999) that examined the relationship between equality and happiness in marriage. Poplau (1983) found that egalitarian spousal relations predict marital satisfaction. Studies examining dual-career couples showed that egalitarian relations predict both marital satisfaction and expected marital continuity (or stability) (Brehm, 1985; Sexfon and Perlman, 1989).

The effect of egalitarian marital relations on marital quality was found to be greater for women than for men. In other words, women are more sensitive to an egalitarian marriage style (Suitor, 1991; Vannoy and Philliber, 1992; Pina and Bengtson, 1993; Tompson, 1993). The impact of egalitarian relations on marriage according to these studies is gender specific. Our study examines the impact of spousal equality (reflected in role division and power relations) on marital quality. This examination is carried out in two communities—the kibbutz and the moshav.

Based on the above literature review, we hypothesize that in a community characterized by low spousal interdependence, a high degree of equality between the partners, and the low price of marriage dissolution—the kibbutz in our study—marital quality will be higher and marital stability will be lower than in a community characterized by high spousal interdependence, non-egalitarian relations between the partners, and the high price of marriage dissolution—the moshav in our study.

Research Hypotheses

1. Spousal interdependence in the kibbutz is lower than that in the moshav.
2. Spousal interdependence in the kibbutz is more symmetrical than that in the moshav.

3. Power gaps between spouses in the kibbutz are smaller than that in the moshav.
4. Role division between spouses in the kibbutz is more egalitarian and flexible than that in the moshav.
5. Marital quality in the kibbutz exceeds marital quality in the moshav.
6. Marital stability in the moshav exceeds that in the kibbutz.
7. Greater mutual dependence between marital partners increases marital stability.

Table 7.1 presents the first six hypotheses comparing patterns of couplehood in the kibbutz and the moshav.

Description of the Research

Study Populations and Samples

The study population consists of members of selected kibbutzim and moshavim in the Jezreel Valley (northern Israel). It includes fifteen thousand residents, members of long-standing communities. The vast majority of them are Ashkenazim (Jews of European/American extraction). The sample consisted of two hundred married couples—one hundred from kibbutzim and one hundred from moshavim (Table 7.2). The average age of the women was 40.75 (SD 6.9) and that of the husbands was 43.6 (SD 7.87). The average number of children per family was 2.96 (SD 0.99), with the average age of the youngest child in the family 6.83 (SD 5.17) and the average number of years of marriage 15.26 (SD 7.99).

The sample was constructed according to the following stages:

Stage 1: Selection of the localities investigated.

The localities were selected by a nonrandom procedure. Local experts (chairpersons of regional councils, directors of social services departments) marked off localities that met the following criteria:

Table 7.1   **Comparison of marital patterns between the kibbutz and moshav communities**

No.	Characteristic	Community type
1	Interdependence between spouses	Kibbutz < moshav
2	Egalitarian role division	Kibbutz > moshav
3	Egalitarian distribution of power	Kibbutz > moshav
4	Marital stability	Kibbutz < moshav
5	Marital quality	Kibbutz > moshav

1. Distribution of age in the locality (only localities old enough to contain at least three generations)
2. Affiliation with a settlement association (i.e., a national settlement federation)
3. Existence of bylaws determining the community's lifestyle and regulating compliance
4. Demographic stability (only slight changes in the size and structure of the local population over the past decades)

These localities became the study population.

One may wonder whether the study was conducted before ten or twenty years since the kibbutz and the moshav have undergone processes of privatization that distance them from the unique attributes of former times. Efforts were made to limit the effect of these processes by selecting settlements that remained as close as possible to the traditional model of kibbutz and moshav.

Stage 2: A quota was determined for each locality, reflecting the population of the locality as a share of the population under study. In each locality, a complete list of couples that fulfilled the following criteria was compiled:

- Legally married
- Aged twenty-five to fifty
- Parents of at least one minor child

Finally, the appropriate quota was selected at random from each local list.

Data Collection

Each family in the sample was contacted by phone and told that the purpose of the study was to investigate family life in rural settlements. The response rate in the kibbutz sample was almost 100 percent.

Table 7.2 Schematic description of the sample

	Men	Women	Sample
Kibbutzim	($N = 100$)	($N = 100$)	Total kibbutz sample ($N = 200$)
Moshavim	($N = 100$)	($N = 100$)	Total moshav sample ($N = 200$)
Total	Total men ($N = 200$)	Total women ($N = 200$)	All respondents ($N = 400$)

Response rate in the moshavim was about 80 percent, and some hesitancy was encountered there. The data were gathered by a multiple-choice questionnaire. Each spouse was instructed to complete his or her questionnaire independently. Since the response rate in the moshav sample was less than perfect, the moshav sample may be biased toward marital satisfaction.

Operationalization of the Main Variables

Spousal Interdependence

This variable was defined as the degree to which one spouse needs the other's resources. To explore spousal interdependence, Lampert's dependency scale was applied (1981). This was done through a questionnaire including items such as the following:

1. "Separation from my wife (husband) would be more difficult for me than for her (him)."
2. "In everyday life my wife (husband) needs me more than I need her (him)."

In our study, the reliability of the dependency scale was found to be rather low: $\alpha = 0.58$.

Egalitarian Role Allocation

This index was designed by Blood and Wolfe (1960) and adapted for Israel by Katz (1980). Subjects were asked to select one of five options to indicate who performs each item in a list of tasks: (1) only the husband, (2) mainly the husband, (3) both, (4) mainly the wife, and (5) only the wife. For example, "Which spouse performs the following tasks in your home?" (1) Washing dishes and (2) taking children to the doctor.

The data were transformed to scales of 1–100, with 100 denoting perfectly egalitarian allocation of roles (we both do the job) and 1 being an inegalitarian allocation of roles (only the husband or only the wife performs this task).

The reliability of the items in this study was found to be $\alpha = 0.71$.

Power Relations

This set of questions, too, was adapted from Blood and Wolfe (1960) as translated by Katz (1980). Subjects were shown a list of family decisions and asked to select one of five options to indicate who usually makes the final decision: (1) always the husband, (2) usually the husband (3) both, (4) usually the wife, and (5) always the wife.

The same transformation was made here as for the allocation of roles. The power questionnaire has been used in numerous studies in various countries (Warner et al., 1986; Aida and Falbo, 1991; Rabin, 1991; Weiss, 1994; Shapira-Berman, 1999). According to these authors, its reliability is high—between 0.8 and 0.9. In our research, the reliability was found to be $\alpha = 0.87$.

Marital Quality

We used an abridged version of ENRICH (Olson et al., 1987) to measure marital quality (or satisfaction). The scale was translated and adapted for Israel by Lavee (1995). This abridged scale includes ten items that examine the degree of satisfaction, agreement, and compatibility of the spouses.

In the present study, the reliability was $\alpha = 0.83$.

Marital Stability

Booth et al. (1983) developed the marital instability index. This instrument examines the couple's expectations regarding the likelihood that their marriage will dissolve. Examples are as follows: "The idea of separation has occurred to one of the spouses" or "I have discussed my thoughts about divorce or separation with a good friend."

In our study, reliability was found to be $\alpha = 0.71$.

Findings

Table 7.3 examines the differences between the samples from the kibbutz and the moshav with respect to the dependent variables applying ANCOVA.

The data in Table 7.3 suggest that the data corroborate most of our hypotheses. The following criteria characterize the kibbutz family more than the moshav family: low and symmetrical dependence between spouses, egalitarian role division and power distribution, and lower marital stability. However with respect to marital satisfaction (marital quality), no significant differences were found.

As suggested in our introduction, spousal interdependence may be the variable linking community type to marital stability. The subjects were classified into two groups according to dependence level (high, above the median; low, below the median). The results are presented in Table 7.4.

Table 7.4 shows that average marital stability in the kibbutz is lower than that in the moshav. The cause of this divergence is the instability of

Table 7.3   The effect of community type and gender on marital characteristics. Results of analysis of covariance (ANCOVA) with control variables, F values, and their statistical significance

Source of variance	Spouse mutual dependence	Power distribution	Role division	Marital quality	Marital stability
Independent variables					
Gender	0.007	0.007	0.39	0.04	0.74
Community	58.8***	8.06**	76.3***	0.67	9.97***
Gender × community	23.1***	0.12	1.37	2.69	0.17
Control variables					
Wife's education	3.06	0.01	0.04	1.03	0.09
Husband's education	7.12**	1.12	0.96	3.73*	1.55

$*p \leq .05; **p \leq .01; ***p \leq .001.$

the kibbutz couples with low interdependence. This finding corroborates hypotheses 6 and 7.

Table 7.5 presents an analysis of variance that examines the main effects of the variables "gender," "community type," and "dependence level," as well as the effects of the interactions between community type, dependence level, and marital stability.

Table 7.5 indicates a statistically significant positive correlation between dependence level and marital stability. In other words, the higher the dependence level, the higher the marital stability. Thus, when the variable "dependence level" is added, the relationship between community type and marital stability is statistically significant. This finding also supports hypotheses 1 and 6.

Figure 7.1 shows a statistically significant difference between men and women in the kibbutz with respect to dependence level and marital stability: the greater the dependence level, the greater is marital stability. This difference was not found between men and women in the moshav. Hence, low marital stability is found when the following two conditions exist in tandem: low dependence and belonging to the kibbutz (egalitarian) community. Under any other combination of conditions (couples in the kibbutz with a high level of spousal dependence or couples in the

Table 7.4   Marital stability by community type (kibbutz/moshav) and dependence level (high/low)—averages and SD

		Place of residence											
		Kibbutz			Moshav			Total					
		Spouse dependence			Spouse dependence			Spouse dependence					
		Low	High	Total	Low	High	Total	Low	High	Total				
Marital stability	Average SD	82.16	92.91	85.28	90.60	91.74	91.44	84.42	92.07	88.36				
		(17.93)	(11.58)	(17.01)	(15.45)	(12.10)	(12.98)	(17.63)	(11.91)	(15.41)				

Table 7.5 **The main effects of community type, dependence level, and gender, and the interaction between them on marital stability—analysis of variance**

		Degrees of freedom	Statistical significance
Main effect—community type	Marital stability	1	2.39
Main effect—dependence level	Marital stability	1	6.42**
Main effect—gender	Marital stability	1	6*
Interaction: dependence level × community	Marital stability	1	4.19*
Interaction: community × gender	Marital stability	1	0.64
Interaction: gender × dependence level	Marital stability	1	0.011
Interaction: gender × community × dependence level	Marital stability	1	0.127

$*p \leq .05; **p \leq .01.$

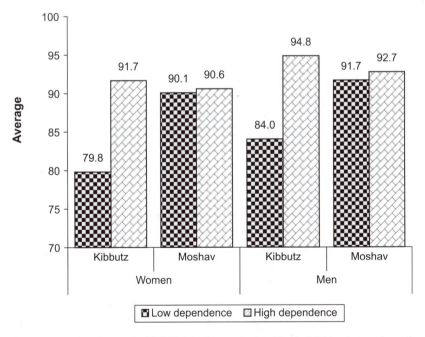

Figure 7.1 Average marital stability in the moshav and in the kibbutz by gender and level of mutual dependence between spouses

moshav irrespective of their dependence), there is a high level of marital stability. In statistical terms, we found an interaction between community type, marital interdependence, and marital stability.

Discussion

Impacts of Community Structure and Functioning on Spousal Relationships

The key finding that emerges from the data is that the structure and functioning of the community have an important impact on the spousal relationship—interdependence, the balance of power, and the sense of marital stability.

We suggest that the community affects spousal relations mainly through spousal interdependence. It should be noted that we speak about dependence as a function of social arrangements rather than as a personality trait. In the kibbutz context (especially in the more "traditional" kibbutzim), the arrangements ensuring lack of dependence between spouses were still intact at the time of data collection (1998). Nonetheless, the subjects were well aware of changes toward privatization taking place in the contemporary kibbutz, and, indeed, about 35 percent of the kibbutz couples expressed a moderate or high perceived dependence level, despite existing kibbutz arrangements.

Spousal dependence versus independence is discussed at length in the academic and therapeutic literature, with most researchers seeing dependence as a reflection of the couple's intrapersonal and interpersonal dynamic (Rusbult, 1983; Rusbult and van Lango, 1996; Malach Pines, 1997). Our findings add the community aspect to the existing knowledge about spousal interdependence. The data indicate that spouses' interdependence is affected by the organizational and economic arrangements prevailing in their community. These arrangements are particularly salient in the event of divorce or separation.

In a community that assigns each individual personal rights irrespective of gender and marital status (the kibbutz model), spousal interdependence is low; hence the cost of separation or divorce is reduced. Moreover, if the community offers effective alternatives to services usually provided by the family, the individual is less dependent on his or her spouse in daily matters. By contrast, in a community in which marriage and divorce arrangements are not egalitarian and in which there are no alternatives to services provided by the family (the moshav model), spousal interdependence is high.

By means of differentiated spousal dependence, the community also affects the power balance between the spouses. In the moshav, the husband's control of the family's economic resources (i.e., the farm) produces a power disparity in the husband's favor.

In both types of community, the attitude toward gender equality is somewhat ambivalent. This ambivalence is at least partially due to an ideological factor: the notion that productive, income-generating, hard work is one of the most important criteria of a person's worth. In this regard there is a gender gap in kibbutzim as well as in moshavim. However, in the kibbutz, this gender gap is balanced by considerable spousal equality in the family.

In this research, we have studied two unique community models that have been undergoing radical changes during the last decade (Ben-Rafael, 1996). These changes affect values and norms that have distinguished these communities from other ways of life. However, in the kibbutz, the egalitarian arrangements concerning marriage and divorce have remained relatively stable. In the moshavim as well, marital relations have remained unchanged.

Theoretical and Practical Implications

The relevance of the findings to family issues in the postindustrial era is not self-evident. There are many differences between the kibbutz family and the postmodern middle-class urban family. However, postmodern (urban) and kibbutz families share several basic traits pertaining to spousal interdependence. In both cases, alternatives to services conventionally provided by the family are accessible to the individuals without family mediation: education, food, laundry, entertainment, and even sex. Furthermore, power and spousal roles are allocated in a more egalitarian way, and there is greater freedom to break up the relationship, hence remaining married becomes more voluntary.

These similarities bring about similar problems. Despite being subject to tight social control, the stability of the kibbutz family is relatively low. Thus, it seems that there is a price to the personal freedom and gender equality typical both of the kibbutz and of the contemporary urban family.

Almost by definition, weak spousal interdependence reduces the cost of divorce. However, the freedom to leave a relationship is more likely to be realized by the husband than by the wife, due to the latter's total commitment to the children. For as long as it lasts, an egalitarian, liberal marriage strengthens the wife's position, but in the event of divorce, the husband's position prevails. Indeed, we found that even in the kibbutz society, women feel less secure in their marriage than do men.

In modern societies, the value of marital stability is controversial. Some see the relative ease of terminating a marriage as an advantage for the individual and also for the quality of couplehood in general. Others see marital stability as a basic human need that is no less valid than personal freedom or gender equality.

A great deal of evidence attests to the positive impact of marital stability on the learning ability, concentration, and emotional development of children (Klein, 1932; Bowlby, 1951; Fairbairn, 1952; Winnicott, 1965; Peres and Pasternack, 1985), as well as on the quality of life of the elderly. Although marital stability may be most important at these two developmental junctures (the beginning and the end) in a person's life (Peres, 2000), its importance in midlife should not be ignored:

"We get married in part out of a desire to find stability in a socially acceptable way" (Rabin, 1991, p. 43).

Family research as well as feminist ideology links spousal equality to marital satisfaction. Pollock et al. (1990) and Altrocchi (1988) found that egalitarian couples communicate better and invest more in improving their relationship. This pattern of behavior predicts a high level of satisfaction in married life (Poplau, 1983; Nicola and Hawkes, 1985; Li and Caldwell, 1987; Shapira-Berman, 1999). By contrast, our findings indicate that marriages characterized by equality are similar in quality to those characterized by strong asymmetric allocation of power and household chores. It seems that the two marriage patterns examined involve a trade-off that balances out in terms of marital quality.

The elements of marital quality contributed by spousal equality, stability, and independence can be visualized as the vertices of a triangle (see Figure 7.2).

There is tension, but not necessarily contradiction, between each pair of goals: equality–stability, independence–stability, independence–equality (equality means lack of hierarchy: consequently, it is a situation in which both spouses must be satisfied for stability to prevail, whereas in a hierarchical situation only the strong partner has to be satisfied.)

Another conclusion implied by our findings is that the modern family's problems should be treated in a community context rather than an individual one. This suggestion accords with Etzioni's communitarian approach (Etzioni, 1993, 1995). We conclude that spousal therapy should take into account the community background of the family in treatment, just as the physician should consider the patient's familial conditions.

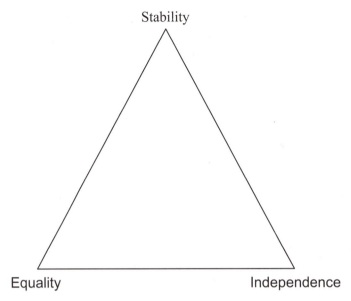

Figure 7.2   Triangle of marital values—equality, stability, and independence

The community's codes, values, resources, and procedures are relevant to all stages of marital life: mate selection, fertility, spousal relationships, and the maintenance of stability. This does not necessarily mean that individuals and couples have to "adjust" to the community to which they happen to belong. In some cases, it might be more practical to encourage the couple to find the "right" community, one that corresponds to their needs. When new communities are planned or founded, the balance between quality and stability should be sought on both community and family levels. The term "balance" is emphasized because any exclusive reliance on one of them might jeopardize the other.

Bibliography

Aida, Y. and T. Falbo. "Relationships between Marital Satisfaction, Resources and Power Strategies." *Sex Roles* 24, no. 1–2 (1991): 43–56.

Altrocchi, J. "Happy Traditional and Egalitarian Marriages." *Journal of Contemporary Social Work* 69 (1988): 434–42.

Applebaum, L. and J. Margulies. *Moshavim and the Test of Time*. Rehovot: Settlement Study Centre, 1979 [in Hebrew].

Bagarozzi, J. *Sourcebook of Marriage and Family Evaluation*. New York: Brunner/ Mazel, 1993.

Ben-Rafael, E. *A Partial Revolution*. Efal: Yad Tabenkin, 1996 [in Hebrew].

Ben-Rafael, E. and S. Weitman. "The Reconstruction of the Family in the Kibbutz." *European Journal of Sociology* 25, no. 1 (1984): 1–27.

von Bertalanffy, L. *Perspectives on General System Theory*. New York: George Braziller, 1975.

Blau, P. M. *Exchange and Power in Social Life*. New York: Wiley, 1964.

Blood, R. O. and D. M. Wolfe. *Husbands and Wives: The Dynamics of Married Living*. New York: Free Press, 1960.

Boehm, A. "Corporate Social Responsibility: A Complementary Perspective of Community and Corporate Leaders." *Business and Society Review* 107 (2002): 171–95.

Booth, A., D. Johnson, and J. Edwards. "Measuring Marital Instability." *Journal of Marriage and the Family* 45 (1983): 387–93.

Bott, E. *Family and Social Network*. New York: Free Press, 1971.

Bowlby, J. *Maternal Care and Mental Health*. Geneva: World Health Organization, 1951.

Brehm, S. S. *Intimate Relationships*. New York: McGraw-Hill, 1985.

Buckner, C. "The Development of an Instrument to Measure Neighborhood Cohesion." *Journal of Community Psychology* 17, no. 3 (1989): 397.

Burr, W. R., R. Hill, F. I. Nye, and I. L. Riess, eds. *Contemporary Theories about the Family*. New York: Free Press, 1979.

Crane, D. R., S. M. Allgood, J. H. Larson, and W. Griffin. "Assessing Marital Quality with Distressed and Non-distressed Couples: A Comparison and Equivalency Table for Three Frequently Used Measures." *Journal of Marriage and the Family* 52 (1990): 87–93.

Crawford, D., R. Houts, T. Huston, and L. George. "Compatibility, Leisure, and Satisfaction in Marital Relationship." *Journal of Marriage and Family* 64 (2002): 433–49.

Doron, H. "Marriage in a Small Community: The Effect of Community Structure and Spousal Interdependence on Marital Equality, Quality, and Stability on Kibbutzim and Moshavim." Doctoral dissertation. Tel Aviv University School of Social Work, 2000 [in Hebrew].

Drake, M., ed. *Time, Family and Community—Perspectives on Family and Community History*. Oxford, UK and Cambridge, MA: Open University and Blackwell, 1994.

Emerson, R. "Social Exchange Theory." In *Annual Review of Sociology*, Vol. 2, edited by A. Inkeles, J. Coleman, and N. Smelser, 335–62. Palo Alto, CA: Annual Reviews, 1976.

Etzioni, A. *The Spirit of Community: Rights, Responsibilities and the Communitarian Agenda*. New York: Crown, 1993.

———, ed. *New Communitarian Thinking*. Charlottesville: University Press of Virginia, 1995.

Fairbairn, W. R. *An Object-Relations Theory of the Personality*. New York: Basic Books, 1952.

Foulker, R. A. "Qualitative Research in Family Therapy: Publication Trends from 1980 to 1999." *Journal of Marital and Family Therapy* 28 (2002): 69–75.

Fowers, B. J. and D. H. Olson. "ENRICH Marital Satisfaction Scale: A Brief Research and Clinical Tool." *Journal of Family Psychology* 7 (1993): 176–85.

Gurman, A. and D. Kniskern. *Handbook of Family Therapy*, Vol. 2. New York: Brunner/Mazel, 1991.

Heaton, T. B. and S. L. Albrecht. "Stable Unhappy Marriages." *Journal of Marriage and the Family* 53 (1991): 747–58.

Holman, T. "The Influence of Community Involvement on Marital Quality." *Journal of Marriage and the Family* 43 (1981): 143–49.

Homans, G. *Social Behavior: Its Elementary Forms*. New York: Harcourt, Brace and Jovanovich, 1974.

Johnson, D. K., L. White, J. Edwards, and A. Booth. "Dimensions of Marital Quality. Towards Methodological and Conceptual Refinement." *Journal of Family Issues* 7, no. 1 (1986): 31–49.

Katz, R. "Power in the Family: The Effect of Resources and Cultural Background on the Balance of Power between Husband and Wife." Doctoral dissertation. Tel Aviv University, 1980 [in Hebrew].

Kaufman, M. "The Father's Role in Collective Education." *Inbal* 6 (1981): 42 [in Hebrew].

Keidan, A. "Successor Sons on the Moshav: The Choice Factor and Marital Quality." Master's thesis. University of Haifa, 1994 [in Hebrew].

Klein, M. *The Psycho-Analysis of Children*. London: Hogarth, 1932.

Lampert, A. "Parental Investment, Harm to Relationships, and Adjustment Difficulties." Ph.D. dissertation. Tel Aviv University, 1981 [in Hebrew].

Lavee, Y. "Marital Assessment Scale: Clinical and Research Uses." *Israel Psychological Association, 25th Academic Conference, Ben-Gurion University*, Beersheva, 1995 [in Hebrew].

Lenthall, G. "Marital Satisfaction and Marital Stability." *Journal of Marriage and the Family* 3 (1977): 25–32.

Levinger, G. "A Three-Level Approach to Attraction: Toward an Understanding of Pair Relatedness." In *Foundations of Interpersonal Attraction*, edited by T. L. Huston, 49–67. New York: Academic Press, 1974.

———. "Duty toward Whom? Reconsidering Attraction and Barriers as Determinants of Commitment in a Relationship." In *Handbook of Interpersonal Commitment and Relationship Stability*, edited by J. M. Adams and W. H. Jones, 3–33. New York: Kluwer Academic, 1999.

Lewin, K. *Field Theory in Social Science*. New York: Harper & Row, 1951.

———. *Conflict Resolution: Papers in Field Theory*. Jerusalem: Keter, 1989 [in Hebrew].

Li, J. and K. A. Caldwell. "Magnified and Directional Effects of Marital Sex Role Incongruent on Marital Adjustment." *Journal of Family Issues* 8, no. 1 (1987): 97–110.

MacMillan, D. and M. Chavis. "Sense of Community? A Definition and Theory." *Journal of Community Psychology* 14 (1986): 6–23.

Malach Pines, A. *Gender Psychology*. Tel Aviv: Open University, 1997 [in Hebrew].

Mintz, S. and S. Kellogg. *Domestic Revolutions: A Social History of American Family Life*. New York: Free Press, 1988.

Nicola, J. S. and G. R. Hawkes. "Marital Satisfaction of Dual-Career Couples: Does Sharing Increase Happiness?" *Journal of Social Behavior and Personality* 1, no. 1 (1985): 47–60.

Nye, I. "Choice, Exchange and the Family." In *Contemporary Theories about the Family*, edited by W. R. Burr. New York: Free Press, 1979.

Olson, D. H., D. M. Fournier, and J. Druckman. *PREPARE/ENRICH Counselor Manual*. Minneapolis: PREPARE/ENRICH, 1987.

Palgi, M. *The Family on the Kibbutz*. Tel Aviv: Na'amat, Division for the Status of Women, Executive Committee of the General Federation of Labor in Israel, 1984 [in Hebrew].

Peres, Y. "Who Will Protect the Family?" *Panim* 12 (2000): 48–52 [in Hebrew].

Peres, Y. and R. Pasternak. "The Importance of Marriage for Socialization: A Comparison of Achievements and Social Adjustment between Offspring of One and Two Parent Families in Israel." In *Marriage: A Comparative Approach*, edited by R. Davis and Grossbard-Schechtman. New York: Sage Publications, 1985.

Pina, D. L. and V. L. Bengtson. "The Division of Household Labor and Wives' Happiness." *Journal of Marriage and the Family* 55 (1993): 901–12.

Pollock, A. D., A. H. Die, and R. G. Marriot. "Relationship of Communication Style to Egalitarian Marital Role Expectation." *Journal of Social Psychology* 130, no. 5 (1990): 619–24.

Poplau, L. "Roles and Gender." In *Close Relationships*, edited by H. H. Kelley, E. Berscheid, A. Christensen, J. H. Harvey, T. Huston, G. Levinger, et al. New York: W. H. Freeman & Company, 1983.

Rabin, K. *Two Are Better: Marriage as a Dialogue*. Tel Aviv: Keshet Meidan, 1991 [in Hebrew].

Rachlin, V. and J. Hansen. "The Impact of Egalitarianism on Dual-career Couples." *Family Therapy* 12, no. 2 (1985): 151–64.

Raley, R. K. and L. Bumpass. "The Topography of the Plateau in Divorce: Levels and Trends in Union Stability after 1980." *Demographic Research* 8 (2003): 246–58.

Rubin, L. B. *Intimate Strangers: Men and Women Together*. New York: Simon & Schuster, 1983.

Rusbult, C. E. "A Longitudinal Test of the Investment Model: The Development of Satisfaction and Commitment in Heterosexual Involvements." *Journal of Personality and Social Psychology* 45 (1983): 101–17.

Rusbult, C. E. and P. A. M. van Lango. "Interdependence Processes." In *Social Psychology: Handbook of Basic Principles*, edited by E. T. Higgins and A. W. Kruglanski, 564–96. New York: Guilford, 1996.

Sabatelli, R. and C. Shehan. "Exchange and Resource Theories." In *Sourcebook of Family Theories and Methods*, edited by P. Boss, W. Doherty, R. LaRossa, W. Schumm, and S. Steinmetz, 385–441. New York: Plenum, 1993.

Scanzoni, J. "From the Normal Family to Alternative Families to the Quest for Diversity with Interdependence." *Journal of Family Issues* 22 (2001): 688–710.

Sexfon, C. S. and D. S. Perlman. "Couples' Career Orientation, Gender Role Orientation, and Perceived Equity as Determinants of Marital Power." *Journal of Marriage and the Family* 51 (1989): 933–41.

Shapira-Berman, O. "Married Life in an Era of Change: The Connection between Assertiveness, Attitudes, de facto Equality, and Quality of Married Life." Doctoral dissertation. Tel Aviv University, 1999 [in Hebrew].

Shepher, J. and S. Fogiel-Bijaoui. *Kibbutz Society: Change and Continuity*. Open University, units 6 and 7, 1992 [in Hebrew].

Shor, S. "The Problem of Equality in the Kibbutz Movement." Doctoral dissertation. Tel Aviv University, 1983 [in Hebrew].

Silver, V. "The Problem of Women—A Problem of Society as a Whole." In *Thinking Kibbutz*. Efal: Yad Tabenkin, 1994 [in Hebrew].

Spanier, G. B. and R. A. Lewis. "Marital Quality: A Review of the Seventies." *Journal of Marriage and the Family* 42 (1980): 825–39.

Suitor, J. J. "Marital Quality and Satisfaction with the Division of Household Labor across the Family Life Cycle." *Journal of Marriage and the Family* 53 (1991): 221–30.

Swim, T. and C. Sura. "Role of Gender in Behavioral Interdependence and Relationship Outcomes for Premarital Couples." *Sex Roles* 41 (1999): 49–70.

Taibaut, J. W. and H. H. Kelley. *The Social Psychology of Groups*. New York: Wiley, 1959.

Tal, A. *Dependence Relationship in Couples on a Kibbutz*. Doctoral Dissertation. Colombia Public University, New York, 1991.

Talmon-Garber, Y. *Individual and Society on a Kibbutz*. Jerusalem: Magnes, Hebrew University, 1970 [in Hebrew].

Tester, K. "Community: Seeking Safety in an Insecure World." *Contemporary Sociology* 31 (2002): 442–44.

Tiger, L. and J. Shepher. *Women in the Kibbutz*. New York: Harcourt Brace Jovanovich, 1975.

Tompson, L. "Conceptualizing Gender in Marriage: The Case of Marital Care." *Journal of Marriage and the Family* 55 (1993): 557–69.

Trost, J. E. "Abandon Adjustment!" *Journal of Marriage and the Family* 47 (1985): 1072–73.

Vannoy, D. and W. W. Philliber. "Wives' Employment and Quality of Marriage." *Journal of Marriage and the Family* 54 (1992): 387–98.

Veroff, J. "Commitment in the Early Years of Marriage." In *Handbook of Interpersonal Commitment and Relationship Stability*, edited by J. Adams and W. Jones, 149–65. New York: Kluwer Plenum Publishers, 1999.

Warner, R. L., G. K. Lee, and J. Lee. "Social Organizations, Spousal Resources and Marital Power: A Cross-Cultural Study." *Journal of Marriage and the Family* 48 (1986): 121–28.

Weiss, Y. "Marital Quality in the Active Parental Stage among Men and Women." Master's thesis. University of Haifa, 1994 [in Hebrew].

Winnicott, D. *The Maturational Process and the Facilitating Environment*. New York: International University, 1965.

8
Kibbutz 2008: A Way, a Place, or a Home?

Amia Lieblich

Thirty-one years have passed since 1978 when I conducted my narrative study of Beit-Hashita (founded in 1928), and, as a result, became "a kibbutz scholar"—despite the fact that I had never belonged to a kibbutz community. The original work was published in English (1982), Hebrew (1983), and Japanese (1993) under the pseudonym *Kibbutz Makom* (place in Hebrew) in order to protect the privacy of the interviewees. The earliest newspapers' reviews of the Hebrew edition, however, immediately identified the kibbutz as Beit-Hashita. Furthermore, since the disguise could not prevent the identification of the narrators by their own family and community, and the kibbutz members were quite satisfied with the authenticity of the work, it became superfluous to conceal its identity. Soon after the publication of the book in Hebrew, the kibbutz chose to be known by its proper name, Beit-Hashita.

In 1978, when I first got to know this community in the fertile Yizrael Valley, Kibbutz Beit-Hashita celebrated its fifty-year jubilee. In fact, the permission to conduct my study in their village, to observe, to interpret, and mainly to interview individuals in their midst was granted to me as part of the jubilee events. I was given a room that I could use for my interviews, and a female member was appointed to take care of my needs and to help in scheduling my activities. Gradually I formed relationships with several men and women in the community, who served as my main informers and contributed to my growing list of interviewees. At that time, Beit-Hashita was one of the largest kibbutzim in terms of its population size and had the reputation of a highly ideological and successful collective.

Although the original research was not planned to have a follow-up study, close, ongoing, and trusting relationships have developed

between the kibbutz members and me. As a result of this involvement, I have visited the kibbutz frequently for community or private
events, corresponded with several members who have become personal
friends, conducted many informal conversations, and was invited to
document certain aspects of this kibbutz life at three additional time
points, as will be detailed below. Members of Beit-Hashita have always
been very verbal and profound in their self-evaluation and critique. The
unique opportunity to participate in these conversations over a long time
period, to observe the kibbutz development, and to witness its struggle
with the various issues confronting its collective identity provided
the materials for this chapter's integrative summary of Beit-Hashita's
evolution over time. The accumulated material produced an intricate,
multifaceted profile of a community in transition because of structural,
political, economic, and ideological changes, as well as the aging of its
membership. While every community has its own specific composition,
character, and history, this profile may provide some insights concerning
similar and different issues faced by other Israeli kibbutzim.

Time 1

The most intensive and extensive stages of this research were occurred
in one year of fieldwork (1978–79), when I interviewed one hundred
members of the kibbutz individually. In addition, I located thirty-two
ex-members who had left the kibbutz either to another kibbutz (during
the 1952–53 division) or to the city. The protocol of my recorded interviews requested the narrators to tell the story of their life in this kibbutz,
starting from whatever was deemed as an appropriate beginning of their
story up to the present moment. This request was naturally not repeated
in the next stages of the follow-up, which focused on the present and
future of the community.

The narratives that I obtained varied greatly. However, at this first
stage of the research—usually conceived as prior to the major crisis of
the Israeli kibbutz—a fairly coherent picture of the community emerged:
this kibbutz members were profoundly proud of their history, identity, and
achievements, and slightly concerned about their future.[1] Beit-Hashita,
as I got to know it in its fiftieth year, was a tightly knit community of
650 members, 400 children, and about 250 temporary residents, living
collectively. A clear system of values, ideals, and norms, as well as an
elaborate structure of kibbutz committees and institutions, supervised
from "above" by the strong kibbutz movement organization governed
its life. Children were raised within the collective education system,

including common lodging for all age-groups, which was strictly enforced on parents and children alike. All kibbutz members worked in positions allocated or approved by the "work committee," the vast majority of them employed in the kibbutz, either in its collective agricultural or industrial enterprises, for men, or education and services, for women. All meals were cooked in the kibbutz kitchen and served in the common dining hall. Since the community provided for all the basic needs of the individual, families received—in accordance with their size—only a small, fixed, monthly "budget" for additional expenses. The kibbutz declared that it observed the ideals of collectivity, equality, and mutual responsibility, and educated the next generation to continue this form of life. It advocated and seemed to practice the slogan "from each according to his/her capacity, to each according to his/her needs."

Members of the first generation, the kibbutz founders, were proud of their present situation, claiming that they had never, in their modest beginning, dreamed of a collective of such size, wealth, or accomplishments. They were particularly proud of the kibbutz members' contribution to the establishment of the state in 1948 by their immense participation in crucial security and immigration activities. In addition, they were highly satisfied with their educational system, which included, at the time, their own comprehensive elementary and high schools in which only their kibbutz children studied, taught by a selective team of kibbutz educators. At the same time, some underlying currents of dissatisfaction and criticism started to emerge. The old-timers worried about deviations from the kibbutz' ideologically based practices, such as the use of hired labor, and suspected that some members kept private savings or received substantial gifts from family members outside the kibbutz. A recent (1978!) decision of a member to build an extra window, although the "building committee" had rejected his request, was cited as an example of disobedience that threatened the harmony and lawfulness of the community. Several kibbutz leaders chastised themselves for the inefficient teaching of kibbutz ethics to younger generations. At the same time, some of the first generation claimed that expressions of concern about the future—such as the notions that a kettle or private bathroom might destroy the collective—had always been part of the kibbutz discourse. A minority of the old-timers reflected with dismay and regret on the tragic events of the "division" of 1952–53. They were keen to persuade me that such a breach could not be repeated. Some existential anxiety permeated the more sensitive of these accounts.

Second-generation members took for granted that their kibbutz was strong, rich, and stable. They manifested other kinds of dissatisfaction: women complained about the limited work opportunities and felt completely harnessed to the low-prestige jobs of childcare, kitchen, and laundry for the entire community. They also started to express criticism and misgivings about the common lodging of children. Several members observed that kibbutz education tended to promote a conforming, unoriginal, and unexpressive personality, and that life in the kibbutz stood in the way of deep friendships or personal creativity. Nevertheless, the general tone of their accounts was as positive as that of the first generation. At the time, the third generation of Beit-Hashita was just crossing the threshold to adulthood. It was unclear whether they would join the collective or how they would affect the kibbutz in the future. Several of these young people expressed the need for individual freedom, which they thought that the kibbutz inhibited. They lamented the fact that in this well-formed, stable community, they might not have any opportunity for innovative action.

Time 2

Fifteen years later, in 1993, Yehuda Yaniv, a documentary film director, invited me to coproduce a movie about Beit-Hashita. The planned movie was to be focused on the reception of the famous High Holidays prayer[2] "Unetane Tokef" by the kibbutz' community, following its composition by Yair Rosenblum—a well-known Israeli folk-composer, who had lived at the time in Beit-Hashita. In addition to the use of some archival materials, I interviewed more than twenty members of the kibbutz individually or in groups, and some interviews were filmed. The interviews explored two related areas—the reaction of the community to the large number of war casualties among the young members of Beit-Hashita in the 1973 Yom Kippur War and the place of Jewish religion in the personal and collective spheres of this secular kibbutz. We did not directly discuss the decline of the kibbutz after its major recent economic crisis. However, the topic hovered in the background of many conversations. I was informed that a large number of singles, as well as some prestigious families, had recently left the kibbutz, which was shrinking in size. At this time, the kibbutz had abandoned the common lodging institutions, and all the children were living with their parents in enlarged apartments. As an outcome of the decrease in the number of children and the high cost of its maintenance, members shut down the comprehensive school of Beit-Hashita and bused the kibbutz children to regional schools on a daily basis.

While an evaluation of the current situation in the kibbutz was not our aim during these interviews, it was implied in many of the filmed as well as informal conversations I had during the months of the production. The general feeling, expressed by older and younger members alike, was of a community in decline, shrinking in size, searching for ways to solve its gradually discovered financial and demographic crises, its sense of loss of prestige and alienation from the Israeli society at large, and the resulting tensions within. The intense mourning process for the eleven men killed in the Yom Kippur War (1973)—which had been hardly expressed in the previous stage—could be understood also as a broader, projected mourning for things that had been lost and as a predicament which consolidated the common ties of the community in spite of its growing disagreements and tensions. At a time when many of the common practices of daily life were being abandoned, mourning could still maintain the powerful bond within this community. The emerging search for the integration of Jewish content and prayer into the secular tradition of the kibbutz could also be constructed as a means to bolster the weaker system of kibbutz ideology or values by old traditions and to establish a closer link between the kibbutz and the wider, historical Jewish–Israeli culture.

Time 3

At the turn of the new millennium, as the kibbutz becomes aware of its troubled existence and increases its concern with the future, my friends invited me often, half jokingly, to write a "second volume of *Kibbutz Makom*." My informers referred to four interrelated processes that took place in the kibbutz around this time:

1. A severe economic crisis in all its forms
2. Questioning whether the basic kibbutz values were adequate to deal with life at present
3. Urgent attempts to establish an alternative, socially just, but "privatized" lifestyle for the members
4. The continuous shrinking and aging of membership as many young families and singles moved out of the kibbutz

As in many other kibbutzim, most of the previously common services were now "privatized," which meant that they were not offered for free to all members. Members had to pay the kibbutz some basic "community taxes." On the other hand, members received a "salary," which was computed—following a long process of consultation with an external expert team—as a combination of a basic "social security" minimum for all, plus the differential income of the employed members, according to the relative market value of their work. Individual members were thus greatly encouraged to be "productive" in the capitalistic sense, and they could not automatically rely on community support. Most of the traditional kibbutz functions and committees were abolished, and a hired team of nonmember administrators managed the community.

While all of these changes were formally adopted through democratic processes, many policies were decided upon following severe and tense disagreements, arguments, persuasion, and counter-persuasion by the different factions, which had almost torn apart the gentle fabric of the community. Several members complained that voting took place before the average member could really understand the complicated, critical issues. My long-term friends reported that the kibbutz was undergoing a severe crisis on all levels.

Realizing their dire straits, I came to Beit-Hashita for a week in the winter of 2003 and conducted fifteen in-depth interviews with members of different generations and positions. I analyzed the material and wrote a summary that was submitted to the concerned members who had invited me. I did not publish a report for external readership.

My most prominent observation was that the pride of the kibbutz members in their community and lifestyle had evaporated and was often replaced by shame, suspicion, and a sense of loss. The questions, "How did we err?" and "How were we misled by our own leadership and authorities?" appeared in all the interviews, whether the narrators took responsibility themselves, saw the decline as part of a global or national processes, or blamed others for the kibbutz mishap. Older, unemployed members felt insecure about their basic livelihood and health care, and often lamented their "wasted" years of dedicated work. Those whose children had left were lonely, but frequently supportive of their children who did "the right thing." Others, whose children had stayed, were deeply worried about their ability to maintain an adequate standard of living and provide their kids with a good education. Middle-aged people were challenged by the need to find employment, and most of them had to work outside of the kibbutz. Younger members often displayed "internal walking away"—a term used to describe an existence focused on oneself or one's family, alienated from the collective's life, and perhaps in search for an opportunity to leave it.

While every narrator provided a different account of the catastrophe and defined its beginning as arising at a different time or event, the lack of hope permeated many of the conversations. Some blamed the kibbutz for its failure to introduce the structural–economic changes as fast and early enough to avoid the crash. Others blamed the community for abandoning its ideals and practices too quickly and widely. A minority of older members expressed acceptance of the changes as a normal process of growth and transition that occurs in every living organism, whether an individual or a collective. They hoped that the community would pull through the present hardships, as it had done previously in its past crises.

Another view, which tried to balance the current discontent, shifted the focus to the kibbutz heroic past. People who expressed this view claimed that while they were dismayed about the present, they were nonetheless proud and satisfied to have been part of the great ideals and achievements of the kibbutz in the past.

Emotionally, I was deeply saddened by this set of conversations and impressions, and hesitated about writing my report, as if my narrative might add grievance to what was bad enough already. I have never attempted to publish my work, but in various opportunities of sharing it, I was given to understand that my picture was not unique within the general map of Israeli kibbutzim's situation at the turn of the millennium.

Time 4

In 2008, as part of the kibbutz' eightieth anniversary celebrations, I was invited to review the original 1978 study and the resulting book in the context of a now thirty-year perspective. This "review" was designed to take place as a kibbutz assembly where many of the original narrators and some of their offspring would provide their view of the kibbutz then and now. Several of the invited speakers wrote their pieces and posted them in an electronic network, which had become an important means of communication within the community. During this daylong, multifaceted dialogue, I could respond to the participants' pieces and integrate them with my own thoughts. All these materials were compiled as a booklet, published with the generous aid of a second-generation ex-member.

Although the celebrative nature of this stage of my acquaintance with Beit-Hashita may be part of the reasons for its more hopeful mood, I am inclined to think that some optimism had indeed replaced the despair of the previous stage. Most of the members adjusted to the change and learned to live within this framework. Symbolically, refreshments for the event were provided by individual members—who cooked and baked "at home"—and not by the general kitchen facilities as in previous times. Indeed, people seemed to have lowered their level of expectations of the collective; most of them learned how to take care of themselves and their families within the system. The previous anger, bitterness, and disappointment at the leadership or anxiety about the future were not as prominent. These feelings were replaced by what I saw as modesty, pride about the past, and deep love and attachment to the nature, location, and landscape of the kibbutz. As the term "new kibbutz" started to appear in public discourse, a new narrative emerged in the members' reflections where accepting the process as a part of a global, historical life transition replaced demonization and deep shame or guilt.

While economic solutions for the kibbutz' problems were still scarce, one of the phenomena that produced positive effects on the community was the introduction of nonmember residency. Following the government agreement to allow private construction on the kibbutz grounds (as part of the government plan to support the kibbutzim in overcoming their economic crisis), Beit-Hashita had decided to build a new neighborhood of private homes. These new homes were sold to young families who chose the location for a variety of reasons. Obviously, the inclusion of these "residents" in the community, in some loose manner of belonging, broke the old, sacred value of equality. The residents were not part of the collective, but, for a fee, could use the old facilities of the kibbutz for their comfort. Thus, the new families revived such services as infant care, child education, common Sabbath and holiday celebrations, and many cultural activities. On the other hand, they conducted their lives as private families in all respects.

As I found out, many of these young families were of kibbutz-born men and women who had left the kibbutz because they did not want to be members, but were glad to return as residents and live next to their parents in a landscape that they cherished. They were hoping to provide their families with a high standard of living, focused on good health, education, and ecological norms—but without any of the old constraints and obligations of the commune. The effect of their presence was amazing: in the kibbutz grounds that had started to look like a nursing home, many young faces could be encountered on the paths. Young voices or music were suddenly heard in the park surrounding the cultural center and the dining hall. In spite of the persistent hardships in the financial and administrative spheres, the ambience was that of a revived community.

An attempt to integrate these follow-up observations and impressions led to the proposal implied in the title of this chapter, namely, that this kibbutz was shifting its major metaphor or meta-narrative from a *"way"* (of life), to a "*place*" (to live), and last to a "*home.*" In their psychological, collective history, "*way*" represents for members of Beit-Hashita the ideological era of the early kibbutz, a "*place*" stands for the mere physical setting of the territory or neighborhood, which threatened to become dominant in the 1990s, and finally, "*home*"—the current term—emphasizes above all the emotional attachment of the members to the kibbutz in its natural location. These three terms appeared in the interviews, in the individuals' efforts to explain and differentiate the nature of their existence and experience in Beit-Hashita over time.

In the first fifty years of its history, the kibbutz members saw their daily lives as outlined by a *way*—namely, a highly articulated ideology. Practices and events were examined *vis-à-vis* this "*way*" and judged as correct or incorrect according to this system of values. The formal network of committees and secretariats and the informal powerful instrument of public opinion were utilized to evaluate every step taken as appropriate or inappropriate for the kibbutz way of life. All these governmental tools could not, however, prevent the downfall of the old system in the late decades of the twentieth century.

As members of the kibbutz came to realize the huge economic crisis of the 1990s, they lost their trust in the "*way.*" They experienced betrayal by their leaders who did not avert the general catastrophe and instead were sometimes blamed for behavior motivated by self-interest. At this painful stage, the alienation among the members, and between them and their leadership, produced a sense of living in a "*place*"—minimizing interpersonal, as well as person-collective, attachments. Mistrust, suspicion, and egoistic considerations dominated the scene. In this atmosphere, none of the members was willing or able to perform administrative or leadership functions in the kibbutz for any length of time. Anomie is the best description for this stage of the affairs.

But as in a living organism, the next phase of this kibbutz history manifests some recuperation and revival. By giving up many of its old ideals and the compulsive nature of the collective framework, Beit-Hashita opened itself to newcomers who were drawn to this particular territory as long as it allowed for a more liberal and flexible lifestyle. The new residents of the "new kibbutz" were offered hospitality on an entirely different contract, suitable for an individualistic rather than a collective era. In their presence, however, they revitalized the community. It is perhaps a paradox that by giving up the major aspects of its character and mission, Beit-Hashita voted for life as a vibrant community.

Notes

1. All of the general statements of this chapter could be demonstrated by quotations from my published book or my private, larger, personal archive of interview transcripts.
2. This central prayer is part of the Rosh Hashanah and Yom Kippur services.

Bibliography

Lieblich, A. *Kibbutz Makom*. New York: Pantheon, 1982.
———. *Kibbutz Makom*. Tel Aviv: Schocken, 1983 [in Hebrew].
———. *Kibbutz Makom*. Tokyo: Mirtos Press, 1993 [in Japanese].

Part II
Representations of Kibbutz Change

Introduction to Part II

Michal Palgi and Shulamit Reinharz

Since the early days of the first kibbutzim, kibbutz members have expressed themselves through the arts. Although the physical hardships that artists endured were numerous and the time/privacy available to engage in the arts was limited, many kibbutz artists developed their skills to become national figures. For example, Rachel Blustein, known always simply as Rachel, came to Palestine as a young woman from Russia. An assimilated Jew, she knew no Hebrew before her arrival. As soon as she felt able to express herself in her new language, Rachel began writing Hebrew poems. Swept up in the enthusiasm of encountering the old–new landscape, she became a member of the first kibbutz—Deganya—near the Kinneret where she lived briefly before succumbing to malaria. Rachel became the poet of the early settlers in general and of the kibbutz in particular and helped define the way that people thought about kibbutz life.

Similarly, famed parachutist Hannah Senesh, member of Kibbutz Sdot Yam, is remembered as a poet, particularly for her iconic "Blessed is the Match." Both Rachel and Hannah Senesh described the way the kibbutz represented the rebirth of the Jewish people. The kibbutz they painted in words was the key to the future. Over time, poets, filmmakers, and novelists have painted the kibbutz differently, but they have all remained true to the idea that the poet's words are crucial in the quest to understand the kibbutz and themselves. Throughout the decades, the kibbutz movements have contributed not only poets themselves, but also have established publishing houses that have produced collections of poetry of non-kibbutz members as dissimilar as "Zelda" and Chaim Gouri. An examination of poetry enables us to see the evolving images of the kibbutz.

Kibbutz contributions to the visual arts are similarly extensive. In her article, "Universal and International: Art in the Kibbutz in the First Decade[1]," Galia Bar Or claims that "the kibbutz movements saw themselves as a vanguard, and established training frameworks for creative people. They also created important cultural projects—publishing houses, museums, art festivals, etc.—for all the state's inhabitants." In the first decade of the state, the kibbutz movements established three art museums. In fact, she claims, "the kibbutz made art a central axis of its core of values, which by any criterion is a distinctive phenomenon and an extraordinary experiment."

While acknowledging the significance of artistic representations of kibbutz life and conflict, artists also began to shape an image of the kibbutz. In this part of our book on *One Hundred Years of Kibbutz Life*, we include five chapters that explore these artistic challenges and discuss the ways contemporary artists—visual and literary—deal with the "remembered kibbutz." In the first chapter, "The Kibbutz and the Disenchanted: Representations in Contemporary Israeli Narratives," Ranen Omer-Sherman offers the provocative thesis that "the kibbutz has impacted the literary imagination in Israel, especially in the context of *the alienated, vulnerable, or skeptical outsider*" [emphasis added]. This literature has legitimized the nonintegrated individual, even in the midst of a tight-knit, seemingly well-integrated, socialist community. Exploration of this thesis begins with Arthur Koestler's 1946 semiautobiographical novel, *Thieves in the Night*, and Amos Oz's *Where the Jackals Howl; Elsewhere, Perhaps; and A Perfect Peace*, which "artfully probe the frail lives of maladjusted individuals and the idiosyncrasies of kibbutz society." Omer-Sherman goes on to discuss Avraham Balaban's *Mourning A Father Lost: A Kibbutz Childhood Remembered*, which "castigates the communal child-rearing system in which he was raised for having created adults who 'evince the selfishness of people who never got enough protection and security." One could argue that these authors and others are not so much maladjusted as they are critical, or that only the marginal become great writers, regardless of the type of society. If the kibbutz was supposed to be utopia, then it was set on a path toward a goal it could never achieve, thus leading to a perpetual state of frustration. These authors and others focus on the disjunction between the real and the ideal, a theme common to writers throughout history but disturbing in light of the utopian ideal. The point is that literature gave people the opportunity to see familiar structures in new ways even if those ways were discomfiting.

For numerous kibbutz members, their memories of living in the children's houses, where they had to share the attention of a caretaker with a whole group of same-aged children, where they felt torn from their parents every evening, and where they did not have their parents to comfort them in the dark of the night, are being translated into cinema as well as literature. Whereas the kibbutz literature of the past concerned the future; the kibbutz literature of today mulls over the past. To explore this topic, Eldad Kedem and Gilad Padva offer the reader a chronological filmography, highlighting the important films of each period, particularly with regard to whether or not, and how, the kibbutz is portrayed. In their chapter, "From *Sabra* to *Children of the Sun*: Kibbutz Films from the 1930s to the 2000s," they explain that the earliest films produced in the Yishuv concerned kibbutz life. "In . . . *Sabra* (*Tzabar*, directed by Alexander Ford, 1933), the first fiction film made in Palestine/Eretz Israel, Jewish settlers . . . from Russia arrive at a desolate place in Palestine. There they establish a communal settlement that will develop into a flourishing kibbutz." Unlike literary products that allowed for the expression of a critical voice, these early films were primarily propagandistic: "The cinematic representation distances the kibbutz and its significant problems from the actual reality and exaggerates it as a romantic, pastoral, harmonious, and perfect place." This early period was followed by twelve years (1936–1948) in which the few films produced were of the documentary or newsreel genres. In the final period covered in the chapter (1999–2009), the authors claim that Israeli films have become postideological and self-critical. It is in this context that *Children of the Sun* appeared to enormous public acclaim. "Children . . ." uses home movies and current interviewing to investigate the pain and joy of collective childrearing.

In her chapter, "Freedom of Expression in an Ideological Society: The Case of Kibbutz Literature," Shula Keshet asserts that the first literature that kibbutz members produced (aside from poetry) were sketches, not full-fledged novels. She claims

"The sketch gave expression to impressionistic moods and philosophical thought. It described scenes from the life of labor while attempting to depict Eretz Yisraeli landscapes and nature in words. Writers chose the sketch as a preferred genre for two main reasons: the harsh conditions of reality compelled them to adopt a minimalist literary form suited to writing after a hard day's work in the fields; the sketch mirrored collective-egalitarianism in offering possibilities of expression for many, without distinction between skilled and lay writers."

What is rewarding in these sketches is that we hear the individual's voice, frequently not only freed from ideological constraints but also in tension with expected beliefs. This freedom, a *sine qua non* for artists, seems to have been created early on. As time passed, however, and daily living conditions became less harsh, novels also began to appear.

It is interesting to consider Irit Amit-Cohen's chapter in this light. While artists conjure up memories of place through words and images, she writes about the preservation of those places themselves. She examines the value of the physical structures that remain from the pre-State years (1910–1948). Amit-Cohen's focus is not on the work of trained architects, but rather on what is called "vernacular architecture," that is, functional buildings constructed with local materials and know-how. Her study explains that there is enormous tourist potential in preserving these sites, but also that kibbutz members are not always aware of the treasures that exist within their setting. Iris Milner's chapter, "Agitated Orders: Early Kibbutz Literature as a Site of Turmoil," relates well to Amit-Cohen's. Milner highlights the significance in literature of revisiting kibbutz sites "that demonstrate the practical applications of . . . revolutionary change, such as the collective dining-room and kitchen, the children's house (beit hayeladim), the clothing storehouse (machsan habegadim) and the communal showers, all of which conventionally symbolize a private family's indoors activity." The unusual nature of these buildings and the activities of kibbutz life in general ignited the attention of talented individuals who drew on their environment to forge a kibbutz literature. The literature was not propagandistic, however, but rather expressed the inner turmoil of individuals adjusting to a new social system nearly overnight.

Given the new forms of kibbutz that are now emerging, including the non-collectivist type with neighborhoods established for nonmembers, one can expect that the vigorous Israeli film industry will soon produce cinematic pieces that explore both the virtues and troublesome underbellies of the continuously evolving kibbutz social structure. The first one hundred years saw a cultural outpouring from the tiny population of Israeli society—members of kibbutzim. The next one hundred years will likely be as culturally rich, but substantively different. Literature will both reflect and spur on this evolution.

Note

1.   Available at artisrael.org. Bar Or is referring to the first decade of the State of Israel, that is, 1948–1958, not the first decade of kibbutz life, circa 1910–1920.

9

The Kibbutz and the Disenchanted: Representations in Contemporary Israeli Narratives

Ranen Omer-Sherman

And afterwards, in the way things have of suddenly touching people from behind, came the electric kettle and the stove and the apartment and the clothes and the phonograph. And again there was an agitated straining. Then the great and furious disputes, the revenge of the world on its re-formers, the revenge of the soul on its reformers. And more: the revelation merciless and unforgiving, of the awful distance between the world of words and the world of deeds and things. The complexity of situations, which shatters even the most beautiful, most subtle and most correct systems of thought.

—Amos Oz

It should come as little surprise that the kibbutz has long played a pervasive and provocative role in the formation of Israel's literary (and more recently cinematic) culture.[1] A remarkable number of Israel's founding generation of writers were raised, or otherwise spent a significant number of years, on a kibbutz. The institution of the kibbutz was always treated with the same spirited skepticism and questioning as any of Israel's other national institutions, but in recent decades, intensely pessimistic portrayals of estrangement and alienation have begun to eclipse more sanguine representations.[2] Indeed, the subject of narrative portrayals of the kibbutz is so vast that it warrants an entire study, but the following essay addresses late twentieth-century exemplars drawn from three genres: the mystery novel, literary fiction, and a memoir. Each of these highly representative narratives by Batya Gur, Savyon Liebrecht, and Avraham Balaban offers the perspectives of skeptical outsiders or those otherwise estranged from the life they observe. This unifying rubric serves to place the fraught relation between the individual and the collective into razor-sharp perspective.

Given that the mystery genre has often been described as preoccupied with the trauma of violent disturbance in a world of ostensible harmony and order,[3] it comes as a surprise that no writer before the late literary critic and novelist Batya Gur (1947–2005) took imaginative advantage of the rich possibilities inherent disparity between the kibbutz's pastoral promise and setting, and the imperfections of human beings. In most installments of Gur's immensely popular mystery series, the sensitive and intellectual Inspector Michael Ohayon struggles with gaining access to various forms of self-contained and closed subcultures whose inner dynamics pose unique challenges.[4] Some of these institutions may be found anywhere in the world—academia, a hermetic neighborhood, a television network, an orchestra—which may partially account for the international popularity of the series.

However, there is one important exception to that generalization: *Murder on a Kibbutz: A Communal Case* (Linah Meshutefet [1991]), in which the accumulating dead seem to embody the demise of the idealistic values for which they once toiled.[5] Ohayon's visible identity as a Mizrahi Jew generally makes his struggle to penetrate the elite, Eurocentric institutions featured throughout the series all the more difficult (a sly irony given his elite education in history and literature at Cambridge). In this regard, the kibbutz, long considered the ideological vanguard of Israel's Ashkenazi establishment, poses perhaps the greatest challenge of his career.[6] As he is warned *ad nauseam* by kibbutzniks and outsiders alike: "if you've never lived on a kibbutz . . . you'll never understand anything" (p. 183). Yet, precisely in this critical context, Gur does a fine job of bringing the unresolved ideological tensions of kibbutzim fully to life.

Murder opens amidst the idyllic surroundings of a veteran kibbutz preparing for a festive celebration of its fiftieth anniversary. One cannot imagine a more appealing scene of community and agrarian life; most of the cherished stereotypes of early Zionist pioneering days seem on display here. Golden bales of hay are stacked high under a dazzling blue sky, a choir of kibbutz members appears dressed in festive blue and white, and even the kibbutz tractors are ornamented with flowers. It is the same sort of inviting scene that actually accommodated most kibbutz festivals and celebrations for many years.[7] But moments after these alluring images are introduced, a sense of dissonance takes over as we encounter the world of the kibbutz through the perspective of Aaron, a member of Knesset who left years ago. This outsider dismisses all he perceives as anachronistic trappings, veiling a more complex and troubled present:

> once you took away the blue and white and the flags on the Caterpillar, the whole ceremony seemed archaic and foreign, as if it were taking place on a collective farm in Soviet Russia . . . it was the farce of an agricultural ceremony in a place where agriculture was almost bankrupt—a kibbutz, a Zionist agricultural commune, that derived its income from an industrial plant that, of all things, manufactured cosmetics, having given its name to an international patent for a face cream . . . No one else seemed to be showing any recognition of the absurdity of celebrating an agricultural rite where only the manufacture and sale of face cream made it possible to go on working the land. (p. 4)

Though raised on the kibbutz, Aaron currently has a more officious relationship to the entire movement as the Knesset has recently begun to debate its economic plight. A relatively minor character, Aaron's insider–outsider perspective is nonetheless crucial for establishing the sheer alterity of kibbutz life. In other words, he serves as a helpful surrogate for the vast majority of the Israeli novel readers who might enjoy visiting a kibbutz but who would find it difficult to tolerate its paucity of distractions, its regimental routines: "The minute you walk into the door of the dining hall, your oxygen supply drops, your productivity declines; that phlegmatic calm, that slowness, they're enough to drive a person crazy" (pp. 5, 6). Aaron's rueful musings efficiently introduce the novel's focus on irreparable change, the disparity between the staunchly socialist, even Soviet leanings, of the early days, and that of the present, in which communal entities struggle to adjust to an increasingly capitalist, globalized society for whom the kibbutz is a quaint and outmoded relic of the past.

In an apparently ironic nod to highly successful enterprises such as Ahava (the famous line of cosmetics based on Dead Sea minerals marketed by a conglomerate of kibbutzim), Gur illustrates the surrender to the very bourgeoisie values—the decadent glorification of the self—against which the kibbutz once defined itself. Aaron nostalgically regrets the uprooting of plum trees to make way for cactuses that produce cosmetics rather than life-giving food—and which he thinks embodies the loss of the old values of individual modesty and simplicity: "how did the women of the founder's generation—with faces that had been weather-beaten and wrinkled . . . how did they feel when they saw the women of the middle generation, looking . . . as fresh and smooth as if they'd never spent a day working in the fields?" (p. 37). And yet Gur's reader is made aware that such nostalgia ignores the hard facts of new realities. As a kibbutz member instructs Aaron, the cosmetics factory's profit margins subsidize the unprofitable agricultural branches, enabling members who work in the fields and orchards to feel productive, while preventing the kibbutz from sinking into debt.

Soon after Aaron's observations of the community's jubilee celebration, Inspector Ohayon is summoned to investigate the death of a young woman named Osnat, a kibbutz leader whose platform for reforming her community included a number of controversial proposals. Violence, let alone murder, is exceptionally rare on kibbutz, and when Ohayon forces the members to accept that the criminal is likely still among them, the result is initially outright shock, a kind of disassociation often linked to posttraumatic stress disorder. Dvorka, a founder and ideological firebrand, draws a bizarre comparison between this threat and the crisis of the early 1950s when the cold war tensions wreaked havoc in the "one big family" that comprises kibbutz society: "I thought we'd already seen everything . . . who could have foreseen what happened in 1951, when ideology and politics split kibbutzim right down the middle? Ever since then I've thought we'd seen everything. Families destroyed. The hatred" (p. 154).[8] Only the prospect of what this veteran perceives as the kibbutz ideal's complete and irreversible betrayal genuinely rattles her composure.[9]

When Ohayon attempts to obtain information about the possible motives of the killer, Dvorka instructs him in what she regards as the true calamity at hand, the triumph of materialism and selfishness over socialism and altruism:

> what went wrong must be put right . . . There's a slow and gradual process of decay! . . . Hired labor on the kibbutz! All the kibbutzim are prostituting themselves today, they're prostituting themselves! . . . it's a process of putting the individual above the group, putting the private person above the general good . . . it's all one long process—you begin by speculating on the stock exchange and profiting from bank shares, and you end up having to give our own members credit points for picking the fruit off our own trees. (p. 155)

In spite of the fact that Dvorka acknowledges changes the kibbutz once weathered, it soon becomes apparent that for Dvorka, *every* change is inherently destructive, especially the new "family sleeping" arrangements sweeping through the entire kibbutz movement. She is similarly irate about the new tendency among residents to take meals in private rooms because that too represents a diminishment of the collective life: "I'm opposed . . . to people shutting themselves up in their rooms . . . Taking meals together is also a value on the kibbutz" (p. 159).[10] When Ohayon, ineptly struggling to win her trust, gushes about the attractively designed dining room (with "all the up-to-date appliances"), she snaps that it too is corrupted by "abundance. The curse of affluence" (p. 160). As this deft portrait of an aging ideologue suggests, *Murder on a Kibbutz* impresses not least for its willingness to examine the necessity for progress, even as it presents a moving portrait of the heroic struggle of the chalutzim whose selfless ideals prove painfully ephemeral in the changing times.

Throughout the novel, both these paradigms (adaptation to globalization and loyalty to socialist roots) are explored sympathetically and intelligently, in insistent counterpoint to one another. As one survivor of those early days of toil poignantly recalls:

> Those were different times, hard times, you can read about them . . . but you won't really understand even then. It's difficult to transmit what the first contact with the land was like. The hardship, the dryness, the water, the hunger . . . Twelve hours at a stretch sometimes, clearing and plowing and gradually building. And the heat in summer, the cold in winter, the poverty and the hunger. The men were weak with hunger and hard labor, all of us were. There were days . . . when all we had to eat were two slices of bread and half an egg a day for a pregnant woman, and a few olives. (p. 169)

Gur presents such recollections in evident reverence for the selfless struggle between human beings and the natural world, just as she creates space for another character's acerbic dismissal of the social naiveté of those early days: "So much spite and envy! What a load of rubbish it is—all that talk about the ideal society! Look what it turned into! But right from the beginning, the idea of a place or a society where people would be equal, from each according to his ability and to each according to his needs—what nonsense! . . . To each according to his ability and the strength of his elbows and the loudness of his yells—that's what really happened" (p. 184). That last rejoinder is of course a scathingly ironic inversion of the founding ethical imperative: "from each according to his ability, to each according to his needs."[11] With that paradigm in mind, Gur proves especially adept at demonstrating that what may strike readers living in the outside world as a relatively benign process of adaptation to changing circumstances is viewed by many of those within as an insidious abandonment of the core value of self-reliance and resistance to hired labor.

Conversely, Aaron, the politician who grew up on kibbutz, complains bitterly about one of its once most highly hallowed institutions; he considers the children's houses to be responsible for adult maladjustment and neurosis due to the individual's early experience of emotional and material deprivation:

> You don't give them a chance to cope with the existential problems of life and the end result is a kind of stunting of the capacity for suffering, for doubt; they take everything for granted, they know nothing except the need to accumulate material possessions. That covetousness, that acquisitiveness of theirs . . . all stems from anxiety, from the fear of an independent life outside the kibbutz, and from the memory of deprivation transposed to a sphere where it didn't exist at all: The real deprivation had nothing to do with material things, it had to do with the stunting of individual growth. (pp. 193–94)

Like a virus, Aaron's candor stimulates doubts and misgivings in the mind of his acquaintance, Moish.[12] In the past, this loyal kibbutznik consciously resisted such moments, but now he begins to grasp the enormity of the malaise he long denied: "The pain of loneliness and questions about the meaning of life seemed to descend on the young people all at once, as soon as they left the stifling greenhouse they were so eager to escape in order to experience new things, disorienting and alienating them from the possibility of returning to that same greenhouse and bringing up their children as they themselves had been brought up, in the sincere belief that this was the very best of all possible ways" (p. 194). Interestingly, the novel's suggestion that the first tentative step toward this often permanent separation usually follows the first expansive encounter with the outside world is supported by critical studies.[13]

A member of the novel's older generation sympathizes, seeing this phenomenon as a healthy corrective to an unavoidable lack of the kind of genuine challenges and ordeals that once gave meaning to their elders' lives, a critical path toward individuation:

> These trips should be seen . . . as a natural and constructive reaction to a spiritual quest. We should encourage them to travel as part of the process of apprenticeship in which a person learns that the meaning of life is to be found within himself. Think about how hard it is for them. They don't have any swamps to drain. They have nothing to protect them from emptiness. It's hard to live without a challenge. (p. 194)

Gur revisits the plight of kibbutz youth later in the novel, where the child rearing experiment, long the subject of admiring interest, is revealed as a callous institution where conformity and dogma overruled both the heart and common sense. Here is Moish again, baring his soul in a cry of protest directed toward Dvorka and her generation of uncompromising ideologues:

I'll tell you exactly what was wrong. There were a lot of things wrong. The first thing wrong is that we never talked about it. You didn't allow it, you didn't want to hear . . . What do you know about us? Maybe you know when we began to walk or talk and when our first tooth arrived, but what goes on inside us you know nothing at all. We never had a chance to talk, only under cover of the jokes and skits we wrote for kibbutz celebrations . . . I'm not saying there wasn't anything good about the way we grew up, but what about the misery, the nights when we woke up to a nonmother instead of a mother and a nonfather instead of a father . . . Where were you before I was eighteen months old, when Miriam [a kibbutz member] told me that the memory she had of me as a baby was of a little toddler walking behind his housemother's [metapel's] dress while the woman keeps pushing the little hand away? Where were you then? . . . What were you thinking about then, on the nights when we were afraid? How did you come to agree to let mothers see their babies for only half an hour a day? (pp. 322, 323)

As this crescendo of long-repressed resentment suggests, *Murder on a Kibbutz* adroitly encompasses the unresolved intergenerational tensions that cause what outsiders might assume is a staunchly settled, even static, society, to be one that is far from free of uneasy questioning and harsh self-criticism.

In what amounts to Moish's *J'accuse*, he repudiates the selfhood-smothering form of child rearing that he and others hope to reform:

For the sake of the ideal of equality you organized things so we would have a group ego, but you destroyed our own, our personal egos. How healthy and secure do you think kids can be who've got only each other to turn to at night? And I'm not even talking about the beginning of adolescence and the communal showers and all your other brilliant ideas! . . . I want to understand what went on in your heads when you locked the doors of the children's house from the outside and told the night watch to check on us twice a night! Two whole times! And we would sometimes stand there the whole night banging on the door and crying and nobody came! I explode every time I think about it! (p. 324)

Interestingly, this wounded character's diatribe actually conforms to recent reassessments of kibbutz education by those who were raised within the system.[14] For those of us who once accepted the wonders of this pedagogy at face value, Moish's denunciation can be painful reading, just as the discourse of the "post-Zionists" can be difficult for those raised on the appealing myths of Israel's establishment. And yet both are essential for coming to terms with complex realities.

As Ohayon's investigation proceeds, he successfully makes inroads into the different social sectors of the community, which means that Gur encompasses marginal perspectives, such as that of newcomers (including recent immigrants) as well as hired workers. Hence, by the novel's conclusion, the reader has been exposed to surprisingly divergent versions of the famous kibbutz "reality." Here for instance is Dave, a Canadian immigrant, surprised that his single status so threatens the community's staid family structure that he is sent off to "all kinds of seminars and ideological weekends" in search of a mate. He confesses that all the ideological reading he did about the creation of the kibbutz movement left him ill-prepared for the social conservatism, the singular devotion to the nuclear family, that he subsequently experienced:

> [H]e would never have expected them to take the institution of the family so seriously. After all, kibbutz society was supposed to be one big family . . . and the family cell was perceived as being inimical to society, and here he was, discovering every single day the conservatism of the kibbutz. In fact, he . . . said unsmilingly, it was such a bourgeois society that they hadn't succeeded in overcoming the family cell at all. (p. 235)

As an outsider, Dave inevitably has a rough encounter with the painful contradictions of kibbutz life. But he is no malcontent and, ultimately, having weathered the loss of his earliest illusions, remains an idealist, one who has had time to carefully consider the kibbutz experiment in all its complexity. When skeptically questioned about his motives for remaining, he ardently insists that the positive attributes greatly outweigh the negative (a point of view that goes unexpressed in Liebrecht's rendering):

> One of the main advantages of living on a kibbutz . . . was the freedom from all kinds of things that people outside enslaved themselves to. Here too you could be a slave to material standards of living . . . but you didn't have to be. Because the minimum you were provided with here was more than enough . . . he was not only talking about material goods but also about other worldly vanities, status and so on. (p. 236)

Hence, through Dave's eyes, readers encounter the sheer potentiality, the open-ended destiny of the kibbutz which, in spite of what other characters deem unacceptable ideological compromises, endures for him.

In contrast, Savyon Liebrecht's short story "Kibbutz" is notable for its unsparingly bleak, ultimately unrealistic, portrayal of unfeeling kibbutzniks whose callous sensibilities seem very far-removed from most expectations of an enlightened community, especially *vis-à-vis* its disadvantaged and vulnerable residents. The collection in which it appears, *A Good Place for the Night* (*Makom Tov La-Laila*), is memorable for its sobering renderings of individuals who are alienated from their ostensible homes and homelands. Liebrecht, born in Munich, Germany, to Holocaust survivors in 1948, has received much acclaim for her novels and short fiction. Yet her rendering of kibbutz life, the fate of its more vulnerable residents, is surprisingly monolithic, lacking the depth of portrayal and moral shadings of the two other works under discussion here.

"Kibbutz" concerns the return of Melech, a young army officer, to his kibbutz origins. His quiet investigation of the evil done to his parents culminates in an outraged *J'accuse* directed toward the institution that was supposed to embody the heart of humanity's most egalitarian and humane ideals but which departed appallingly far from those principles. The chief protagonist, Devora, a matronly kibbutz nurse, is startled one day by Melech's unexpected reappearance, with whom she has had a special bond since his infancy. Brimming with affection at the sight of him, Devora soon notices that her onetime charge is strangely distant and agitated. After Devora informs Melech that she has proudly followed his career and posted a notice about his "outstanding officer award" on the communal bulletin board, the young man responds with hostile doubt about the goodwill of the community.

Soon it emerges that Melech's visit is not motivated by casual affection but by an urgent need to press his old caregiver for details of certain remote events concerning his parents' unhappy lives. And Devora is the most apt address for his painful questions as throughout his early childhood she had inculcated him with an unvarying account of his origins, told "in the same voice she used for fairy tales" (p. 63). With the best intentions, Devora indoctrinated the boy with an attractive and reassuring myth of his early life: "She would tell him the story of his father and the story of his mother and the story of their meeting, their love, their happiness which grew greater every day until, when it was absolutely perfect, a child was born to them, the most beautiful child in the kibbutz . . . He grew and became their pride and joy until his sixth birthday party, which was memorialized in the last picture of the three of them" (p. 63). In the past, this was always the juncture where Devora would tactically halt the reassuring narrative. The details are so well known to both of them that in years past "they knew the sentences by heart and would say them in unison" (p. 63), but now Melech pressures her to tell the story again. Devora senses a menace behind the request but in the difficult dance of interrogation and evasion that ensues, Melech coaxes her to tell it just as she had in years past ("Once upon a time"). Soon it becomes clear that he intends to penetrate the truth that Devora's gentle artifice sought to shield him from. Inexorably, Melech forces Devora to acknowledge a far more painful past than the benign version with which she has nurtured him.

As Melech and Devora revisit this ancient story, we learn how Melech's father David, born in a DP camp shortly after the Holocaust, was brought by his survivor parents to Israel. After his mother's death, David spent his days working with his father in the family grocery store which eventually failed, leaving David with few options in life. One day he learns that the kibbutzim are interested in hardworking youth and applies for the program. Already in love with farms and the countryside, David bursts with so much excitement that he never even arrives at his formally assigned kibbutz but simply descends from the bus at his first glimpse of a cowshed: "Stunned with joy." In love at first sight, "David shouted a passionate 'Shalom' and almost fainted from the impact of the delightful smell and the velvety eyes of the cows. He had no doubt, this was where he belonged" (p. 71). Informed there is no work available by the cowherd's manager, David collapses in tears and throws "his arms around the neck of the cow Attalia," refusing to leave.

From this startling beginning, the kibbutzniks acidly dismiss David as an idiot unworthy of their respect or even goodwill. Cynically, they "welcome" him into the community only when the realization sinks in that he is prepared to immediately surrender the Tel Aviv apartment his late parents willed him. Nor does David's selflessness dissuade the kibbutz members from refraining from cruel taunts and sadistic pranks:

> Not out of malice, but out of a lack of a generosity, after teasing David, the people on the kibbutz began abusing him . . . in an imperceptible, ongoing deterioration that blurred the horror of it . . . because David was amiable and seemed not to always understand the affronts, the kibbutz members could tell themselves that they teased him out of their affection . . . At first, they merely added salt to his coffee . . . Later they involved him in escapades that provided them with hours of laughter: how he slept on the rickety roof of the cowshed from midnight till dawn, his socks full of ice, to protect his cows from thieves; how they stood him in front of a pan of Atida's dung to look for a precious stone she'd swallowed; how they starved him for a whole day so he could do his part to help cut expenses. He was an eager participant in their schemes, keeping awake with the help of the ice he'd poured into his socks, bringing the lumps of dung close to his eyes, enduring hunger without complaint for the sake of the kibbutz budget. (pp. 76–77)

David's complicity in his maltreatment presents the reader with a bitingly ironic portrait of the fate of the truly selfless individual devoted to serving the community that the kibbutz as an institution sought to foster. At the same time, Liebrecht's unrelenting vision of the community's overarching maliciousness wears the reader down, diminishing our confidence that she is interested in presenting a realistically diverse community.

One day, Devora, noticing David's increasing retreat to solitude, sits down with him for a conversation. She discovers that the one item tying David to his late parents, an album of family photographs, was callously abandoned by the kibbutzniks who sold his apartment and turned the profit over to the kibbutz budget: "They didn't take you to the apartment so you could get what you wanted?" "No. They said it was a shame to waste a day's work" (p. 78).[15] When Devora confronts the culprit responsible for David's loss of the only photos of his Holocaust survivor parents, this character attempts to placate her with a secret: a wife has been found for David, in hopes of weaning him from his supposed amorous attachments to the kibbutz cows.

From here, the story shifts back into Devora's fairy-tale version of events, which Melech perversely demands she recount for him again. In this tale, Rachel (Melech's mother) is discovered working in the storeroom of the Haifa-based garage where the kibbutzniks often purchase parts for the kibbutz vehicles. They immediately notice her mental deficiency. As anticipated, David and Rachel eventually fall in love and she joins him on the kibbutz.[16] Once married, the kibbutz members initially treat Rachel as a grotesque object just as they did her husband, but she proves herself a suspicious and fierce "buffer between the abusive kibbutz members and her husband fighting his fights energetically and fearlessly" (p. 85). Though a specialist has warned Devora that the couple is unlikely to have a child of "normal intelligence," she nevertheless takes it upon herself to present the reproductive facts of life to Rachel (poignantly using illustrations from a children's book). Six months after their wedding, Rachel is pregnant with Melech. In the coming weeks, Devora appears in the couple's house regularly to explain about the fetus's stages of development. But she cannot shield the isolated couple from her comrades' enduring interest in exploiting them as objects of hilarity and learns that the kibbutz secretary has insisted that the couple adapt "a name worthy of their baby—Melech (king)." Furious (it's a name that invites abuse), she tries to persuade Rachel to change her mind but to no avail.

One day, when Melech (who turns out to be a healthy, normal baby after all) is still a toddler, David and Rachel ask Devora to promise to care for him should anything ever happen to them. Years later after his parents' deaths, the two have become very close. For instance, after Melech's class is assigned a family history project, Devora accompanies Melech to Beersheba to visit a cousin of his father, nearly the sole survivor of David's entire extended family who were murdered in the

Holocaust. As he takes in old black and white photos of the deceased, Melech asks the old man why nobody rescued them and is told that "there were a lot of other bad people, not only the Nazis" (p. 90). Melech presses further: "And there weren't any good people?" to which his old relative responds tersely, "There weren't enough good people" (p. 90). At this critical moment, it seems clear that Liebrecht is quietly insinuating a connection between the amoral bystanders of the Holocaust and the cruelty we have witnessed in the kibbutz. As they prepare to depart, the old man suddenly seizes Melech, nearly smothering him in an emotional embrace, which moves Melech intensely. Aside from Devora, he is clearly unaccustomed to experiencing such affection.

Unlike his parents, Melech proves a precocious learner and high achiever, skips two grades, wins sports medals, and enjoys immense popularity. But before all this, he was only little Melech, aware only of the love of his parents and Devora. He tells her gratefully that she has been the most "stable thing in my life since I was six. Without you, I wouldn't have survived in this place" (p. 92). Devora is disturbed by what might lie behind this utterance and indeed the nature of the mystery that has provoked Melech's sudden visit. At this crucial juncture, the narrative becomes a suspenseful interrogation as Melech presses ahead to demand the raw data of his parents' lives: the nature of their "retardation," the gift of the apartment that apparently ensured his father's acceptance, the harsh exploitation of his father at work. Most critically, Melech is anguished by his father's status as the "kibbutz clown" and what that meant to his own identity in childhood: "Is it funny to call the sons of retards 'Melech'? Is that a kind of humor?" (p. 94). But his deepest concern is with something far more ominous.

Officially, the tractor involved in his parents' death was said to be an Oliver, but Melech has somehow learned that this was substituted in the evidence submitted to the police for a John Deere that was known to be dangerous and obsolete. When Devora, now fearing Melech's anger, insists that their death was a tragic accident, Melech angrily prevents her from leaving, forcing her to listen to a new version of the tale that his erstwhile protector repeated throughout his childhood:

> Once upon a time there was a beautiful place, like in a fairytale, that was called a kibbutz. The people there were very hard-hearted and mean-spirited, and more than anything, they were very bored, and that's why they were always looking for entertainment. One day, a good, hard-working young man who was mildly retarded came to their kibbutz. He loved the cowshed and the cows, and he loved the people and their kibbutz, but that didn't make them really like him, because they had a great need for entertainment. (p. 95)

In his "revisionist" narrative, Melech asserts that after his birth, the kibbutzniks were pleased that "their fun would be tripled because the circus had really expanded . . . but alas, the boy didn't suffer from mild retardation . . . He was a pretty smart kid, and that's why he was also very sad, because unlike his parents, he understood very well what he saw" (p. 96). Devora weeps in the face of this version of events "that mocked the stories she had told him with so much love" (p. 96). But Melech is relentless in elaborating on the chilling revelation concerning the John Deere's fatal defect, which set the stage for "the circus people's last and best performance" (p. 96). After all these years, a witness to the events has come forward, telling Melech that his parents were murdered, a crime that remained a secret known only to the three conspirators. One of them is dead, another, who became intensely religious and left the kibbutz, revealed these facts to Melech. The third "stayed on the kibbutz with his beloved wife and two lovely daughters as if nothing had happened" (p. 97). It appears that this man is Devora's husband.

This final revelation forces Devora to confront "with profound clarity . . . the things that had simmered at the edge of her consciousness all those years, never flowing over the edge but never subsiding either" (p. 97). At last, the anger she has long felt toward her husband and most of all "toward the soul-crushing kibbutz" (p. 98) rises to the surface. Melech presents her with a heartbreakingly unadorned account of the reality she rationalized away, what was done to this couple:

> who were so . . . retarded that they thought they were members of the kibbutz, a couple like all the others, a couple with a child. They didn't know they lived here to be the kibbutz clowns. They didn't know they were taking risks that circus people take. They probably didn't even know they were actually murdered . . . They wanted to live here in peace with the cows and the flowers and the plum cakes, and their little boy. (pp. 98–99)

The story's concluding words chillingly reinforce the earlier bridge to the Holocaust (and its amoral bystanders) as Melech completes the retold story that he has appropriated to give his life authentic, if tragic, meaning: "Once upon a time there were a few bad people and a few indifferent people . . . There was also one good woman, but that wasn't enough" (p. 99). Dramatically powerful, deeply moving, Liebrecht's "Kibbutz" ultimately presents a monochrome society whose singular cruelty bears little resemblance to the moral complexity of its real-world counterpart. In imagining a thoroughly dystopic environment utterly adrift from its moral antecedents, this gifted writer misses an opportunity to grapple with the deeper possibility of moral autonomy and selflessness alongside all the foibles and pettiness that, as any reasonable interlocutor must assume, invariably informs any human community.

Suffering is also present in the kibbutz lives examined in *Mourning a Father Lost: a Kibbutz Childhood Remembered* (first published in Hebrew in 2000) but so are more redemptive dynamics, enabling a more multifaceted portrait to emerge on the page. Though ostensibly dedicated to the author's difficult relationship with his late father whose death serves as a bookending device, Avraham Balaban's raw memoir is actually one of the most fully realized literary examinations of kibbutz childhood to date, filled with anger, compassion, irony, love. Above all, *Mourning* is a powerful examination of the strangely alienating childhoods the dreamers of utopia inadvertently bestowed on their progeny. Balaban, who grew up in the classic days of the children's houses, begins with scenes that immediately establish the socially engineered distances between children and their parents. After briefly relating how he first learned of his father's death in Israel, Balaban (now a college professor based in Florida) sends the reader backward through time to a primal experience of childhood terror.

It is nighttime on Kibbutz Hulda and the darkness fills with the screams of jackals[17]:

> The jackals know when the nurse leaves the children's house, as if her departure were an agreed signal. The first wail comes over the kibbutz's rusty fence, which passes near our children's house, rises at once to its pitch, drops for a moment, gathers strength, and tries to reach its peak again. It is joined, before it falls silent, by fresh wails from the dark field. Now they rise and fall continually, rasping the darkness. The shadows in the room move around, the scraping of their nails on the floor makes the air tremble. I breathe softly, I don't turn to the wall, to avoid exposing my back to the room beasts. They stir restlessly . . . They stop beside the beds, stand and crouch . . . I don't move my arms and legs. (p. 7)

In the characteristically poetic prose that distinguishes *Mourning*, Balaban succeeds in making his childhood recollection of raw fear and plaintive vulnerability a visceral thing. Hence, the reader has no subsequent difficulty comprehending how the "New Jews" of the laboratory experiment, having no choice but to rapidly learn strategies to suppress outward signs of fear and other forms of neediness, grew up with an acute sense of deprivation.[18] Balaban notes the insidious power with which this ideology took hold and the glib self-assurance of its pedagogues: "'A child cannot long for what it has never had, it cannot miss what it has never known,' the lecturers at the ideological seminars . . . persuaded one another" (p. 13). Balaban effectively renders his own experience with this objectifying dogma, its chilly logic of duty, sacrifice, and substitution, as an ironic echo of the emotional detachment with which he and his peers were indoctrinated:

> Mom and Father are busy building up this place, and if they can't finish their work in time to fetch their children from the nursery or kindergarten, they ask a friend or neighbor to do this—for are we not all brothers? The few visits by people from their hometown . . . offer the nearest thing to a hug from an uncle or aunt. Mom and Father are very busy, laboring to put flesh and sinews on the skeleton of this settlement, and normally they only see their children for a little while before they put them to bed. These few moments are all it takes to remind the children of the existence of a warm body to snuggle against and all it takes to revive the fear of abandonment. The children are sheltered by the finest theories, surrounded by nurses and educators but . . . .[t]he children develop survival strategies, like street kids, toughening their skin to the best of their abilities. When they grow up they will evince the selfishness of people who never got enough protection and security. (pp. 8–9)

Many former kibbutz children of that era have recalled parents who withheld emotion and even physical affection (during their brief visits) and Balaban is no exception.[19]

In fairness, today he seems to believe that their parents' days were so arduous that they simply were left too exhausted to conjure up what was missing. For instance, his mother, even as a young woman:

> never played ball or hopscotch with me, never laughed with me. Eventually I understood that when she came to me at the end of the day her gravity was purely exhaustion—her love had been drained during the day by a dozen greedy mouths. The movement's gurus also did the damage. The old family is obsolete, the educationalists proclaimed. We shall create a new family, the education committee told her. Away from mother's apron strings we shall bring up natural, healthy children, echoed the general meeting. And she believed everything she was told, as a Hassid believes his rabbi. (p. 12)

The same tone of near-incredulity is expressed by one of his childhood friends: "What amazes me, when I think about our childhood, is the members' conviction that we were a clean slate on which they could write whatever they saw fit. So they wrote on us: be brave and not afraid of the dark and the jackals . . . be loyal to the kibbutz. And they were naïve . . . or stupid enough, to believe that this is what would happen" (p. 97).[20] As for his father, Balaban recalls a remote figure fiercely devoted to the collective good and protecting the kibbutz apple orchard, and ill at ease and impatient during the short periods designated for his children:

> The time assigned to his children was the gap between his shower and supper. He would lie down, cover his face with a sheet or a newspaper, and we would walk

around on tiptoe, as in a sickroom. We clearly felt we were a nuisance to him . . . The apple varieties, Delicious, Nonpareil, even the delicate Gala Beauty, reached the Tel Aviv market safely, despite all the hardships of . . . picking, sorting, and packaging. But how to touch us, his children, that he didn't know. On stormy nights he would rush out, like a true farmer, to ensure that his tender saplings were unhurt by the blast. (p. 21)

Even today, whenever he cares for a plant or a tree, Balaban says he instantly recalls that agrarian dedication, his "father's sunburnt hands showing me how to plant a cypress tree, or stroking a cluster of apples with the affection he reserved for his trees" (p. 23).

Only toward the end of this often wrenching book does the portrayal of Balaban's father take on a hint of how the two might have reconciled, but by then it is late, both for Balaban and the reader, and of course that is the point—the narrative aesthetically and emotively circling around its irrecoverable absence, a yearned-for figure who was never there.[21] Yet in spite of its aching notes of loss, *Mourning* never descends to self-pity nor condemnation; rather it is a chronicle of complex, sympathetic individuals caught up in a lofty dream whose vast social goals were, inevitably, never quite fulfilled. Moreover, for all its bitterness, there are moments of unabashed love for the daring experiment, for what was attempted.

At one point, while lecturing to the old people on his former kibbutz, Balaban is struck by what they represent: "They were humanity's finest dream in this century, the most consistent attempt to forget humanity's inglorious origins" (p. 37). After so much pain and disappointment, this surprising affirmation seems all the more authentic. The fact that Gur, Liebrecht, and Balaban each investigates the shadowy areas of kibbutz life, exposing troubling aspects concerning the fate of the vulnerable individual, indicates that the kibbutz continues to serve Israel's literary world as a sort of moral barometer. As this brief examination of three disparate works suggests, even after its shimmering promise has faded, the kibbutz ideal endures as a profound catalyst for the moral imagination of Israel's writers.

Notes

1.   As Jo-Ann Mort and Gary Brenner observe: "Until the end of the 1970s, most Israelis knew someone on a kibbutz. If you weren't a kibbutznik yourself, you had family on a kibbutz that you visited on holidays; or maybe your parents sent you to spend the summer holiday with the kibbutz cousins. And young people in the city were sent to the youth movements with the possibility of going through the IDF Nahal (agricultural settlement corps) and eventually becoming a kibbutz member" (p. 14).

2. In fact, there have been notable literary encounters with the kibbutz ever since the early years of statehood. These include Aliza Amir (b. 1932), Yossl Birstein (1920–2003), Zvi Luz (b. 1930), David Maletz (1900–1981), Amos Oz (b. 1939), Nathan Shaham (b. 1925), Moshe Shamir (1921–2004), Amnon Shamosh (b. 1929), and Dan Shavit (b. 1944). Most importantly, there is an important emerging critical discourse that, as Rachel Elboim-Dror asserts, "present a new and important dimension: the subjective and first-hand experiences of utopia's children, as viewed from their present, mature and adult perspective" (p. 158). Cinematically, the quasi-autobiographical film *Sweet Mud* (2006) and Ran Tal's film documentary *Children of the Sun* (2007) are also important examples of works that have lately intensified the public perception of the kibbutz as a site of alienation more than utopia.

3. As Marvin Heiferman and Carole Kismaric note, "The golden age of detective fiction began with high-class amateur detectives sniffing out murderers lurking in rose gardens, down country lanes, and in picturesque villages" (p. 56). In this regard, such "golden age" detective novels might be considered as reenactments of the primal murder scene of Genesis wherein the agrarian landscape is irreparably violated by fratricide until the divine utterance renders up the guilty Cain. Other ancient works that have been considered as possible antecedents to the genre include the story of Susanna and the Elders (Daniel 13) and Sophocles' *Oedipus Rex*, wherein Oedipus struggles to discover the fate of his murdered father.

4. It is not at all to her discredit that what most enlivens Gur's books are not the crimes themselves but rather her keen grasp of the peculiar sociology and the arcane rules that operate within the insular worlds that Ohayon must learn to solve the mystery.

5. The English version of the novel's title is not a precise translation; the Hebrew alludes directly to the institution of cooperative children's housing which proves critical to the violence Ohayon investigates.

6. In each of his cases, and in spite of promotions, Ohayon fears being " 'out of his element,' . . . the alienation that caused the tension he felt every morning upon awakening, an acute, indefinable, unfocused anxiety, which also produced the insomnia characteristic of the periods when he was working on a particularly difficult case" (pp. 139–40). Confronted by the necessity of upsetting the cream of the Ashkenazi Zionist establishment, Ohayon's angst is often present during this case.

7. Gur's portrayal of the classic rhythms of kibbutz life offer a distinct verisimilitude, nearly echoing Balaban's memoir that recalls "Harvest and vintage, bushel and scythe, furrow, first fruits and husbandry. The voices lifted in song at Passover, Pentecost, and *Tu Bishvat* reveled in the festive words, and the speakers set them like jewels in their speech . . . . girls come up on the stage, which is edged with rolls of hay, to do the dance of the priestesses. Their white dresses glow against their wheat-colored suntan, their eyes are wide open, as though they're listening to a melody the rest of us can't hear. Blushing a little, aware of their beauty, they turn slowly, like sorceresses, their arms holding up invisible sheaves—they seem to be offering their youth to the four winds. The audience is sitting . . . on bundles of straw, amid festive decorations and slogans. The biblical verses ringing in the afternoon breeze turn the prickly straw into bricks of gold. If we're patient, we shall see Boaz and Ruth coming in from the field" (*Mourning A Father Lost*, pp. 38, 39). This evocative passage aptly sums up the kibbutz movement's strategic way to forge a bridge of decorous continuity between Jewish antiquity and the Jewish reclamation of the land.

8. The same pivotal historical crisis informs *Noa at Seventeen* (1982), Yitzhak Yeshurun's film about the stormy politics that tear a family apart during the cold war.

9. Dvorka (taking the murder of her comrade a bit too coolly in stride) insinuates that, just as that destabilizing schism had once seemed to herald the end of the kibbutz movement, the present crisis would be overcome.

10. Even though, as an old woman, she often has little appetite, Dvorka imposes the discipline of attendance at all meals on herself, which she elaborates on here in the plainspoken, robust language characteristic of her generation: "because that's when you can meet people and sit around the same table, discussing your day and keeping in touch on a daily level, which is really what it's all about . . . . We're a nonalienated society, the last bastion of a lack of alienation in today's horror-ridden world" (pp. 159–60).

11. It is increasingly observed throughout the kibbutz movement that this dictum has been effectively revised to: "from each according to his preferences, to each according to his needs."

12. Once again, Gur's novel successfully delineates a source of pervasive unease in actual kibbutzim, for in her numerous conversations with former kibbutzniks, Naama Sabar often heard "complaints that . . . ideology was imparted, not in open discussion or through open persuasion but by preaching . . . . [w]hile their parents had chosen kibbutz life for ideological reasons, the next generation never had experienced the challenge of having to choose a life, but were born into the kibbutz reality." Elsewhere she reports that "Many spoke of the intense frustration they experienced at having been deprived of the ability and the right to make their own decisions, either big or small. As they put it, they tried to make up for this deprivation by later establishing a family whose lifestyle was decided exclusively by the two spouses." See *Kibbutzniks in the Diaspora*, pp. 123, 128.

13. Many Israeli young people fresh out of the army travel abroad, but those raised on kibbutz often exhibit an even greater sense of claustrophobia and restlessness, trekking around the globe and often risking their lives in dangerous environments. See Chaim Noy and Erik Cohen's *Israeli Backpackers and Their Society*.

14. It is striking, perhaps even uncanny, to note the extent to which Gur's novel anticipates many of the voices recently heard in Ran Tal's acclaimed documentary, *Children of the Sun*.

15. The kibbutzniks' cynical disregard for David's altruism appears in an even worse light when we learn that two veteran members of the kibbutz who inherited apartments have held onto them as private property.

16. At this point, the blissful tale on which Melech was raised is abruptly interrupted by the omniscient narrator's less appealing but 'truthful' rendering in which David was initially repulsed by the photograph of Rachel with which he is presented: "she's black as a Negro . . . I can't marry a black woman" (p. 81). Whether by instinct or assimilation, David shares the Eurocentric biases of his comrades and is repelled by the prospect of marriage to the Iranian-born immigrant. But when told that Rachel desires him, David proves pliable.

17. The distressing nighttime cry of jackals is a surprisingly prevalent motif in the memoirs of Zionist childhoods of that period.

18. Kibbutz Hulda was one of the early communities influenced by famous theorists of utopian Zionism (Siegfrid Bernfeld, Boris Schatz, among others) who insisted that the revolutionary utopians would only succeed if they overcame the bourgeois institution of the family and raise the children apart from the corrupting influences of their parents.

19. In her examination of young people who left their kibbutzim to live as expatriates in Los Angeles, Sabar cites a study conducted during the 1970s in which "half" the participants (all raised on kibbutz) spoke of "their relationship with their parents as complex, filled with tension and frustration . . . . Most of the interviewees spoke about the weakness of the parent-child relationship on the kibbutz, a relationship they would not want to return to under any circumstances. The main point of criticism was the parents' limited involvement in the children's lives . . . beginning with the toddlers' group through the children's house and the elementary or high school." See *Kibbutzniks in the Diaspora*, p. 117.

20. This speaker nearly echoes Balaban's own sense of abandonment: "How they chucked us, aged two or three, into a children's house that was the furthest building in the kibbutz, right by the fence. You remember that poem—'Wizened and quiet, my mother laid me down by the fence'—it was read out on some occasion in school, and for a moment I thought it was a poem about me" (*Mourning A Father Lost*, p. 97).

21. Interestingly, Rachel Elboim-Dror (who grew up in moshavim and is a scholar of Zionist education practices) concludes her largely favorable review of Balaban's *Mourning* by calling for a "dialectical synthesis" between "the sweet, but false nostalgia for a reality that never was, and the empty rhetorical slogans [and] the equally false bitter anger and alienation towards the pioneering heroics of that early period" (p. 159).

Bibliography

Balaban, A. *Mourning a Father Lost: A Kibbutz Childhood Remembered*. New York: Rowman & Littlefield, 2004.

Elboim-Dror, R. "Review: Mourning a Father Lost." *Utopian Studies* 16, no. 1 (2005): 155–59.

Gur, B. *Murder on a Kibbutz: A Communal Case*. New York: HarperCollins Publishers, 1994.

Heiferman, M. and C. Kismaric. *The Mysterious Case of Nancy Drew and the Hardy Boys*. New York: Simon & Shuster, 1998.

Liebrecht, S. "Kibbutz." In *A Good Place for the Night*. Translated by Sondra Silverston. New York: Persea Books, 2005.

———. *Makom Tov La-Laila*. Tel Aviv: Keter, 2002 [in Hebrew].

Mort, J. and G. Brenner. *Our Hearts Invented a Place: Can Kibbutzim Survive in Today's Israel?* Ithaca: Cornell University Press, 2003.

Noy, C. and E. Cohen, eds. *Israeli Backpackers and Their Society*. Albany, NY: State University of New York Press, 2005.

Oz, A. *Artzot Ha-Tan*. Tel Aviv: Massada Press, 1965 [in Hebrew].

———. *Where the Jackals Howl*. New York: Random House, 2005.

Sabar, N. *Kibbutzniks in the Diaspora*. Translated by Chaya Naor. Albany, NY: State University of New York Press, 2000.

Shaul, D., dir. *Sweet Mud*. (Adama Meshuga'at.) GlobusUnited, 2006.

Sophocles. *Oedipus Rex*, edited by E.H. Plumptre. New York: Digireads.com, 2005.

Tal, R., dir. *Children of the Sun*. (Yaldey hashemesh.) Lama Films, 2007.

Yeshurun, Y., dir. *Noa at Seventeen*. (*Noa Bat Sheva-Esrey*.) United King Films, 1982.

10

Agitated Orders: Early Kibbutz Literature as a Site of Turmoil

Iris Milner

Ever since their earliest appearance on the ideological horizon of Zionism in the first decades of the twentieth century, kibbutz ideology and practices became the focus of attention in the works of prominent Hebrew writers. Y. H. Brenner's short story "Agav Urcha" ("By the Way") is an outstanding example: written in 1909, before the first kibbutz actually came into being, it describes the rise and fall of an experiment in communal life involving six fervent Zionist pioneers, on their way to Eretz Yisrael on an express ship from Trieste to Alexandria.[1]

Brenner's piece is an early herald of a wide corpus of prose fiction that started to appear in the 1920s in which kibbutz life and ideology were a central issue. Within the context of Hebrew literature's major concern with the initiation and growth of modern Jewish national revival, these works accompanied the formation of the idea of communal life in the land of Israel, observed its initial practical applications, and testified to its growing role in the Israeli nation-building process. Fulfilling its function as a medium through which criticism and doubt may be raised and reflected upon, and the hegemonic order questioned, literature also gave voice to some problematic aspects of this revolutionary ideology and explored its limits. Thus, as the kibbutzim rapidly developed into a dense network of settlements and started to be conceived of—both inside and outside kibbutz society—as the core of the "new Israeliness" and the place of its ultimate realization, their literary representations became an important virtual site where critical reflections on the benefits of the Zionist ethos, particularly in its socialist version, which was the dominant political current of the time, were expressed.[2] As Hannah Naveh demonstrates in specific reference to Brenner's "Agav Urcha," these works were, already at a very early stage, sensitive not only to the inherent problematics of kibbutz life, but also to the charged relations between the kibbutz ideology and that of other components of the Jewish national revival (Naveh, 2000). While in the 1920s and 1930s critical and doubtful expressions in other media, such as the visual arts, were only marginal, skeptical literary voices were more open and explicit.[3]

This chapter explores the phenomenon of kibbutz representation in Hebrew prose fiction during the first three decades of the kibbutz— from the early 1920s to the end of the 1940s (the pre-state period)— from both these angles: literature's attempt to establish a strong link between kibbutz ideology and the Israeli nation-building project on the one hand and the possibilities it provided for the expression of subversive misgivings regarding its exclusive position as well as its redemptive power on the other.[4] The corpus referred to is a selection of prose fiction works—novels and short stories that are often mentioned in kibbutz-literature taxonomies.[5] Some of the novels are "historical" ones, in the sense that they follow the history and development of individual communal settlements, often associated with specific, identifiable kibbutzim, such as kibbutz Kfar Giladi in Ever Hadani's *Tzrif ha-Etz* (*Wooden Hut*) (1930), kibbutz Ein Harod and kibbutz Tel Yosef in Shlomo Reichenstein's *Raishit* (*Genesis*) (1943), and kibbutz Revivim in Yonat and Alexander Sened's *Adama Lelo Tzel* (*A Land without a Shadow*) (1950). Other novels, as well as the short stories, are more concisely organized around more specific dramatic events. They, too, however, have similarly broad implications concerning the place and status of the kibbutz in the Israeli social, cultural, and political arena of the time.[6]

The literary value of the works under consideration is varied: some of them are of high artistic quality and are worthy of study and exploration due to their place in the modern Hebrew prose canon; others arouse interest solely in terms of their role as a cultural phenomenon, which is the subject matter of the present essay, namely, the presence of the kibbutz in the Israeli collective consciousness, as mediated by literature. Despite their differences, and the variety of individual artistic voices they express, many of the works in the relevant corpus share some principal poetic characteristics, on which the present chapter focuses. The discussion begins with a demonstration of the poetic language—themes, motives, and structures—by which a "literary model" of the kibbutz is constructed. This is followed by an analysis of the dynamic forces that generate the literary plots and a suggestion of a common conflict through which the opposing narratives they produce are presented—a recruiting narrative on the one hand and a hesitant, subversive one on the other. Finally, the texts' varying literary closures are presented as anticipators of an ongoing, often turbulent struggle for more pluralistic and democratic approaches to collective interests and goals.

Communal Spaces and a Communal Soul
(Hanefesh Hakibbutzit)

Collectivity in early kibbutz ideology was designed to apply to all aspects of life, including material, emotional, and intellectual issues. Early kibbutz literature attempts to simultaneously concretize and mythologize the commitment to such a totally demanding system, by thoroughly and minutely portraying the mundane structures and practices through which it was carried out, while at the same time endowing them with an aura of sublimity and transforming them into symbolic components of the process of constituting a collective national identity.

Both the novels and the short stories invest significant efforts in the establishment of a rich catalog of the institutions and functions—most of them located in the public sphere—initiated by the pioneering kibbutzim members for the management of their communal life and the reinforcement of their communal ideology. Elements that commonly compose the background (exposition) of a literary plot—in this case those that constitute the kibbutz milieu—are brought to center stage and given a central role in the stories' dynamics. Rather than serving as the setting only, they function as the geographical and psychological magnetic center of the literary texts, the nucleus of a concentric architecture (of both the kibbutz and the text representing it) to which the literary figures are constantly drawn and attempt to adjust.

Particular emphasis is placed on those sites that embody the replacement of traditionally private, familial functions and the renunciation of private property. Kibbutz literature thus works to establish the kibbutz as a place of a total realization of the Zionist agenda of fostering the collective over the private sphere, which is a critical move in the formation of the collective, national identity and a crucial aspect of Socialist Zionism. Indeed, the constitution of a "collective family" in place of the private one—a change which this literature is deeply committed to portraying—represents the twofold ideological rebellion of Socialist Zionism against both Capitalism (represented by the traditional bourgeois family) and Diasporic Judaism (represented by the traditional religious Jewish family).[7]

The constantly revisited kibbutz "sites" are therefore those that demonstrate the practical applications of this revolutionary change, such as the collective dining room and kitchen, the children's house (*beit hayeladim*), the clothing storehouse (*machsan habgadim*), and the communal showers, all of which conventionally symbolize a private family's indoor activity. Similarly highlighted are *functions* that had been previously handled within the closed circle of the family and in the kibbutz are transferred to the public domain, as well as the *functionaries* in charge of them, who in fact take over the traditional responsibilities of the individual family members (particularly of parents) and empty the allegedly anachronistic institution of the individual family of its content and status. Among these functions and functionaries are the kibbutz secretary (*mazkir*), the work coordinator (*sadran avoda*), the children's caretakers (*metaplot*), the kitchen workers (*mevashlot*), the night guards, the members' assembly (*asefat chaverim*), and the various committees (*vaadot*) in charge of all aspects of life. All are described with particular emphasis on the habits and rituals connected to them and are loaded with national significance. These include, for example, the habit of assembling to the sound of the kibbutz bell (which serves both as a call to duty and as an alarm),[8] the nightly heated arguments around the work coordinator's table in the dining room,[9] the routine, habitual reading of the bulletin board (*luach modaot*), the discussions of the members' assembly,[10] gossip (stereotypically attributed particularly to women), the move into a "family room" as a declaration of marriage,[11] and the collective singing and dancing of the hora in hasidic fashion as a spontaneous expression of close and intimate relations among kibbutz members.[12] These rituals are commonly described in an elevated tone, in a manner that acts out the members' enthusiastic, religious-like devotion and marks its ceremonial quality.

Other minutely described elements are the sites of the working life of the kibbutz member as a "new Jew," representing a fulfillment of the aspiration to adopt a productive way of life on the land. The catalog of kibbutz life as represented by literature thus includes numerous agriculture branches as well as a variety of workshops that established the kibbutz as an economically self-sufficient entity: the cowshed and the routine of milking the sheep and shepherds, the wheat and alfalfa fields with their watering ducts, the orchards, the plant nursery, the vegetable garden, the silage production, the locksmith's workshop, the carpentry—all these places, and the narrow footpaths connecting them, are compiled in kibbutz literary representations to constitute the kibbutz mythological landscape.

The literary texts are self-consciously preoccupied with such a minute description of kibbutz "places" for the purpose of constituting such archetypical profile of the kibbutz, based on a "complete dictionary" of its items, which are transformed into iconic components of "Israeliness." As the novel *Adama Lelo Tzel*, for example, returns time and again to the inside of the collective dining room, following its changes at times of battle with neighboring Arab villages, its narrator openly declares that this central public site faithfully reflects the changes and developments, for better and worse, in the well-being of the community: "The dining room has grown old [. . .] Bad news hit the dining room. We have abandoned it. [. . .] The very few who are left back home try to fill the emptiness of the dining room [. . .]. I have a feeling that the dining room, *our society's barometer*, will finally celebrate its victory" (Sened and Sened, 1950, pp. 161, 171, my translation from Hebrew, my emphasis).

The totality of the collective experience is textually reproduced also through the use of a common style of literary composition and strategy of narration. Despite the existence of an identifiable plotline and specific protagonists, the scheme of most of the works, including the short stories, which are usually more compactly arranged around a single dramatic event, often appears anecdotal. Episodes take place at different sites of the relatively closed kibbutz area and enable a comprehensive view of its layout. The limited boundaries of the small settlement are often juxtaposed with the surrounding open landscapes, which are ambivalently experienced as both attracting and threatening, due to the dangerous maladies and potential enemies they hide. When the story sometimes leaves the closed territory of the kibbutz (going back in time to the biographical history of different members, as in Bistritski's *Yamim ve-Leilot* (*Days and Nights*) and Yaari's *Keor Yahel* (*Like a Burning Light*) (1937) or to an urban environment, as in Avigdor Hameiri's *Tnuva* (1946 [1934]), and in the rare cases in which the kibbutz is looked at from the outside (as in Itzhak Shenhar's "Prazon" 1960 [1939][13]), the resulting oppositions that emerge declaratively reinforce and confirm the advantages of the kibbutz over any other way of life in the newly settled land.

The narrating voice of the texts is typically auctorial (an all-knowing narrating voice, not identified with any of the literary characters) and seldom conceals its freedom to witness private affairs and to enter the inner lives of all participants alike: it follows the different figures along the narrow footpaths between the various public sites and their family or bachelor tents or rooms, peeps through windows, walks into the nursery and the communal showers, stops by the tables at the collective dining room and listens to conversations, goes out to the working places and catches details of tensions and disputes, and follows the kibbutz members' inner thoughts and reveals their most hidden secrets.

This composition of materials and narrative strategy combine to create a puzzle of interconnected life stories and relationships, tightly interweaving the identities of the individuals and blurring the borders between them. The focus of the stories moves from one character to another, allowing each one a similar amount of attention, so that it is sometimes hard to determine who, if anyone at all, is the specific protagonist of the text (which is clearly the case in Bistritski's *Yamim ve-Leilot*, Ever Hadani's *Tzrif ha-Etz*, Emma Levin-Talmai's *Leet Ohalim* (*In the Time of Tents*) (1949), and the Sened's *Adama Lelo Tzel*, and to a lesser extent in many other works, such as Zvi Schatz's "Batia" (1918), Hameiri's *Tnuva* (1946 [1934]) and Valfovski's "Yeled Yulad Lanu" (1950 [1940])).

The literary figures are themselves iconic. Although they usually represent specific (fictive) personalities, involved in specific affairs, their characters are usually only superficially drawn, as their importance stems from their role in the collective organization rather than from their individual personalities and needs. Particular persons or events are thus presented as the cornerstones of a general model of the kibbutz as a preferred framework for life, which early kibbutz literature is highly committed to portray.

Conflicting Voices: Textual Dynamics and Tensions

The first decades of the kibbutz were marked by a consistent rise in its status as a leading, indispensable factor in the Israeli social and political milieu. Literature's commitment to the support and reinforcement of this status is apparent not only in its treatment of the kibbutz setting (as discussed above), but also in the dramatic narratives that it presents. This is particularly obvious in the historical novels that follow the development of specific kibbutzim through their initial stages. The chain of events these novels commonly recount starts from the very first steps of the communal group and leads to its successful establishment. The overt message thus relayed clearly relates to the advantages of kibbutz ideology and practices in "conquering" the land of Israel and in accomplishing the desired metamorphosis of the allegedly sick diasporic "Jewish" body into a vital, manly, cured Israeli one.[14] The achievement, against all odds, of the almost impossible undertaking of taking over the harsh land and overcoming the rough physical conditions is attributed in all these novels exclusively to the communal efforts and the collaboration among the kibbutz members in terms of work, distribution of income, and expenses and the maintenance of a system of physical and psychological mutual support. Egalitarianism and equality are thus presented not only as just and moral social causes, but also as crucial conditions for the realization of national, Zionist aspirations.

Indeed the kibbutz attempted to define itself, from its very beginning, as the spearhead of national revival, its holy shrine, and an "order" of the most devoted few who took upon themselves to comply with its strictest demands and lead the way for the entire people seeking redemption in the ancient homeland. "The kibbutz is a revolutionary cell, a cell that prepares a new regime and a new way of life. I see it as a framework in which the utmost can be done for this country and this future regime," declares one of the members of the group of settlers in *Adama Lelo Tzel* (Sened and Sened, 1950, p. 217). Such a self-conceptualization turns the kibbutz into a closed entity, as closed as "a pond quarried within the limits of its rocks, a pond which any strange elements thrown into it storm and boil it," in the words of writer Shlomo Zemach.[15] It is this self-conceptualization that engenders a critical component of the narrative of many of the literary texts, including the historical ones—in fact the core of their dynamic structure: a recurrent conflict, centering on the very question of belonging to the closed circle of the kibbutz society in which the protagonists are repeatedly placed and with which they recurrently struggle.

The specific dilemma that reflects this conflict may vary: In some cases it is an outsider who is considering the possibility of joining the kibbutz[16]; in others a kibbutz member is thinking of leaving it on his or her own initiative or is being forced to leave by others.[17] Sometimes the concrete question of belonging is indirectly suggested, in a struggle over status or adherence to rules (as in S. Yizhar's "Efrayim Hozer la-Aspeset" ("Efrayim Returns to the Alfalfa") and in Maletz's *Maaglot (Circles)*). The immediate triggers that arouse the dilemmas also differ: they may be the harsh struggle for survival in face of an extremely demanding reality, or more personal issues such as loneliness, envy, homesickness (for the home abandoned back in Europe), a frustrated desire for individual expression, love intrigues (usually quite simplistically drawn), or bitter disputes between a single member of the kibbutz and the entire commune. The personas involved may be central figures or marginal ones, veterans, or newcomers. In all cases alike, however, the options of joining in or staying on the outside, holding on or abandoning, being accepted or being rejected expose a constant collision between centrifugal and centripetal forces, drawing the protagonists into and out of the communal entity and what it stands for. In stories like "Batya," *Tnuva, Tzrif ha-Etz, Maaglot,* and others, it is the woman protagonist's either excessive or deficient libido, or her strong motherly feelings, that interfere with her readiness to comply with the group norms. Thus, women are stereotypically defined in these works, which are supposed to represent a tolerant society that erases all difference between men and women, as obstacles to the embodiment of the national goals.

As a result of this conflictual situation, both the kibbutz and its individual members are in fact repeatedly involved in mutual acceptance tests and initiation rites that sharpen the definitions of both the kibbutz society's rules and norms and those of a fit, committed kibbutz member. "This life [in the kibbutz], what is its true essence?" asks Chava Mohar, an urban young woman in Shenhar's "Prazon," who is contemplating the possibility of joining the kibbutz after an old friend from her home town in Europe, whom she now falls in love with (Shenhar, 1960 [1939], p. 94). In this sense, the common narrative of early kibbutz literature echoes that of the *Bildungsroman*. As in the *Bildungsroman*, the protagonists—very often young men and women—are indeed positioned in a transitory, reflective, liminal stage from which they are expected to emerge as obedient, submissive subjects of the hegemonic social order. From this transitory, liminal position, some normally denied insights are acquired that may shatter the stability of the kibbutz system and its ideological agenda. This is, then, how the critical attitude of early kibbutz literature is constructed: the recurrent conflictive situation sheds light on various incongruences, faults, and imperfections. The list of flaws that emerges includes the great distance between ideological propaganda and real life, where egalitarianism is very partially implemented, social classes do not cease to exist, and discriminatory, double standard relations prevail; the refusal of the private domain and the private family to be taken over by the public sphere; the resistance of individuals to enforced uniformity; the suppressive and exploitive nature of the leadership; and the many instances of extreme suffering under the unforgiving, intolerant pressure of the group. Observed from this intermediary focal point, and experienced from the agitated conflictive position, the kibbutz atmosphere is thus often presented as a chokingly dense network of physical and psychological pressures. The blurring of borders and the auctorial narration mentioned above turn out to constitute literary devices that are used to represent a panoptic strategy of regulation and control, where every place and every move is constantly under surveillance, with no available hiding place from the watchful collective eye.

The social atmosphere that is created in this way echoes the aspiration of the most radical kibbutz founders to unite in the creation of a "collective soul" (*nefesh kibbutzit*). The participants of the collective text *Kehiliyateinu* (Bistritski, 1922) and their literary representatives in Bistritski's *Yamim ve-Leilot* and Yaari's *Keor Yahel*—all of them reconstructing the short-lived settlement in Bytannia Ilit—confess to their belief in this utopist idea.[18] At the same time this atmosphere of closeness exposes the infeasibility of the revolutionary idea of an absolute and exclusive commitment to collectivity in all areas of life. It conveys the experience of steady exposure to the public gaze as extremely oppressive, arousing stress and rejection, as it in fact constitutes a strategy of indoctrination that allows no personal variations in the expression of devotion to the national cause.

Varying Closures: Against Monolithic Narratives

Centripetal forces in many of the texts do gain victory over the oppositional forces. This is apparent in the common "positive" narrative closures: a decision is made in favor of the kibbutz (joining in, staying in, obeying the rules, and being accepted by the group) and a cohesive group is successfully formed, whose members agree to the uniformity it demands. The necessary compromises in most of these texts are made by the individual, who agrees to pay the price of private inconvenience for the sake of participation in the collective project. The case of the couple Menachem and Hannah in Maletz's *Maaglot* is a most obvious example: despite the continuous humiliation they suffer and the various pressures inflicted upon them, and albeit their acknowledgment of the malfunctioning of the commune in terms of care for and support of the individual, and its rigid adherence to irrational rules, they develop a strong sense of belonging to the kibbutz and experience it as their extended family. A long and detailed portrayal of their sufferings ends with a conciliatory springtime scene describing their satisfaction in an evening walk with their three sons on the kibbutz footpaths. "It was all worthwhile," Menachem whispers to his wife in the concluding line of the novel (Maletz, 1945, p. 260).

In the mid-1960s, Amos Oz suggests such a conciliatory closure to his kibbutz novel *Makom Acher* (*Another Place*) (1966): at the end of a series of scandalous affairs that expose strong subversive currents, a harmonious final scene erases all estrangements and disruptions and restores the initial supposedly balanced, tranquil state.[19] Oz's *Makom Acher* may be read as an ironic parody on the earlier narratives, in which the reconciliatory final scene is part of the rhetoric of indoctrination: Rachel who decides to join the kibbutz in Ever Hadani's novel despite her understanding of the uniquely problematic position of women in it,[20] Efrayim who goes back to the Alfalfa, Miriam, the urban woman of Shenhar's "Prazon," who at a moment of crisis recognizes her love of a kibbutz member (thus affirming the model of vital manhood dictated by the kibbutz norms) and decides to join him there—all these and many other hesitant literary protagonists end up voting for the system they at least partially resent and agree to take their place in it as responsible, committed members.

Whatever the direct circumstances under which such an outcome is achieved (very often it is a love affair that is successfully realized), it produces a fortified trust in the collective goals and a sense of their satisfactory achievement. This is obviously a recruiting narrative at its best: it constitutes a powerful affirmation of the ruling norms and strongly advocates the superiority of the kibbutz and what it represents as the sole route for realizing national agendas. The suppression of opposing tendencies is conceptualized as due concession for a worthy cause. The conclusions thus established are that only an absolute eradication of individual interests and needs, with no exception, may enable the accomplishment of the hopes of resettlement in the extremely harsh and demanding Jewish homeland.

A small number of texts end with an outright rejection of the kibbutz, embodied in departure or suicide. Even in these relatively rare cases, it may be claimed that what in fact takes place is a removal of negative elements for the benefit of a stronger, more cohesive group. Nevertheless, these open rejections, as well as the undercurrents that emerge in the more conciliatory narrative, point to uncertainty and doubt that the texts acknowledge and to which they give voice. The insights acquired due to the constant mobility of the protagonists—in and out of the kibbutz entity—remain present in the blood stream of the cultural and political system that literature represents. A recognition is allowed of the implications of the indoctrinating demand of early Social Zionism, to which the kibbutz most rigidly obeyed, for an elimination of any personal variations in the commitment and devotion to the national cause. This exposes the hidden seams of the unifying Israeli meta-narrative at the time of its creation. Literature thus anticipates the counter-narrative of the second and third generations of the national revolution in general and its manifestation in second and third generations of Kibbutz literature in particular. Before the melting-pot ethos' strict demand for homogeneity reached its climax, it had already been refuted in early kibbutz literature, which manifested a remarkable sensitivity to its possible oppressiveness and to the need of a more pluralistic, multiculturalist and democratic approach.

Notes

1. Brenner (1955 [1909]).
2. On the kibbutz as an ultimate realization of "Israeliness" and the holy shrine of the social Zionist ideology, see Oz Almog (1997), particularly pp. 351–82.
3. On the kibbutz in the visual arts in the first half of the twentieth century, see Tali Tamir (2005).
4. The definition of the period under discussion relies on the assumption that the 1950s were years of change in terms of collective consciousness and its literary correlates. These changes, which began following the establishment of the State of Israel, are of relevance to the issue of the kibbutz: a shift toward the ethos of *mamlachtiyut* (republicanism), which led to the kibbutz's loss of status as a principal site of re-alization of national agendas and as an elite society leading historical processes. A discussion of the reflection of these changes in literature and consequent develop-ments in kibbutz literary representations in the following decades are beyond the scope of the present chapter.
5. See the list of works referred to in this chapter in the bibliography section. Tax-onomies of kibbutz literature are included in Schorr and Hadomi (1990) and Kritz and Kritz (1997).
6. The works composing the corpus under consideration were written both by authors who were kibbutz members and by outsiders. The intricate issue of the confronta-tion between kibbutz-member writers and their audiences inside the kibbutzim, and the effect of this confrontation on the literary materials, is a most crucial one and has been dealt with elsewhere (see Shula Keshet, 1994, 1995). The present discussion investigates kibbutz representations in literature regardless of the specific interpersonal circumstance within which they were created.
7. See a discussion of the private and collective family in the kibbutz in writer Zvi Schatz's short essay "Al ha-Kvutza" ("About the Group," 1929 [1918]): "The working people in their land will constitute a new family based on a new religion. On the foundation of the closeness of the souls rather than blood relations this fam-ily will arise" writes Schatz, who was among the leading initiators of the idea of communal settlement (Ibid., p. 93). Researchers who have written on the issue of the kibbutz as an extended family are, among others, Yonina Talmon in her *Family and Community in the Kibbutz* (1972), Oz Almog in *ha-Tsabar—Dyokan* (1997, p. 353), and Yaara Bar-On, in her analytical–autobiographical notes entitled "The Family in the Kibbutz" (2004).
8. The ritual of assembling to the sound of the kibbutz bell is a significant component of Nathan Bistritski's novel *Yamim ve-Leilot* (*Days and Nights*) (1940; an extended version of the novel was initially published in 1926). The bell is one of the many symbolic items in this novel, all of which are recruited to the mythologization of communal ceremonies.
9. The coordination of work assignment is a most crucial function in the kibbutz life as represented in literature. Such works as S. Yizhar's "Efrayim Hozer la-Aspeset"

("Efrayim Returns to the Alfalfa") (1978 [1938]), M. Z. Valfovski's story *Yeled Yulad Lanu* (*A Child Will Be Born to Us*) (1940), David Maletz's novel *Maaglot* (*Circles*) (1945), and many others demonstrate how the work coordinator's responsibility for the just and equal division of work, which may best serve the various branches of the kibbutz economy and the principal economic interest of the kibbutz, and at the same time support national goals, arose deepest passions of anger, envy, and discontent. Often it generated feelings of inferiority and bitter resentment on the part of individual members. Some of the vehement conflicts that literature portrays (which will be discussed later in this chapter) therefore start, or find their overt expression, around the work coordinator's table after the evening meal, where preparations for the following working day are carried out.

10. Bistritski's *Yamim ve-Leilot* (which follows the collective text that he had edited, *Kehiliyateinu* (1922)) builds up the drama of the formation (and destruction) of the group in a series of meetings of the commune members for the purpose of carrying out personal "confessions," as was the habit in ha-Shomer ha-Tsair movement (see an extensive discussion of this drama in Keshet, 1995). A version of such meetings is the routine weekly assemblies of all kibbutz members for the discussion and vote on all private and collective matters. Yizhar's "Efrayim Chozer la-Aspeset" and Maletz's *Maaglot* are among the texts that focus on the significant, sometimes tragic, implications of the decisions thus taken.

11. As in Moshe Shamir's *Hu Halach ba-Sadot* (*His Beat Led through the Fields*) (1947).

12. Collective singing and dancing is a ritual performed by the literary figures in almost all literary representation of the time and is a most dominant signifier of collective life. It commonly generates the group intimate union. It appears, as a crucial act of unification (sometimes ironically portrayed), in times of happiness and in times of crises. One famous collective singing scene, echoing many others, is the opening scene of Yizhar's "Efrayim Hozer la-Aspeset." The irony with which it is described anticipates the problematics of communal life that the story presents through the eyes of its agitated protagonist.

13. The biblical Hebrew word "prazon" means an open town, with no surrounding defense walls.

14. On "conquering" (*kibbush*) as the common terminology used to express the successful achievement of collective goals in the discourse of the early settlement era, see Naveh (2000, p. 82).

15. Quoted from Zemach's story "Shimshon u-Miriam Banu Beitam" ("Samson and Miriam Built Their Home") (1965 [1938]), p. 239. My translation from Hebrew.

16. As, for example, is the case of Batia in Schatz's "Batia," Miriam in Zemach's "Shlomo u-Miriam Banu Beitam," Rachel in Ever Hadani's *Tzrif ha-Etz*, Chava in Shenhar's "Prazon," Teo and Geula in Shenhar's "Lehof ha-Kineret" (1960 [–]), Cahva in Valfovski's "Yeled Yulad Lanu," and Hirsh Malech in Yehuda Yaari's "Darchei Ish" ("A Man's Ways") (1969 [1938]).

17. Ernst and Franz Reinish in Bistritski's *Yamim ve-Leilot,* Yosef Landa in Yaari's *Keor Yahel,* Shulamit and Rivka in Ever Hadani's *Tzrif ha-Etz,* Hirsh Malech in Yaari's "Darchei Ish," Tnuva in Hameiri's *Tnuva,* the group that splits from the settlers of the Negev in the Sened's *Adama Lelo Tzel,* Gershon in Maletz's short story "Resulkot" ("Crushes"), and Yaakov and Miriam in his "Sdakim" ("Cracks") (1947).

18. See, among other instances of such a confession, the short text entitled "Kvuzateinu ha-Rishona" ("Our first Group") signed "Dror," in the opening section of *Kehiliyateinu* (pp. 19–23).

19. See my discussion of these subversive currents in my essay on Amos Oz's early literature (Milner, 2005).

20. Rachel openly expresses her reservation regarding women's statues in the kibbutz and her suspicion that the conventional system of exploitation had not ceased to exit in it (Ever Hadani, 1930, pp. 92–96). She nevertheless obeys the orders of her heart and joins kibbutz Tzrif ha-Etz, ready to pay the unique prices demanded of women.

Bibliography

Kibbutz Novels and Short Stories

Bistritski, N. ed. *Kehiliyateinu* (Our Community). Kibbutz Alef, Haifa-Jedda Road: ha-Shomer ha-Tsair Movement, 1922.

———. *Yamim ve-Leilot* (*Days and Nights*). Merchavia: Sifriat Poalim, 1940.

Brenner, Y. H. "Agav Urcha" ("By the Way"). In *The Complete Works of Y. H. Brenner*, Vol. 1. 275–82. Tel Aviv: Hakibbutz Hameuchad Publishing, 1955.

Ever Hadani, A. *Tzrif ha-Etz* (*Wooden Hut*). Tel Aviv: Mizpah Publishing, 1930.

Hameiri, A. *Tnuva*. Tel Aviv: Shreberk Publishing, 1946 [1934].

Levin-Talmai, E. *Leet Ohalim* (*In the Time of Tents*). Mercahvia: Sifriat Poalim, 1949.

Maletz, D. *Maaglot* (*Circles*). Tel Aviv: Am Oved Publishing, 1945.

———. "Resulkot" ("Crushes"); "Sdakim" (Cracks). In *Hathatim ba-Derech*, 17–44, 45–62. Tel Aviv: Beterm Publishing, 1947.

Oz, A. *Makom Acher* (*Another Place*). Tel Aviv: Sifriat Poalim, 1966.

Reichenstein, S. *Raishit* (*Genesis*). Tel Aviv: Am Oved Publishing and Kibbutz Ein Harod, 1943.

Schatz, Z. "Batia." In *Al Gvul ha-Dmama* (*On the Verge of Silence*), 16–70. Tel Aviv: Davar Publishing, 1918.

———. "Al ha-Kvutza" ("About the Group"). In *Al Gvul ha-Dmama* (*On the Verge of Silence*), 87–98. Tel Aviv: Davar Publishing, 1929 [1918].

Sened, Y. and A. Sened. *Adama Lelo Tzel* (*A Land without a Shadow*). Tel Aviv: Hakibbutz Hameuchad Publishing, 1950.

Shamir, M. *Hu Halach ba-Sadot* (*His Beat Led through the Field*s). Merchavia: Sifriat Poalim, 1929 [1918].

Shenhar, I. "Prazon." In *Short Stories*, 81–114. Jerusalem: Bialik Institution, 1960 [1939].

———. "Lehof ha-Kineret" ("On the Beach of the Kineret"). In *Sipurei Itzhak Shenhar* (*The Stories of Itzhak Shenhar*), 118–41. Jerusalem: Bialik Institution, 1960.

Valfovski, M. Z. "Yeled Yulad Lanu" ("A Child will be Born to Us"). In *Yeled Yulad Lanu*, 7–40. Tel Aviv: Hakibbutz Hameuchad Publishing, 1950 [1940].

Yaari, Y. *Keor Yahel* (*Like a Burning Light*). Merchavia: Sifriat Poalim, 1937.

———. "Darchei Ish" ("A Man's Ways"). In *Drachimn ve-Ohalim* (*Roads and Tents*), 5–64. Jerusalem: Ogdan Publishing, 1969 [1938].

Yizhar's, S. "Efrayim Hozer la-Aspeset" ("Efrayim Returns to the Alfalfa"). Tel Aviv: Hakibbutz Hameuchad Publishing, 1978 [1938].

Zemach, S. "Shimshon u-Miriam Banu Beitam" ("Samson and Miriam Built Their Home"). In *Stories*, 231–72. Jerusalem: Ydidim Publishing, 1965 [1938].

Research and Criticism

Almog, O. *ha-Tsabar—Dyokan* (*The Sabra—A Profile*). Tel Aviv: Am Oved Publishing, 1997.

Bar-On, Y. "ha-Mishpacha ba-Kibbutz" ("The Family in the Kibbutz"). In *Al Ahavat Em Umora Av—Mabat Acher Al ha-Mishpacha* (*On Mother's Love and Fear of Father—Another Look at the Family*), edited by Aviad Kleinberg, 20–79. Tel Aviv and Jerusalem: Tel Aviv University Publishing and Keter, 2004.

Keshet, S. "Raishit ha-Roman ha-Kibbutzi, Safrut Idiologit Bein Korim, Yotzer ve-Yetzira." Dissertation, Tel Aviv University, 1994.

———. *ha-Machteret ha-Nafshit: Al Raishit ha-Roman ha-Kibbutzi* (*Underground Soul. Ideological Literature: The Case of the Early Kibbutz Novel*). Tel Aviv: The Porter Institute for Poetics and Semiotics and Hakibbutz Hameuchad Publishing, 1995.

Kritz, R. and O. Kritz. *Stories of the Kibbutz*. 3 Vols. Tel Aviv: Pura Publishers, 1997.

Milner, Iris. "Sipur Mishpachti—Yezirato ha-Mukdemet shel Amos Oz Leor *Sipur Al Ahava ve-Choshech*" ("A Family Story: the Early Works of Amos Oz in Light of his *A Tale of Love and Darkness*"). *Yisrael: Ktav Et le-Cheker ha-Zionut u-Medinat Yisrael—Historia, Tarbut ve-Chevra* (*Israel: a Journal for the Study of Zionism and the State of Israel—History, Culture and Society*) 7 (Spring 2005): 73–106.

Naveh, H. "Dyokan ha-Kvutza Agav Urcha—Haya O Lo Haya? Od Meshel Y. H. Brenner" ("A Portrait of the Group By the Way: Had it Ever Existed? More of Y. H. Brenner"). In *Safrut ve-Chevra ba-Tarbut ha-Ivrit ha-Chadasha (Literature and Society in the New Hebrew Culture*), edited by Yehuydit Bar-El, Yigal Schwartz, and Tamar Hess, 82–100. Tel Aviv and Jerusalem: Hakibbutz Hameuchad & Keter, 2000.

Schorr, S. and L. Hadomi. *Recounting the Kibbutz*. Tel Aviv: Poalim Publishers, 1990.

Talmon, Y. *Family and Community in the Kibbutz*. Cambridge, MA and London: Harvard University Press, 1972.

Tamir, T. *Lina Meshutefet—Kvutza ve-Kibbutz ba-Todaa ha-Israelit* (*Togetherness: The 'Group' and the Kibbutz in Collective Israeli Consciousness*). Tel Aviv: Tel Aviv Museum Publishers, 2005. A catalog of an exhibition in Tel Aviv Museum.

11

From *Sabra* to *Children of the Sun*: Kibbutz Films from the 1930s to the 2000s

Eldad Kedem and Gilad Padva

In the film *Sabra* (*Tzabar*, dir. Alexander Ford, 1933), the first fiction film made in Palestine/Eretz Israel, Jewish settlers ("pioneers," *halutzim*) from Russia arrive at a desolate place in Palestine. There they establish a communal settlement that will develop into a flourishing kibbutz. Seven decades later, in *The Galilee Eskimos* (*Eskimosim ba'Galeel*, dir. Jonathan Paz, 2007), these settlers are now elderly people, residents in a nursing home. They discover that their families and the youth have all left and their kibbutz has been sold to a private entrepreneur. What has happened between these two periods? How does the Israeli cinematic representation of the kibbutz reflect the changes, problems, and dilemmas of the kibbutzim in Israeli society? How does the metamorphosis of the kibbutz in Israeli cinema relate to significant changes in that cinema itself? And, what are the ideological implications embodied in these kibbutz films?

This article presents a review of the cinematic discourse on the kibbutz, as reflected in about thirty films that engage with the kibbutz, from the 1930s onward. This is an invitation to a journey, one that is nostalgic but also critical, a journey that follows the portrayal of the kibbutz in Israeli cinema, mainly in fiction films, from 1930 to 2009.

Myths of Beginning and Continuity: 1930–1939

The kibbutz first appears on-screen, in the earliest films ever made in Palestine/Eretz Israel, in the 1930s. These are mainly documentaries, propaganda films, and docudramas that glorify the Zionist Jewish immigration ("going up," *aliyah*) to Israel and the establishment of kibbutzim in the frontier areas near the borders. The cinema pioneers in this period not only documented the Zionist enterprise, but were also deeply identified with it, and considered themselves as a significant part of the efforts to establish a Zionist national home in Palestine. These early films, with their typical pathos, embrace the landscapes, the Biblical antiquities, the urban and peripheral settlements, and mainly the construction of the country: developing roads, water supply, electricity, agriculture, and industry; building houses and institutions, as well as the developing leisure culture in the bigger cities. The films are characterized by pathos-replete dialogues, glorifying voice-overs, emotional subtitles, and sentimental, stirring sound track.[1]

Documentaries and docudramas like *Sabra* (*Tzabar*), *Land of Promise* (*Le'Chaim Hadashim*, dir. Yehuda Lehman, 1933), and *This Is the Land* (*Zot Hee Ha'Aretz*, dir. Baruch Agadati, 1935) manifest a selective testimony and memory of a complicated, crucial period, full of hardship and agonies, mystifying the consolidation and realization of the communal vision. These films highlight the settlers' arrival in the land, their making a place for themselves, and their agricultural production on the kibbutz. The films function as a genuine platform for an idealistic synthesis of the return of the Jews to the land of their forefathers and the renewal and repossession of the land. The narrative of these films—particularly the opening scenes—echoes another sort of memory: the mythical, Biblical tale of arrival in the promised land. As in the Biblical story, the new immigrants are going on a journey to their new/old land, seeking to find themselves and to survive in a harsh environment. Possessing the land—the soil—embodies a temporal and physical connection, an experience that reflects both the ancient contact with this land, and a tradition passed down from farmers to sons.

Panoramic views of the kibbutzim reveal fields and settlements, reflecting both the real and symbolic aspects of the Zionist socialist ideas. Sequences presenting agricultural work on the kibbutz (edited in a *montage* technique) create a magic and fascination, symbolizing a cosmic, actual sequence of nature's progress and the natural cyclicality of human labor: plowing, sowing, fruition, blossoming, harvest, rest, and so on. Sights of people working in the field embody a primordial memory of ownership and belonging, an ancient scene, in which possessing the land is embodied in the plow and the furrow. Labor is idealized in these films as the "productivization" of the exilic Jewish nation according to the socialist trends of the Zionist movement. In the consolidation of the Zionist discourse, the Zionist pioneer and the kibbutz were prototypes of the Zionist revolution and its high ideals: return to the Jewish homeland, redemption of the land, making the country flourish, creating a solidarity between the many types of immigrants, and embracing communality and a volunteer spirit for national missions.

The focus on the human body and its daily hard work in the fields, often embodied as a semi-naked male physique, emphasizes and even (homo) eroticizes the organic connection of the farmers to this particular land.[2] The pioneer's body is instrumentalized according to the Socialist Zionist ideology that glorified physical labor as its greatest achievement because such labor was signifier of modern qualities and efficiency. Beside the corporeal and physical aspects, these films emphasize the importance of cultural rituals and ceremonies and their transcendental, spiritual meanings. For example, in the film *Land of Promise*, the famous composer Daniel Sambursky performs his new song "Song of the Valley" (in Hebrew: "Shir Ha'Emek" *aka* "Ba'ah Menuha La'Yage'a") at the kibbutz dining room. These rituals constitute a mystical (mythical) manifestation of belonging to the land and a sort of secular alternative to ultra-Orthodox Jewish practices, as Almog Oz (1997) suggests: "Like the Hora dancing, singing was also a constitutive in the ecstatic worship of the community—a stimulating and unifying mechanism, which is fundamentally similar to the choir singing at the synagogue."[3]

The cinematic collective memory idealizes life on the kibbutz in an era in which this life was extremely arduous, both physically and mentally. The cinematic representation distances the kibbutz and its significant problems from the actual reality and exaggerates it as a romantic, pastoral, harmonious, and perfect place. This ideological encoding of the kibbutz includes sequences of herds of cattle and flocks of sheep, agricultural machinery, and vistas of sunrises and sunsets that evoke a sort of "transplanted memory" of the Russian or German countryside, rather than the aridity of the Middle East. One of the effects of this mystification is the perception of the kibbutz as a manifestation of endless vitality and omnipotence: a plethora of spaces, animals, flowing water, etc. Such a description is detached from the concrete experience of the kibbutzim, which were (and still are) constrained by the market economy and struggling with a dearth of means of production and a lack of equity capital.

Absorption of Holocaust Survivors and Rituals of Initiation: 1939–1947

Between 1936 and 1948, only a few fiction films were made in Palestine/Eretz Israel, and most of these were documentaries and newsreels. After 1936, film production ground to a halt, partly because of the technical difficulties in moving to new sound systems, but mostly because of the local political events, including murderous Palestinian attacks on Jews in Jaffa and neighborhoods in south Tel Aviv, and the World War II. Until the end of the 1948 War of Independence, and the establishment of the State of Israel, a very limited number of fiction films were produced, and most of these were English-speaking copro-ductions. The films of this period relate mainly to the World War II and the Holocaust.

In the films *My Father's House* (*Beit Avi*, dir. Herbert Klein, 1947–1949), *The Great Promise* (*Dim'at Ha'Nehama Ha'Gdolah*, dir. Joseph Leitz, 1947–1950), and *Out of Evil* (*Mi'Klalah le'Bracha*, dir. Helmer Larsky, 1947–1950), a thematic change can be seen in the cinematic portrayal of the kibbutz. The depiction of making the land flourish and of agricultural production is replaced by a portrayal of the kibbutz as a haven, an institution that can both contain and heal the traumas of the Holocaust survivors. This change is also manifested in the characteriza-tion of the kibbutz space: the former space of production now becomes a place of initiation and integration of the newcomers and of transforming them into Zionist subjectivities. Additional motives of pioneering, agri-cultural working, and communality support the image of the kibbutz as one big family, a personal and collective home, supporting and nurturing the Holocaust survivors.

Considering the dramatic events of this period, the kibbutz is perceived and represented in these films as a counter-metaphor to the crisis and trauma of the Holocaust and its consequent sense of annihilation, and perhaps also to the Zionist establishment's feelings of guilt and helpless-ness. This theme is embodied in these films by a passage from destruction and annihilation to revival and rebirth; from orphanhood to family; from detachment and estrangement to solidarity, belonging, and continuity. The kibbutz, as an open environment, characterized by physical work-ing in the fields, is contrasted to the closed ghetto and the stereotype of the Jew who lives by *luft gescheft* (in Yiddish: "air business"), that is, nonproductive or nonphysical, intellectual work.

In a way, kibbutz life is merely the background in these films. Instead of its *production value*, the kibbutz is now represented according to an *exchange value*, embracing the national Zionist mechanism of absorption, of ingathering of the exiles. It functions as a refuge and provides social and mental support to the children and older refugees, helping them to overcome numerous obstacles: the trauma of the Holocaust, their loss of family members, and the social and cultural difficulties inherent in relocating themselves to a new place. Mythologized as a sort of paradise with endless vitality, the kibbutz is represented as an ideal site for education and reeducation, transforming the foreigner, the other, into "one of us." The earlier socialist themes—redemption of the land and of the human being—are now bound up with the idea of salvation and rebirth of the survivors, and the ethos of ingathering of the exiles and transforming them into native Jews of Palestine/Eretz Israel. Miri Talmon suggests: "One of the significant manifestations of this identity change, is the immigrants' melting into the circle of the dancing children, or the group of children working in the field."[4]

The narrative of initiation of the Holocaust survivors accompanied by rituals of passage is a prevalent theme in the kibbutz films of this period. Rites of passage are rituals that follow any change in space, condition, social location, or age. Victor Turner, following van Gennep, suggests that rituals of passage are characterized by three stages: detachment, liminality, and reunion.[5] The arrival of the Holocaust survivors at the kibbutz manifests the first two stages of the initiation ritual, both the detachment and the entering into a liminal state. It specifies a detachment from their previous social structure and cultural conditions. Their entry into kibbutz life involves an initial alienation that evolves into a transitional state in which the subjects first detach and then attach themselves in their efforts to become part of the new society. According to Turner, liminal entities are neither here nor there; they exist in between the social loci formed by law, costume, tradition, and ritual.[6] This process necessitates learning and ends in an acceptance by the collective. Acceptance by the kibbutz, or the symbolic order, or the nation, marks an entrance into a new historical and cultural phase. At the same time, the idealization of kibbutz life as paradise is bound in these films with an idealization of the absorption of Holocaust survivors that actually was difficult in the kibbutz, as it was in any other place in Israel before and after the 1948 War of Independence.

From Heroic Memories to Nostalgia: 1948–1964

Only a few fiction films were produced in Israel in the 1950s, again mostly coproductions and English-speaking films. More established and organized filmmaking started only in the early 1960s. A significant portion of the 1950 films focus on diverse aspects of the kibbutz: *Ceasefire* (*Hafugah*, dir. Amar, 1950), *Pillar of Fire* (*Amud Ha'Esh*, dir. Larry Frisch, 1959), *They Were Ten* (*Hem Hayu Assarah*, dir. Baruch Dinar,

1960), the Hollywood production *Exodus* (dir. Otto Preminger, 1960), *Blazing Sands* (*Holot Lohatim*, dir. Raphael Nussbaum, 1960), *I Like Mike* (dir. Peter Frye, Israel 1960), *What a Gang!* (*Havurah She'Kazot*, dir. Ze'ev Havatzelet, 1962), *The Hero's Wife* (*Eshet Ha'Gibor*, dir. Peter Frei, 1963), and *Eight against One* (*Shmonah Be'I'kvot Ehad*, dir. Menahem Golan, 1964).[7] The films are part of a large group that portrayed the Zionist struggle in the War of Independence and the establishment of the State.

Defined as National Heroic Cinema, these films center around a brave protagonist who is a warrior with high ideals, willing to sacrifice himself for the State. In an era in which a local cinematic tradition of narratives and genres had not yet developed, the films are based on Hollywood war films: the main plot focuses on a hero, a group of combatants and a national militaristic mission, obstacles, and physical and mental difficulties. Sometimes, this plot is accompanied by a subplot of a love story between the male warrior-hero and a woman (e.g., in *Pillar of Fire* and *Ceasefire*). Zionist nationalism is manifested in glorifying the "illegal" Jewish immigration of Holocaust survivors, their absorption, and the socialization of the newcomers (particularly the so-called Oriental Jews), and recruitment of gentile supporters who are identified with the Zionist struggle (e.g., *Exodus* and *Hill 24 Doesn't Answer*). Notably, the same national and heroic themes were also popular in other cultural domains in the late 1940s and the 1950s including literature, poetry, theater, and folk songs.[8]

Significantly, the kibbutz in this third set of films is located on the frontier, near the borders. Its protagonists are part of the genealogy of stories and myths of the birth of the nation. Indeed, the plot of *They Were Ten* (nine male pioneers and one female pioneer establish a colony in a remote place) repeats the story of *Sabra* (1933) and returns to the chronotype of a story of origins, by dramatizing and theatricalizing the hardships of the first communes in the country in the late nineteenth century. *Exodus* and *What a Gang!* retell the story of the founders, the underground movements, the illegal Jewish immigration, the Palmach (the military wing of the Hagana, the precursor of the Israel Defense Forces), and more. All of these films offer a sort of genealogy of the stories of heroism and sacrifice, a struggle that is taken up not only by men, but also by women and children.

Stories of war and frontiers are usually associated with the definition of a border between the inside and the outside, between the nation and its enemies. These films, however, were aimed at creating a common ethos, in an era in which about half of the Jewish population in the country was comprised of immigrants who had arrived in Israel during the 1950s.[9] The construction of a common denominator on the frontier is manifested by the socialization of the newcomer into the combat unit and the kibbutz, a metonym of their assimilation and subordination to the symbolic order of the State. For example, the Oriental (i.e., Sephardi or Mizrachi or Yemenite) protagonist in *Ceasefire* is a kibbutz member and a Palmach combatant who eventually returns to the kibbutz. The recruited bunch in *What a Gang!* and the children's group in *Eight against One* absorb and educate an immigrant of Oriental Jewish origins who becomes an integral part of the group/kibbutz. In *Pillar of Fire*, American Jews join the struggle. The wish to create consensus, integration, and brotherhood between newcomers and veteran immigrants is also embodied, in some of these films, by a romantic subplot that transgresses ethnic and cultural boundaries. In the Israeli version of the Hollywood war films, the love story is not only a union between the male protagonist and his sweetheart, but also an ethnic and intersocial union, endorsing the ideology of the melting pot.

Some of these films present the traces of a native Jewish generation— the Sabra culture with emphasis on exploring the country on foot (*Exodus*), a dangerous trek with backpack and water canteen (*Blazing Sands*), eating and sleeping in tents (*What a Gang!*), or revealing a landscape of Eucalyptus trees, dusty trails, and oases (*The Hero's Wife* and *Eight against One*). These characteristics of a native Jewish culture are identified with the kibbutzim and youth movements. This culture nurtures the connection between body and land, and of group trips around the country as Almog suggests: "patrols and navigations were part of the didactic menu, and practiced the field studies that were learned in the youth movements."[10]

In regard to the changing cinematic presentation of the kibbutz during this phase, there was a transition from expressivity to instrumentality, which we can term as the National Security Code: the kibbutz becomes heavily instrumentalized by the State, while its everyday life is misrepresented. The cinematic articulation does not include the communal life of the kibbutz or the individual's life *per se*, but emphasizes the national values and imperatives, particularly with regard to issues of security and defense. The land is perceived as a territory that must be possessed and defended, and holding on to the territory becomes the main purpose of the protagonists. The spatial language of the State appears to be taking over the space of the kibbutz. The films presuppose the existence of the kibbutz and represent only its national aspects, glorifying the Zionist struggle.[11]

In this phase of the establishment of the Israeli film industry, the kibbutz functions as a familiar brand. Films of this period are inspired by popular genres and formulas. For example, *They Were Ten* is a sort of Western; *The Hero's Wife* is a melodrama; *Pillar of Fire* is a war film; *Eight against One* is a youth and adventure film. *Exodus*, which appealed to an American audience, emphasized the kibbutz as a brand or label. The use of the kibbutz as a brand, and the National Security Code, reflects the ideological function of the kibbutz films in this period. In actuality, although kibbutzim are still privileged and appreciated, the option of living on a kibbutz is becoming less popular. Consequently, these films try to persuade viewers to volunteer to work on or live on a kibbutz. This message is emphasized by the glorification of the kibbutz as a sort of frontier and heroic enterprise.

Detachment and Disappearance: 1964–1980

From the 1950s and 1960s, Israeli society underwent dramatic changes.[12] The collectivist norms and socialist values were weakened in favor of individualist and more capitalistic norms. Individual aspirations for material achievement, paralleling the development of a consumer, leisure, and recreation culture, became dominant. Generally, the diverse energies—economic, social, and mental motivations—were channeled into existential and material practices relating to the present and future, rather than the past and its ethos of a socialist, pioneering kibbutz. These changes in the cultural and artistic fields meant liberation from the need to create a didactic, recruited art, and an opening up to the dynamics of the market forces, as well as artistic and individual autonomy. These dynamics gradually became part of the Israeli cinema. The most significant change was the gradual decline of the National Heroic Cinema and the emergence of two different cinema types—individualist/personal cinema and popular ethnic cinema ("Bourekas" films).[13] Established in the 1960s, Judd Ne'eman perceives these two cinema genres as opposing the ideological and aesthetic values of Zionist Realism.[14]

Two films that are considered as the beginning of the individualist cinema and the ethnic cinema, *A Hole in the Moon* (*Hor Ba'Levanah*, dir. Uri Zohar, 1965) and *Sallah Shabati* (dir. Ephraim Kishon, 1964), use the kibbutz as a starting point. Both criticize it and prefer to concentrate on other themes and values. In effect, by the mid-1960s, the cinematic kibbutz had lost its power. The innovative and avant-garde film *A Hole in the Moon* is an anarchistic parody on Zionist myths and the socialist ethos of the pioneers. The ridiculing of the kibbutz ethos takes place in the first sequence of this film. The new immigrant arrives in Palestine on a raft, wearing a smart suit and tie, smoking a cigar, and drinking whiskey. Shortly after, he goes to the desert, opens a kiosk, and lives idly. After a few days, he discovers that another kiosk has opened opposite his own. The two merchants argue with each other and then decide to go downtown together and establish a cinema industry in Eretz Israel. The parody operates to demonstrate the decadence of archaic norms and ideals. *A Hole in the Moon* parodies the images of the pioneer and the kibbutz as represented in the local cinema of the 1930s and 1940s: the pioneer who wears khaki shorts and shirt, uses a hoe, makes the desert bloom, and works from sunrise to sunset in agriculture, building a flourishing kibbutz. This pioneer is also a part of the collective, working in the name of his homeland, rather than a private entrepreneur. For the younger generation of filmmakers of individualist cinema, inspired by global modernism and existentialist cinema and literature, the kibbutz is associated with provinciality, conservatism, and anachronism. This negative perspective offers a sort of Oedipal rebellion against the "founding fathers" of the Heroic National Cinema and against the national Zionist founders of the kibbutz.[15]

Sallah Shabati (1964)—a (mostly) comic story about a family of Jewish immigrants of North African origins in the 1950s—demonstrates a similar paradigm in regard to the representation of the kibbutz, which it exploits as a narrative and ideological starting point. *Sallah Shabati* criticizes kibbutz values and opens the way to a new ethnic cinema (which prefers not to relate to kibbutzim at all). This film explicitly and genuinely criticizes the Zionist establishment, and particularly the kibbutz. It represents kibbutz members as paternalistic and arrogant. It sees kibbutz members as operating out of selfish interests and using newcomers as a cheap labor force, contrasted to the original socialist vision of equality. Implicitly, the film embodies a new set of values, which is partly a petit bourgeois and capitalist ethos (the newcomers' wish to buy an apartment and their caring for the material future of their family and siblings), and partly ethnic and religious (the association of the North African immigrant with the Jewish tradition and religion, in contrast to secular Zionism). Ne'eman contends that the protagonist in *Sallah Shabati* is "all-Oriental," ridiculing the Western Ashkenazi myth of pioneering, and denying the most sacred value of Zionist socialism— the religion of labor.[16] This film, however, also ridicules American

Jews who help Israel by planting trees and are constantly deceived by the corrupted establishment.

Diverse expressions of individualism, particularly that of leaving the kibbutz, appear in some of the films of this period. Implicitly and explicitly featured as a space of transition, the kibbutz can be left easily in favor of another place. In *Every Bastard, a King* (*Kol Mamzer Melekh*, dir. Uri Zohar, 1967), for example, the kibbutz is a place seen only in passing, while in *He Walked in the Fields* and *Three Days and a Child* (*Shlosha Yamim Ve'Yeled*, dir. Uri Zohar, 1968), the kibbutz is a place to be left behind. The kibbutz in *Sallah Shabati* is also a place in which the protagonist neither lives nor belongs to, while the kibbutz members themselves represent a space without a location, a sort of ethos-in-motion. The protagonists in these films do not follow the values of continuity and holding the ground but, rather, live in temporary spaces: the newcomers' transit camp (in Hebrew: *Ma'abarah*), the spaces of the military and war (in *He Walked in the Fields* and the female-soldier in *Every Bastard, a King*), or the feeling of urban detachment in the big city (in *Three Days and a Child*).

In terms of genres, some motives from the previous period are explicitly expressed: leaving the kibbutz, the kibbutz as a place merely to be seen in passing, and issues of loyalty and betrayal. For example, Uri's preference in the cinematic version of *He Walked in the Fields*, for military service over kibbutz life, is interconnected with his father's "betrayal" (the latter prefers to continue his missions abroad) and the "betrayal" of his mother (who has an affair with another kibbutz member). The kibbutz is strictly represented in films of this period according to the National Security Code: soldiers and frontier people (*Every Bastard, a King*), Palmach and heroism (*He Walked in the Fields*), absorption of immigrants and the melting pot (*Sallah Shabati*), and archaic pioneering (*A Hole in the Moon* and *Three Days and a Child*).[17] Moreover, the geographical, moral, and emotional distancing from the kibbutz, and the alienation of some of the characters toward the kibbutz, indicates that the kibbutz has undergone change from a familiar place into a site of memory, an estranged different space. Only in the 1980s did the Israeli cinema begin to focus again on the kibbutz, particularly in films that challenge and provoke the ideals and values of the kibbutz society.[18]

Broken Myths and Critical Historiography: 1980–1990

In the 1980s, the Israeli cinema returned to a discussion of social, ethnic, and national conflicts, as well as comedies, teen films, candid-camera films, etc. In particular, there are two film categories that became canonical. One that criticized the norms and values prevalent in Israeli society—the military, the educational system, the kibbutz, and the various marginalized others, for example, Holocaust survivors, gay men, etc. The other was films of conflict, focusing on the conflict between Israelis and Palestinians and encounters between Arabs and Jews. Nurit Gertz classifies the films of the 1980s as "films of the foreigner and the transgressor," suggesting that this cinema concentrated on the political reality in Israel, focusing on the issue of Israel's social identity and its relationships with the surrounding world.[19] These two categories of films express and reflect a feeling of discontent and a growing contempt among Israeli leftist circles toward the militaristic heritage and the stagnation of the Labor Party. This process began in the crisis of trust between this party and its voters following the 1973 Yom Kippur War and the exposure of political corruption. The process intensified in the wake of dramatic political change—the upheaval of the Likud party's winning the election in 1977, the nationalist tendencies as reflected in the intensification of the Jewish settlements in the West Bank and Gaza Strip, and the Israeli invasion of Lebanon in 1982. The criticism of the kibbutz in the 1980s films can be perceived as a part of a broader moral crisis and reexamination of the Zionist ethos.

At the same time, the return to the kibbutz is present in many films in this period, a significant group of which return to the past in order to criticize the values and ethos of the Kibbutz: *Noa at 17* (*Noa Bat 17*, dir. Itzhak Tzepel Yeshurun, 1981), *Atalyah* (dir. Akiva Tevet, 1984), *Stalin's Disciples* (*Yaldei Stalin*, dir. Nadav Leviathan, 1987), *The Dreamers* (*Ha'Holmim*, dir. Uri Barbash, 1987), and, to a certain extent, *Intimate Story* (*Sipur Intimy*, dir. Nadav Leviathan, 1981), *On a Thin Rope* (*Al Hevel Dak*, dir. Michal Bat-Adam, 1981) and *Boy Meets Girl* (*Ben Loke'ach Bat*, dir. Michal Bat-Adam, 1982).[20] *Atalya, Stalin's Disciples, The Dreamers,* and *Noa at 17* return to the past by integrating two perspectives. One is the creation of a historical distance that enables a rational, sober, and critical perspective; the second is a political and ideological focusing that reflects an *a priori* discontent with the moral decadence and the present nationalist trends in Israeli society. Although the Likud party was in power during that period, the colonization of the occupied territories is also associated with the activist heritage of Zionism and the Labor Party. The Israeli public identifies the kibbutzim with the Labor Party. These films reflect significant changes in Israeli society and its relation to its national past, and particularly in regard to the kibbutz.

A significant theme in these films is the clash between the values and ideals of the kibbutz, and the desires and needs of the individual. Ideal collectivism and the demand for total equality are represented as the causes of the suppression of the individual, particularly the transgressor. In *The Dreamers*, it is the demand to give up all private property to the collective, including one's personal belongings, as much as unrequited love, that lead to the suicide of a young woman. The requirement that Noa will dress like everybody else, particularly in the uniform of the youth movement, generates anger, alienation, and despair in *Noa at 17*. The demand that the female Holocaust survivor will not claim individual reparation from Germany, or, rather, that she transfer the money to the communal fund in her kibbutz, is represented as an abusive and cruel attitude toward the ailing survivor in *Stalin's Disciples*. This film also mocks three cobblers, all of whom sport a big Stalin-like mustache.

The ideological totality and the life in a small, closed community severely damage the individual. Communal life encroaches upon even the most intimate moments in the lives of the individual kibbutz members. People perceive Atalya's different wardrobe (in *Atalya*) as a sexual provocation. Disturbing gazes and wicked gossip accompany her affair with an eighteen-year-old youth (Atalya, who is a war widow, is even nicknamed "The Black Widow," like a female spider who eats her male partner immediately after their copulation), and she is stigmatized as the kibbutz whore. Later she is almost raped by another kibbutz member. In *Stalin's Disciples*, kibbutz members belittle and look upon the male painter, who is not considered to be doing "productive" work, with contempt; and in *Noa at 17*, Noa's friends abandon her because of her desire for personal fulfillment, which transgresses the collective norms.

Israeli society now perceived the public nature of the discourse on personal needs as both an invasion of the private world of the kibbutz member and an avenue into the negative side of the community's life—the hypocrisy, gossip, stubbornness, arbitrariness, aggression, and wickedness that collective members express toward the individual. The films of the 1980s return to the kibbutz in order to expose, criticize, and undermine its myths and ethos in Israeli culture. Rather than a society of harmony, equality, and solidarity, the kibbutz becomes a conflicted site of quarrels and fights, a space in which the utopian dreams of social justice have degenerated into a violent, destructive society. Miri Talmon argues that *Noa at 17* reflects the decline both of collectivism and socialism and of social and moral norms. The kibbutz society and the Jewish rural settlement began to be exposed as disintegrating frameworks, stubbornly adhering to the now weakened ideals of Israeli society.[21] Meir Schnitzer refers to another film of this period, *Boy Meets Girl* (a story about a young city girl who joins a traumatizing children's group on a kibbutz), noting that this ostensive children's film is in effect the filmmaker Michal Bat-Adam's critique on the very idea of the kibbutz.[22]

The 1980s films on the kibbutz do not return to tell a story of dedication, continuity, or rearrangement. Rather, they return to it in order to continue their critique, which had already started in the mid-1960s. The kibbutz in the films of the 1980s continues to function as an available platform for a projection of historical lessons.[23] The use of the kibbutz as a site for the discussion of social and national conflicts had already been manifested in *Sallah Shabati* and, to a certain extent, in *He Walked in the Fields* and *Three Days and a Child*. This return to the kibbutz does not, however, offer the kibbutz an autonomous voice, but rather continues to subordinate the representation of the kibbutz to the National Code and to the political standpoint of the Israeli *auteur*, the critical left-wing filmmaker, who expressed his doubts about the kibbutz as early as the 1960s.

In a different perspective, the return to the familiar and recognized kibbutz, represented as conservative and archaic place—that same kibbutz which had become detached from the Israeli cinema in the late 1960s—was neither interesting nor attractive enough for the heterogeneous audience of the 1980s. In contrast, a return to the kibbutz that is articulated as "a place of otherness," strange and estranged—a place of sensations, scandals, sex, and even some hints of orgies and perversions—was much more appealing. In 1980s, in comparison to the 1960s and 1970s cinema, the kibbutz regained its status as a "sexy," tempting, and arousing domain. The spectacle of the 1930s (tractors and agricultural machinery) and of the 1950s and 1960s (war technologies) turned into a spectacle of sensations in the 1980s.

The (Broken) Dream, Memory, and Archive: 1991–2009

Since the end of the 1980s, Israeli cinema has entered a period that we define as postideological. This is an era of the gradual penetration of marginal audiences, for example, North African, Orthodox, and ultra-Orthodox Jews, into the center of the Israeli political map. Israeli culture has become more open to alternative narratives, new sensitivities, and a developing multiculturalism. The migration of about one million people from the former Soviet Union to Israel since the early 1990s has also contributed to this tendency of ethnic and cultural diversity and a discussion of other groups of new and old immigrants. This dynamic has become integrated in, and perhaps also stimulated some critical processes in Israeli culture, primarily the discourse of the new (post-Zionist) historians, centered in academia and the arts. This discourse combines criticism and the undermining of the hegemonic and homogeneous identity ruled by Zionism, with the employment of other narratives and identities that were previously repressed or silenced. According to Yael Munk, some of these films express a post-Sabra world, in which the Ashkenazi Israeli (of Western origin), a symbol of this hegemony, becomes a stranger and an exile in his own country and/or is involved in personal and family conflicts that are related to an unstable identity.[24]

In the films *No Names on the Doors* (*Ein Shemot Al He'Dlatot*, dir. Nadav Leviathan, 1996) and *No Longer 17* (*Lo Bat 17*, dir. Yitzhak Tzepel Yeshurun, 2003), *Sweet Mud* (*Adama Meshuga'at*, dir. Dror Shaul, 2006), *The Galilee Eskimos* (*Eskimosim ba'Galeel*, dir. Jonathan Paz, 2007), and, to a certain extent, *Operation Grandma* (*Mivtza Savta*, dir. Dror Shaul, 1999), and documentaries like *Mother of the Giv'atron* (*Imma Shel Ha'Giv'atron* [singing group], dir. Shahar Magen and Ayelet Gil, 2003), *Eight Twenty Eight* (*Shmoneh Esrim Ve'Shmoneh*, dir. Lavie Ben-Gal), *Children of the Sun* (*Yaldei Ha'Shemesh*, dir. Ran Tal, 2007), and *The Last Battle for Deganya* (*Ha'Krav Ha'Aharon Al Deganya*, dir. Yitzhak Rubin, 2009), the internal conflicts in the kibbutz society depicted in the films of the 1980s now become individual traumas and devastated feelings. The sense of trauma and loss is manifested in narratives and themes of deconstruction, displacement, homelessness, wanderings, transience, and internal or external exile. The family is spread across the world. In *No Longer 17*, the kibbutz founders are building a temporary encampment. Three brothers, former members of the kibbutz, cannot find a permanent home in *Operation Grandma*. Suicide and deportation feature in *No Names on the Doors*, childhood traumas in *Sweet Mud*, and traumas related to the long-traditional communal children's houses in *Children of the Sun*. These films constitute an inventory, listing what remains of memory, partly subjective and authentic and partly based on the recorded memory accumulated in the kibbutz archives. They reveal a closed circle: the kibbutz, which previously symbolized an antimodel to the exilic Jew—through rootedness, physical work in the field, a permanent, absorbing, and supportive home—is now represented through exilic themes: a sense of displacement, wandering, transience, and homelessness.

Intensifying the sense of crisis and trauma, these films directly and indirectly echoed the kibbutz society crisis, experienced from the mid-1980s onward, a crisis expressed in financial debts, followed by social and demographic fall out. Toward the end of the 1980s, a few clear voices forecasted the end of the kibbutz in its historical, communal form. In a continuous process, a large number of kibbutzim have been "privatized," transferring their responsibility for ensuring a livelihood from the kibbutz to its individual members. In privatized kibbutz, there is a separation between the kibbutz business and that of the community, a reduction in dependency of the members on their kibbutz, and a drastic reduction in the organization's staff. This (over) enthusiastic privatization, however, has resulted in a certain amount of social and personal injustice and tragedy, including physical violence, murder, and suicide, as some kibbutz members have been downgraded overnight to the lowest sector of the emergent privatized, capitalistic society.

Privatization now appears in all domains of Israeli society, witness the emergence of populist TV politics and demise of the smaller political parties; privatization of the media and commercialization of radio and television broadcasting; privatization of lands and corporations; privatization in education and sports, etc. Because privatization in kibbutz society is part of the overall capitalization and globalization of Israeli society, these kibbutz films can be interpreted as a national allegory and a reflection of the processes taking place in the Israeli society at large, in particular, the collapse of the welfare state.

In *No Longer 17*, the kibbutz, a former symbol of harmony and solidarity, is presented as a conflicted site and as a space that can no longer contain the wishes and needs of all its members. Instead of communality and group action, it is characterized by a bitter struggle between the different interests of the generation of the founding fathers and the younger generation. The ideals of equality and of helping the weak have been replaced by "capitalist" considerations of market forces: efficiency and utility, profit and loss. The reorganization and the need to survive are forcing the young new leaders of the kibbutz to ignore moral or sentimental considerations and to act according to rational and utilitarian logic. The implicit moral meaning of the removal of their elderly to an external nursing home is an admitted failure of the kibbutz utopia. In *The Galilee Eskimos,* the older generation wakes one morning and finds that all their families have left the kibbutz and their property has been sold to a private entrepreneur.

In a similar spirit, *Operation Grandma* (about a young man's efforts to bury his deceased grandmother) parodies themes, institutions, and rituals identified with the kibbutz by presenting them in an absurd manner. This film mocks the kibbutz bureaucracy and its adherence to those regulations, ceremonies, and behaviors that once symbolized kibbutz solidarity and its essence as one big family. The film presents characters that care only for themselves. The kibbutz becomes a microcosm in which everyone fights everyone and all the members attempt to fool each other. This pattern is associated with the argument that in recent years Israeli society has become a divided and tribal society, in which each group cares only for itself: Jewish settlers in the West Bank, ultra-Orthodox Jews, Sephardi and Mizrachi Jews, Russian Jews, kibbutzim, villages, workers' unions, etc. The film comically articulates the younger generation's abandonment of the kibbutz, their sense of displacement and homelessness, and their yearning for a different place and time. The older brother is a temporary resident on the kibbutz; the middle brother immigrates to America; and the youngest brother is unable to find his place anywhere. The motif of temporality also appears, in different variations, in *No Longer 17*, *The Galilee Eskimos*, and *Children of the Sun*.

These films express feelings of foreignness, alienation, and an inability to integrate in this particular place, resulting in wandering and transience. These themes are radicalized in the representation of death, suicide, deportation, leaving, or a sense of detachment and alienation. They are associated with the experience of a borderline existence and a crisis, a detachment between past and present, and an uncertainty about the future. In archival footage featured in *Children of the Sun*, *The Mother of the Giv'atron*, and, to a certain extent, the communal rituals in *Sweet Mud*, the past of the kibbutzim is exposed as meaningless, a sort of remains of a memory of what used to be the fundamentals of collective, spontaneous life, which have now been deconstructed as something remote, out of context, veiled in myth, time, and place.

Some of the characters in the films of the 2000s are located in-between, in a gloomy and unstable space. They are no longer in the kibbutz, but neither do they feel that they have arrived at a different place. The sense of having lost one's direction is supported and enhanced by thematic codes of orphanhood and variations of the notion of the absent father in *Operation Grandma*, *No Names on the Doors*, *No Longer 17*, and *Sweet Mud*. These offer a sort of allegory on the deconstruction of the organic family, the kibbutz family, and the national symbolic order in general.

The film *Sweet Mud* (the traumatic story of a kibbutz child who lives with his alienated brother and his mother, who suffers from mental illness) returns to the past from a personal point of view, moving between an experienced memory and a lost memory. Like the other films, it features a clash between the values and ideals of the kibbutz, and the wishes and needs of the individual. Life in the small community causes real damage to the personal and changing needs of the individual. For example, the decision of the kibbutz general assembly to expel Stephan, the Swiss male lover of Miri, the female kibbutz protagonist, triggers the processes of segregation and mental deterioration. This dynamic exposes the negative side of community life: arbitrariness, aggression, and malicious attitudes of the collective members toward the individual. The persistent collectivist ideology becomes a stimulus for intolerance, sentimental blindness, and bluntness toward the individual.

As is true in many of the aforementioned films, the kibbutz in *Sweet Mud* conveys the tension between the outsiders and the kibbutz establishment (i.e., the kibbutz secretary, the general assembly). The kibbutz outsiders create liminal phenomena and situations that the kibbutz cannot contain. They threaten the family and communal order. Characters like temporary residents, the bachelor, the widow, the old man, the sick, or handicapped person express this sensitive periphery of the social order. Their liminal situations include loss, an unaccepted affair, betrayal, madness, or suicide. This narrative structure oscillates between two poles: the transcendental idea (the past) and its degenerated fulfillment (the present).

In *Children of the Sun,* the smarting, bitter memories of veteran kibbutz members are voice-overs, while the screen images present authentic documentation of typical kibbutz rituals practiced over the decades. These include the ritual of the festival of Shavuot (Feast of Weeks), rituals of the socialist youth movements, and, of course, ceremonies on May 1 commemorating International Labor Day. The mimicry and gestures of happiness, the joy of youth, and the youngsters' idealism in the archival footage acquire an ironic, even sarcastic meaning because they are combined with the critical sound track. What emerges is a picture of veteran kibbutz members settling their accounts with the creation of their personalities and ideological perspectives by the collective, sometimes aggressively and sometimes by means of intense self-persuasion. The kibbutz members, whose faces are shown only at the end of the film, still resent their kibbutzim for social experiments like that of communal housing; for preferring the collective rather than the nuclear family; and for ignoring the individual's agonies and their subordination to high ideals even to the extent of abusing and belittling the individual.

Conclusion

The dramatic changes in the cinematic representation of the kibbutz over eighty years of Israeli cinema reflect the significant moral and ethical changes that have taken place in Israeli society and culture. The Zionist collectivist values and positive empathetic attitude toward labor, solidarity, social justice, equality, and communality have been vacated and replaced by a new agenda, encouraged by the authority which is aggressively capitalist and supports free initiative, individualism, and abandoning the communal social frameworks in favor of social Darwinism. The founding generation and their descendants' profound sense of guilt accompany these radical changes. At the same time, they express profound, often merciless, and highly masochistic criticism of the very idea of the kibbutz and Zionist socialist communality.

The cultural demand for reconsideration of the form and formulation of the kibbutz is a demand for reexamination of the fundamentals in Israeli society in an age of globalization and Americanization, an era characterized by ideological unification and a surrender to strict economic imperatives, even if this results in trampling upon subordinate groups. Cinema, as an interdisciplinary and multidisciplinary art, provides Israeli culture with some visual, persuasive, sentimental, and emotional instruments for dealing with and reevaluating the nostalgic vision of the kibbutz, which was aimed at improving and sublimating the individual human being and concomitantly at displaying conformity and solidarity. The changes in the cinematic articulation of the kibbutz mirror the emergence of new, alternative attitudes in Israeli society with regard to the commitment (or, rather, indifference) of the individual toward the collective and the commitment (or, rather, indifference) of the society toward its citizens, particularly with regard to those individuals who are considered as *others*, the different kinds of transgressors and dissidents who do not wish, or are unable, to conform to the collectivist imperatives.[25]

The deconstruction of the kibbutz, as reflected in Israeli cinema, offers a problematic deconstruction of basic moral values in Israeli society, as well as a liberating aspiration to focus on the individual as a free, autonomous human being. This tension is fundamental to the kibbutz in its many incarnations, from the Spartan settlement of idealistic Zionist socialist youngsters in the film *Sabra*; the abandoned elderly veterans of the kibbutz in *The Galilee Eskimos*; the new suburbs of bourgeois villas, which are rapidly being built on the former agricultural fields of privatized kibbutzim; up to the sentimental memory of the kibbutz and its values, which still beats in the hearts of many former kibbutz members who have chosen to migrate to the enticing big city.

Recently, the kibbutz is highly represented, however, in the Israeli culture, including television (e.g., the dramatic series *Loving Anna* and *Pillars of Smoke*), art (e.g., the installation Communal Sleeping at the Helena Rubinstein Pavilion of Art in Tel Aviv), literature (e.g., Assaf Inbari's *Home*, Ada Lampart's *Naked Soul,* and Smadar Gonen's *Intimate Reminiscence*), and many films which have been discussed in this article. The kibbutz is now a potential or virtual power that repeats in many different variations and an endless plateau of new, innovative combinations and rearticulations. In Nietzschean terms, it is an eternal recurrence, an eternal return.

Notes

1. These films were categorized as Zionist Realism, following the Socialist Realism in the Soviet cinema of that period (see Shohat, 1991, p. 30; Ne'eman, 1998, p. 12).
2. See Yosef (2004), *Beyond Flesh: Queer Masculinities and Nationalism in Israeli Cinema.*
3. Almog (1997), p. 3. In this respect, many of the kibbutz members came from a religious background, and they tried to integrate diverse religious rituals into the kibbutz's secular life (see Zur et al., 1981, pp. 105–20).
4. Miri Talmon (2001), p. 144.
5. Victor Turner (2004), p. 87.
6. Ibid., p. 88.
7. Another famous nationalist film is Thorold Dickinson's *Hill 24 Doesn't Answer* (1955) about four fighters in the 1948 war, although there is no representation of the kibbutzim in this film.
8. See, for example, Hannan Hever (1999), pp. 12–46. The films *What a Gang!*, *Eight against One*, and *He Walked in the Fields* (which were produced in the late 1960s) are adaptations of popular books and stories.
9. Between 1949 and 1951, the population was doubled. More than 650,000 immigrants arrived in Israel, half of them from North Africa (Morocco, Libya, Tunis, and Algiers) and Asia (Yemen, Iraq, Iran, and Turkey) (see Cohen, 2004, pp. 54–85; Almog, 1997, p. 263).
10. Almog (1997), p. 263.
11. This development echoes the transition from the defensive to the offensive ethos, as theorized by Shapira (1998), pp. 460–62.
12. After the difficult period of the war, the complicated absorption of the large immigration, and the harsh recession, an economic growth began. This growth was generated by the government and labor union's control and direction, and the growth of the private sector (Eisenstadt, 1989, p. 225). These changes were supported by the relative peace between the 1956 war and the 1967 war, significant changes in

the demographic and socioeconomic structure after the massive immigrations, as much as well as the economic advantages of the nationalization of lands after the 1948 war.

13. Nitzan Ben-Shaul (1998) argues that both the popular "Bourekas" melodramas and comedies, and the sophisticated individualist cinema, share a capitalist, liberal, and autonomous ideology (p. 128).

14. Ne'eman (1998), p. 12.

15. In this respect, see the early stories by Amos Oz (then a young kibbutz member) about the kibbutz: *Elsewhere* (*Makom Acher*, 1966) and *A Perfect Peace* (*Menuha Nehonah*, 1982).

16. Ne'eman (1998), p. 17.

17. The kibbutz representations in the cinema of the 1960s also reflect noncinematic artistic manifestations from earlier decades (the 1940s and the 1950s): books like *Such a Bunch*, *Eight after One*, *He Walked in the Fields*, and *Three Days and a Child*; a play like *I Like Mike*, and *Sallah Shabati* which is based on short sketches of the Nahal band, a military entertainment band.

18. In the 1970s, about one hundred fiction films were made in Israel, but only about five of them engage with the kibbutz: *Opposite* (*Mineged*, dir. Menahem Binetzky, 1970), *Queen of the Road* (*Malkat Ha'Kvish*, dir. Menahem Golan, 1970), *They Call Me Shmil* (*Kor'i'm Li Shimil*, dir. George Ovadia 1973), and *Belfer* (Yigal Bursztein, 1976).

19. Nurit Gertz (1993), pp. 175–217.

20. Other films are less familiar, including *On a Bright Day You Can See Damascus* (*Be'Yom Bahir Ro'im et Damesek*, dir. Eran Riklis, 1982), and nostalgic films of initiation and adolescence like: *The Valley Train* (*Rakevet He'Emek*, dir. Jonathan Paz, 1989), *Yossaleh, How Did It Happen?* (*Yossaleh, Eich Ze Kara?*, dir. Tal Ron, 1989), *Children of the Stairs* (*Yaldei Ha'Madregot*, dir. Yigal Pe'eri, 1984). Other films that include a kibbutz character or a scene in the kibbutz: *The Hawk* (*Ha'Ait*, dir. Yaki Yosha, 1981), *First Love* (*Ahava Rishona*, dir. Uzi Peres, 1982), *Again, Forever* (*Roman Be'Hemshachim*, dir. Oded Kotler, 1985), *The Silver Trace* (*Magash Ha'Kesef*, Judd Ne'eman, 1983), and *Avanti Popolo* (dir. Rafi Bukai, 1986).

21. This idea is discussed, albeit in a different context, in Zuckermann (1993), p. 92.

22. Schnitzer (1994), p. 229. Yes. 1994, p. 229

23. This idea is also discussed, in a different context, in Zuckermann (1993), p. 92.

24. See Munk (2006).

25. See, for example, Padva (2005) on the (mis)representation of queer subjectivities in the Israeli cinema.

Bibliography

Almog, Oz. *The Sabra: A Portrait*. Tel Aviv, Israel: Am Oved, 1997 [in Hebrew].

Ben-Shaul, N. "The Subtle Connection between the Bourekas Films and the Individualistic Films." In *Fictive Looks: On Israeli Cinema*, edited by N. Gertz, O. Lubin, and J. Ne'eman, 128–34. Tel Aviv, Israel: Open University of Israel, 1998 [in Hebrew].

Bursztein, Y. *Face as a Battlefield*. Tel Aviv, Israel: Ha'Kibbutz Ha'Meuchad, 1990 [in Hebrew].

Cohen-Fridheim, R. *The Kibbutz Movement and the Absorption of the Mass Immigration 1948–1953*. Dissertation, Department of Land and Israel Studies, University of Bar-Ilan, 2004 [in Hebrew].

Eisenstadt, S. N. *The Israeli Society and Its Changes*. Jerusalem, Israel: Magnes, 1989 [in Hebrew].

Hever, H. *A Literature Which Is Been Written from Here: Shortening the Israeli Literature*. Tel Aviv, Israel: Yedioth Aharonoth and Hemed Books, 1999 [in Hebrew].

Kedem, E. *The Kibbutz and Israeli Cinema: Deterritorializing Representation and Ideology* (a dissertation). Amsterdam, The Netherlands: University of Amsterdam, 2007.

Munk, Y. "Major Trends in Contemporary Israeli Cinema." In *The Routledge Encyclopedia of Modern Jewish Culture*, edited by G. Abramson. Oxford, UK: Oxford University Press, 2004.

———. "Borderline Cinema: Space and Identity in Israeli Cinema of the Nineties." A Ph.D. thesis. The Department of Literature at Tel Aviv University, Tel Aviv, Israel, 2006 [in Hebrew].

Ne'eman, J. "Zero Degree in Cinema." In *Introduction to Israeli Cinema: A Reader,* edited by J. Ne'eman and R. Schwartz, 144–47. Tel Aviv, Israel: Tel Aviv University, 1982 [1979] [in Hebrew].

———. "The Modernists: The Genealogy of the New Sensitivity." In *Fictive Looks: On Israeli Cinema,* edited by N. Gertz, O. Lubin, and J. Ne'eman, 9–32. Tel Aviv, Israel: Open University of Israel, 1998 [in Hebrew].

Oz, Amos. *Somewhere Else*. Tel Aviv: Syfriat Hapoalim, 1969 [in Hebrew].

Oz, A. *Where the Jackals Howl*. Tel Aviv: Am Oved Press, 1976 [in Hebrew].

Padva, G. "Israel, Filmmaking." In *Routledge International Encyclopedia of Queer Culture: Gay, Lesbian, Bisexual and Transsexual Contemporary Cultures,* edited by David Gerstner, 312–13. New York and London: Routledge, 2005.

Schnitzer, M. *Israeli Cinema: All Facts, All Plots, All Directors, and the Film Criticisms*. Tel Aviv, Israel: Kinnereth, 1994 [in Hebrew].

Shapira, A. *New Jews, Old Jews*. Tel Aviv: Am Oved Press, 1998 [in Hebrew].

Shohat, E. *Israeli Cinema: East/West and the Politics of Representation*. Austin, TX: University of Texas Press, 1989.

———. *Israeli Cinema, History and Ideology*. Translated into Hebrew by A. Glickman. Tel Aviv, Israel: Breirot, 1991.

Talmon, M. *Israeli Graffiti: Nostalgia, Groups, and Collective Identity in Israeli Cinema*. Tel Aviv and Haifa, Israel: The Open University Press and Haifa University, 2001 [in Hebrew].

Turner, V. *The Ritual Process: Structure and Anti-Structure*. Translated into Hebrew by Noam Rachmilevitz. Tel Aviv, Israel: Resling, 2004 [1969].

Yosef, R. *Beyond Flesh: Queer Masculinities and Nationalism in Israeli Cinema*. New Brunswick, NJ: Rutgers University Press, 2004.

Zuckermann, M. "A Past Which Is Not a Past." *Zmanim* 45 (1993): 86–95. Tel Aviv, Israel: Tel Aviv University Press and Zmora-Bitan, [in Hebrew].

Zur, M., T. Zevulun, and H. Porat, eds. *Here on Earth*. Tel Aviv, Israel: Ha'Kibbutz Ha'Meuchad and Sifriyat Poalim, 1981 [in Hebrew].

12

Freedom of Expression in an Ideological Society: The Case of Kibbutz Literature

Shula Keshet

Introduction

Ever since the early kibbutz settlement of the Jordan and Jezreel valleys, the kibbutz concept has been perceived by many as the principal innovation of the Jewish people in Eretz Yisrael. The utopianist lifestyle, which was not put in abeyance until the End of Days but realized in everyday life, was set in the collective consciousness as a symbolic site that represented pioneering Israeliness at its best. The human experiment touched not only the people who lived it but also many others who found the dream captivating, even if they were unable to fulfill it themselves. This fact is manifested both in the expectations that preceded the literary work created within kibbutz society and in the wide appreciation the unique products of "kibbutz literature" gained in kibbutz and Israeli public life alike.

The social invitation was unconcealed. Communication between writers and readers was direct, overt, and, more particularly, public. The "outline plan" for the literature still to be written from within kibbutz society was in the public domain before the opening word of the first kibbutz novel was written. Like every society living in messianic tension (even if it is secular), kibbutz society also had what Ya'akov Talmon (1956, p. 126) called a prepared model of reality "written in pencil," and the expectations from worthy kibbutz literature became part of other expectations in every sphere of life.

The texts, mainly from the novel genre, will serve as representative examples, and we shall examine the ways in which the works met these expectations. The present chapter will focus on three coordinates through which the main trends can be marked: the various representations of the kibbutz as a "topos," a place (realistic, symbolic, surrealistic); the tension between collective and individual forms of expression; and the conflict between the "superego" of the kibbutz as a total ideological system and what I call the "underground soul," which did not place itself at the disposal of the dominant ideology out of total self-denial (see Keshet, 1995).

The Staring Point: Pioneering Life Is the Work of Art

In the first two decades, "literature" was hardly written at all. In its first steps, the settlement enterprise swept up the kibbutz members and imbued them, first and foremost, with endeavor, hard physical labor, mainly on the land. Literary–artistic writing written by professional writers was rejected and halted. In the wake of Brenner's central poetic article, "The Eretz Yisrael Genre and Its Adjuncts" (written 1911, published 1930), the opinion became rooted in Hebrew critique that the Eretz Yisrael reality did not yet possess permanence and typification, and thus could not serve as a model for literary writing; in Brenner's opinion, the writers writing from Eretz Yisrael presented a sham model of life experience and thus did not succeed in creating superior artistic work (see Govrin, 1978). Meanwhile, Brenner proposed that only memoirs should be written—"an examination of memories and impressions from the dynamic situation"; A. D. Gordon's demand from writers was even more stringent: he thought that the transition to "right living," undetached from the land, from nature, demanded man's all and that only when individuals redeem themselves and become whole people, their work would in any case become living work. Gordon accused the Hebrew writers who did not physically take part in the new life of pioneering of having a sterile "aesthetic" approach and demanded that they first of all invest all their efforts in creating life itself. In his view, even Bialik's work did not pass the test: "If Bialik were here," Gordon dared to say, "working and living a life of labor and nature and seeing life purely as a life of work (for in any other way he would not achieve what there is to achieve here), and sing us the song of labor and the life of labor, then I would now give all his poems for that . . ." (1928, p. 236). Berl Katznelson, too, who founded the *Davar* newspaper and the Am Oved Publishing House and encouraged writers from the kibbutz movement taking their first steps, was in thrall to the conception that saw, at this stage, no legitimacy for intellectual creation without combining it with physical labor (see Shapira, 1980, pp. 259–60). The entire generation was preoccupied with converting spiritual energies to the practical and all aspired toward a common aim: turning the Jewish people into a working people. The pioneers tried to translate "the religion of labor" into action and spoke of this conversion in religious terms. Joining the "Order of Pioneers" was perceived as ritual and called for enlistment of all the forces. Drab quotidian life became holy and the simple road became "a heavenly road"—"And like phylactery straps, the highways that palms have paved glide down," as Shlonsky wrote in his famous poem.

This perception of the spiritual aspect as weakness, as one of the ills of the Diaspora, drove kibbutz writers into silence, or at best to writing in secret, in stolen hours, just before dawn before going out to work in the fields. The majority tried to physically maintain the difficult, perhaps impossible, combination of "worker–writer." Only after many years of paralysis of their creative power and their voluntary inhibition did some dare to critically address the early days: "The heroic and barbaric times alike, at the beginning of our road, the times of the rite of muscles and contempt for the spirit" (see Neuberger, 1937, pp. 60–65). In the first years, only a few attempts were made at literary–artistic writing by writers from communal groups. *On the Border of Silence*, by Zvi Schatz, is a posthumously published work. Schatz, together with Brenner and Louidor, was murdered by Arab rioters on May 2, 1921. Only one novel was published in his lifetime, *Without Words*, whose previous title was *On the Border of Silence*. His second novel, *Batya*, was published only after his death (*Ha'adama* 12, March 1923). He wrote the stories found in his literary remains during the three years he served in the Jewish Brigade. Only there were his living conditions more or less conducive to writing (see Keshet, 1990, pp. 47–65). The first novel to deal with life in the kvutza, *Days and Nights*, by Natan Bistritsky (1926), based on the events of Bitaniya Ilit, was written by a professional writer who was close to the founders of the Hashomer Hatzair movement but was never a kibbutz member and thus was not shackled by the practical commandments of "the pioneering religion."

Collective Texts

In the early years, the collectivist trend encouraged the writing of collective anthologies that documented the experiences, troubles, and dreams of groups of pioneers. The groundbreaking anthology, *Kehilyatenu* (*Our Community*), written by the founders of Hashomer Hatzair, was the best known of these. In the course of the summer of 1920 and winter of 1921, a small select Hashomer Hatzair group settled at Bitaniya Illit, on a slope overlooking the Sea of Galilee, and was engaged in preparing the ground for planting for the Jewish Colonization Association's experimental farm. This site has special significance in the history of Hashomer Hatzair as the movement views it as its cradle in Eretz Yisrael. During the day, the group worked at removing rocks, uprooting jujube bushes, and digging holes for planting olive trees and vineyards, and at night devoted themselves to the ritual of confessional talks, hoping to thus bring about reformation of the self and the world alike. About a year after coming down from the mountain, the group set down its experiences in a collective anthology entitled *Kehilyatenu* (Spring, 1922). This is not the place to discuss the singular story of the Bitaniya Illit group, which became a defining myth in the history of the pioneering tribe. In the framework of the present discussion, we shall only say that the anthology constitutes a particularly fascinating example of this kind of writing. *Kehilyatenu* offered a unique lexicon, a system of symbols, images, and dreams; the expressive language and raw structure of the text that was intermingled with various writing genres—group discussions, journal extracts, things written in the group's notebook, articles, and letters—held the potential of a primal canon that is still uncompleted. And indeed years later, three Hebrew writers found provocative and stirring raw material for their literary–artistic writing in the Bitaniya Illit episode and the *Kehilyatenu* anthology: Natan Bistritsky wrote his novel *Days and Nights* in 1926, Yehuda Ya'ari's novel *Like Glittering Light* was published in 1937, and Yoshua Sobol wrote his play *The Night of the Twentieth*, first performed in 1976 (translated into English: 1978). Other group journals, like the Kvutzat Hasharon *Book of the Kvutza* or the Kvutzat Kiryat Anavim *The Book of Life*, which for years were kept in the archives of these kibbutzim, were only published in the 1990s as part of a retrospective research effort (see Ofaz, 1996, 2001).

This genre, which left its mark in the early days, reappears after more than forty years in the wake of the Six-Day War. The anthologies, *The Seventh Day* (1968) and *Between Young People* (1969), which were published by the Allied Kibbutz Movement, continue the tradition of *Kehilyatenu*. The second and third generations, which had recently emerged from the experience of that war, make the kibbutz community as a whole part of their confessions, thoughts, and observations.

The Sketch Genre

Over a long period of more than two decades (1920–40), the sketch genre claimed a central place in the sphere of literary production. Its characteristics were simple: a short, flexible text of elementary form that attempted to come close to reality. The words with which the experiences were transmitted did not attempt to draw attention to themselves, but rather to convey the authentic experience. The sketch gave expression to impressionistic moods and philosophical thought, and described scenes from the life of labor while attempting to depict Eretz Yisraeli landscapes and nature in words. The writers chose the sketch as a preferred genre for two main reasons: the harsh conditions of reality that compelled them to find their expression in a minimalist literary form that enabled them to fulfill it even after a hard day's work in the fields and the collective-egalitarian reason that in the sketch there were possibilities of expression for many, without distinction between skilled writers and the rank and file.

Ha'adama edited by Y. H. Brenner and *Hapoel Hatzair* edited by J. Aharonovitz were the first journals to open their platform to sketches expressing the authentic feelings of the pioneers. Brenner, and Berl Katznelson too, viewed the initial attempts of workers as a fount of vitality and originality that would influence the entire literary spectrum. Katznelson even viewed workers' literature as a continuation of the popular genre of Hasidic literature, folk literature, that would be written by the people and speak to the people (see Berlowitz, 1984; Miron, 1987). The workers' press of the third aliyah pioneers—*Hasolel*, the road workers' journal, and *Mihayenu*, that of the Labor Battalion, which were handwritten, duplicated, and distributed among the groups between 1921 and 1929—continued the tradition. The kibbutz movement journals, too, whose publication commenced in the 1920s—*Mibifnim* (1923 onward), *Niv Hakvutza* (1929 onward), and *Hedim* (which first appeared in 1927)—gave pride of place to sketches and in them can be found examples by Fanya Bergstein, David Maletz, and Shlomo Reichenstein, alongside sketches by almost anonymous authors who published but one or two on the public platform and usually signed them using only their first name or a pseudonym. This genre, which befitted a revolutionary period, was close to life, and its writers—members of the rank and file—viewed themselves as expressing truths deriving from the depths of the pioneering experience, not as professional writers.

It was during this period that a sort of dialectical equilibrium was formed between community and individual. With this conjoining into a kind of collective mosaic, the sketches expressed the community, but in this choir solo voices could still be heard, giving expression to individual hardship, the difficulties, and heavy toll of pioneering realization.

The degree of anonymity that characterized some of the sketch writers enabled the expression of doubt, self-criticism, and nonacceptance. On the overt level, the genre mainly served the dominant ideological dictates. Sketches describing landscape and nature, descriptions of work, and the seasons, which appear with great frequency, were an umbrella for collective endeavor and reinforced the consensus of "the building line" and the "return to the roots" of the Jewish people, after Zemach's coinage (1925). But there were also sketches that voiced loneliness and disillusionment with the gray everyday life that came in place of the great dream.

The Thirties and Forties: A Renewed Commission

With the institutionalization and stabilization of kibbutz life, there appeared in the various kibbutz movement journals an explicit call to abandon the sketch form and replace it with more complex literary forms. The feeling in the kibbutz community of the late 1930s was that the reality of life had indeed undergone a revolution. During the Arab riots, which broke out in 1936 and continued almost up to World War II, thirty-nine new kibbutzim were founded, and in the following six years, from 1941 to 1947, the number of kibbutzim in Eretz Yisrael was almost doubled, reaching 145. With the advent of the "Tower and Stockade" settlements, kibbutz settlement spread through most regions of the country; in the overall Jewish population, the kibbutz population increased, as did the area of land worked by it. The sense of mission and pride in its achievements gave rise to a lexical–ideological vocabulary in which pathos lurked; its speakers spoke in absolute terms of creating a "new man" and a "new society," and the communal way of life was presented as a worthy alternative to the sham European civilization and old Jewish culture alike (see Almog, 1993).

From now on kibbutz literature was required, as M. Braslavsky, editor of *Mibifnim* put it, to be "more than literature," for it now had the mission of influencing and shaping the life of the entire generation, of becoming a lever for the greater needs of Eretz Yisrael reality, and contending with shaping the image of a new societal type, "the Jewish pioneer," a unique synthesis of intellectual and farmer (see Shimoni, 1937; Braslavski, 1938).

Poetic recommendations also joined this ideological–didactical demand: the renewed commission called upon writers to keep any conflict quiet, ignore the psychological schism, and focus on "externalized" descriptions of the conquest of the wilderness (see, e.g., Vulcani, 1930).

Malaria, the life of poverty, the hard physical labor under the burning sun, and the voices of despair were all concealed. To bridge the chasms in the soul, an "amendment" to the concept of happiness was proposed that included the self-sacrifice component, the total identification of the individual with the aims of the community.

Creating the Topos

The license now given to kibbutz writers to describe the new reality through sophisticated literary–artistic writing that would serve as an educational tool and shape the "spirit of the generation" yielded but few results. In the 1940s, only three novels were published: *Beginnings* by Shlomo Reichenstein (1943), *Circles* by David Maletz (1945), and *Time of Tents* by Emma Levin-Talmi (1949). Two more novels, *Land without Shade* by Yonat and Alexander Sened, and *A Man's Home* by Zvi Arad, were published in 1951, after the war of independence.

To a great degree all these early novels met Gordon's demand to integrate life into literature, and documentary elements are clearly evident in them. The works were based on events from a life of labor and self-realization, and in his work the narrator "documents" the first period of the "pioneering tribe." Bistritsky's *Days and Nights* and Yehuda Ya'ari's *Like Glittering Light* based their plot schema on the Bitaniya Illit episode; *Beginnings* by Shlomo Reichenstein, a member of Tel Yosef and later Ein Harod, tells of the first years of Kibbutz Tel Yosef and the split in the "Labor Battalion"; *Time of Tents* by Emma Levin-Talmi, a member of Mishmar Haemek, tells of the early days of the Hashomer Hatzair groups on the roads; and *Land without Shade* by Yonat and Alexander Sened, members of Kibbutz Revivim, describes the outpost settlement enterprise in the Negev and the early days of Revivim.

The early novels were the first and foremost works that created a "topos." They mimetically and accurately reconstruct the rituals sanctified by the kibbutz society and mainly make room for descriptions of working on the land in the Eretz Yisrael landscape. These descriptions create a singular atmosphere, a kind of rhythm of epic width that dwells on details of the description. A new type of novel is created here, a "spatial" text that attempts to restore the lost harmony of the epos to the world, to heal the rift between the Jew and the world, and to reconnect literature with the concrete material of life.

Beginnings by Shlomo Reichenstein (1943) is a good example: step by step, the text describes the conquest of the site of Kibbutz Tel Yosef: the removal of rocks, the first plowing, the first planting, harvesting, threshing, building the cowshed, and so on. The meticulous description of agricultural work (one can learn, e.g., how a broken down threshing machine is repaired) ends with a big ceremony, the first harvest festival in the kibbutz. The novel's title, *Beginnings*, alludes to the main theme: the re-creation of the world out of chaos, the creation of paradise on earth. Raphael, the novel's leading protagonist, is a kind of first Man, discovering nature's deepest secrets each day, learning to cultivate and maintain the Garden of Eden. The novel ends with a harmonious scene: Raphael is walking through the kibbutz fields, seeing the abundance of the world that he and his comrades have built, and like God, he sees that it is good. The secular pioneer has become a god on earth, and his deeds are praised in religious language.

Land without Shade by Yonat and Alexander Sened (1951) is also a novel that creates a topos. This work, too, describes, step by step, faithfully and accurately, the stages of the establishment of the place, the first plowing, the planting of the first tree, a carob, laying the foundation stone of the fort, establishing the experimental vegetable garden, storing water in bitumen ponds, and so on. Here, too, the struggle against the forces of the desert is described as a mythical struggle against the forces of chaos. The creation theme places the pioneers inside an all-embracing framework of the tension between desert and culture, between Jewish detachment and the rooting of Hebrew, and turns the pioneering endeavor into a cultural pole advancing humanity.

The close familiarity of the authors of these novels with the Eretz Yisrael landscape and climate, which came from personal experience, endowed their writing with sensual details of reality, scenes, feelings, smells, and colors that were all grounded in a specific landscape. A deep connection with the tracts of the Jezreel Valley landscape stands out in the writing of Reichenstein and also of David Maletz, who for many years worked in the forage crops branch. The descriptions of flora and fauna in *Beginnings* present a realistic catalog of the valley in its first stages of clearing: numerous jujubes, wild shrubs, reeds and rushes, clover and alfalfa, and oats and other cereals all growing wild; in the fields larks, red-legged and red-billed storks, hares, and jackals could all be seen. The agricultural landscape in those years was the wide-open spaces of fields of grain, and center stage was occupied by scenes of plowing and harvesting, stacking the sheaves, and threshing. In the spring, ranunculus stood out among the wild flowers and, with the commencement of the harvest, the blue cornflowers. This is an inventory amazing in its richness when compared with that found in other works of the "settlement novel" genre that were not written by kibbutz members.

Individual and Society: The *Circles* Episode

The novel *Circles* by David Maletz, a member of Kibbutz Ein Harod, published in 1945, marks a different trend whose influence would be felt later in the works of second- and third-generation writers. The epic description, which focuses on the external plot of conquest of the topos, does not stand at the center of the novel, and the narrator's view is directed to the social plot.

Maletz joined the Emek group in Ein Harod in 1923. In the initial period, the act of creating life was attended by a sense of great pride, but after about five years his articles reveal a tone of profound concern alongside the spiritual aspect of life in the new culture, which concentrated itself almost exclusively on a life of endeavor. In an article he wrote in 1929, Maletz expresses concern that the diversion of all physical and spiritual effort to labor, following Gordon's recommendation, holds the great danger of diminishment, for "we have elevated the 'material' in general to the status of sanctity," and the material is likely to take over life in its entirety like the golem lurking for its creator, Rabbi Yehuda Löw of Prague (see Maletz, 1929). Hence Maletz is gravely concerned that the new kibbutz lifestyle would be unable to equal that offered by the previous Jewish experience. A social life that is not controlled by an overall spiritual basis that endows the endeavor with reason and logic, he claimed, may become, due to its detachment from its transcendental source, relations of "a terrible indifference," and the immeasurable over-endeavor necessary for living the new life would probably lead to a sudden laxness in which the effort would be replaced by "emptiness between people and between hearts" (Ibid.)

Maletz, too, endeavored to observe the commandments of the religion of labor with every fiber of his being. He wrote his first novel, *Circles* (1945), in the early hours of the morning before going out to work in the fields. His naive protagonist, Menachemke, clashes with a social world whose rules he finds difficult to comprehend. He encounters social institutions, falls victim to them, and cannot, as it were, solve the secrets of customs and conventions formed within kibbutz society.

> The big group machine, organization of life in the big group economy, requires the ordinary man. People who are equal. Who do their deeds communally, at the same rate [...] the machine must work rhythmically. The special man, who demands particular attention, the exceptional, disrupts the working of the machine. (*Circles*, p. 123)

On its publication, *Circles* caused a storm both inside and outside the kibbutz movement. Many kibbutzim held meetings and discussions attended by the author, something akin to "literary tribunals." Dozens of responses and critiques appeared in the general press, in the kibbutz movement journals, and in kibbutz newsletters. The author also received scores of personal letters that were kept in his archive.

The poetic guideline that recommended the production of texts built upon the integration of life into literature, texts structured on documentary material, created a situation whereby reading the work led to a blurring of the line between the real and fictional worlds. The novel was perceived by its readers as a reflection of their real life, as a book that evaluated and judged their kibbutz way of life. The twenty years that had elapsed since settlement in the Jezreel Valley commenced facilitated a stocktaking of the generation, and the stocktaking undertaken by the author of the most ambitious human experiment of the Zionist dream found it flawed. The kibbutz members, who stubbornly adhered to the dream and whose new life demanded numerous concessions from them, hard work, and a Spartan life, could not accept with equanimity a book that questioned the worthiness of the sacrifice.

The case of *Circles* is a well-documented, instructive example of the way in which a controversial literary work is accepted in an ideological society (see Keshet, 1995). It emerges that the ideological baggage that the kibbutz readers brought with them into the reading process offered an *a priori* model for organizing the human experiment as the only, exclusive possibility. The rigid scale of values influenced aesthetic judgment and created a dynamic of "ideological refusal." The novel's arousing potential, since it mandated adjustments to the group's scale of values, was not realized. The majority of readers remained stuck at the referential level of their life and dealt intensively with rehabilitating the normative system that had been damaged, as if the novel were a documentary document and not a literary–artistic work. The stifling atmosphere and yearning for another place would also be revealed in later works like *On Narrow Paths* by Yossl Birstein (1959), who was a member of Kibbutz Gvat when he wrote the novel that was translated from Yiddish, and also Amos Oz's *Elsewhere, Perhaps* (1966 Hebrew, in English: 1985).

The 1948 Generation: Kibbutz Collectivism
Is Also a National Mission

The war of independence was a watershed from which literary writing in the kibbutz began addressing subjects outside its internal world.

National missions were now added to the communal value system. At the beginning of their careers, the majority of the young prose writers of the 1948 generation was graduates of the pioneering youth movements and was kibbutz members. In their works, the "kibbutz" topos becomes a symbolic place, the most representative topos of committed Israeliness. Moshe Shamir wrote *He Walked in the Fields* in 1947 when he was a member of Kibbutz Mishmar Haemek; the figure of Alik from his novel *With His Own Hands* became a symbolic founding figure in the eyes of that generation; Yigal Mossensohn, who was educated at Beit Alpha and later joined Na'an, wrote *Gray as a Sack* (1949); Aharon Megged, who wrote *Hedva and I* (1954), went to Kibbutz Sdot Yam with his agricultural core group; and Nathan Shaham, who wrote *Grain and Lead* (1948) and *Always Us* (1952), became a member of Beit Alpha. Abba Kovner's 1955 novel *Face to Face* should also be part of this circle as it deals with Kibbutz Negba's stand against the shelling and attacks of the Egyptian army (Kovner's biography was different from those of the above-mentioned authors since he had been an underground fighter in the Vilna ghetto). The books describe the coming of age of Israeli youth in the period prior to and during the war of independence, a process that included the young peoples' willingness to sacrifice themselves on the altar of society. Quite naturally, the Bildungsroman includes dealing with the parents' generation and with the overidealistic image of kibbutz society as it had been fixed in the collective consciousness (see Shaked, 1993). In the opinion of Gershon Shaked, the writers of this generation are not distinguished by an innovative, groundbreaking style. The writing is realistic and even naturalistic, with the main thrust being the external dramatic plot; the protagonists are mainly characterized by means of practical action and not through soul searching.

A notable example of writing that represented the national kibbutz consensus is the novel *Land without Shade* (1951) by Yonat and Alexander Sened, members of Kibbutz Revivim. The years between 1949 and 1951 were replete with political tension that ultimately led to the split in the Kibbutz Hameuchad movement. In the sociopolitical space in which the book was received, there was a radicalization of positions that was manifested, *inter alia*, in increasing fanaticism for the kibbutz way of life. Many kibbutz members acknowledged the fact that the state was starting to execute missions that had thus far been under the sole control of the kibbutz movement. The change threatened to leave the movement behind. It is against this background that the sweeping enthusiasm with which the Seneds' novel was received should be examined. The novel's plot, which was based on the Negev settlement enterprise, was perceived as a representative example of the national implementation potential still inherent in the kibbutz movement and as telling proof of the rightness of its path.

The novel achieved unprecedented success. It was published in eleven editions, between seventy thousand and eighty thousand copies (up to 1970, the number of copies of a Hebrew book sold in a regular edition did not exceed three thousand). The authors received hundreds of readers' letters and were invited to scores of meetings in kibbutz movement settlements and at youth movements. A dramatized version was staged by dozens of amateur theater groups. Chapters were translated into other languages, Yiddish and Portuguese, and were used in educational activities in the Diaspora. Readers praised the work as a "heroic epos" written in a simple tone, without romantic pathos, and admired the authors' success in shaping the figure of a collective protagonist that succeeds in attaining the aims of the community. Many years later, in 1990, in an interview I conducted with him, Alexander Sened defined *Land without Shade* as a "protectionist book": "The public wanted a book like this. It wanted a book of 'Who will speak of the valor of Israel,' and we spoke of the valor of Israel . . ." In the first kibbutz–Israeli novel, they wrote there is no allusion to the biographies of the two authors, which contain Alexander's mission to the Diaspora after the Holocaust and Yanka-Yonat's activities in the Warsaw ghetto and the underground. The collective protagonist they created is mainly described from the outside; the characters live without conflict and actually have no internal life. Yonat and Alexander Sened, who created a unique genre of collaborative writing, would later write employing a complex and totally different literary technique. *The Land Inhabited* (1981) is based on the metaphor of "living in glasshouses" and relates ambivalently to the intimacy imposed on the individual in the kibbutz; the "communal confession" on which the book's narrative is based (a continuation of the confessional nights at Bitaniya?) creates not only a kind of "communal memory box," but also a dynamic of incessant mutual judgment; *Oasis* (1988), the couple's next novel, is an intellectual book that attempts to document the compiling of the kibbutz code of living. The book casts doubt on the ability of the human experiment (of the kibbutz, perhaps of humans in general) to impose rational authority on a life so full of contradictions.

The first cracks that became evident in the attitude of the young guard kibbutz writers were first seen in *Hedva and I* (1954), Aharon Megged's humoristic–satirical book. The story gained great success, was published in several editions, and was even dramatized. It relates the adventures of a couple, former kibbutz members Hedva and Shmulik, who open a new chapter in their life in the big city. The humoristic tone, which for the first time brings the two worlds of the kibbutz and the city into confrontation and settles scores with both, contributed to the book's popularity. Other books by writers of that generation—Nathan Shaham's *Veterans' Housing* (1958) and *First Person Plural* (1968), Hanoch Bartov's *Heart of the Wise* (1969), and Aharon Megged's *Israeli Folk* (1956)—also express a kind of moderate social critique. In the kibbutz too, it seems, there are waifs and strays and there are the powers that be, here too, in this apparently utopianist place, society does not succeed in resolving the problems of the exceptions and loners. The organized establishments designed to solve the problems of the individual are impervious, and those who obsessively give themselves up to the dictates of the community suffer a voiding of the soul.

Elsewhere, Perhaps

The ideological guideline of the 1940s and 1950s recommending that authors give priority to the deeds of kibbutz society while suppressing internal contradictions and conflicts completely evaporated in the 1960s. In the collection of stories *Where the Jackals Howl* (1965, translated into English: 1982) and the novel *Elsewhere, Perhaps* (1966) by Amos Oz, the realistic topos, "kibbutz," undergoes an allegorical transformation. The enlightened, sane world of the kibbutz is no more than a remote island in the land "where jackals howl," and the attempt to impose rational order on the forces of chaos—white, red-roofed houses, lawns, paths dividing the lawns into square, tilled, rectangular agricultural areas—is frequently threatened by the hostile world all around, and the demonic and dark drives of the soul. Amos Oz elevates what was relegated to the subconscious by the kibbutz "superego." There are characters that uphold the accepted norms and ideological dictates and impose the kibbutz superego on their soul, and there are the plotting "others" that break the rules of the pioneering ethos while undermining the norms sanctified by the community.

"Kibbutz," the symbolic topos, is also the most appropriate place to present the conflicts between the generation of founders, the Titans, and the second generation, the "doers." The story "The Way of the Wind" from *Where the Jackals Howl* became a prime example. Shimshon, the founding father, who is the movement's ideologue and also in charge of landscape gardening in the kibbutz—the uncontested representative of the ordered, sane world—is cruel to his delicate, poetic son who does not fit the stereotype of the ideal "sabra." The son, Gideon, who despite his nature endeavors to meet his father's expectations, is trapped in a tragic situation: in the course of a parachute display over the kibbutz fields, his parachute becomes entangled in a high-tension wire and he is unable to free himself. The outcome—perhaps an accident, perhaps suicide—comes about with the destructive influence of the father. Shimshon also has an illegitimate son, Zaki, a kind of Esau-like twin of Gideon. Zaki is agile, strong, and uninhibited. Is he the desirable type of the younger generation, the ideal model of the new Israeliness? Sixteen years later, Oz would return to the dilemma of the second generation with the novel *A Perfect Peace* (1982, translated into English: 1993). Yonatan, the sabra, the biological offspring of the founding generation, whose talents lie in the technical–practical field, has to exile himself from the kibbutz to the desert to find the meaning of his life; his wife, Rimona, who cannot become pregnant by him, does so with the foreign young man of ghetto mentality, Azaria Gitlin, who came to the kibbutz from outside and who carries in his genes the identity components of the "old Jew." The outcome in *A Perfect Peace* is through synthesis: Yonatan, Rimona, and Azaria will live as a *ménage á trois* and raise their "common" baby together.

The 1960s and 1970s, in which the kibbutz was relatively economically sound, widened the gap between the utopian vision and its fulfillment in real life. This economic prosperity linked up with ideological failure. The kibbutz underwent its own industrial revolution, employed hired labor that later created a gap between the executive level and the rank-and-file members, and exacerbated inequality. It still preserved its symbolic value but became a secondary sector, one isolated sector among others that competed for influence and allocation of resources in Israeli society. Many kibbutz members, including writers, left.

The books written during these years take a sober look at the kibbutz. The ideological crisis was no longer denied. In the majority the kibbutz is presented to one degree or another as a partner to repressing the individual and creating a stifling atmosphere. The narrator projects, as it were, the real situation over that of the vision, and the comparison calls for rectification (Hanoch Bartov, *Heart of the Wise*, 1969; Nathan Shaham, *First Person Plural*, 1968; and Dan Shavit, *The Last Bus*, 1972).

An exception is the trilogy by Zvi Luz, a member of Deganya Aleph: *A Place and Its Legends* (1972), *Going Around* (1975), and *Receding*

Wave (1977). In an interview with Yehiel Hazak (1981), Luz stated that he chose the name "place" and not "kibbutz" because he sought to free himself from the accepted model of "kibbutz literature" (albeit he was still connected to the principle of "the place"). In his trilogy, there are three generations of the same family. The traditional description of the kibbutz establishment is deliberately absent, work relations play a minor role, and clashes between the individual and the kibbutz do not stand at the center of the plot. The author focuses on the deep-rooted sense of place of the Segal family, which created a founding myth of its own that is kept in the family, not the collective, museum and hands it down from generation to generation.

Surrealistic Escape Routes

At the end of the 1980s, the kibbutz was in a deep economic and demographic crisis in which it was compelled to relinquish most of the components that characterized the utopian worldview of its early days. Many kibbutzim embarked on a process of deep privatization. In the literature written during those years, there is a proliferation of indications of the collapse of the human experiment and thoughts about its approaching end. Study of the second- and third-generation kibbutz literature shows that the younger generation created, from numerous standpoints, a discourse antithetical to that of the first generations, but do not propose a real rebellion. Instead of the expected rebellion indicated by their critical position, imaginative "escape routes" suffice. In the surrealistic space, the imagination of the individual subject imposes itself on the collective world that is trying to eradicate its uniqueness, creates new images, and opens possibilities free of the world of accepted representations of the dominant ideology (see Laor, 1995, pp. 7–11).

As opposed to the founders' discourse, which extolled the building enterprise and the life of a new society, *The Black Hills of Dakota* (1987), the novel by Meir Agassi, a son of Kibbutz Ramat Hakovesh, is dominated by death. The novel opens with a scene that reconstructs the moment of the death of two-year-old Gidi Dimant, brother of Zali the boy narrator; continues through the suicide of Walter Minkowitz, a lone, elderly bachelor; and concludes with the news of the death of Aviva and Ze'ev, two of the prominent figures of the kibbutz, in a road accident. Alongside the experience of death, the novel reveals numerous signs of the malignant disease inside many of the characters. Unlike the novels of Oz that present the founding generation as castrating giants, Agassi's narrator adopts a more sober view. His founding-generation heroes are neither giants nor heroic figures. They find themselves in midlife, exiles in their own land—many of them still speak Yiddish— "A *shtetl* masquerading as something else," as Eli Shai puts it (1987). People's lives have become a continuous series of doing one's duty, and their dreams exchanged for the gray routine of the quotidian. This is a world without hiding places—everyone sees everyone else all the time and knows "everything" about them. Furthermore, the symbolic order of the old society has stagnated to such a degree that it is no longer open to the touch of the subject. Instead of receiving the frequency of human pain, it prefers to exclude it. Only death or madness can liberate from the routine.

Unlike the Freudian schema that elevates coping with the father to a mythical level, as employed by Amos Oz, for example, the material of the struggle in Agassi's novel is trivial to the point of becoming comedy. And since kibbutz society, not the parents, functions as a "superego," the struggle for self-realization is with the external, not the internal world. The ideological system also enslaves the parents who live their life in accordance with the kibbutz way of life without really believing in it, and the son, Zali, behind the father's helplessness and mother's sick exhaustion, and out of his own helplessness, exposes an entire world of mini-enslavement in which his parents are merely acquiescent slaves, and to which they try to enslave him.

A further option presenting itself to the boy is a surrealistic escape on the wings of imagination. The moments of surrealistic illusion increase as the plot progresses, and he seeks escape alternately in thoughts of death, hallucinations of soaring over the earth inside the padded capsule of a Sputnik in which he can lie curled up like a fetus, and thoughts of "America," the land of unlimited opportunity, where he will get rich and marry a blonde film star (like Doris Day, who sings "Take me back to the Black Hills of Dakota").

Avraham Kantor's short story, "Nails in the Coffin," from a collection of the same name (1988), tells of the surrealistic funeral of a founder member, Haim Leibedicke (twice "life"). From the coffin the voice of the deceased is heard. It orders the young man taking the body from the morgue to the kibbutz to take him directly to the cemetery and bury him right away, without an announcement, eulogies, and mourning ceremonies. To put him in the ground and fill in the grave: "That's that. Haim Leibedicke is finished, disappeared!" And in Dan Shavit's novel, *Like a Last Night* (2001), an eminent author who has not published anything for years, and his wife arrive one evening at a remote kibbutz, all of whose members are packing up to leave in the morning.

In conclusion, I shall present as my final and interesting example the book written by Doron Avigad, a third-generation son of Givat Brenner, a novella with the odd title, *The False Cards of the Last on the List* (1992). This is the story of a group of young people, kibbutz children, after their military service. According to the kibbutz rules, they must contribute a "year at home" before embarking on their "year out," that is, traveling abroad, studies, or any other activity outside kibbutz life. Avigad does not give his protagonists first names since they will reveal individual existence and identity. The group's members are numbered from 1 to 13. The serial number represents the hierarchical status of each within the group, and the author differentiates between them solely by small recurring "rituals." The novella's strange title is taken from one of these rituals, card playing, a kind of poker based on truth and lying— bluffing. The winner is the one who manages to bluff the other players by presenting his false cards as the real thing.

In the end, boredom and emptiness lead to a sort of revolt. No. 1, the leader of the party, and no. 3, its political brain, take a group decision: to engage the group in digging a deep pit with no purpose. As expected, the new initiative does not bring salvation. The pit gradually widens and deepens and represents the devouring oblivion that has taken over their lives. In the end the pit claims its tragic victim. No. 4, the narrator's nonconformist beloved, the only one that did not take part in the obsessive digging, falls into the pit that has reached surrealistic dimensions. An accident? Suicide? Perhaps an act of murder directed against the odd one out who separated herself from the community? The body, too, was never found; it is as if it had been swallowed up and vanished into thin air.

If we examine the structure of this work, we cannot but discern the similarities of Avigad's novella with the mythical–classical model. The protagonist is the group, not the individual; the group is united around a common aim; the calling becomes a sacred objective for whose sake they are prepared to toil day and night. Even the kibbutz, elders are happy with the pioneering venture that brings the well-loved hoe back to center stage. As in Agassi's novel, here too the Oedipal struggle is voided of true meaning. The third generation was handed down only a meaningless ritual. The deed, which so to speak still focuses on tilling the soil, became a pointless Sisyphean exercise. The huge pit becomes a ravening, empty grave, a kind of black hole. The author places on the stage the empty forms of the symbols of the past that compel the protagonists to perform a pointless ritual of endeavor and which does not allow them true freedom. In the course of the game, the third generation was dealt "false cards." They are incapable of reconstructing the great plot of the pioneers, but they are also incapable of the act liberation, the true act of rebellion.

Bibliography

Almog, S. "Pioneering as an Alternative Culture." *Zion* 58 (1993): 329–46 [in Hebrew].

Berlowitz, Y. "A Young Branch on an Ancient Trunk." *Iton* 77 (1984): 21–23 [in Hebrew].

Braslavski, M. "On the Question of Literary Expression in the Kibbutz." *Mibifnim*, June–August (1938): 314–18 [in Hebrew].

Brenner, Y. H. "The Eretz Yisrael Genre and Its Adjuncts." In *The Works of Y. H. Brenner*, 160–67. Tel Aviv, 1930 [in Hebrew].

Gordon, A. D. "From Reading." In *The Works of A. D. Gordon*, 210–37. Tel Aviv, 1928 [in Hebrew].

Govrin, N. *Keys*. Tel Aviv: Tel Aviv University-Hakibbutz Hamehuhad, 1978 [in Hebrew].

Hazak, Y. "Interview with Zvi Luz." *Hotam*, January 9, 1981 [in Hebrew].

Keshet, S. "The Art of Life or the Art of the Expression of Life: On Zvi Schatz, the First Storyteller of the Kvutza." *Hakibbutz* 13 (1990): 47–65 [in Hebrew].

———. *Underground Soul: Ideological Literature, The Case of the Early Kibbutz Novel.* Tel Aviv: Tel Aviv University-Hakibbutz Hamehuhad, 1995 [in Hebrew].

Laor, Y. *We Are Writing You, Homeland.* Tel Aviv: Hakibbutz Hamehuhad, 1995 [in Hebrew].

Maletz, D. *Around the Essence: On the Image of a Generation*, 39–42. Tel Aviv: Tarbut Vehinuch, 1970 (An article dated 1929, Hebrew).

Miron, D. *If There Is No Jerusalem: Hebrew Literature in a Cultural-Political Context.* Tel Aviv: Hakibbutz Hamehuhad, 1987 [in Hebrew].

Neuberger, H. "Art and Artist in the Commune." *Mibifnim*, July (1937): 60–65 [in Hebrew].

Ofaz, A. *Sefer Hakvutza—Kvutzat Hasharon.* Jerusalem: Yad Ben-Zvi, 1996 [in Hebrew].

———. *The Book of Life: The Diary of Kvutzat Kiriat Ananvim.* Jerusalem: Yad Ben-Zvi, 2001 [in Hebrew].

Shai, E. "A Rainier Rain." *Yedioth Ahronoth*, September 18, 1987 [in Hebrew].

Shaked, G. *Hebrew Narrative Fiction 1880–1980*, Vol. 4. Tel Aviv: Keter-Hakibbutz Hamehuad, 1993 [in Hebrew].

Shapira, A. *Berl: The Biography of a Socialist Zionist, Berl Kaznelson, 1887–1944.* Tel Aviv: Am Oved, 1980 [in Hebrew].

Shimoni, Y. "Reader's Impressions." *Mibifnim*, December (1937): 74–81 [in Hebrew].

Talmon, Y. *On Totalitarian Democracy.* Tel Aviv: Dvir, 1956 [in Hebrew].

Vulcani, E. (signed "E. Zioni"). "The Literature of Labor." *Hapoel Hatzair* 23 (1930): 12–16 [in Hebrew].

Zemach, S. "The Building Line." *Hapoel Hatzair*, January 2, 1925 [in Hebrew].

Literary Works Translated into English

Oz, A. *Where the Jackals Howl.* Translated by Nicholas de Lange and Philip Simpson. New York: Bantam Books, 1982 (paperback).

————. *Elsewhere, Perhaps*. Translated by Nicholas de Lange. New York: Harvest Books, 1985 (paperback).

————. *A Perfect Peace*. Translated by Nicholas de Lange. New York: Harvest Books, 1993 (paperback).

Sobol, J. *The Night of the Twentieth*. Translated into English by Chanah Hoffman. Tel Aviv: Or-Am, 1978.

13

Values and Sites, Attitudes, and Development—The Status of Cultural "Built Heritage" in the Kibbutz

Irit Amit-Cohen

Research Aim

The purpose of this chapter is to discuss the important role of vernacular[1] heritage for the economic developments of the kibbutzim in Israel by examining their location and potential for tourist development. This purpose is part of a wider effort to encourage kibbutz members to preserve their built cultural heritage. One way of convincing them to do this is to discover its historical value and its potential for tourist development, but also to emphasize that this development is not contradictory to their way of life.

The kibbutzim are rural settlements and, as in the entire Western world, they are undergoing significant identity-shaping changes. Pressures to urbanize kibbutzim stem from (a) Israel's population growth, which has increased the value of land for real estate development, (b) the development of nonagricultural businesses, and (c) ideological changes among "new" generations, which are different from the kibbutz founders. Alongside the decrease in agriculture and the increase in demand for privatization, the kibbutzim are attracting new residents as part of community expansion. These new populations are looking for homes as well as a high quality of life and new economic opportunities. These changes have greatly influenced the kibbutzim's existing built heritages.

A large inventory of sites and buildings with historical and architectural values reflecting historical events, social ideology, and lifestyles that no longer exist can be found in the vicinity of many kibbutzim. Most of the buildings reflect "everyday life"—agricultural use and technology, vernacular architecture, local building materials, residential buildings, and ordinary community facilities. Since the mid-1980s, economic changes, together with social and ideological shifts, have threatened this cultural heritage.

Kibbutz members are often unaware of the economic potential of vernacular assets, and therefore do not include them in either preservation or conservation projects, nor in the kibbutz's new physical and economic development plans. Since vernacular assets represent mundane culture, and since they are regarded as common buildings with common uses, both kibbutz members and planning authorities have negative attitudes toward them. An increased awareness of the relationship between the historical value of the buildings and their economic potential for tourist development could change vernacular sites' status in the eyes of kibbutz members.

Method

In order to understand the important role of vernacular heritage in past and present kibbutz development, this chapter defines vernacular heritage, explains how it reflects kibbutz history, explores its spatial distribution in and around the kibbutz, and assesses its economic potential for tourist development.

To study the inventory of sites, their location, their values, and the attitude of the kibbutzim's members to their cultural landscape and their tourism potential, I conducted a survey in five kibbutzim that represent their distribution in Israel: two in the north, two in the center, and one in the south of Israel. All five were founded before 1948, the year Israel became an independent state. In these kibbutzim, I interviewed 123 members—out of a population of 926 (January–April 2007). The members' positions regarding preservation of cultural built heritages and tourist development in the kibbutzim were examined in personal interviews conducted in April 2007. In each kibbutz, the interviewees were divided into three groups: members born in the kibbutz—aged twenty to forty; members born in the kibbutz who were forty years old and above; and "newcomers"—most of them were not members, that is, who were not born in the kibbutz, and were twenty years old and above.

Vernacular Built Heritage and Its Status in Rural Areas

The importance of vernacular heritage was described in 1997 by Groth and Bessi: "Ordinary landscape denotes the interaction of people and place: a social group and its spaces, particularly the spaces to which the group belongs and from which its members derive some part of their shared identity and meaning" (1997, p. 1).

The explanations and demands for preserving vernacular assets can be found also in ICOMOS decision in 1999 to adopt a new charter concerning the protection of vernacular landscapes and sites. The need for a separate charter was explained in the treaty: "The built vernacular heritage is important; it is the fundamental expression of the culture of a community, of its relationship with its territory and, at the same time, the expression of the world's cultural diversity. The vernacular embraces not only the physical form and fabric of buildings, structures and spaces, but the ways in which they are used and understood, and the traditions and the intangible associations which attach to them" (*Charter on the built Vernacular Heritage*, 1999, p. 2). Since then more countries became aware of their vernacular heritage, especially in rural areas, where there are buildings that represent old crafts, agricultural work, or rural life-styles, of which some were left as monuments to commemorate the past, while others became tourist attractions, or were utilized for entertainment and commercial uses (Marshall, 1981, 1989–90, 1990–91; Turan, 1990; Lane, 1993; Saleh, 1996; Pickard, 1997; Birnbaum, 2005).

Recently, research on historical remains in rural areas has been gaining momentum, focusing primarily on three issues: (1) the representative role of the remains, their symbols and values (Meinig, 1979; Jackson, 1994, 1997; Amit-Cohen, 2004, 2006); (2) the remains' location and distribution (Abbott, 1993; Amit-Cohen, 2005a, 2006); and (3) the functional changes and the integration of the remains in rural development and renovation (Graham et al., 1999; Amit-Cohen, 2006).

The decisions to choose objects of the cultural built heritage and leave them in the landscape, as well as to integrate them in the development of rural areas, are driven by three motives:

- Reinforcing communal identity and patriotism, nationally or locally (Ashworth, 1994; Antrop, 2005).
- Conservation for economic purposes: utilizing the volume of the old building for new functions; to refer to historical buildings' cultural value as an "added value" (which increases the property value and the economic value of its newly chosen function) (Xavier, 2004). This topic has been extensively researched, especially the tourist attractions and uses of historical buildings for leisure and entertainment purposes (Ashworth and Tunbridge, 1990). In the past ten years, new economic functions have been observed in structures listed for residency, high-rent offices, and economic services (Leichhenko et al., 2001; Amit-Cohen, 2005b). This process is also part of an accelerated demand for suburban living, mainly by middle-class groups (Wilson, 2004).

- Politically motivated preservation: to advance the interests and power of a specific group, to represent its ideology, or to glorify its deeds and leaders (Young, 1989; Duncan and Ley, 1993).

The influence of these three motives is not uniform; they change from one period to another and from one institutional planning framework to the next. They are dependent on the historical and economic status of the assets, on their appearance, and on the political atmosphere. Exposing the story and values of the historical objects can alter their status for the present and future generations and encourage their preservation and integration in rural landscape renewal. This approach also holds true for vernacular heritages.

Based on the universal and local charters that were adopted throughout the world, the Israel Charter was adopted in 1991. This charter presented seven criteria for preserving historic sites, including bearing witness to an event of historic importance, of a famous person or group, and of a building style. In addition, the site is typical of the culture and atmosphere of the period, a site unique in its building techniques and use of materials, a historical layer in the building culture (*Israel Charter for Preservation of Building and Sites 1991*, 1995).

Israel is not different from other countries in that its planning authorities neglect its vernacular heritage in urban and rural areas because of pressure coupled with preference for preserving just a few sites. Thus the building materials deteriorate and the building technology is ignored, giving rise to a perception that old is ugly, and above all, exacerbating the lack of knowledge about the building technology, the materials, and the events related to this vernacular phenomenon. Kibbutzim have the same attitude—vernacular cultural heritage is hardly preserved.

If vernacular building assets in the kibbutzim reflect "the culture and atmosphere of the period" (ibid.), they should be preserved and, more so, made prominent in planning and development.

Kibbutzim in Israel—Cultural Built Heritage and Its Location

In the kibbutz settlements there is a high inventory of sites and buildings with historical and architectural values that represent local memories and national memories. All are part of the legacy of the kibbutz and of Israel.

The Kibbutz's Cultural Heritage Inventory

By looking at the kibbutz image (which was drawn by a member of a kibbutz in the 1980s), we may expose its cultural built heritage (see Figure 13.1). Most of the sites are vernacular: farming sheds, industrial and residential buildings, water tower, and a dining hall.

We can get the impression of vernacularism also from a signboard that is located at the entrance of a kibbutz in the north of Israel. The reality is very much different from the image that is presented by the sign. See Figure 13.2.

Interviews and field research showed that the kibbutz members divide their cultural heritage sites into two parts comprising three categories:

1. *Kibbutz public landscapes*:
   a. National landscapes embodying national (collective) memories.
   b. Ideological landscapes reflecting the kibbutz movement's ideology and uniqueness.
2. *Kibbutz local landscapes*:
   a. Local landscapes containing intimate memories of each specific kibbutz.[2]

Kibbutz national landscapes include defense and security buildings; water towers and wells; archaeological sites in open spaces (Biblical sites, Old and New Testaments); memorial sites; and sites associated with national historical figures.

Kibbutz ideological landscapes celebrate the kibbutz ideology and include sites that reflect its main principles of cooperation, equality, mutual guarantee, mutual aid, children's education, and independent work without relying on hired worker. Such sites could be dining halls, agriculture buildings, industrial and workshop buildings, educational buildings, children's houses, gardens and open spaces, or agricultural lands.

Kibbutz local landscapes comprise heritage sites reflecting each kibbutz's local legacy: the first location; buildings in unique styles or employing unique construction technologies, memorial gardens, cemeteries, buildings connected to local events or persons, and scenery associated with local memory.

Each of these three "landscapes" has specific location in the kibbutz area. Figure 13.3 shows these distribution and location.

Kibbutz Vernacular Heritage and Its Location

Ideological landscapes are located in two areas.

1. The kibbutz's *public space* or the *central lawn*, which is located next to the dining hall. This area contains buildings for children, the Secretariat, and Security Building (which was usually the first cement-constructed building

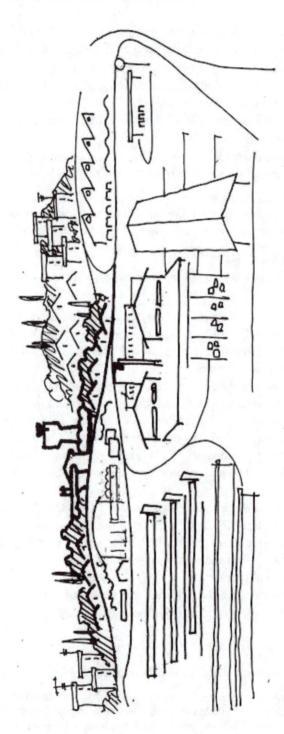

Figure 13.1   The kibbutz image—landscape and legacy

Figure 13.2   Reality and image (Kibbutz Ramat-David, 2008)

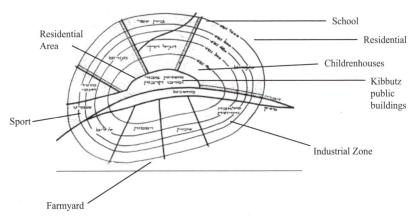

Figure 13.3   Location of vernacular heritage in the kibbutz vicinity

Source: Feinmesser (1984).

in most kibbutzim). Its large lawn is decorated with monuments (by local sculptors or even famous artists) and trees, most of them planted during the settlement's first years. Children's buildings are located adjacent to the garden.

2. An area that is named by its function—*the kibbutz farmyard*. In most kibbutzim, it is located at the entrance and includes the silo, a water tower, cowsheds, barns, storehouses, and workshops. For many years, this area served as the kibbutz's *visiting card* and a *window* to its ideology.

Nowadays, because of their dominating size, the buildings in these two areas are often allocated new functions (most of them at the request of private entrepreneurs): as storage areas, workshops, and wholesale distribution points. These new functions often lead to the building's deterioration and neglected appearance.

The kibbutz national landscape has no clear location. Archaeological sites or battlefields are mostly located outside the kibbutz. Water towers that sometimes trigger memories of a historical event are found in the *kibbutz farmyard*. Buildings dedicated to a national event or a person can often be located in the *kibbutz public space*. And, a historical building (a studio, a private room) can often be found in the residential area, which is part of the *kibbutz local landscape*.

The kibbutz local landscape is located at the outskirts of the *kibbutz public area*, which often separates the farmyard and residences to ensure the privacy and environmental quality of the latter. Residential zones are characterized by low buildings, gardens with no fences, and narrow sidewalks. The name of each neighborhood recalls an important local historical event.

Location versus Tourist Developments: Attitudes of the Kibbutz Members

The three groups of interviewees reported previously were asked several questions regarding their attitudes for preservation of cultural built heritages and tourist development:

1. Characterize your attitude (awareness for preservation and willingness to be involved) to the act of preserving historical heritages in your kibbutz: positive/indifferent/negative.
2. Where would you prefer the development of tourism to take place: on the kibbutz public space; in the kibbutz farmyard; in the kibbutz historical core; at the outskirts; location unimportant?
3. Which activity would you prefer to take place at a conserved site: economic–tourist activity or educational–cultural tourism?
4. Of the following activities connected to preservation and development of tourism at preserved sites in your kibbutz, in which would you choose to be involved: economic–cultural activity for residents and tourists; activities only for tourists; economic–educational–cultural (museum, memorial room, library, and educational center) activities?

Findings

Findings on awareness and involvement of the population and its perception of preservation and development in cultural built heritages are presented in the following tables:

Table 13.1: Answers to questions 1, 2, and 3.

Table 13.2: Answers to question 4.

1. In the answers to questions on residents' relationship to the cultural built heritages (Table 13.1), gaps were observed between the tested populations. While 64 percent of the population born on the kibbutz (aged forty-one plus) supported conservation, only 15 percent of the younger population (aged twenty to forty) supported it; 52 percent did not relate to the topic seriously. The "newcomers" who had only come to the kibbutzim in the last decade were close in their position to the group aged forty-one plus, who were born in the kibbutz—58% supported conservation.

2. In the answers to the question on the connection between activities that integrate conservation, tourist development, and location of the heritage site, 47 percent of those born on the kibbutz had a clear preference for tourist activity in conserved heritage sites located "not in the centre of the kibbutz, the 'Public Space' should remain for the kibbutz uses." "It's part of our private life." "It reflects our intimate uniqueness." In other words, from their point of view, the historical center of the kibbutz is worth developing because of its significance and status—it reflects the kibbutz ideology, *but* it should preserve the kibbutz's privacy. The young people born in the kibbutz (aged twenty to forty) also preferred preserving the historical center of the kibbutz, but not for tourist development (55 percent); the newcomers, even if they welcomed the economic–tourist activity in built heritage, preferred development in the historical assets that are on the periphery of the kibbutz—mainly in the farmyard zone.

3. As far as the type of tourist activity at the conserved site was concerned, the kibbutz-born preferred economic development connected to educational–cultural activity (70 percent); the young generation kibbutz-born (twenty to forty years) and the newcomers preferred economic–commercial and cultural activity, and as somebody said, "I would like to stay and spend my time as much as I can in the frame of the 'Kibbutz Yard,' which became my new home" (March 22, 2007).

4. Table 13.2 concerns the population's involvement with development. Newcomers in the kibbutzim preferred tourist economic–commercial activity. They did not show great interest in economic–educational–cultural activity such as galleries or museums that charge an entry fee. Those forty-one plus who were kibbutz-born requested to be involved primarily in economic activity connected to educational and cultural topics. The young generation (twenty to forty) who were kibbutz-born showed interest in economic activities connected to commercial tourism development—pubs, restaurants, and boutique hotels.

Summary and Conclusions

Built assets were declared cultural built heritages for representing "the past," the intimate story, and the collective memory. Like every prod-

Table 13.1 Relationship of the population in the kibbutzim to conservation and tourist development (%)

Groups of population	Relationship to conservation			Connection between tourist activity and the location of conserved site			Relationship to characteristics of tourism development	
	Positive	Indifferent	Negative	In the public space (the center)	On the farmyard	Unimportant	Economic–commercial development, leisure, entertainment, and tourist development	Economic–educational–cultural development
41+ born on the kibbutz 18%	64	22	14	22	47	31	30	70
20–40 born on the kibbutz 36%	15	33	52	20	55	25	92	8
Newcomers (not born on the kibbutz) 42%	58	12	30	23	61	16	82	18

Table 13.2   Different types of tourism activities in conserved heritage assets, in which the residents of the kibbutzim are willing to be involved (%)

Activity	Born on the kibbutz 41+ on)	Born on the kibbutz 20–40	New
Economic–commercial	27	27	48
Economic–leisure entertainment tourist	20	42	33
Economic–educational–cultural	53	31	
Total (%)	100	100	100

uct, they also undergo a process of choice, classification, and filtering, but the choice is not uniform and there are different criteria for every community. These criteria can be checked by the physical state of the asset, its location, and adaptability to the existing development plans in the environment. But these criteria are insufficient, and because of the asset's uniqueness and value, there is also room to examine the population's relationship to it. In a period of awareness of quality of life and environment, there is also a demand for cultural quality; in other words, to be concerned about sustainable development, which recognizes the contribution of cultural built heritages to the contemporary population and for generations to come. This approach stems from an awareness of the several functions of cultural built heritages: (1) They are a reflection of the past—events, lifestyles, building styles, cultural values, settlement ideology, symbols, and myths. (2) Cultural built heritages contribute in creating local pride: the more the population is aware of its heritage assets, the more it is involved in shaping its environment. (3) Cultural built heritage has an economic value. Their volume and location in dynamic environment allow them to be integrated into the new planning and renovation of old settlements. In that case, the values of "the place"—its appearance and the heritage values—contribute to the demand for new function chosen for the old structure.

This research examined the future of vernacular cultural built heritages in the kibbutz settlement in Israel. The research assumed that the demographic changes occurring in the kibbutz (age and place of birth) will have influence on several matters concerning preservation of the vernacular historical assets and their economic development as tourist attraction: willingness to preserve, being involved in economic development of the vernacular heritage assets, and taking under consideration not only their values but also their location in the kibbutz vicinity. These assumptions were based on the idea that the veterans of the kibbutz (the founders or the children who were born during the first years of the settlement) are closely related to the local history and the basic principles of the settlement. The younger members, who live through the changes and transformations and newcomers (not born on the kibbutz), will be involved in the physical and economical development of the settlement and will be less concerned in its historical values but more in its location—especially when it comes to vernacular heritage.

The data analysis below demonstrates social and economic differences of opinion in the perception of conservation of vernacular heritage as a lever for tourism development in the kibbutzim.

1. There is a difference between the three main social groups: the "old-timers" (forty-one plus) born on the kibbutz are very aware of the kibbutz's historical assets. They have extensive familiarity with historical events and historical images connected to the history of the settlement (its local memories). Their answers show a clear connection between their awareness of the historical values of the kibbutz assets and their relationship to conserving cultural built heritages—monumental assets as vernacular.

    For the kibbutz-born youth, the historical events are distant and awareness of the place's values and historical heritage stems from individual interest in the topic. The new residents who came to the kibbutzim in the late 1990s have scant familiarity with the kibbutz and its history. The two groups are less concerned with the historical values of the vernacular assets, but they show interest in their location and potential for tourist development.

2. The old-timers, the carriers of intimate memory, are interested in the conservation of vernacular built heritages as a means of preserving the local historical story (the kibbutz intimate memories); therefore, they prefer economic activity surrounding the preserved assets and activities connected with education and culture. They also want to be involved, a preference connected with the fact that this population has free time and a desire to volunteer.

3. The newcomers encourage preservation, like the old-timers, but for different reasons. Their point of view is that preservation reinforces their decision to live in a rural environment, which also includes social, nostalgic, and cultural characteristics. Although they know less of the kibbutz history— its intimate and national memories—they believe in its necessity for their demand for high quality of life.

4. On the relationship of the kibbutz population to site location, approximately half of the old-timers, who were born in the kibbutz, preferred to preserve the vernacular sites of the *kibbutz public space* but not as tourist attraction. They prefer economic development connected to educational– cultural activity for the kibbutz population alone. This preference is not based only on accessibility (the center of the kibbutz and its open-space

characteristics), but also on the emotional relationship to assets and development possibilities. They perceive the kibbutz center as *the heart of the kibbutz* that should not be changed. They are aware of the values of the vernacular heritage sites and their potential for economic development, but as long as they do not negatively affect the lifestyle and the image of the kibbutz settlement.

Therefore, the old-timers prefer economic–tourist activities—commercial, leisure, entertainment, and recreation—in preserved sites on the outskirts of the kibbutz center. According to their perceptions, the farmyard zone is fit for such development. Economic development in the center of the kibbutz should be oriented to education and culture—free of charge (70 percent). These differences stem from the older populations' emotional relationship to historical values—local and national—rather than an economic perspective. The young kibbutz-born prefers tourist–economic development that is oriented to commerce, leisure, entertainment, and vacation (92 percent).

The discussion about different populations' relationship to economic development in cultural built heritages—although most of them are presenting vernacular heritage—strengthens the assumption of this research. There is a connection between the population's attitude toward tourism development in a preserved heritage, their demographic changes (age and place of birth), the type of development, and the location of the preserved heritage site. However, the attitudes are varied from one group to the other. The differences are expressed in the extent of the population's familiarity with the history of the site, the image of the kibbutz area, and participation in the profit of tourism development.

Analysis of the positions of the different populations in "now-a-day" kibbutz and familiarity with their expectations will encourage involvement with planning and development of the settlement. The populations' different perceptions in relation to development and conservation in the kibbutz require a strategic planning perspective, using many sites and their availability for the good of advancing the kibbutz. In other words, this is a combined policy of conservation, with awareness of the historical importance of the structures, their location, and the landscape, with existing economic development, in order to increase population involvement in what is happening in the settlement. The functional development of these structures, and in this case for tourist development, must be evaluated according to its contribution to the development of the kibbutz, the attitudes of its varied populations, and the design of its image as a separate and unique type of settlement.

Notes

1. Vernacular buildings and architecture: a term used to categorize methods of con-
    struction that use locally available resources to address local needs. Vernacular
    architecture tends to evolve over time to reflect the environmental, historical,
    and cultural context in which it exists. It has often been dismissed as crude and
    unrefined, but also has proponents who highlight its importance in current design.
    In contrast to planned architecture by architects, the building knowledge in ver-
    nacular architecture is often transported by local traditions and is thus more—but
    not only—based on knowledge achieved by trial and error and often handed down
    through the generations rather than calculated on knowledge of geometry and
    physics.
2. The three categories are based on a research of twenty kibbutzim that was conducted
    by the author of this chapter in the years 2007–2008. The results are going to be
    presented in a book *Assets and Values in the Israeli Kibbutz*. See also Irit Amit-
    Cohen (2007).

Bibliography

Abbott, C. "Five Downtown Strategies: Policy Discourse and Downtown Planning Since
    1945." *Journal of Policy History* 5 (1993): 5–27.
Amit-Cohen, I. "Cultural Built Heritage in Rural Areas: Values and Assets." In *The
    Regional Dimension and Contemporary Challenges to Rural Sustainability*, ed-
    ited by A. M. de Souza Mello Bicalho and S. W. Hoefle, 448–66. Rio de Jenero:
    Laboratorio de Gesttao Do Territorio, 2004.
———. "Cultural Built Heritage and Tourist Development in Rural Areas: The Case
    of the Israeli Moshavot (Jewish Colony of Small Farms)." In *Land Use and Rural
    Sustainability*, edited by A. S. Mather, 144–52. Aberdeen, Scotland: Aberdeen
    University Press, 2005a.
———. "Synergy between Urban Planning, Conservation of Cultural Built Heritage
    and Functional Changes in the Old Urban Center—The Case of Tel Aviv." *Land
    Use Policy* 22 (2005b): 291–300.
———. "Cultural Heritage Landscapes in the Kibbutz: Values, Assets and Develop-
    ment." *Horizons in Geography* 66 (2006): 154–75 [in Hebrew].
———. "Cultural Heritage and Cultural Landscapes: Implications for the Planning and
    Preservation of Rural Landscapes, the Case of the Kibbutz in Israel." In *Progress in
    Sustainable Rural Development*, edited by Tony Sorensen, 90–98. Cairns, Australia:
    Cairns University Press, 2007.
Antrop, M. "Why Landscapes of the Past Are Important for the Future." *Landscape and
    Urban Planning* 70 (2005): 21–34.
Ashworth, G. J. "From History to Heritage; from Heritage to Identity: In Search of
    Concepts and Models." In *Building a New Heritage, Tourism, Culture and Identity
    in the New Europe*, edited by G. J. Ashworth and P. J. Larkham, 13–30. London
    and New York: Routledge, 1994.
Ashworth, G. J. and J. E. Tunbridge. *The Tourist-Historic City*. London: Behaven,
    1990.
Birnbaum, C. A. *Protecting Cultural Landscapes: Planning, Treatment and Management
    of Historic Landscapes*. National Parks Services 36. Washington, DC: Department
    of the Interior, 2005.
Charter on the Built Vernacular Heritage 1999. Paris: World Cultural Center, 1999.

Duncan, J. and D. Ley. *Place Culture Representation*. London and New York: Routledge, 1993.

Feinmesser, Y. *The Kibbutz and Its Planning*. Tel Aviv: Sifriat Hapoalim, 1984 [in Hebrew].

Graham, B., G. J. Ashworth, and J. E. Tunbridge. *A Geography of Heritage: Power, Culture and Economy*. London: Arnold Publishers, 1999.

Groth, P. and T. W. Bessi. *Understanding Ordinary Landscapes*. London: Yale University Press, 1997.

Israel Charter for Preservation of Building and Sites 1991. Haifa and Jerusalem: Technion, Center of Architecture and Heritage, 1995, p. 41 [in Hebrew].

Jackson, J. B. *A Sense of Place, a Sense of Time*. New Haven and London: Yale University Press, 1994.

———. *Landscape in Sight: Looking at America*. Edited by Helen Lefkowitz Horowitz. New Haven and London: Yale University Press, 1997.

Lane, B. "Sustainable Rural Tourism Strategies: A Tool for Development and Conservation." In *Rural Tourism and Sustainable Rural Development*, edited by B. Bramwell and L. Bernard, 102–11. Clevedon, Philadelphia, and Adelaide: Channel View Publications, 1993.

Leichhenko, R. M., N. E. Coulson, and D. Listokin. "Historic Preservation and Residential Property Values." *Urban Studies* 38 (2001): 1973–87.

Marshall, H. W. *Folk Architecture in Little Dixie, A Regional Culture in Missouri*. Columbia: Colombia University Press, 1981.

———. "The British Single-cell House in the American Cultural Landscape Folk Life." *Journal of Ethnological Studies* 28 (1989–90, 1990–91): 31–40, 29, 97–98.

Meinig, D. W., ed. *The Interpretation of Ordinary Landscapes, Geographical Assays*. New York: Oxford University Press, 1979.

Pavin, A. *The Kibbutz Movement Facts and Figures*. Ramat Efal: Yad Tabenkin, 2006.

Pickard, J. "Rural Fences: Perhaps the Most Common (and Most Commonly Neglected) Component of European Cultural Landscapes in Australia." *Historic Environment* 13 (1997): 3–4, 19–22.

Saleh, M. A. E. "Al-Alkhalaf Vernacular Landscape: The Planning and Management of Land in Insular Context, Asir Region Southwestern Saudi Arabia." *Landscape and Urban Planning* 34 (1996): 79–95.

Turan, M., ed. *Vernacular Architecture: Paradigms of Environmental Response. Ethnoscapes Vol. 4*. Hampshire: Gower Publishing Group, 1990.

Wilson, D. "Making Historical Preservation in Chicago: Discourse and Spatiality in Neo-Liberal Times." *Space and Polity* 8 (2004): 43–59.

Xavier, G. "Is Heritage an Asset or a Liability." *Journal of Cultural Heritage* 5 (2004): 301–09.

Young, A. R. "We Throw the Torch: Canadian Memorials of the Great War and the Mythology of Heroic Sacrifice." *Journal of Canadian Studies* 24 (1989): 5–28.

Part III
Reinventing the Kibbutz

Introduction to Part III

Michal Palgi and Shulamit Reinharz

The concluding part of this book looks at the unprecedented directions and surprising ideas evolving in a large majority of kibbutzim today. It starts with the kibbutz movement's global placement, continues with its new local statutory position in Israel, and then describes and analyzes the inventive solutions the kibbutzim are implementing to keep the kibbutz alive. During the first seven decades after the establishment of the earliest kibbutzim, the people involved in this movement devoted their human and physical resources to creating collective, economically viable, egalitarian agricultural communities and to contributing militarily and geographically to building the State of Israel. Kibbutz founders became the heroes of the nation. Despite kibbutz effectiveness in coordination with the Labor Party that had been in power since 1948, the opposition, capitalist-oriented Likud Party, won the national elections in 1977. All of a sudden new bodies and political forces entered the national arena. With these unexpected upheavals, the centrality and importance of the kibbutz as an institution declined.

While the political status of the kibbutz was diminishing within Israel, the kibbutz took a few steps to establish ties among communes internationally. The global community knew of the existence of the kibbutzim through informal visits and somewhat more formal study. But hitherto there had been no real attempt on the part of the kibbutzim to participate in any organization of international collectives. It is as if the kibbutzim saw themselves as Zionist first and socialist second until the shift in power. Only then did they begin to emphasize their links to other socialist utopian communities. In his chapter, Yaacov Oved analyzes the attempt by kibbutzim to form an international federation of kibbutzim and communes. Although this endeavor failed, the International

233

Communes Desk for cultivating international ties was established. In addition, Oved describes the formation of the International Communal Studies Association that maintains ties among scholars who study the kibbutz and communal life. Both these associations have helped place the kibbutz intellectually in the domain of global communes.

The kibbutz's well known and staggering economic crisis of the 1980s had many roots. The first was that the Labor government previously had adopted a policy of guaranteeing the kibbutz debt because of the party's affinity to the kibbutz movement. These guarantees led to poor economic planning. The Likud government, by contrast, was not willing to assume the debt. Instead it adopted an economic plan that halted inflation and led to the accumulation of even larger debts. In 1989 and 1996, the Israeli government, the Israeli banks, and the kibbutz movements agreed upon two debt arrangements to help resolve the economic crisis. Some of the kibbutzim that had remained unscathed by the crisis helped repay the debt of the "weaker" kibbutzim.

With its formerly romantic, pristine image tarnished, the status of the kibbutz in Israeli society and among its own members was questioned. People began to redefine the kibbutz "safety net" negatively as a system by which individuals could be economically irresponsible. As young people began to move away from kibbutzim, few young people joined, and the graying of the remaining population ensued. Kibbutz members soon realized that more than belt-tightening was needed. New ideas, new structures, and new arrangements would have to be considered to stem the steady decline in population and revenues. With the introduction of these significant changes, kibbutz members, the public at large, politicians, and writers began to ask, "When does a kibbutz stop being a kibbutz? If members receive differential salaries and have different standards of living, and if apartments are privatized and nonmember neighborhoods are established, is this entity still a kibbutz? Does it deserve any special treatment from the government? Does it retain any Zionist tasks?"

In response to these questions, the Israeli government convened a public committee to classify and define the kibbutz for legal purposes. Committee chair, *Eliezer Ben-Rafael*, and *Menachem Topel* describe the processes that developed within the committee. Their chapter outlines the discussions, debates, and resulting formal definition of a kibbutz in Israel. The common denominator essential for all kibbutzim, according to the ruling of the committee and agreed to by the kibbutz movement, is the principle of *unconditional extended social security*. Ben-Rafael and Topel tested the committee's definition among kibbutz members and found agreement on the principle of unconditional extended social security, but disagreement on many other issues.

Perhaps the most dramatic action the kibbutzim took to rejuvenate their dwindling and aging communities was to build residential neighborhoods for nonmembers. These new areas were intended to attract young couples with children, including, among the adults, people who were born on the particular kibbutz but had left. Kibbutz leaders thought this would be a win-win situation. The newcomers would enjoy the benefits of the kibbutz "lifestyle," including the use of its educational services, its social and cultural life, and its rural environment. The kibbutz, on the other hand, would have a younger population to fill its ranks and would have an income stream from the allocation of its land to home-buyers. The chapter by *Yigal Charney and Michal Palgi* and that by *Zeev Greenberg* examine this ten-year-old phenomenon. Charney and Palgi analyzed the obstacles that *border* kibbutzim[1] face as they establish residential neighborhoods for nonmembers. After detailing the main barriers to initiating these projects, they explain the criteria used for admission to the neighborhoods and whether the kibbutz communities have achieved their rejuvenation goal. As it turns out, even though this initiative faced major hurdles, it *did yield satisfactory outcomes in terms of revitalizing the demographically skewed kibbutzim that were on the verge of collapse.* Nonetheless, discontent and conflicts arose primarily as a result of unrealistic expectations on both sides. In addition, the tactics used for integrating the newcomers into the community were sometimes unappealing.

Greenberg looks at this same phenomenon from another angle. He studies communications between kibbutz members and new residents and their effect on the process of constructing a partnership between the two. The misunderstanding and conflicts that Greenberg identifies demonstrate that progress in improving the quality of life in the kibbutz requires communication channels for the sharing of information, the exchange of opinions, and sustaining open dialogue for all who wish to participate. Mutual understanding is reached only when kibbutz members (i.e., the "owners" of the kibbutz) accept the rights of the newcomers and the latter understand the needs of the kibbutz.

Part of the economic crisis that was not politically driven derived from the fact that the kibbutz economy had been rooted in agriculture, but agricultural branches were no longer financially sufficient to support the kibbutzim. *Marjorie Strom* depicts the struggle of kibbutzim in the south of Israel to "stay above water" when agriculture became less profitable and markets more competitive. In her chapter, the conflict between acting on one's values and the need to survive economically hinges on the old, endlessly discussed issue of self-labor, that is, a condition in which the kibbutz relies entirely for its needs on the labor of its own members rather than on hiring employees. The concept of kibbutz self-sufficiency played a major role in the ideological development of a Jewish state. But if adhered to completely, it would destroy kibbutzim that need more labor than their membership can provide. The limited alternatives facing three such kibbutzim are the core of her research: a kibbutz that hired workers from Thailand, a kibbutz that attempted to live by self-labor alone, and a kibbutz that hovered in between. Strom found that when kibbutz values and actions are consistent, whether by changing the ideology wholeheartedly or by changing the actions, the kibbutz succeeded in its enterprise. But when values and practice contradicted each other, the enterprise failed. This finding has practical implications for both *differential kibbutzim* (i.e., those with areas of privatization) and *egalitarian kibbutzim* (i.e., those that try to preserve socialist principles), new terms that describe the emerging types of kibbutzim.

The kibbutz has always been a group of people and a set of ideas, not only a set of actions and structures or places. The last two chapters in this part of the book examine a new set of ideas for kibbutzim, a new vision for collective life. There are many such re-visioned or reinvented kibbutzim, each one somewhat different from the next. *Michael Livni* describes the rationale and ideology behind the decision of one community in the southernmost part of Israel to become an eco-Zionist kibbutz. He maintains that an ecological mission overlaps with the goals of intentional communities and could provide a new *raison d'être* for the kibbutz in Israeli society and the increasingly environmentally conscious world.

In his concluding chapter, *Yuval Dror* describes and analyzes the formation of communal groups who have revolted against the traditional kibbutz pattern. Most members of these urban or rural experiments are kibbutz-born young adults or people who graduated from Israeli youth movements where they internalized kibbutz ideals. This small population and the communities they are forging mark a fresh direction for collective intentional communities in Israel. Some have created their collective within Israeli "development towns," traditionally poor cities populated with immigrants who have not assimilated well into Israeli society. Other groups have located in rural areas where the communities they are building are neither agricultural nor industrial. Rather, they are education-community centered and have psychological goals. These "new kibbutzim" limit the number of their members in order to form close relationships with one another. The goal of the members is to enable self-actualization[2] while adhering to basic rules of equality. Moreover, the members study together on a weekly basis. Were this idea to take root, it would mean a remarkable transformation, because the kibbutz would be understood as "for the individual" rather than the individual striving to sustain the kibbutz. Regardless of the potential popularity of this idea or others mentioned above (i.e., new neighborhoods, new goals, and privatization), it is clear that while some kibbutzim remain immune from the forces for change, most are reinventing themselves. This concluding chapter shows that the communal ideal is not dead in Israel but is valued to such an extent that unprecedented initiatives are being undertaken in order to sustain it beyond its first century.

Notes

1. Border kibbutzim are a subset of kibbutzim located physically on the 1967 borders of Israel. They are located on the Lebanese, Syrian, Jordanian, Egyptian, and now Gazan borders.
2. Although he did not invent the term, American psychologist Abraham Maslow popularized the concept of "self-actualization" by placing it at the apex of his theory of the hierarchy of needs. Self-actualization is conceptualized as the ultimate level of psychological development and is similar among the various people who have reached it. A person is self-actualized when all basic and mental needs are fulfilled and the "actualization" of her/his full personal potential takes place.

14

The International Association of
Kibbutzim and Communes

Yaacov Oved

Kibbutzim and communes share social and economic structures based on the principle "to each according to his/her needs from each according to his/her capacity." These two types of social organization also differ from each other. Whereas communes are a worldwide phenomenon present throughout history; kibbutzim are confined to the Zionist movement. Their roots originated in Jewish history, and their existence is limited to Israel. During the first decades of the twentieth century, the kibbutz movement had a few transient connections with communes. Deeper contacts began to develop only after the end of World War II. At that time, kibbutz members were sent on missions to the United States and Canada where they were surprised to discover the existence of communes. This discovery led to contact with these communes for the purpose of learning about their way of life. Kibbutz members were amazed to learn of the similarities between the communes and kibbutzim. Descriptions of visits to American communes can be found in articles in kibbutz movement's weekly publications during the 1950s. These articles were characterized by the discovery that other societies were leading a communal lifestyle and attempting to deal with problems similar to those of the kibbutz. As the initial amazement over the similarities waned, kibbutz writers began to examine the other societies more carefully in order to make meaningful comparisons.

The person who brought the most extensive information about communes in America to kibbutz members' attention was Shalom Wurm, a member of Kibbutz Ramat Yochanan who wrote a series of articles in the 1950s in *Niv Hakvutza*, a periodical published by one of the kibbutz movements. Wurm had been an emissary to the American Zionist

Youth Movement in the 1940s. Later, he reissued these articles as a book (Wurm, 1968). In the 1960s, American commune members became aware of the kibbutz movement in Israel. Some of these Americans were interested in learning from the kibbutz experience. Contacts started on a personal level and gradually expanded to more formal relationships. Concomitantly, books on communes published in the USA reached members of the kibbutzim and aroused great interest. One of these influential books was Kat Kinkade's (1973) A *Walden Two Experiment,* which described the early years of the Twin Oaks commune in Virginia. Mordechai Bentov, a founder of one of the federations of kibbutzim, was enormously impressed by the similarity of the descriptions, particularly with regard to the early years of the kibbutzim. Bentov invited Kinkade to visit the kibbutz movement in Israel, a visit made possible by a grant from the Kibbutz Artzi Federation. When Kinkade returned to the United States, she wrote an article describing the commonalities between communes in the USA and the kibbutzim in Israel. She concluded that the American communes should create a federation that would maintain connections with the kibbutz federations. This idea led her and some of her colleagues to lay the foundation for the Federation of Egalitarian Communities in the United States.

This development, in turn, moved Mordechai Bentov to found the "International Communes Desk (ICD)" (1976) as a central communications office for the publication of an informative newsletter sent to communes throughout the world. His personality and experience as a kibbutz veteran aided him in creating personal relationships with members of American communes and enabled him to get the endorsement of the Kibbutz Artzi Federation for this enterprise. The success of these contacts stimulated Bentov to convene an international conference of commune members in Israel in 1981. Bentov envisaged the establishment of an international federation of communes and believed that the conference would become the starting point of this endeavor. Approximately fifty commune members from fifteen countries participated in the conference. The lectures and discussions dealt with diverse aspects of communal living in the spheres of modern technological society, communal values, work, gender, interpersonal dynamics, economy, education, politics, ecology, and the relations between alternative communities and the world at large. Proceedings were published a year later in book form (Agassi and Darom, 1982). The atmosphere at the conference was friendly but did not create a basis for an international association in part because the worldviews of the communes and kibbutzim differed. Thus the suggestion to establish an international organization was overruled. Instead, a general nonbinding proclamation of mutual ties was endorsed, expressing the following recommendations:

> As a radical alternative to the development of society, we recommend the exchange of experiences and perspectives concerning our lifestyle and our attempts to create social change . . . We recommend that our respective movements . . . coordinate our efforts in persuading the governments of our respective countries to extend their help in supporting communal development as a means to combat problems of unemployment . . . We recommend that our movements call upon the ideological commitment of our own membership to support in any practical manner the continued creation of a World Communities network through which we can not only enhance the viability and survivability of our own communities but offer to all the world the challenge of freedom and equality in community life . . . We suggest that an international community directory be composed listing the addresses plus the historic, demographic and economic data of all the communities of the world . . . This conference represents an immense achievement and step forward in establishing a World Wide Network . . . It stands as a testimony to the vision and dedication of Mordechai Bentov . . . We delegates wish to extend our thanks and admiration to Bentov and to our comrades in the kibbutz movement for bringing us together in this conference. (Agassi and Darom, 1982, pp. 100–02)

Mordechai Bentov died in 1985, and with his demise, the hope for an international organization of communes was put aside. Contacts were renewed some years later by a group of kibbutz members who reactivated the ICD. This group continued to cultivate ties between communes and the kibbutz movement through mutual visits and the circulation of magazines. These connections had their ups and downs but continue to exist to this day.

In the early 1980s, a new stage of scholarly contacts began as a result of the participation by some Israeli kibbutz scholars in the conference of the American Communal Studies Association (CSA). Later, Professor Donald Pitzer of the University of Southern Indiana and the author of this chapter (Oved) decided to initiate an international conference of communal scholars. As a result, a conference of commune and kibbutz scholars was held in 1985 under the auspices of Yad Tabenkin (The Research and Documentation Center of the Kibbutz movement) in which three hundred academics, commune members, and kibbutz members participated. The sessions dealt with issues related to communal life that were common to communes and kibbutzim. Transaction Publishers and Yad Tabenkin published the full text of the conference proceedings (Gorni et al., 1987).

The extensive, multifaceted research on the kibbutz attracted a great deal of attention from foreign participants. They were impressed by the significance of the kibbutz's universal message and by its longevity, which demonstrated to them that human beings are capable of living together communally. The speakers realized that the kibbutz has great potential for offering socialist answers to modern problems. One of the large communal groups whose members attended the conference was the Bruderhof, who followed up with visits to kibbutzim. Upon their return to the United States, the Bruderhof sent letters comparing their way of life to that of the kibbutz. One of their veterans wrote, "We both see our communal way of life as a forerunner of a future social order . . . we feel closeness to you, since for many years we have both lived a way of life based on community of goods" (Oved, 1993, p. 53). Following the first visit after the conference, reciprocal visits followed between kibbutz members and members of the Bruderhof.

The success of the conference encouraged scholars from Israel and abroad to establish the International Communal Studies Association (ICSA) to provide a common framework for the scholarly exchange of information regarding communal life throughout the world. The association was to be multidisciplinary and to serve as a clearinghouse for research projects and for the encouragement of comparative studies. The association's aim was to convene international meetings every three years, to publish the proceedings of these conferences, and to maintain and distribute a list of communes and a list of scholars active in kibbutz and communal research. Its board of directors was international: Pearl Bartelt (USA), Dennis Hardy (England), Bill Metcalf (Australia), Timothy Miller (USA), Yaacov Oved (Israel), Michal Palgi (Israel), and Saskia Poldervaart (Holland). As an international association, the ICSA began to develop contacts with such parallel associations as the CSA and the Associations for Utopian Studies in the USA, and it triggered the establishment of the European Utopian Studies Association resulting from the participation of UK scholars at the second ICSA conference in Scotland. The international conferences of the ICSA enabled scholars and members of kibbutzim and communes to meet and exchange views and research. The participation of scholars at these conferences triggered many reciprocal visits of kibbutz and communal scholars to kibbutzim and communes.

At this stage, the ICD found it advantageous to combine efforts with the ICSA on the assumption that the academic world offers a valuable entry to the wider society that could boost the outreach efforts of communities. On the other hand, combined efforts could benefit ICSA because regular contacts with living communitarians offer an unparalleled opportunity to experience the communal phenomenon. These contacts occurred during the years when kibbutzim believed they had a message for communes and for the society at large. In the 1970s, the noted Israeli writer, Amos Oz, expressed the evaluation that the kibbutz, despite its deficiencies, is the only attempt to create a communal, egalitarian society without oppression. The kibbutz shows how to maintain, within a materialistic, competitive reality, a community with structured mutual help and collective responsibility for its welfare.

Some years after the establishment of the international kibbutz and commune associations, a substantial change took place in the general make up of the kibbutzim. During the 1980s, an economic crisis swept over Israel hurting the national economy and damaging numerous kibbutzim whose debt rose significantly, thus affecting the economic situation of the entire kibbutz movement. People experienced this crisis as an earthquake that shocked the economic and social structures of the kibbutz, leading to doubts about the way the kibbutz system functioned and about its ability to survive and sustain its values and quality of life.

These socioeconomic problems also shook the self-assurance of kibbutz members. Alarmed by the gravity of the economic crisis, many members felt that their community model had lost its aura as a sustainable utopia. These uncertainties generated radical changes in the kibbutz movement, and soon, two-thirds of all the kibbutzim sought new arrangements of privatization in most areas of social and economic activities. Information about the kibbutz crisis and subsequent privatization spread rapidly throughout the world. What was once regarded as a successful secular,[1] communal experience that Martin Buber defined as "the experiment that did not fail" began to be considered as another failure in the attempt to realize a utopian experiment and weakened the status of the kibbutz as a source of inspiration for secular communes. During those years, many secular communes worldwide underwent similar changes, leading to the privatization of the communal economy. The new communities that arose during these years were partial communes only. As a result, the sector of integral (or classic) communes decreased. With this change in the overall spectrum of communities, "Intentional Communities" became the generic term.

Over time it became clear that the problems of kibbutzim and communes are similar and that the kibbutz was not unique in its challenges. Kibbutz members emphasized problems with the quality of life (rather than political ideology), thus bringing kibbutzim closer to the issues that are the main concern of commune members. This sharing of experiences may account for the fact that interest by commune members and scholars in the kibbutz experience did not diminish even though the kibbutz had become less concerned with its universal message and more with the intricacies of privatization. Currently, there is a great deal of interest in research carried out by kibbutz scholars about the roots of the crisis. Arthur Keene, an American anthropologist who studied the kibbutz for many years, claimed that changes bring the kibbutz closer to the Western materialistic way of life in which there is only a weak ideological component. "Although the kibbutz will not become more attractive and will not inspire people to believe that it is the ideal alternative society," he asserts, "its search for solutions to its problems in these new circumstances will evoke much interest" (dialogue with the author, 1998).

The new circumstances of privatization in the kibbutz movement and among many of the intentional communities did not limit or weaken the international activities of ICSA. From 1988 to 2010, it held nine conferences that took place in Scotland (1988), the United States (1991, 1993), Israel (1995), Holland (1998), Germany (2001), the United States (2004), and Italy (2007). The 2010 conference was held in Israel and was part of the centenary celebration of the founding of Deganya (the first kvutza). In these nine conferences, 950 papers were delivered by commune and kibbutz scholars, the vast majority of whom came from Israel and the United States, with smaller contingents from the United Kingdom, Germany, Holland, Australia, and Denmark, and a few individuals from Canada, Italy, Sweden, Switzerland, Spain, Ireland, Japan, South Korea, Poland, Hungary, Serbia, Russia, Portugal, and India. The proceedings of three conferences were published as books (Gorni et al., 1987; Hardy and Davidson, 1989; Poldervaart, 2001). Most of the scholars presented papers dealing with issues related to communes in their respective countries. But the international convergence enabled the exchange of views and triggered comparative studies. Approximately thirty scholars delivered papers with a comparative perspective. Some comparative studies were published as books during the last twenty years: Michel Tyldesly, *No Heavenly Delusion: Comparative Study of Three Communal Movements* (2003); William Metcalf, *Sharing Visions Sharing Lives: Communal Living Around Half of the Globe* (1996); Yaacov Oved, *Communes and Intentional Communities in the Second Half of the 20th Century* (2009); Maria Folling Albers, *The Transformation of Collective Education in the Kibbutz: The End of Utopia* (1999).

Since the 1990s, the ICD has renewed and strengthened its activities, but it did not create an international framework like the ICSA. It remained an Israeli entity, a contact office that maintained international links with communes all over the world. In 1992, the ICD began to publish its bulletin *CALL,* which became a platform for connections between the kibbutz movement and the communes. *CALL*'s goal was to have representatives of different types of communal life become acquainted with one another so that they could learn from each other's experiences, changes, achievements, and setbacks. *CALL* also hoped that knowing that many groups succeed in leading lives of solidarity, sharing and disseminating a utopian message, would boost people's spirit.

Despite the privatization trend, members of egalitarian communes continued to have a sense of connection and identification with each other. An indication can be found in several articles that appeared in *Communities Magazine* #109 (Winter 2000). One member of Twin Oaks contributed a piece about the introduction of changes in his commune and in the kibbutzim: "The Israeli kibbutzim offer a close parallel with our larger Federation purpose. Many kibbutz members are from the same Western individualistic culture which values personal freedom highly" (Brian in *Leaves of Twin Oaks*, Winter 2000). Valerie Renwick Poter, a member of Twin Oaks, has corresponded with the ICD for several years sharing thoughts and observations about communal life.

An additional example of the connections between egalitarian communities and the ICD occurred in February 2002 with the arrival of a delegation of five members from the East Wind commune who made a month long visit to Israel and visited twelve kibbutzim. Located in Tecumseh, Missouri, the East Wind commune is "interested in creating an alternative society based on a vision of peace and social justice." Its Web site continues:

> Once thought to be a relic of the sixties, the communal living movement is enjoying renewed interest. There are now hundreds of "intentional communities" spread throughout North America. East Wind is one such community, owned, operated and governed by its members. All income and expenses are shared in common. We are located on 1045 acres of land in the beautiful Ozark mountains of southern Missouri. Presently we number about 60 adults and 5 children. (http://www.eastwind.org/)

The organizer of the East Wind delegation wrote about the two purposes of the visit: To experience life in the kibbutzim and compare it with life in the communities belonging to the Federation of Egalitarian Communities, and to establish a network between these two movements, hoping kibbutz members will be inspired to visit the communities in the United States. The ICD has ongoing contact with communes and with a variety of communities worldwide. For example, Richard Jandel of the Swedish organization "Co-housing Now," author of a book in Swedish on the history of the kibbutz, has been in contact with ICD and invited its secretary to attend the International Co-housing conference in Sweden in the summer of 2010. Members of the Bruderhof communities have been in contact with the ICD for many years. Recently several delegations came to visit kibbutzim and had several contacts with the Desk. The ICD also has strong contacts with the German Catholic "Integrierte Gemeinde." In recent years they formed "The Urfeld Circle" that meets with their German counterparts both in Israel and Germany to discuss religious and community topics.

Modern communes and various types of intentional communities are facing shared problems, including their small size. They are tiny islands, no more than small isolated cells within the larger society. Moreover being inherently selective, their general social contribution is limited. Their experience and way of life represent a social laboratory, an opportunity to study a realistic form of cooperative life that espouses equality within voluntary communities. The communal framework represents the free choice of its members and not the imposition of an external coercive regime. Kibbutzim and communes display moral behavior that is willingly accepted and internalized as normative. Thus in modern pluralistic society, kibbutzim, communes, and intentional communities offer an option for social reform within a community framework where members lead their lives voluntarily on the basis of social justice. In a world in which the end of ideology and the demise of utopia are discussed, these alternative communities represent a "mini utopia." The establishment of international links and associations is essential to boost the possibilities of having an impact on society at large. The continuation of international and national connections among communes, intentional communities, and kibbutzim may be able to advance this goal.

Note

1. Communes in many parts of the world are based on shared religion. Most kibbutzim are only minimally involved in traditional Jewish religion. Sixteen kibbutzim (10,000 members) are considered "religious kibbutzim."

Bibliography

Agassi, Y. and Y. Darom, eds. "The Alternative Way of Life." *The 1st International Conference on Communal Living*. Tel Aviv: ICD, 1982.

Brian. "Reports from a Visit to the Kibbutz." *Leaves of Twin Oaks, Bulletin of the Community Twin Oaks*, Winter 2000.

Folling Albers, M. *The Transformation of the Collective Education in the Kibbutz: The End of Utopia*. Frankfurt am Main: Peter Lang, 1999.

Gorni, Y., Y. Oved, and I. Paz, eds. *Communal Life: An International Perspective.* Tel Aviv: Yad Tabenkin and NY: Transaction Books, 1987.

Hardy, D. and Lorna Davidson, eds. *Utopian Thought and Communal Experience.* Enfield: Middlesex Polytechnic, 1989.

Kinkade, K. *A Walden Two Experiment.* New York: William Morrow, 1973.

Metcalf, W. *Sharing Visions Sharing Lives: Communal Living Around Half of the Globe.* Findhorn: Findhorn Press, 1996.

Oved, Y. *Distant Brothers—History of the Relations between the Bruderhof and the Kibbutz.* Tel Aviv: Yad Tabenkin, 1993.

———. *Communes and Intentional Communities in the Second Half of the 20th Century.* Tel Aviv: Yad Tabenkin, 2009.

Poldervaart, S., ed. *Contemporary Utopian Struggles.* Amsterdam: Aksant, 2001.

Tyldesly, M. *No Heavenly Delusion: Comparative Study of Three Communal Movements.* Liverpool : Liverpool University Press, 2003.

Wurm, S. *Communal Societies and Their Way of Life.* Tel Aviv: Ayanot, 1968 [Hebrew].

15

Redefining the Kibbutz

Eliezer Ben-Rafael and Menachem Topel

Recent changes within kibbutzim since the 1990s (Ben-Rafael, 1997), demonstrating how far they have strayed far from the kibbutz model, raise the question of whether it is still appropriate to use the term "kibbutz" with regard to these communities. And if it is appropriate, what does the word "kibbutz" mean? The research summarized in this chapter confronts the fundamental question of whether these changes represent the end or a new phase of the kibbutz. The temptation is great to answer this question peremptorily and conclude that "the kibbutz is over" and that it has exhausted its historic mission. Nevertheless, even when introducing the most radical changes, kibbutzniks (i.e., kibbutz members) still insist that their communities be called "kibbutzim."

We contend that changes have gone so far that a definition is needed to clarify the parameters of a contemporary kibbutz. Civil servants in the national administration have an interest in this new definition as well, as they deal with kibbutzniks in matters of income tax, land use, physical planning, social services, school budgets, and many other matters linking kibbutzim to official agencies. The kibbutz, indeed, had always enjoyed a special status and complied with special regulations as long as it conformed to the definitions of what a kibbutz is (Lapidot et al., 2000). Since these definitions are inadequate today for a growing number of kibbutzim, civil servants need reformulations to allow them to adjust their policies *vis-à-vis* the kibbutz sector. Thus, on May 19, 2002, the Israeli government formed the Public Committee for the Classification of Kibbutzim. The debates of this committee together with a survey organized by the authors (through the Yad Tabenkin Institute) provided the material of our analyses.

After more than one year of work, the Ben-Rafael Committee (named for its chair) reached conclusions regarding the kibbutz as well as a concept that compared the various models of kibbutzim as they take shape in practice. The committee's composition reflected its goal. Members included leaders of the kibbutz movement, including representatives of the pro-change and the conservative camps; public figures outside the kibbutz movement; academics in relevant fields; and representatives of the civil service. In addition, the committee invited a considerable number of specialists—kibbutzniks and non-kibbutzniks—to evaluate and analyze selected developments. Considerable information from varied sources fueled the debates during the fifteen monthly meetings, each of which lasted from four to five hours. Large differences of opinion existed among the members of the committee. However, after several crises, the committee succeeded in reaching an agreed formulation regarding all points of its agenda. Its complex process made the committee itself a central scene where the fate of the kibbutz movement was played out as an entity with internal diversity.

Based on committee documents, testimonies, and discussions, this chapter critically examines the actual transformations that a large part of the kibbutz sector is undergoing. We use the notion of "collective rebuilding" to emphasize that the collective persists despite its transformation. Rebuilding raises the question of whether the new reality represents a reinterpretation or a discontinuation of basic kibbutz codes. The work of the committee constitutes the ideal material for considering most aspects of collective rebuilding, as the committee's decisions were formalized into official government regulations, later endorsed by the Kibbutz Movement. It is through this work that the most impressive efforts took place to stabilize communities that started transformations but did not always know where to stop, each of them acting according to its own drives, at its own pace, and with different goals in mind. Moreover, it was unclear to what extent kibbutzniks involved in these processes, which pushed in very different directions, still shared the conviction that they make up one collective identity, sufficiently distinct from its environment.

In this study, the three basic issues of collective rebuilding were considered:

1. the implementation of new arrangements in place of former ones;
2. the eventual renewed crystallization of the collective so that the kibbutz remains distinct organizationally;
3. the formulation of new forms of collective identity and their relation to former ones.

Our investigation of the first two issues was based on material gathered by the Ben-Rafael Committee, while the third was based on a survey carried out by the authors in a large sample of kibbutzim (see Ben-Rafael and Topel, 2009). The survey explored the relation between structure and identity: to what extent do members of kibbutzim that develop differently adopt different approaches to kibbutz collective identity? The three basic issues—implementation of new arrangements, redefinition of the kibbutz's "uniqueness," and the reformulation of collective identity—should shed light on the process of collective rebuilding that the Ben-Rafael Committee endorsed. Two categories of kibbutzim emerged—the "renewing kibbutz" (in Hebrew: kibbutz *mitkhadesh*) and the "collective kibbutz" (in Hebrew: kibbutz *shitufi*). The second refers to kibbutzim that decided to remain loyal to the longstanding models; the first refers to a kibbutz that has instituted at least one of the following: (a) privatization of apartments; (b) differential salary among members; (c) distribution to members of cooperative shares in kibbutz economic enterprises (see Sabbagh and Dar, 2002). It is to note here that kibbutzim *shitufiim* are often among the richer kibbutzim, which means that members of this type of kibbutz may be willing to remain loyal to the original value orientations provided that their kibbutz can "afford" it.

Concerning the replacement of "classical" arrangements with new ones, our research assesses the extent and ways the kibbutz sector has become pluralistic in terms—among other issues—of education, distribution of resources, salaries, relations between the family and the collective, the rights and duties of individual members, the social contract between the collective and individual members, the organization of work branches, or policies regarding employment. As a result of this diversity, the kibbutz movement's institutions are also shifting their orientation. They increasingly resemble an umbrella organization of a variety of associations and decreasingly resemble central bodies of a social–political movement (Chapter 3 of this book).

What continues to bind the communities that define themselves as kibbutzim? Committee material leads us to one essential common denominator—the principle of unconditional extended social security, in Hebrew *arevut hadadit*. In kibbutzim *shitufiim*, this principle lies at the core of the collective experience. In kibbutzim *mitkhadshim*, however, things are different. In this type, life is much more individualistic, and the community's response to people's demands is regulated by formal and specified regulations, according to the availability of resources. Elucidating this notion in practical terms is a major activity of the kibbutz movement as well as of individual kibbutzim. The operation of welfare services, minimum guaranteed wage to any member regardless of his/her input, rights to education, individual rights in the community or retirement funds are major concerns of kibbutzim *mitkhadshim*. Kibbutzim are quick to declare themselves of the *mitkhadshim* type, but then have to struggle to respond to the commitments demanded by this status. Paradoxically, while kibbutzim often aspire to become kibbutzim *mitkhadshim* because of economic difficulties, to become one, they need resources they may not have.

At the same time, it is relatively easy for a kibbutz to morph into a *mitkhadesh* type because partial and relatively moderate moves do not require the authorization of an external body, like the Registrar of Collective Associations. These gradual changes may lead later, however, to the completion of the formal transformation into a kibbutz *mitkhadesh*. Data from the field show that many kibbutzim *mitkhadshim* that were previously confronted with acute difficulties have recently undergone economic, social, and demographic improvement following the endorsement of reforms.

On the other hand, it is undeniable that many contemporary kibbutzim reach a stage where traditional values of equality and sharing are no longer central values of the community (see Rosner, 2004). However, even when supporters of the transformation lead the harshest attack on the original values, the rules of legitimate kibbutz discourse are rarely violated. Critics use the idea of a "new interpretation" so that they can retain the notion of "kibbutz" to describe themselves. New interpretations are indeed essential for kibbutzim *mitkhadshim* to rebuild their institutions. These interpretations include personal responsibility, achievement motives, respect for authority, and profitability of work. Concomitantly, one observes the kibbutz's adoption of a newly legitimate management terminology that was rejected in the past because it was symbolic of the "other society." Instead of "Economic Committee," these kibbutzim use the term "Board of Management," "the Secretary" is now the "Community Director," and so on. Above all, privatization of apartments is one of the conspicuous denominators of kibbutzim *mitkhadshim*. This change decollectivizes a main communal resource and breaks the kibbutz's longstanding refusal to accept internal private real estate property. Advocates of "privatization of apartments" do not present this shift as a rupture with the past, but rather as a new phase of the familization of kibbutz life. The beginning of familization, they claim, reaches back to the recognition of the family as a budgetary unit entitled to authority in specific domains of collective life (education, health, or children's problems). In this perspective, one may speak of the privatization of apartments as the completion of a process that does not directly question allegiance to other kibbutz values.

The privatization of means of production, however, is a different matter. This concept means that members are allotted shares that represent their part in the collective capital invested in factories, agricultural crops, and other productive activities. Kibbutz economic branches remain organized on the basis of collective enterprise that binds the settlement's membership, but, as a result of the distribution of shares, individuals have a direct relation to production, with a projected higher work motivation. Hence, profitability becomes the major, if not the sole, evaluative criterion. Any emotional or symbolic value of work becomes obsolete and irrelevant when pondering, for example, continuing or discontinuing the cotton crop or dairy farming. In this climate, humanistic considerations that, in the past, could lead a kibbutz to retain a branch only because it provided handicapped people jobs that gave them feelings of contributing to the collective welfare need not be continued. Technocrats who are now solidly in command stress the practical outcomes, in purely economic terms, of any decision-making, and they are weakly challenged by people sensitive to other arguments.

This development of kibbutzim *mitkhadshim* damages one of the most important kibbutz resources—its social capital. This resource was generated by close cooperation between members' informal ties and deepened their commitment to the collective welfare. Social capital expressed itself in member responsiveness to urgent tasks even after regular work hours and to a readiness to adjust to changing circumstances and new constraints. It was also expressed in voluntary involvement in committees in charge of various social and cultural spheres. This responsiveness depends on the cohesiveness of the community, which is scarcer now that the kibbutz distributes differential salaries and endorses the privatization of social life (Pavin, 2007). The decline in social capital demonstrates the extent to which the kibbutz *mitkhadesh* is definitely not "like before." In contrast to the past, kibbutzim *mitkhadshim* define social exchange between individual members and the collective in specific and concrete terms—precise financial rewards for precise contributions to the welfare of the community (see also Warhurst, 1994). One is "worth" what one produces and gets rewarded for it in quantitative terms. Money becomes a direct and open means of measurement of power and status, and above all, a determinant of the standard of living.

Furthermore, in some kibbutzim *mitkhadshim*, a "community extension" or in Hebrew, *harkhava kehilatit*, has been created. These are new neighborhoods to be populated by nonmember residents who build their apartments and pay for the services they receive from the kibbutz. When the number of such residents reaches a certain size, they are entitled to participate in elected municipal bodies that are expected to act on their behalf as well as that of kibbutzniks. For the latter, the residents are "others" but not "outsiders." While this new development does not destroy kibbutz reality—especially when many of the nonmembers are the offspring of kibbutz members, as is often the case—it is still a drastic move. In the past, numerous nonmembers did live among kibbutz members—students of Hebrew programs (*ulpanim*), groups from youth movements in stages of preparation for kibbutz life, voluntary workers, tourists, or parents of members--yet the creation of neighborhoods specifically for permanent nonmember residents is a novelty. It signals a transgression of the traditional principle according to which a kibbutz is a community, distinct from its environment in terms of territory, structure, and social life. While this change is not a brutal rupture with the past, it indicates the readiness to legitimize the non-kibbutz way of life within the physical boundaries of the community.

In this context, the second unavoidable basic issue of collective rebuilding is kibbutz members' search for answers to the question: "What is a kibbutz?" This question is difficult to answer today. Yet, we found that the main answer given by the rank and file, as well as by the leaders and technocrats in the most innovative kibbutzim, revolves around the concept already mentioned and defined in the above, namely, *arevut hadadit*. This notion signifies that the kibbutz retains its commitment to the welfare of its individual members, at least with respect to basic privileges. Regarding rights, the kibbutz *mitkhadesh* provides its members with conditions of life that far surpass anything comparable in contemporary welfare states. This principle warrants a partial common ground with the kibbutz *shitufi* and constitutes the ultimate justification for the retention of the title "kibbutz" as a unique social setting.

In principle, the practical definition of *arevut hadadit* is primarily the responsibility of the central bodies of the national kibbutz movement, which convenes commissions of experts to elaborate regulations and submits them to individual kibbutzim. In reality, and as noted, kibbutzim are increasingly demonstrating autonomy *vis-à-vis* these central institutions. This overall weakening of the movement's authority has persisted even after the two large kibbutz federations found the way to merge, ending up more than eighty years of separate existence and endless quarrels. Privatization and partial decollectivization undermine the newly unified movement's cohesion and position *vis-à-vis* kibbutzim. At most, movement bodies may try to provide kibbutzim with services. But this is not easy when kibbutzim exist in a multiplicity of forms stemming from divergent interests that can hardly be encompassed by central policies. Yet, it is also to emphasize that despite the growing and ever more ramified pluralism of the kibbutz sector, one does not witness serious attempt to split it up the kibbutz sector. Less than a handful of kibbutzim have concluded that they can no longer define themselves as a kibbutz, thus confirming that transformation and pluralization are not "fatal" to the kibbutz idea. Moreover, despite the weakening of the kibbutz movement and the existence of extremist kibbutzim *mitkhadshim*, people continue to perceive kibbutzim as constituting a "movement," however "movement" is understood.

All of the above brings us to the third issue of the kibbutz's collective rebuilding—how do kibbutzniks perceive themselves within all of this change? This issue touches upon the three components of collective identity, namely, the perceptions by members of their commitment to the collective, their perceptions of the collective's singularity in terms of values and ethos, and their self-positioning as kibbutzniks *vis-à-vis* "others" who "are not." To examine these questions, we designed and administered a special survey (2005) to reach members of the largest range of kibbutz models.

The research sample numbered 312 respondents who are members of twenty-five diverse kibbutzim. In brief, this research revealed that kibbutzniks believe the kibbutz has rejected its original values and aspirations—especially the value of equality and involvement in Israeli society. Furthermore, they believe that the kibbutz now stresses individualistic values such as the search for quality of life and economic security. What remains of the "old" values is the appreciation of common ownership of material means of production and *arevut hadadit*. As mentioned, it is on this basis that a consensus remains among kibbutzniks that the kibbutz still constitutes a distinct and unique social setting. However, the less a kibbutz is bound by the original model, the less its members tend also to appreciate those original values.

The survey revealed that there are significant differences between kibbutzniks who belong to the two extremes on the kibbutz continuum, running from "firmly *shitufi*" to "determinedly *mitkhadesh*." Members of the first type show significantly stronger loyalty to "classic" kibbutz values than do members of the second. It is not surprising that kibbutzniks who are members of in-between categories of kibbutzim—somehow *shitufi* and somehow *mitkhadesh*—are less confident regarding which values should be emphasized in the operation of a kibbutz. This lack of clarity applies to a large part of the kibbutz sector and certainly prevents the crystallization of two polarized antagonistic camps. Confirming our earlier analysis, the large majority of kibbutzniks of all types are determined to remain kibbutz members and bind their destiny to their communities even though many refuse to answer whether they would have chosen to join a kibbutz "if they had to do it over again." In addition, a commitment to collective challenges is not a high priority of kibbutz members of any type.

As for the third aspect of collective identity, the self-positioning of kibbutzniks *vis-à-vis* "others," survey respondents tend to identify themselves more with the urban middle class than with any other segment of the Israeli population. Concomitantly, the group perceived as most remote consists of underprivileged populations in poor towns and neighborhoods, their geographical proximity to kibbutzim notwithstanding. Yet, in this latter respect, we found significant differences among kibbutz members according to the kinds of kibbutz to which they belong. As opposed to the more *mitkhadesh* kibbutz, members of the more *shitufi* kibbutz type express a stronger allegiance, at least rhetorically, to non-kibbutz members who eke out a living from blue-collar work. Moreover, the kibbutzniks of more *shitufi* kibbutzim are also more convinced that the kibbutz has contributed positively to society as a whole. These findings indicate that the collective identity of kibbutzniks in kibbutzim *shitufiim* is closer to classical ideology than is that of members of kibbutzim *mitkhadshim* (see also Palgi, 2002).

Israeliness and Jewishness are primary features of the various identities of kibbutz members. In numerous cases, however, professional diplomas and positions matter more than does kibbutz membership. In this respect, kibbutz members are not substantially different from individuals outside the kibbutz. Nevertheless, respondents do mention kibbutz membership as a factor of identification. Only when exploring this identity further do we see differences between types of kibbutzniks: the more *shitufi* their kibbutz, the more respondents stress their kibbutz identity; the more *mitkhadesh* the kibbutz, the less importance respondents give to their kibbutz identity.

In sum, we may speak of a plurality of contemporary kibbutz models, of formulations of collective identities, and of members' identification with them. Furthermore, most kibbutzim belong to intermediate categories on both the structural and subjective dimensions. The majority of the interviewees present collective identities in which varying allegiances to old values intermingle with new preoccupations (Achouch, 2000). It is true that in the 1950s and 1960s, kibbutzniks would also speak of themselves in terms of "better" or "less good" kibbutzim according to their perceptions of kibbutzim's observance of kibbutz ethical and normative rules. Today, however, the ends of the continuum have been displaced: what was once "very liberal" often seems today close to "classical" or *shitufi*, and what is now "more *mitkhadesh*" would not have qualified as "kibbutz" at all.

It is also to evince at this concluding stage of these pages that structural changes in the entire kibbutz sector that have taken place in recent years—and still expand—have not been coordinated nor planned by any party or leadership. Although members in individual kibbutzim knew what was happening in other kibbutzim, there were no joint considerations. One is rather to speak of a "chain phenomenon" illustrating a process well known from other places and times. Some examples are the decolonization that spread from one colony to another during the 1960s, the students' revolts in the 1960s and early 1970s, which crossed countries and continents, or the crumbling of communist regimes in Central and Eastern Europe in the late 1980s and the early 1990s. One more case that is still ongoing at the hour that these lines are written (April 2011), is the set of uprisings taking place in the Arab world. In each of these chains of events, local actors were aware of what others were doing in other places but were confronting unique circumstances and acted by their own. This kind of development applies to kibbutzim as well. In each case, members faced specific problems in general circumstances of crisis that hit the kibbutz sector as a whole. In many kibbutzim, this crisis caused a genuine breakdown of legitimacy of the social order that brought about claims for radical change and the invention of new patterns. These new patterns took on a variety of forms among the various kibbutzim.

Even today, however, *arevut hadadit* that guarantees that membership in a kibbutz community is much more than mere residency plus the feeling of being part of a "movement" have remained basic characteristics of a kibbutz. To this is to add the quasi-constitutional stipulation of the kibbutz official regulations according to which decision-making about matters implying essential structural changes in the community requires an overwhelming majority of the members. Hence, whatever the category of a kibbutz, the collective remains the focus of reference for its members. It is in the collective that the conditions of life and the engineering of social structures are determined. As such, members remain, for all practical purposes, *members*. This is, to be sure, the privilege of kibbutzniks. As opposed to city dwellers or those living in other social forms, members determine the arrangements of the community where they live and continue to be sovereign over their social order. Though it is also not less obvious that remaining a kibbutznik is now more than ever a permanent choice, because, unlike in the past, privatization of apartments, differential salaries, and, where applicable, the means of production guarantee the possibility of widening decollectivization to other domains of activity. That this drive may lead kibbutzniks to decide to push transformation far beyond even the most flexible definition of "what a kibbutz is" makes the kibbutz a particular illustration of what Ulrich Beck (1992) defines as a "risk society."

Bibliography

Achouch, Y. "To Reconstruct Inequality: Remuneration for Work and Strategies to Increase Income in the Kibbutz." *Journal of Rural Cooperation* 28 (2000): 3–18.

Beck, U. *Risk Society: Towards a New Modernity.* London: Sage Publications, 1992.

Ben-Rafael, E. *Crisis and Transformation: The Kibbutz at Century's End.* Albany, NY: SUNY, 1997.

Ben-Rafael, E. and M. Topel. *The Kibbutz on Path Apart.* Jerusalem: Bialik and Yad Tabenkin, 2009 [in Hebrew with English abstract].

Lapidot, A., L. Applebaum, and M. Yehudai. *From Protection to Competition.* Ramat Efal: Yad Tabenkin, 2000 [in Hebrew with English abstract].

Palgi, M. *Organizational Change and Ideology: The Case of the Kibbutz.* Haifa: The Institute for Study and Research of the Kibbutz and the Cooperative Idea, University of Haifa, 2002.

Pavin, A. *Communital Resilience: Social Capital in the Kibbutz.* Ramat Efal: Yad Tabenkin, 2007 [in Hebrew with English abstract].

Rosner, M. *Distributive Justice in Kibbutz Communities That Have Changed.* Haifa: The Institute for Study and Research of the Kibbutz and the Cooperative Idea, University of Haifa, 2004.

Sabbagh, C. and Y. Dar. "'Spheres of Justice' in the Israeli Kibbutz and Urban Sectors: Adolescents' View." *Comparative Sociology* 1 (2002): 193–213.

Warhurst, C. "The Nature and Transformation of Communal Socialism: A Case Study of Kibbutz Industry." Ph.D. Department of Organization Studies, University of Central Lancashire, 1994.

16

Reinventing the Kibbutz:
The "Community Expansion" Project

Igal Charney and Michal Palgi[1]

Introduction

This chapter outlines the origins and characteristics of community expansion projects in kibbutzim. Community expansions are neighborhoods for non-kibbutz members located adjacent to the residential built-up area of the kibbutz. Arising since the mid-1990s, demographic needs and legal changes have led many kibbutzim to promote such projects. The goal was to attract young kibbutz-born adults and other young families who wished to take advantage of the quality of life in a small, rural, well-kept community at a fairly reasonable price tag. Living in the kibbutz—rather than being a member of the kibbutz—became a preferred option. Community expansions were of paramount importance in saving troubled and aged kibbutzim from physical degeneration.

As mentioned in many chapters of this book, over the past hundred years, but particularly in the last two decades, the essence and characteristics of the kibbutz as the ideal type have changed dramatically. Specifically, values of equality among members, as well as among kibbutzim, direct democracy, and self-labor were relaxed. These modifications resulted in openness to further economic, educational, and social integration with the non-kibbutz society. Moreover, the "privatization" of communal services arose, that is, the transference of many communal services to the responsibility of the family. In addition, members were allowed to have more private property (for a more detailed description, see Rosner and Getz, 1994, 1996; Palgi, 2002, 2004; Getz, 2009). These changes were prompted mainly by the economic failure of some kibbutzim during the national economic crisis of the mid-1980s. Another impetus to innovation was the change in the kibbutz population, which became more heterogeneous demographically and ideologically. Finally, kibbutzim felt pressure from Israeli society, which no longer venerated this collective way of life (Rosolio, 1999; Palgi, 2002, 2004; Palgi and Orchan, 2009). As a result of these structural and ideological changes, two-thirds of the kibbutzim have transformed from communal (or collective) to restructured quasi-cooperative communities over the past couple of decades. Even so, the kibbutz still retains communal assets and offers specific services as well as constituting a unique social and cultural fabric.

Origins of Community Expansion Projects

For decades, the major and often the exclusive means of demographic growth in the kibbutz was to "recruit" new members who would engage in the collective idea. Nonmembers lived in the kibbutz as residents for many years, but they were "merely" apartment renters. Continued decline in the number of kibbutz members made kibbutzim realize that attracting people for membership was no longer a viable option. Attracting nonmembers, an option previously considered unthinkable, became a matter of necessity for demographic growth. During the past decade, more than 150 kibbutzim have initiated "community expansion" projects; in more than eighty of them, people have already moved into their homes. Many of these expansions are in the periphery of the country, especially in the north (Figure 16.1). The first kibbutzim to initiate expansion projects were those that experienced severe social and economic distress as well as those located on the periphery. For them, the influx of newcomers was a lifeline.

Community expansion means the creation of neighborhoods of private homes on land previously zoned for agriculture. These new neighborhoods are adjacent to the existing residential area of the kibbutz. Neighborhoods vary in size: from small (30–40 homes) to very large (150–200 homes). Admittance is not open to everyone: although newcomers are nonmembers, an internal kibbutz committee approves applicants who may build their homes in the new neighborhood. Such neighborhoods have been built by two principal methods. Since kibbutzim have no experience in real estate development, they had to join forces with private real estate firms. This association forced kibbutzim to surrender to the ultimate goal of capitalism: profits achieved by selling as many homes as quickly as possible. The other method involved leasing land from the Israel Land Administration (ILA; public agency

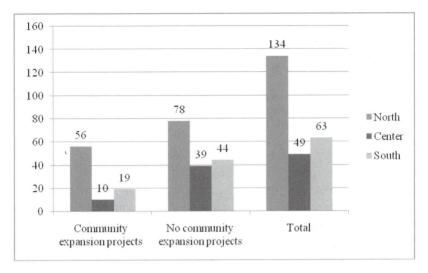

Figure 16.1 Community expansion projects in kibbutzim, by region (Kibbutz Movement, 2009)

that manages more than 90% of the land in Israel) and building one's own homes. The development of such neighborhoods signifies a clear departure from past actions taken to enlarge and strengthen the kibbutz. First, dwellers in these neighborhoods are non-kibbutz members; instead, they belong to a new community, known as the municipal corporation, which functions as a service provider for kibbutz and neighborhood members. In legal terms, the municipal corporation is detached from the collective entity of the kibbutz, which is an agricultural corporation that owns kibbutz assets. Second, unlike homes in the kibbutz, which are collective assets, homes in these neighborhoods are private properties owned by their respective dwellers.

At first, kibbutz movements were hesitant about this move, resisting the proposed change. Their main objection was that such projects would have an irreversible impact on the kibbutz and thus destroy the kibbutz lifestyle, ending in a so-called "community settlement," which would not resemble the traditional kibbutz (Arbel and Czamanski, 2001). Pressure exerted by kibbutzim that wished to pursue the development of such neighborhoods and the acknowledgment that it was the only practical option made kibbutz movements relinquish their objection.

What made kibbutzim realize that such a move is needed? The secretary of the Kibbutz Movement explained:

In the mid-1990s many kibbutzim found themselves without a next generation, a situation which endangered the ability of the kibbutz to run regular communal life. Worse still, it put the very future of the kibbutz at risk. The idea of community expansion projects adjoining the kibbutz was intended to provide solutions in several dimensions. It would be an option for people brought up in the kibbutz and who wished to live in the setting they were raised, in particular close to their families, without the commitment of kibbutz members. It would allow preservation of communal services, strengthening social and cultural life in the kibbutz, and support of a multiage society. (Bargil, 2006)

This view stresses the importance of demographic factors and the need for demographic revival (Arbel and Czamanski, 2001). The aging of kibbutz populations (in some, a mean age of fifty-five or even sixty was not uncommon) and the tendency of the younger generation to leave the kibbutz as young adults triggered the rethinking of regeneration efforts.

Willingness to expand could not be put into practice without a groundbreaking legal amendment. Until the mid-1990s, rezoning agricultural land into land for nonagricultural uses (e.g., housing, industrial, and commercial) was not common practice. As a public agency, the ILA was committed to national objectives, among them the need to strengthen agricultural cooperative communities. By allowing rezoning, such communities, especially on the periphery, could pursue regeneration and growth. In December 1995, a decision by the ILA board permitted a certain degree of flexibility by allowing rezoning of agricultural land into land for residential development. In practice, this resolution was translated into the building of neighborhoods for non-kibbutz members. These projects were profitable as they permitted kibbutzim to charge a fee that was used for specific purposes such as upgrading their aging infrastructure.

The development of community expansion projects corresponded with the growing preferences of many Israelis to live in detached homes. Instead of living in relatively small and crowded apartments in the city close to their workplaces, people were willing to commute and live in larger homes (accessibility—space trade-off). At a fairly similar price to that of an average apartment in a town, a spacious private home could be owned in the more peripheral areas of the country. This preference was supplemented by the desire to live in a village-like environment, where community values were best served and children were safe. Kibbutzim were able to cash in on these two processes and preferences.

The formation of this type of neighborhoods made many who left the kibbutz for ideological reasons rethink homecoming. A couple who grew up in a kibbutz explained why they preferred to join the community expansion and not the kibbutz:

> We did not want to become members. The kibbutz lifestyle, where the community is highly involved and has a great influence on the individual, wasn't for us. On the other hand, we wanted to remain in a rural atmosphere, with good education, and our economic circumstances suited the expansion program. (Mirovsky, 2008)

The driving force for those who came from the city was the exurban dream:

> Among our considerations for moving to the kibbutz was the desire that our children would be educated here, where the schools are better than in the city . . . Other than that, there are the broad lawns and the tranquil atmosphere. The kibbutz is not far from the city and the price is relatively cheap. (Yediot Aharonot, 2002).

Conflicts and Disagreements: A Divided Community?

Initial euphoria notwithstanding, major disagreements and difficulties soon arose, reflecting a possible rift in the newly formed community. These differences revolved around material issues and stemmed from the dissonance between expectations and reality. The notion that the cost of living was cheap soon proved illusory. Life in a private home in small communities, even on the periphery, was not cheap:

> They [newcomers] came to the dream of the kibbutz: green lawns, swimming pool, high-quality education, beautiful scenery . . . In the daily life the cost of living is not cheap, you pay for everything. (Official of a regional council, 2009)

Another individual stated:

> Some of those who came here did not understand the place they were entering into . . . There were those who did not realize that living on the periphery was more costly, that education was more expensive, that you needed two cars. (Director of a municipal corporation, 2009)

This rude awakening made newcomers more suspicious of kibbutz motives and honesty. They were particularly upset by the lack of transparency, which caused some of them to think that the kibbutz was using them. In one kibbutz disagreements with the newcomers reached a point of profound mistrust:

> We argue that the community expansion project is a kibbutz "factory" designed to make money through payments for extras which are not recognized by us [newcomers]. The kibbutz is the supervisor and we are its subordinates; it is no coincidence

that all service providers are from the kibbutz and all the money goes to it. (*Mynet*, 2009)

Unlike kibbutz members, who trusted elected officials, newcomers demanded full transparency. This led to the notion that "the kibbutz is stealing from us." When kibbutz members realized that if were to act in full transparency and in cooperation, the number of conflicts would diminish, they detached the budget of the cooperative corporation from the municipal corporation. To illustrate more vividly the process of building a community expansion, a case study of Kibbutz Galil is next described.

A Case Study

We chose Kibbutz Galil for our case study because it was among the first to engage in a community expansion project. We followed its development in two phases: the first when it had just started to build the new neighborhood in 2003, and the second when the neighborhood was already well established in 2009. In 2003, we held in-depth interviews with four key people in the regional council (the municipal organization for nonurban communities) and two in Kibbutz Galil, and we conducted telephone interviews with sixty-one kibbutz inhabitants (members and nonmembers). In 2009, we held in-depth interviews with two key people in the regional council and two in the kibbutz. Situated in the northwestern part of Israel and close to the Lebanese border, Kibbutz Galil was founded in 1949. At the end of the twentieth century, the number of its members started to diminish. In 1997, there were 204 members, and five years later, the figure was 178, that is, 13% fewer. The same occurred with the number of children, which in the same years declined from 103 to 79. Of the 153 kibbutz-born children, only 22 stayed in the kibbutz.

The idea of building a neighborhood of private homes for non-kibbutz members originated at a time of economic collapse and social distress, two tightly related problems. The Kibbutz Galil deficit was NIS 126 million, or NIS 716,000 for each kibbutz member (Livne, 2004). In a transitional period beginning in 1996, the kibbutz was reshaped. It separated the community from the economy, that is, decisions in the economic sector were made, for the first time, by boards of directors and not by the kibbutz assembly, although the community received some of its profits. By 1998, the kibbutz had established a pension fund, and the transition from a communal budget to differential salaries was completed. This was accompanied by the closure of the communal dining room. Other services were also privatized. In 2004, the kibbutz was the first to complete the process of transferring the property rights to a home from the kibbutz to its members (private homes). These changes were not the result of a carefully thought-out plan or ideology, but were pragmatic, based on immediate necessity.

Initial thoughts about the need to rejuvenate the kibbutz began in the late 1990s. The kibbutz took advantage of its location on the periphery to get government approval to parcel part of its lands for real estate development. The tract of land was designed to have two hundred private homes on land parcels of approximately five hundred square meters each. Two major factors propelled the decision to engage in developing a neighborhood for nonmembers. The first was pure financial logic. Through ILA decisions, kibbutzim were allowed to profit from the development of private homes on their lands. Funds obtained from this development helped Kibbutz Galil erase its debt, repay its loans to the banks, and renew its infrastructure. The second factor was demographics: "In fact, the principle catalyst was demographic" (key person in the kibbutz, 2009). At that time, it was an aging kibbutz experiencing out-migration and having very few young families with children. Without new blood, it was assumed that the kibbutz would collapse.

In 2003, just before the first families entered the new neighborhood, the kibbutz permanent population was approximately 110 households; another 100 households rented houses in the kibbutz. In early 2009, the number of permanent households increased to almost 250 and that of renters declined to fifty. This was the result of two hundred families moving in, creating a ratio of one-third kibbutz members and two-thirds residents in the new neighborhood.

Screening and Acceptance Process

Screening of buyers of the new homes involved a two-phase process. First, the real estate firm that built the neighborhood interviewed all applicants, primarily to ascertain that they could afford the cost of buying a house. Then applicants had to complete a questionnaire for the kibbutz committee and produce a certificate of good character from the police and other formal documents. Next, the committee interviewed applicants, and if its members were not certain about someone, she/he was sent for psychological assessment: "if I remember aright, about 15% of them were sent . . . The main reason for not accepting people was 'social incompatibility'" (key person in the kibbutz, 2009). The process in the second screening phase was rather different because newcomers from the first phase were now on the committee:

They [newcomers] argued that the kibbutz was not strict enough in the selection. They made two dramatic changes in the process. First, before the interview they required that every newcomer be given a thorough explanation about the kibbutz and kibbutz life—an entire day with a kibbutz representative. They said that newcomers had no idea where they were going . . . The second change, which came about due to a constitutional change in Israel, was to require all applicants to undergo psychological assessment. (key person in the kibbutz, 2009)

According to a member of this committee:

. . . the interview today is much less friendly than in the past . . . It is more like a job interview. People are asked: why did you come here? Why didn't you go to another place? What do the neighbors tell you? . . . There are people who after these interviews decide not to come here. (key person in the kibbutz, 2009)

Our informants assess that there are about ten to fifteen families out of the two hundred accepted that will not last in the kibbutz expansion neighborhood for economical or cultural reasons.

Most newcomers are people from the surrounding towns, villages, and kibbutzim who wanted to improve their quality of life and who are able to afford a house in the kibbutz. They are relatively young (the majority younger than forty-five) with children; only 16% did not have children when they came to the new neighborhood. Their education averaged 15.3 years of studies. Half of the newcomers had their own private apartment before moving to the kibbutz and the rest had rented or lived with their parents. In terms of professional occupation, newcomers are extremely diverse, including lawyers, economists, physicians, high-tech operatives, and members of the defense forces (military and police).

Conflicts and Mechanisms for Their Resolution

The new residents moved in over a short period of time, a fact which somewhat impeded absorption. In the first nine months, ninety new families arrived; thereafter the annual rate has been about twenty-five families. Their arrival coincided with a time of near disintegration of the local and communal organization. Committees to handle different aspects of social life, such as the education and cultural committees, were nonexistent, and members were worn out and becoming desperate: "The plan was that each newly arriving family would have an adopting kibbutz family, but soon this idea dissolved and the newcomers formed a separate social unit . . ." (key person in the kibbutz, 2009). This, and the newcomers' ignorance of several aspects of kibbutz life, made conflict unavoidable:

> The kibbutz did not know what it was getting and they [newcomers] did not know what they were getting into. The newcomers thought that they had come to a kibbutz that would provide them everything for free; the kibbutz members thought that newcomers would think like they did. (key person in the kibbutz, 2009)

At Kibbutz Galil, the primary issue that is the root of many conflicts is education, including after-school activities. On this subject, there was a wide gap between expectations and reality. Parents complained that the school buildings needed renovation, that decisions on the extracurricular classes were made by the kibbutz education committee and not by them, that the cost of education was higher than allowed by the Ministry of Education, that the size of the classes was not what they expected (too small or too large), and that the focus of studies was not what it should be (achievement–oriented or value–oriented). Clearly, attaining the aspired-for education was a factor of its cost. A second issue of contention concerned culture, and more specifically the location of the synagogue. The growing number of people who attended synagogue resulted in the need for a new building. To date, people use the bomb shelter located in the center of the kibbutz as their prayer house. Kibbutz members suggested that the new synagogue be situated in the educational center and not in the cultural center of the kibbutz so as to distance the synagogue from the playgrounds and youth clubs that have activities at times of service. The other group composed primarily of residents in the new neighborhood and wanted the synagogue to remain at the center of the kibbutz.

Conflicts over money and assets were not limited to education. They also existed with regard to municipal taxes because the newcomers were unwilling to pay for an unkempt infrastructure—the pavements and roads in and around the kibbutz needed renovation; the electricity cables could not carry the power required for the new neighborhood. Another issue was the decision on the annual budget and investment priorities. Newcomers did not always agree with kibbutz officials on the budget allocations.

Kibbutz Galil "is a very liberal kibbutz" (key person in the kibbutz, 2009) and looked for ways to resolve these conflicts. To this end it created a parents' committee that would decide on educational issues. As most of the children were from the community expansion, their parents formed the majority on this committee. In addition, the kibbutz managed to get help from the regional council and from the Ministry of Transport for repair of the roads and pavements. The kibbutz invested in new school buildings to the parents' satisfaction. Also, before bringing up the annual budget, the kibbutz canvassed its inhabitants for their priorities and allocated the budget accordingly. Thus it reduced the chances of a conflict around the budget. It also forestalled another conflict by insightful thought over the functioning of the swimming pool. Before the new neighborhood was created, the pool's operating rights were transferred to a private vendor, thus sidestepping the need for any negotiations over the price for use of the pool.

Discussion and Conclusions

This chapter attempted to elucidate the processes of attracting nonmembers to a kibbutz and building a partnership between kibbutz and the new neighborhood. It explored the outcomes of such collaboration in terms of building a new community. Specifically, we focused on the following dimensions:

1. the kibbutz's motives for building the new neighborhood;
2. the newcomers' motives for moving to this neighborhood; and
3. points of contention and the nature of the partnership formed between the two parts of the community.

The motivation of the kibbutz to venture into building a "community expansion" was twofold. First, there was an economic crisis that made it necessary to find additional economic resources, and second, there was demographic depletion which demanded "out of the box" solutions to bring back kibbutz-born youngsters and bring in other young people. The kibbutz hoped to inspire a new spirit and fresh energy in its dwindling population. This objective was helped by the changing ideology, which enabled the kibbutz to change its way of life, and an amendment in land regulations that made it feasible to rezone agricultural land for development.

Newcomers hoped to improve their quality of life by moving into the tranquil countryside, where they could find a high standard of education and safety for their children, a bigger and affordable house in the countryside, and a lively community life. Contrary to previous times, this was possible without obliging newcomers to become kibbutz members.

The expectation of both sides was a harmonious, well-developed community. Achieving this was not easy. In the beginning, the unfulfilled expectations were accompanied by open conflict centering mainly on who paid for what and how much. In addition, submerged conflicts focused around three poles. The first was control of community affairs. The kibbutz, as a self-managed community, was accustomed to deciding on its own on how to run the community and the business. The newcomers constituted an unknown body of inhabitants that wanted to take part in decision-making on community matters, and even join official bodies to do so. The second pole was ownership rights over community assets. The kibbutz built and accumulated its assets through the work of its members. Newcomers wished to acquire some of those rights without paying for them, as well as to decide how the kibbutz budget should be distributed. The third set of conflicts was distrust. Newcomers were sure the kibbutz wanted to "rip" them off and was charging them for goods and services they did not receive, or overcharging them for those they did receive. A major conflict centered on payments for education, which was considered to be of high quality but was also more expensive than regular public education. Kibbutz veterans were sure that the newcomers wanted to "rip" them off! The feeling of "we and they" was very strong in the beginning, but slowly ebbed only to resurface when another clash arose. The continuous question is in what areas are "we" (residents of the new neighborhood) equal in the community and in what areas are we not?

As noted, the processes of community partnership entailed coordination, personal and collective concessions, and conflicts and mechanisms for their resolution. To succeed, it is crucial for the partners to negotiate the meaning of this partnership, with consideration of constraints and opportunities in the specific context of its implementation.

Our case study clearly evinces dialectic relationships of cooperation and conflict in the process of building the new community. Such a joint venture reflects inherent tension between these two types of interactions. As posited by Zeng and Chen (2003), management of a partnership entails a sort of "social dilemma," with each partner's immediate temptation to adopt the competitive posture: who will decide each issue and how the decision will be made. But in the long run, as the partnership develops and trust builds between the partners, they tend to make a rational choice to cooperate. The competitive component, however, does not wholly vanish.

We have found that the community building process calls for a continuous dialogue and a bidirectional influence. For this, the partners must overcome defensive mind-sets, share responsibility, and develop mutual accountability.

Note

1. The authors' names are presented in alphabetic order, but their contributions are equal. This research was supported by the Israel Science Foundation, grant no. 438/08.

Bibliography

Arbel, M. and D. Czamanski. *Residential Neighborhoods Next to Kibbutzim*. Ramat Efal: Yad Tabenkin, 2001 [in Hebrew].

Bargil, G. "Opinion on a Challenge that Requires a Response." *Ha'Daf Ha'Yarok*, October 5, 2006, 2 [in Hebrew].

Getz, S. *Changes in the Kibbutz—2008*. Haifa: Institute for the Research of the Kibbutz and the Cooperative Idea, University of Haifa, 2009 [in Hebrew].

Interviews with key persons in a kibbutz (2009).

Kibbutz Movement. *Kibbutzim Yearbook*, Tel Aviv: The United Kibbutz Movement, 2009 [in Hebrew].

Livne, N. "The First Private Kibbutz." *Ha'aretz Daily*, January 23, 2004 [in Hebrew].

Mirovsky, A. "The Kibbutz Movement-Round Two." *The Marker*, March 24, 2008, 11.

Mynet. "Residents of the Expansion in Eilon Filed a Lawsuit against the Kibbutz." June 18, 2009 [in Hebrew].

Palgi, M. "Organizational Change and Ideology: The Case of the Kibbutz." *International Review of Sociology* 12, no. 3 (2002): 389–402.

———. "Social Dilemmas and Their Solution." In *Wirtschaft, Demokratie und Soziale Verantwortung*, edited by Wolfgang G. Weber, Pier-Paolo Pasqualoni, and Christian Burtscher, 317–32. Gottingen: Vandenhoeck & Ruprecht, 2004.

Palgi, M. and E. Orchan. *Opinion Polls in the Kibbutz-XVIII*. Haifa: Institute for the Research of the Kibbutz and the Cooperative Idea, University of Haifa, 2009 [in Hebrew].

Rosner, M. and S. Getz. "Towards a Theory of Changes in the Kibbutz." *Journal of Rural Cooperation* 22, no. 1–2 (1994): 41–62.

———. *The Kibbutz in an Era of Changes*. Tel Aviv: Ha'kibbutz Ha'meuchad Publishing House, 1996 [in Hebrew].

Rosolio, D. *System and Crisis in the Kibbutz Movement*. Tel Aviv: Am Oved, 1999 [in Hebrew].

Yediot Aharonot. "Surprise: Private Homes in the Kibbutz." February 21, 2002 [in Hebrew].

Zeng, M. and X. Chen. "Achieving Cooperation in Multiparty Alliances: A Social Dilemma Approach to Partnership Management." *Academy of Management Review* 28, no. 4 (2003): 587–605.

17

Kibbutz Neighborhoods and New Communities: The Development of a Sense of Belonging among the Residents of New Community Neighborhoods on Kibbutzim

Zeev Greenberg

It was always us against them; that's the way all of our discussions began.

Community expansion neighborhoods on kibbutzim are innovative and unique. In the past, kibbutzim accepted new people who applied to become kibbutz members. Now community expansion neighborhoods enable people who are *not* kibbutz members to live in neighborhoods alongside the kibbutz and to enjoy the quality of life that characterizes these settlements. The residents of the new neighborhoods have a different and unusual status. They reside in, but are not members of, the kibbutz. The fact that residents of the expansion neighborhoods are inhabitants of the kibbutz with permanent homes has created a novel situation for the kibbutz, which must somehow integrate residents who are not members. This chapter deals with that process and with the organizational and social obstacles that affect the formation of connections and a sense of partnership between the kibbutz and its expansion neighborhoods.

To elucidate these matters, I interviewed both kibbutz officeholders and representatives of the expansion neighborhoods in fourteen kibbutzim located in the Galilee and in the Golan Heights. Analysis of the interviews makes it possible to understand the complexity of the partnership between the kibbutz and the residents of the expansion. The interviews reveal organizational and functional obstacles in the building of the connection between the new residents and the kibbutz. These difficulties stem from the sense of exclusion and the invitation to participate but not become a partner. In this chapter, I present information about the feelings of the new residents and of kibbutz members regarding this process.

The occupants of community expansions live in agricultural areas, build their houses adjacent to the kibbutz, and become settlement residents. They are permanent members of the settlement but not members of the cooperative agricultural association to which kibbutz members belong. The expansion neighborhoods provide the challenge of constructing a new partnership between the kibbutz and the neighborhood. This chapter describes the stages of partnership construction between the existing kibbutz and the expansion neighborhoods and discusses the processes experienced by the new residents and by those who are integrating them into the kibbutz.

The Development of Community Expansion Neighborhoods in Agricultural Settlements

In Israel and in the Yishuv that preceded the formation of the state, agricultural settlements, also termed "worker settlements," adopted the aims of "conquering the land" and settling the country. In order to achieve these aims, the agricultural settlements, both moshavim and kibbutzim, organized as agricultural cooperative associations that dealt with coordinated purchasing and marketing agricultural produce in every settlement. The cooperative agricultural association was the body that managed the settlement. New immigrants who wanted to live in these settlements were required to be accepted and to become members of the cooperative associations. In moshavim, candidates were required to purchase a farm as a condition for membership in the cooperative corporation (Applebaum, 1999). The deep connection between residence in the settlement and membership in the corporation is expressed in the statutory status of moshav and kibbutz members (Lapidot et al., 2006). Only association members were partners in discussions, and only they participated in decision-making about everything pertaining to the administration of the agricultural association and the settlement.

Through the years, there were always a few (temporary) residents who were not members of the association but lived in the moshavim and kibbutzim (Greenberg, 1995). This status prevented them from being partners in the administration and agricultural cooperative association. They were subject to decisions made in the association committee without the possibility of appeal. This structure of agricultural settlements, in both moshavim and kibbutzim, indicates the deep connection between agricultural employment and land ownership (Ratz, 1995). The crisis in agriculture, which began during the second half of the 1980s, greatly harmed the kibbutzim and the moshavim and brought about changes in the structure and function of the cooperative agricultural associations. The crisis had many features. Because the economic base of many of these settlements was undermined, the associations became entangled in heavy debts stemming from the high rate of inflation and the traditional credit arrangements. This economic crisis also had social and demographic features (Schwartz et al., 1994; Applebaum and Newman, 1997; Greenberg, 1999). People began migrating from the settlements to the city with its abundance of employment opportunities. As a result, the agricultural communities experienced a negative rate of population growth and a rise in the average age of settlement members. This process is familiar in many undeveloped worlds (Sofer, 2001, 2004; Ceccato and Persson, 2002; Mindy and Bruce, 2004; Stanford and Hogeland, 2004).

At the same time, the Ministry of Agriculture prepared plans for the rehabilitation of rural settlements enabling people to live in agricultural settlements without purchasing a farm and without working in agriculture. Expansion plans on moshavim were meant to ensure demographic growth by adding a young population who did not work in agriculture. These plans responded to those who wished to live near the cities but not in them, in order to enjoy a rural lifestyle. Economically, the change in the function of land from agriculture to residence enabled the cooperative associations to return a portion of their debt to the banks and, thus, to do their part in the debt repayment arrangements.

The community expansion neighborhoods began to develop alongside the kibbutzim near the big cities in the central region of the country. Today they are dispersed throughout the country including peripheral areas (Palgi and Orchan, 2003). By definition, expansions were intended first and foremost for the young generation who wished to continue to live in the settlement where they grew up, but without working in agriculture and without taking part in the agricultural cooperative (Glass, 2008). For kibbutzim in outlying areas, these neighborhoods increase kibbutz population, lower the average age, and encourage growth in educational and cultural activities as a part of the unique kibbutz lifestyle. In some of the regional councils, the aim of demographic growth is part of long-term strategic planning that includes the addition of these community expansion neighborhoods (Razin, 1996; Applebaum, 1999; Sofer and Applebaum, 2006; Ressissi and Applebaum, 2009). Constructing a system of cooperative life for kibbutz members and residents of the new neighborhoods requires the development of a common organizational, administrative, and social infrastructure. This presents a challenge to both the kibbutz leadership and the new residents. The development of the ability to work together, the process of building trust and communication between expansion neighborhood residents and kibbutz members, greatly affects the feelings of the new people, their sense of belonging to the kibbutz, and their being part of the settlement's human capital (Barak and Sadan, 2003; Amit, 2007; Shemer and Schmid, 2007).

In the past, a kibbutz committee investigated the suitability and readiness of candidates who wished to join the kibbutz. The system for accepting and integrating new members into the kibbutz maintained kibbutz member homogeneity. The arrival of the new neighborhood residents challenged the kibbutz to deal with a population that was "different," with a wide range of positions, professions, and motivations to move in (Applebaum, 1999; Orchan et al., 2001; Arnon and Shamai, 2009). Thus, these new residents contributed to kibbutz heterogeneity.

Previous Research

Extensive research explores the integration of migrants into a new place (Ward and Searle, 1994; Akhter, 1999; Ahren, 2000; Shamai, 2000; Orchan et al., 2001; Palgi and Orchan, 2003; Ressissi and Applebaum, 2009). These studies suggest that we can expect integration difficulties of the community expansion residents who must deal with the pressures posed by the nature of the settlement and its administrative methods. Similarly, the kibbutz members are wary of the new and unknown population. Shamai (2000) investigated integration among young people from the Former Soviet Union who migrated to a new settlement and cites four stages in their psychological adjustment: *The idealization stage* begins with the decision to immigrate and continues until the first stages of actually carrying out the decision. *The crisis stage* occurs at the meeting between the cultures of the immigrant and the surrounding society. New immigrants sense that they do not understand the spatial environment or the new place in which they reside (Amit, 2008). Mischel (1973) defined the crisis stage as characterized by disorientation and unclear expectations. *The realistic acclimation stage* unfolds when the process of learning begins. *The full acclimation stage* occurs when the former identity becomes indistinct and the individual identifies and is identified by others as a member of the new culture.

Marsh and Fisher (1992) studied the significance of mutual listening when building a partnership. They state that listening intensifies the acquisition of new knowledge and reveals the existing gaps between the partners. Understanding the gaps enables the partnership to provide more accurate responses to the partners' needs. Glass (2008) conducted a study that uncovered the sense of crisis that precedes the realistic acclimation stage, the significance of the crisis for the receiving kibbutz and for the new residents. Glass stressed both the opposing and the common interests between the neighborhoods and the kibbutz. She also highlighted the importance of preliminary attitudes in the kibbutz on the new relationship.

The Study

This chapter investigates the communications between kibbutz members and new residents and their effect on the process of constructing a partnership between the two. Fourteen kibbutzim were chosen in which residents had been present for more than two years. In these settlements, far from the large cities and core regions, a partnership had to be established between new residents and the kibbutz for the supply of services. We hypothesized that during this period, the construction of a partnership between the kibbutz and the new residents had begun and that the residents had experienced the "crisis stage" and were now at the stage of "realistic acclimation."

Qualitative interviews were conducted in each kibbutz with two team members who deal with cooperation between the kibbutz and the new neighborhoods. One of these was a kibbutz officeholder and the other was a representative of the new neighborhood, active on the partnership-building team. In many of the kibbutzim, partnership building took place in the municipal committee or in the association committee. In each kibbutz, three interviews were conducted. Two were individual interviews while the third took place jointly with the two representatives in each community. In this mutual interview, the representatives were requested to discuss a successful example of partnership building between the kibbutz and the new neighborhood. I conducted a content analysis of the interviews that included a deductive analysis according to the objectives of the research and an inductive analysis of identifying and formulating themes. During the research, complementary interviews were conducted with officeholders dealing with welfare and society who worked in the Upper Galilee Regional Council.

Findings

Tension exists because the new resident must meet a large number of officeholders. In many of the kibbutzim, an external entrepreneur built the expansion neighborhood. The relations between the kibbutz and the external entrepreneur were often unclear to the new resident. After the residents chose an expansion neighborhood in which to build their houses, they met with the acceptance committee made up mostly or completely of kibbutz members. The marketer, often a kibbutz member, but actually a representative of the developer, presents the neighborhood to the new resident. Those who wish to live in an expansion neighborhood must meet with the marketer. Then they meet with representatives of the kibbutz and go through the process of being accepted. After a recommendation to accept, the new residents must sign documents relating to their membership in the municipal committee of the kibbutz, a plot-leasing agreement with the Israel Land Administration, and a building and developing contract with the entrepreneur. It is the entrepreneur's responsibility to provide the infrastructure for the neighborhood and to build the new houses. The residents of the expansion neighborhood did not understand the division of tasks between the kibbutz and the entrepreneur.

> I am not willing to pay for the gardening in the open spaces of the kibbutz. I have been living in the neighborhood for a year and a half already and nothing has changed. I am living on a building site. We have requested dozens of times; why doesn't the kibbutz invest in the gardening of the new neighborhood? Why haven't sidewalks been laid out? Why isn't there lighting? I would be happy to pay the moment I begin receiving this service in our neighborhood as well. Until then, you don't have the right to ask me for money for public landscaping.

In another kibbutz, the kibbutz manager argued during a discussion about setting up a bus stop in the expansion neighborhood: "Setting up a bus stop is not a trivial matter. We have to obtain permits to set it up, safety permits, to make sure there is access and a bus approach, and the most important question, who pays for this?" A resident of the expansion answered: "Even in the planning stage we were told that a bus stop would be built by the suppliers, in this case the kibbutz." The kibbutz representative replied: "The kibbutz? The money paid to the construction company was supposed to take care of it. It's not the responsibility of the kibbutz." The resident of the expansion retorted: "You are the service suppliers and the kibbutz has to take care of it."

These quotes indicate the complexity of the partnership between the new residents, the kibbutz, and the entrepreneur. The discussion regarding the construction of a bus stop for the schoolchildren of the new neighborhood illustrates the effect of the infrastructure gaps between the kibbutz and the new neighborhood. The combination of the incomplete infrastructure of the new neighborhood, the lack of control of the kibbutz over the construction of the neighborhood, and the need to collect municipal taxes angered the new residents. The negative feelings of the residents toward the kibbutz directorate indicated that they viewed the kibbutz as responsible for everything that occurs in the new neighborhood and for all of the difficulties in the building progress. Many times, they expected that the kibbutz would handle problems included in the contract with the entrepreneur. When these expectations were not fulfilled, the expansion inhabitants became frustrated.

Complexity as a Source of Frustration

The arrival of community expansion residents requires the formation of a new organizational framework that will give them full rights in municipal affairs. Neither kibbutz members nor new residents, however, were aware of the complexity of this process. In discussions between kibbutz officeholders and representatives of the new neighborhoods, terms and concepts were used that were not clear to the new residents. Interviews with the new residents indicated that they were frustrated with the use of concepts without explanations of their full meanings.

> The kibbutz wants to act fairly. They brought a lawyer to the preparation meetings to explain the new structure of the association. A representative of the kibbutz was there and he began to argue with the lawyer. I wanted to get up and say . . . Just a minute, I don't understand what you are arguing about . . . Could you just explain the meanings of each of the concepts? The truth is that I was embarrassed. I went home and I began to look up the terms he was using on the Internet.

Another example is a discussion dealing with "dual taxation," which the new residents (as well as kibbutz members) pay both to the kibbutz and to the regional council.

> One of the new residents asked the representative of the association a number of times for details about the level of taxes as the new neighborhood residents felt that taxes were very high and that they had to pay taxes to two bodies: the kibbutz and the regional council, and they suspected that they were making double payments.

Clearly, information regarding the cooperation between the members of the expansion and the members of the kibbutz was neither complete nor orderly. The first quote indicates a process in which learning and discussion could have existed simultaneously. But instead of knowledge acquisition, the meeting turned into a debate. The representative of the expansion expressed the residents' sense of powerlessness regarding the knowledge gaps between themselves and the representatives of the kibbutz when discussing the municipality. The ignorance of the new residents regarding the concepts raised in the discussion intensifies feelings of nonacceptance and raises a barricade between the two sides. The quote dealing with the community tax also illustrates the knowledge gap among the residents regarding everything concerning the settlement system and the interface between the settlement and the regional council. The new residents, most of whom come from urban communities, compare the rural settlement system that they have chosen with the urban system they know. The residents are dealing with these issues for the first time and are forced to confront a world of new and unknown information. This quote also demonstrates the gaps between kibbutz officers and new residents and their effect on the tensions.

The revised settlement organization requires a partnership between the expansion neighborhood and the kibbutz. The planners of the community expansions were unaware that the partnership-building process would be complex especially since they accuse the kibbutz members of having "concealed knowledge." The kibbutz is often the guardian of information as well as the initiator of the learning process, but it is also one of the sides in the discussion, promoting its own interests. The proximity of the learning process to the discussions dealing with the issues and the conflict of interests that exist between the residents and the kibbutz members frustrate the residents and make them feel excluded. The sense of common purpose is eroded.

From Ownership of Knowledge to Full Transparency

Community taxes enable the settlement to supply services to its inhabitants based on an agreement by those living on kibbutz to pay these taxes. The kibbutz collects the community tax. The quality of life on the kibbutz comes at a high price. In many cases, the community tax is higher than the municipal taxes the residents paid in their former communities. The tax is optional rather than legally binding and is based on the agreement of kibbutz inhabitants to pay it. It is not surprising that questions arise regarding the components of the tax, its use, and the possibility of its reduction. The new residents want to understand and be involved in determining the level of the taxes and the costs of services. Kibbutz officers, on the other hand, initially opposed these discussions:

The representatives of the expansion want the right to appeal/decide in areas that involve payment. (Examples are the kibbutz clinic, security, landscaping, the cemetery, among others.) On the other hand, the members of the kibbutz reject these attempts aggressively in their desire to protect and maintain existing services.

A representative of the new neighborhood said:

The kibbutz views us—expansion residents—as being in the same community as members. We wanted to know how it operated, whether the level of taxation is correct. Is there a surplus or a deficit? A situation developed in which some of the kibbutz members felt that they were financing most of the kibbutz activity and the community residents were getting the benefits. Some community residents felt the opposite. They believed that they were paying high taxes and that the kibbutz was using these funds for other purposes and not only for community objectives. This was not based on hard facts; it was just a feeling.

I wanted to check this out with the kibbutz secretariat and I asked for figures, to see the community budget, what the level of the budget was, and to check the level of community taxes, to check whether the level of taxes corresponded to actual community expenses. I felt that as a representative, I was raising legitimate questions and not personal questions. Even if it is unpleasant, it has to be done. There was a sense of coercion at the beginning of the discussion. It was not pleasant, but it was necessary in order to deal with the issue.

The language used by the two sides expresses the difficulty the kibbutz had in involving the new residents in the issue of community taxes. The kibbutz perceived itself historically as having power over the management of operations, services, and their budgets. Kibbutz officers did not understand the meaning of full partnership between the kibbutz and the new neighborhood. On the one hand, the kibbutz and the expansion were supposed to be one community. But in actuality, one side supplied the services, operated the services, and set the level of payment for these services. The kibbutz had knowledge and information regarding costs of services and controlled the procedures for using the taxes paid by kibbutz residents.

In the first stages of building a partnership, the members of the new neighborhoods were included only as service recipients. Thus, the new neighborhood representative's frustration was understandable when she encountered resistance to her requests for information. On the other hand, her complaint illustrates the learning process that kibbutz officers had to undertake. The assertive action by the neighborhood representative led to the publicizing of budget figures and thus made the budget the property of the entire community, both kibbutz members and new neighborhood residents. The neighborhood representative indicated that she saw her role as representing the entire population and not only one sector. She emphasized: "This wasn't my personal question. I did it because I was a public representative."

A kibbutz officer acknowledged:

I think there is a problem, in principle. People don't know what they are paying for and we have to provide them with details. In addition, there is a problem of trust between the new residents and the members of the former committee and, in order to build their trust in us, we must change our attitude.

As the partnership formation progressed, both sides, and especially the kibbutz, learned that financial transparency would create the trust that was lacking and would make it possible to reach agreement enabling a cooperative way of life. The opinion expressed by the kibbutz representative indicated that the kibbutz leadership understood the importance of publicizing figures as a method of building the partnership between the kibbutz and the community expansion neighborhood. Later in the discussion, the kibbutz representative continued:

> I propose that the level of taxes go down and, in the meanwhile, the sum of money which is collected from the new neighborhood be used only for the needs of that neighborhood. The sum will not include kibbutz services (extracurricular education, use of the swimming pool, and others) and this will help the committee to collect money more easily from the new neighborhood residents.

The speaker's language makes it clear that the kibbutz officer understands the sensitive nature of taxation. This helpful proposal indicated the significance of reaching agreement and the need for dialogue and cooperation between the kibbutz and the new residents. It signifies the process of change that the kibbutz leadership is undergoing with regard to the partnership between the kibbutz and the expansion neighborhood.

Her statement indicates the beginning of a dialogue between officeholders of the kibbutz and the new residents. This has been the outcome of the deep conflict between the kibbutz and the homeowners of the new neighborhood, resulting in the refusal of the homeowners to pay the community tax as set by the kibbutz. The quote was taken from a meeting held to find a solution to the problem and reach new understandings. The fact that the statement was made by a kibbutz member indicates understanding among the kibbutz officeholders of the difference between absorption of the new residents and that of members who had joined the kibbutz in the past. The kibbutz has been required to exhibit openness, attentiveness, and understanding in considering the unknown and unfamiliar aspects of these new dwellers who have come to live among them in the expansion neighborhoods.

Building the partnership between the new residents and the kibbutz, and the openness and flexibility exhibited by the kibbutz officeholders have involved training community workers specializing in the creation of community cooperation, formation of joint planning teams, and revision of the committee and organizational structure to include representatives of the entire community, both kibbutz members and new homeowners. Progress in improving the quality of life in the kibbutz has required the formulation of communication channels to enable sharing of information, exchanging opinions, and sustaining open dialogue for all who wish to participate.

The Effect of the Internal Group Communication on the Connection between the New Residents and the Kibbutz Leadership

The sense of obligation is different among kibbutz and expansion representatives. Perhaps because they are volunteers, the turnover rate among expansion representatives active in kibbutz bodies is high. Few remain active for long periods. High turnover expresses and contributes to a lack of a sense of obligation. At the same time it reflects the lack of trust and the sense of exclusion that officeholders on the kibbutz induce:

> It was always us against them . . . You could feel it when you came to meetings. Sometimes we arrived and they were already sitting with the kibbutz manager. We thought to ourselves: What have they already decided even before the discussion has begun?

The alertness and the concern of the new residents, however, are striking in comparison with the lack of involvement and the apathy among kibbutz members with regard to the integration of the new neighborhood.

New residents saw these as discussions not among partners but rather against sides, as the term "us against them" illustrates. When this quote was read during interviews with kibbutz officers, they asserted that the kibbutz initiates most discussions. The kibbutz representatives consider themselves responsible for preparing the discussions, for presenting documents including articles of association and agreements. Thus, they believe it is logical that discussions and internal debates take place in advance of the meetings.

The representatives of the new neighborhood viewed the situation completely differently. They felt that they were not real partners in preparing the discussions. They sensed compartmentalization and a lack of communication that only intensified the feeling of "us against them." The kibbutz officeholders also experienced exclusion and lack of communication. One of the kibbutz managers reported the following:

> The members of the expansion neighborhood carried on their own communications network, leaving us out. One of the representatives would summarize the debate and send it by e-mail to the members of the expansion. That was problematic. It wasn't an official summary but rather his personal summary. The e-mails he sent would open the door to another discussion, a repeat, among the members of the expansion after having read the e-mail. The representatives of the expansion would come with comments and additional requests. All of the agreements of the previous week became irrelevant. I told them, "Listen, this isn't the way to do things. You can't

carry on every discussion twice [once in the cooperative forum and a second time among the expansion members by e-mail]." I didn't want them to interpret this as if I was shutting them up or cutting off discussion, but the situation was intolerable. We couldn't progress.

Both formal and informal communications were at play. Mail distribution and the use of computers enabled a wide variety of means of communication. In addition to official communication in public discussions, internal and informal communications took place among the residents of the expansion neighborhood. The e-mails filled the need to transmit information, and, to a certain extent, complement the communication missing in kibbutz reports of the mutual discussion. The communication among the members of the expansion community is significant in enabling expansion representatives to inform residents about the discussions and to receive feedback regarding them. This type of communication contributes to group cohesion and cooperation among the members of the group. The reactions of the residents after every report of a discussion empowered their representatives and became a source of support when they came to discussions with kibbutz representatives.

At first the community manager felt threatened by the new residents' internal communication. There was also a dilemma involved. On the one hand, publicizing the summary of the discussion by e-mail represents the positive values of openness and fairness. On the other hand, it leads to another discussion. The community manager does not want to request that they stop publicizing these summaries lest he be accused of "shutting them up."

Another community manager reported:

> I did not feel threatened by the e-mails. When I asked to be on their mailing list, they checked it out and in a few days I was receiving their mail. I know, because we talked about it, it came up in discussions, that the mails evoked hard feelings among other members on the community management committee; maybe fear, a feeling that things were going on which were not on the table. In retrospect, I think that there was jealousy. In the new neighborhood everyone was very involved, informed, reacting. Among kibbutz members there was silence. The kibbutz representatives felt that they were "running on empty."

In this quote, the community manager reports being allowed to join the "other side's" e-mail list probably because the resident responsible for this communications network understood the significance of opening up this channel to kibbutz officeholders. The quote illustrates that the communications network is not meant to be concealed or secret. It fulfills a significant role in building the partnership even though kibbutz members do not know that it exists and enables the new neighborhood residents to express their opinions about decisions and to mobilize support. It also enables kibbutz representatives to understand the feelings of the new residents. Opening these channels of communication to kibbutz representatives is not threatening. It leads to progress in communication between the groups and reveals the feelings of the residents. The internal communications network raises a number of difficulties, however, because residents did not censor their comments. They tried to understand the (hidden) motives of kibbutz representatives, adding comments about what was happening in other kibbutzim and expressing thoughts that testified to the tension and lack of trust between the residents of the expansion neighborhood and the kibbutz representatives.

Discussion

Glass conducted her research in 2003. In the ensuing six years, the number of kibbutzim with community expansion neighborhoods has grown leading to a significant change in Israeli rural settlement and in kibbutzim, in particular. Her preliminary work pointed to trends that were beginning to develop between the kibbutz and the new neighborhoods (ibid., p. 130). My research describes the complexity of these connections and the difficulties in creating a partnership between the expansion neighborhoods and the kibbutz (see also Orchan et al., 2001). Key factors were the lack of familiarity and absence of information about the partnership, leading to misunderstandings regarding areas of responsibility, followed by feelings of dissatisfaction and discrimination among the new residents. The residents erroneously see the kibbutz as bearing general responsibility for everything that happens in the expansion neighborhood. The residents do not understand who is responsible for the different areas of building and development, and this leads to the feeling that the kibbutz is not taking the project seriously.

The testimony from the interviews indicates the importance of openness by the kibbutz in integrating the new residents and forming a partnership. Provision of data and explanations as regards the costs of operating the kibbutz systems greatly affects the sense of cooperation among the new residents. During the early stages of developing the cooperation, the new residents felt that they were not full partners. The fact that the community expansion is based on the use of systems that already exist and have been operating on the kibbutz turns the new residents into passive participants rather than full and active partners. The result is essentially a "top-down" partnership (Shemer and Schmid, 2007). The kibbutz is the initiator, the host who decides the pace of progress and the domains of the partnership. An incomplete partnership leads to frustration, lack of control, and the absence of meaning for the residents of the expansion neighborhood (Glass, 2008; Arnon and Shamai, 2009).

Shamai (2000) defined the "realistic acclimation stage" as one in which the immigrant undergoes a process of learning about the new place. This stage involves learning the values that comprise life in the new place and finding ways to assimilate. The historical integrating systems on kibbutz made it possible for those who had chosen kibbutz life to investigate whether they were suited to this lifestyle. Theirs was a process of acquaintance, reception, and acceptance. The kibbutz investigation of the suitability of the prospective member softened his/her integration into kibbutz. However, these conditions also created a kibbutz demand for total assimilation. This model of integration is unsuited to those who have come to live in the community expansion neighborhoods. These new residents must assimilate according to a different model (Shemer and Schmid, 2007).

Based on interviews with officers of kibbutzim and of regional councils, I believe that residents and kibbutz members are now exhibiting characteristics of the "realistic acclimation stage." This stage includes three dimensions of knowledge acquisition and compatibility. The first is *internal knowledge acquisition by the residents*. In this stage, the residents become a group based on common characteristics and needs. The mutual interests of the new residents, especially when dealing with the entrepreneur and the contractors, help to develop contacts and a common communications network among these residents.

The second dimension of knowledge acquisition is *the acclimation of the kibbutz to a new reality*. The new status of community residents who are not kibbutz members and the necessity of quickly integrating large numbers of people required that the kibbutz make adjustments. The historical model of integration based on assimilation of the new member to the kibbutz is no longer appropriate. The kibbutz is now required to adapt to the unique characteristics of the residents of the expansion neighborhood. Building expansion neighborhoods is one step in the series of changes that rural settlements and kibbutzim have been undergoing (Rosner et al., 1989; Getz, 2001; Palgi and Orchan, 2004; Greenberg, 2009). As in previous processes of change, integration of the new neighborhoods requires internal knowledge acquisition on the part of the kibbutz. Nevertheless, it is primarily the kibbutz leadership and less the majority of members of the kibbutz who deal with integrating the new neighborhood.

I do not believe that there are set principles for integrating the new residents. Kibbutzim that have experienced similar processes can learn from one another, and regional councils can play a significant role in advancing this internal learning process but only if neighborhood representatives take part.

A third dimension is *common knowledge acquisition by the kibbutz and the new residents*. "Realistic assimilation," defined by Shamai (2000) as a stage when the new residents learn about their new place, is taking place both by the new residents and by those who are receiving them, the officeholders and the members of the kibbutz. At the same time, both groups experience suspicion and lack of trust. In the kibbutz leadership, this suspicion stems from the insecurity about the continuing function of kibbutz society in its new and unknown status and form. On the part of the residents, the suspicion stems from having to live by decisions to which they were not a party. This study indicates that, despite these feelings among the new residents and kibbutz members, it is possible to develop a process of partnership building. If successful, each member of both groups will enjoy new human capital established in this process.

Bibliography

Amit, K. *The Role of Social Networks and Leadership in the Decision to Emigrate from the Developing Countries: The Case of Immigrants from North Africa*. Publication 8. The Institute for Immigration and Social Integration, The Ruppin Academic Center, 2007.

———. *The Social Integration of Western Immigrants to Israel, Satisfaction from Life in Israel and the Explaining Factors*. The Institute for Immigration and Social Integration, The Ruppin Academic Center, 2008.

Applebaum, L. *The Future of Local Government in Rural Space*. Florsheimer Research Publication 1/15. Jerusalem: Hebrew University, 1999.

Applebaum, L. and D. Newman. *Changes in Rural Space in Israel and Their Affects on Local Government*. Florsheimer Research Publication 1/32. Jerusalem: Hebrew University, 1997.

Arnon, S. and S. Shamai. "White House, Red Room, Green Grass and Community. Migration to the Northern Periphery: Characteristics, Motives, and Satisfaction." In *New Research of the Galilee, Tenth Anniversary Volume of Galilee Research Conferences*, edited by T. Grossmark, H. Goren, et al. Tel Hai Academic College, 2009.

Barak, D. and A. Sadan. "Empowerment and Partnership, Deceptive Terminology." In *Participation, Your Way to Influence*, edited by A. Zimmerman and A. Sadan, 106–24. Tel Aviv: Kibbutz Hameuchad, 2003.

Ceccato, C. and D. Persson. "Dynamics of Rural Areas: An Assessment of Clusters of Employment in Sweden." *Journal of Rural Studies* 18, no. 1 (2002): 49–63.

Getz, S. *The Development of Changes on Kibbutz*. Publication 164. The Institute for Research of the Kibbutz, University of Haifa, 2001.

Glass, M. *Together or Alone. The Kibbutz and the Community Expansion Neighborhood*. Yad Tabenkin, 2008.

Greenberg, Z. "Kibbutz in Rural Fringe. Green Fingers in the Soot—The Kibbutz in a Process of Urbanization." A collection of articles. Background and clarification pages. In *The Kibbutz at the Turn of the Century*, 17–32. Efal: Yad Tabenkin, 1995 [in Hebrew].
———. "The Effect of Metropolitan Space on Kibbutz Society, Geographical Aspects of Society and Economy." M.A. thesis. Social Sciences and Mathematics Faculty, Haifa University, 1999.
———. "The Effect of Spatial and Settlement Factors on the Functioning of the Regional Councils as Focuses of New Power in Peripheral Spaces." In *New Research of the Galilee, Tenth Anniversary Volume of Galilee Research Conferences*, edited by T. Grossmark, H. Goren, et al., 388–417. Tel Hai Academic College, 2009.
Lapidot, A., L. Applebaum, and M. Yehudai. "The Kibbutz in a Changing Environment—Between Survival and Safeguarding Values." *Ofakim B'geographia* 66 (2006): 7–27.
Lester, L. H. "Immigrants Satisfaction: What Is It? Does It matter?" NILS working paper No. 154, pp. 2–103, 2005.
Mindy, S. C. and A. Bruce. "Local Social and Economic Condition, Spatial Concentrations of Poverty, and Poverty Dynamics." *American Journal of Agricultural Economics* 5 (2004): 1276–81.
Orchan, A., G. Adar, D. Rosolio, and Y. Ashoosh. *Research on the Community Neighborhoods on Moshavim*. Publication 169. The Institute for Research of the Kibbutz, University of Haifa, 2001.
Palgi, M. and E. Orchan. *Potential Settlers in the Expansion Communities*. Publication 184. The Institute for Research of the Kibbutz, University of Haifa, 2003.
———. *Public Opinion Survey in Kibbutzim*. The Institute for Research of the Kibbutz, University of Haifa, 2004.
Ratz, M. *With Unlimited Guarantees—History and Economic Policy in Cooperative Agriculture of Israel: Moshavim and Purchasing Organizations—Before the Crisis and in Its Wake*. Beersheba: Ben Gurion University Press, 1995.
Razin, A. *Changes on the Urban Rural Margins and Their Implications for Organization of Local Government in Israel*. Florsheimer Research Publication. Jerusalem: Hebrew University, 1996.
Ressissi, S. and L. Applebaum. *Rural Government in Israel in the Legal Mirror*. Florsheimer Research Publication 1/68. Jerusalem: Hebrew University, 2009.
Rosner, M., Y. Glick, and H. Goldenberg. *Value Orientations and Directions of Change in the Kibbutz*. Publication 90. The Institute for Research of the Kibbutz, University of Haifa, 1989.
Schwartz, M., L. Applebaum, P. Kedar, and T. Binyan. *Regional Councils in an Era of Change—The Challenge of Planning and Development*. Rehovot: The Center for Developmental Education, 1994.
Shamai, S. "The Intercultural Meeting, Immigrant Youth from the FSU Studying on Kibbutz." Doctoral dissertation. Department of Education, University of Haifa, 2000a.
———. *Organization Merging—Intercultural Integration*. University of Haifa, 2000b.
Shamai, S. and S. Arnon, "Survey of Migrant Integration in the Golan Heights." In *New Research of the Galilee, Tenth Anniversary Volume of the Galilee Research Conferences*, edited by T. Grossmark, H. Goren, Y. Zeltenreich, and M. Abbasi. Tel Hai Academic College, 2009.

Shemer, A. and H. Schmid. "Towards a Renewed Definition of Community Cooperation: A Three-Dimensional Approach." *Hevra v'Rivakha* 27 (2007): 327–54.

Sofer, M. "Pluriactivity in the Moshav: Family Farming in Israel." *Journal of Rural Studies* 17 (2001): 363–75.

———. "The Second Generation in the Moshav: Agriculture and Pluriactivity." *Horizons in Geography* 60–61 (2004): 119–26.

Sofer, M. and L. Applebaum. "The Rural Space in Israel in Search of Renewed Identity: The Case of the Moshav." *Journal of Rural Studies* 22, no. 3 (2006): 323–36.

Stanford, L. and J. A. Hogeland. "Designing Organization for Globalized World: Calavo's Transition from Cooperative to Corporation." *American Journal of Agricultural Economics* 5 (2004): 1269–75.

Ward, C. and W. Searle. "The Prediction of Psychological and Sociocultural Adjustment During Cross-Cultural Transitions." *International Journal of Intercultural Relations* 18, no. 3 (1994): 329–43.

18

The Thai Revolution: The Changes in Agriculture in the Kibbutzim and Moshavim of the Arava in the 1990s

Marjorie Strom

Imagine a region separated by geography, climate, and ideology from the economic and social forces that affect the rest of the country. Physical isolation prohibits inhabitants of this area from utilizing many resources available to all other citizens, including inexpensive labor markets and direct consumer markets. On the other hand, the region contains a water supply unavailable to the rest of the country and unaffected by local weather conditions, and is naturally quarantined from agricultural diseases.

Imagine that this region, while climatically and geographically unified, is divided demographically and politically into two distinct subregions, differentiated by their ideological approach to social and economic organizations.

Despite the region's isolation, it is connected to the rest of the country legally and economically. It depends on government funding and support to develop, and trades in the same markets as other citizens. It is subject to government restrictions such as production quotas and labor laws.

One day, the powers-that-be decide to change the rules. The support once provided to agriculture is lowered considerably, while simultaneously a supply of low-cost labor previously denied to this area is made available. Although many of the ideological differences between the two regions have dissolved, the institutional and cultural differences remain in place, causing the inhabitants to react differently to the changed conditions.

It sounds like a case study written in an economic textbook, but this region actually exists. It is the Arava Valley, a long narrow desert running along the Syrian-African rift from the Dead Sea to the Gulf of Eilat. Sparsely settled since the late 1950s, the region today includes approximately five thousand permanent residents. The southern half of the valley, reaching to about one hundred kilometers north of Eilat, is in the jurisdiction of the Hevel Eilot Regional Council and includes ten kibbutzim. The northern half is in the jurisdiction of the Arava Tichona Regional Council and includes five moshavim. Both areas subsist mainly through agriculture.

The kibbutzim and moshavim of the Arava are in many ways different from their cousins in other regions. Four of the ten kibbutzim were founded by groups of immigrants from North America who made aliyah for ideological rather than economic reasons. These immigrants arrived with a higher education level than the average kibbutz member, but with no experience in agriculture. The other kibbutzim were founded by graduates of Israeli youth movements and children of established kibbutzim. The moshavim of the Arava Tichona were founded mainly by descendents of kibbutz and moshav members, with previous agricultural experience. Most literature on moshav settlement divides the moshavim between "veteran" settlements, created in pre-state Palestine by European immigrants, and "new" moshavim, settled in the 1950s by North African and Asian immigrants. The moshavim of the Arava were founded at about the same time as the "new" moshavim, but by children of veteran moshavim and kibbutzim.

The 1990s saw major changes in the economic environment of the region—the "changing of the rules" referred to above. This chapter will examine the forces that brought about different reactions between the kibbutzim and the moshavim, and among the different kibbutzim.

Self-Labor

Both the kibbutz and the moshav movements were founded on the ideal of self-labor, but demographic changes in the communities and in Israel as a whole during the 1950s and 1960s led to at least partial abandonment of that ideal. During the 1950s, the kibbutzim developed an industrial sector, which employed hired workers from nearby development towns. As Israeli cities expanded, many moshav members left agriculture for other types of work, "renting" their land to neighbors. Those who remained in agriculture were now farming plots larger than one family can work alone. With the 1967 occupation of the Palestinian territories, a large number of low-cost workers became available. By 1980, nearly a third of all agricultural workers were hired, 36 percent of them coming from the territories. The 2000 intifada closed off this labor group, but by then foreign workers more than made up for them, and in 2000 about two-thirds of all agricultural workers were employees, 45 percent of these foreign (see Figures 18.1 and 18.2).

Because of a combination of ideology and opportunity, the Arava settlements related differently to self-labor and, through the end of the

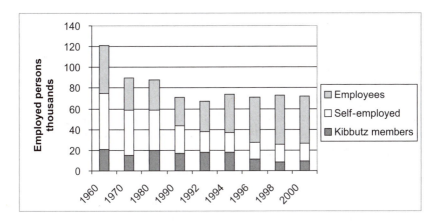

Figure 18.1   Self-employed, kibbutz members, and employees in agriculture (1960–2000)

Source: Central Bureau of Statistics.

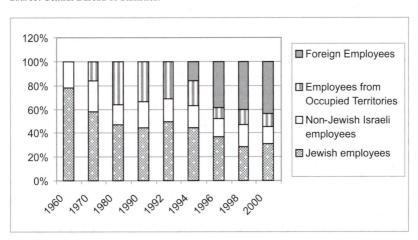

Figure 18.2   Agricultural employees by nationality

Source: Central Bureau of Statistics.

1980s, added only small numbers of volunteers and soldiers to their workforces. The stated basis for this practice was ideological, but practical reasons reinforced the ideology. The kibbutzim remained agricultural, with relatively little industry, and the moshav members nearly all farmed their own land, preventing the situation of having a plot too large for one family. The only city close enough to provide workers, Eilat, has never suffered from unemployment as many development towns did. The occupied territories were too far away to provide day workers. The connection of several of the kibbutzim to Zionist youth movements abroad ensured a population of volunteers to help with the unskilled labor and reinforced the ideology of the kibbutzim. Finally, the young settlements of the Arava in the 1970s and 1980s were demographically similar to their pre-state counterparts: young, healthy members committed ideologically to creating a new society, willing and able to engage in hard physical labor.

Within this common framework, differences existed among the kibbutzim from the beginning. The following discussion will examine the changes in attitudes toward self-labor in two of the kibbutzim—Ketura and Yahel—and the adherence to the principle in one—Samar. The other kibbutzim followed similar patterns.

The move from self-labor at Ketura was incremental and caused major social unrest in the community. "When I arrived here twenty-two years ago, the idea of bringing in volunteers for the harvest was considered extreme," says Bill Slott, former general secretary of Kibbutz Ketura. Eventually the kibbutz decided to supplement its workforce with volunteers. In 1994, Ed Hopland, economic manager of Ketura, tried and failed to convince the kibbutz members to bring Arab laborers to work in the fields. Three years later, when the kibbutz was struggling financially, the general assembly approved a plan to bring in laborers for the melon and watermelon harvests—but with many restrictions: only Israeli citizens would be employed, and they would work only in the fields, located across the highway from the living area of the kibbutz. Eventually Thais replaced the Arab workers, for practical reasons: "forty kibbutz members pick as many melons as twenty volunteers, ten Arabs, or five Thais," according to Slott.

While Slott desired to restrict the employment of foreign workers for ideological reasons, Hopland saw the issue as managerial. "Hired workers are a drug, and Thais are a hard drug, because they're so good," he explains. He feared that allowing any Thais to work inside the kibbutz will cause an uncontrollable flood that would eventually replace kibbutz members, who do not all have an alternative livelihood. Today Ketura employs Thai workers in the date plantations only—the kibbutz no longer raises field crops. According to kibbutz leaders, the decision to stop growing field crops was mainly economic, but was helped by the community's discomfort with foreign workers and ecological issues.

Samar, founded in 1976 mainly by children of established kibbutzim, describes itself as anarchic. Decisions of the general assembly are nonbinding recommendations, and all workers run their enterprises autonomously. At the time that many of the neighboring kibbutzim began expanding the melon crop by employing Arab laborers, the general manager of Samar tried to convince the kibbutz to do the same. The field crop staff, however, refused to consider the possibility, and the issue never even reached the assembly. Since small-scale production of vegetables has become unprofitable, the kibbutz has grown only organic dates and crops that can be tended and harvested mechanically, for which kibbutz members have developed technologies.

Yahel, like Samar, was founded in 1976, but there the similarity ends. After facing an economic crisis in the mid-1980s, Yahel's members decided to take several steps toward privatization, including increasing the number of hired workers. Several families left the kibbutz in the wake of these decisions, but since then the community has been in consensus regarding the issue of hired workers, deciding whether to continue in a work branch or to hire an outside worker on an economic, not ideological basis. In the late 1980s, Yahel began employing Arab laborers in the fields, replacing them with Thai workers "as soon as they became available," reported Matthew Sperber, the then general manager of the kibbutz.

The moshavim all followed the same path to relying on hired labor. Until the 1980s, the climatic advantage of the Arava allowed them to grow small fields of vegetables for the local market profitably in seasons that were too cold in the rest of the country. The development of hothouses lowered this advantage and caused the moshavim to begin growing almost entirely for the export market, which demands much higher quality produce, which in turn demands more—and more professional—labor. The first Thai workers arrived in the late 1980s, and in 2000 there were twenty-five hundred in the region. "If you take away the Thai workers, there will be no agriculture here," Ami Shaham, Arava Tichona water commissioner, states. These workers are known for their reliability and stability; they come for long periods and can be trusted to work alone in the fields. In the packing houses, they preserve a high level of quality.

Crops and Technology

Since the 1990s, the settlements of the Arava have differed not only in their labor decisions, but also in which crops they farmed and by what technologies. The kibbutzim took one of two tracks in the face of the changing conditions: either they greatly increased the amount of land being cultivated or they discontinued labor-intensive field crops altogether. A close examination of the economies of three representative kibbutzim in 1995 and 2001 shows the changes that took place between these years. Table 18.1 shows the contribution to profit from self-labor of agricultural branches of Ketura, Samar, and Yahel as a percentage of the kibbutz total in 1995 and 2001 (negative numbers indicate losses).

In 1995, the three kibbutzim were similar: agriculture provided about 60 percent of the income of the kibbutz, with 24 percent coming from dairy farms and 33 percent coming from field crops and dates together. Yahel and Ketura relied mainly on field crops and Samar on dates. In 2001, the three show very different pictures: Samar has increased the weight of agriculture in its economy to 73 percent while the other two have lowered it to about 45 percent. Dairies now provide only 15 percent of the income, and field crops are significant only at Yahel. Aquaculture, the Red Sea fishery owned jointly by five kibbutzim (not including Yahel), is a major branch for Samar and Ketura. Samar's date orchard provides a significantly larger percentage of the income than the other two.

Table 18.1 Contribution to profit from self-labor of agricultural branches as percentage of kibbutz total, Ketura, Samar, Yahel

Year	Kibbutz	Aquaculture (%)	Citrus (%)	Dairy (%)	Dates (%)	Fields (%)	Other livestock (%)	Total (%)
1995	Ketura	3	−1	18	12	26	3	60
	Samar	4		23	34	3	−2	63
	Yahel		−1	31	5	21	−2	53
Average 1995		4%	−1	24	17	16	0	59
2001	Ketura	15		9	18	1		44
	Samar	23		15	33	2	−1	73
	Yahel		3	19	15	10		48
Average 2001		19	3	15	22	4	−1	55

During the 1980s, the moshavim moved from raising crops in open fields to enclosed buildings. As a result, farmers who had grown several types of vegetables in open fields began specializing in one crop—at Paran, peppers—for export. According to Simha Yudovitch, deputy director of the Ministry of Agriculture, the government encouraged reluctant farmers to move to hothouses by providing grants on the investment and refusing to award grants for investments that did not include hothouses or net houses.

Paran is located at a higher altitude than the other moshavim, with an increased danger of frost in the winter. As a result of this disadvantage, according to Paran member Hemi Barkan, the changes in the late 1980s completely forced members out of the market for a mix of vegetables including some grown in open fields. Since then, they have specialized in growing peppers in enclosed structures for export.

Table 18.2 shows the type of fields used for each crop, and Table 18.3 shows the distribution of vegetables grown at the different moshavim. Hothouses and net houses have little advantage over open fields in growing melons, onions, and watermelons, and therefore those crops are hardly grown at Paran and Tzofar. Barkan explains the complete reliance on peppers (as opposed to tomatoes or other hothouse crops) at Paran as a "copycat" syndrome. In addition, local residents agree that the conditions for growing peppers are best on Paran.

Economic Success

Table 18.4 summarizes the ability of each region to profit from its limited resources from 1999 to 2002. We see that agriculture is a much bigger business in the Arava Tichona than in Hevel Eilot. The Arava Tichona uses three times as much land, five times as much operator labor, ten times as much foreign labor, and four times as much capital

Table 18.2   Production technologies of different crops, Arava Tichona, 2001–2002: number of dunam per crop and technology

	Tomatoes	Cherry tomatoes	Peppers	Melons	Watermelons	Onions
Hothouses	801	272	1,854	38		17
Net houses	15	20	4,038			10
Tunnels	18	55	491	1,523	891	10
Open fields	72	428	91	448	30	572

Table 18.3   Distribution of vegetables grown at the different moshavim,
2001–2002: number of dunam per crop

Product	Ein Yahav	Hatzeva	Paran	Tzofar	Idan
Tomatoes	335	213		116	242
Cherry tomatoes	459	161		80	75
Eggplant	305	60		12	82
Peppers	1,810	513	2,450	1,476	224
Melons	1,486	289		118	116
Onions	20	188	8	47	346
Herbs	137	159		42	
Watermelon	93	484	10	20	314
Other	174	198	343	133	67
Total	4,819	2,263	2,811	2,044	1,467

to create four times as much value-added (profit) as Hevel Eilot. Hevel Eilot farmers maximize profit from labor, both self and hired, while Arava Tichona farmers maximize profit from water and land. Both areas bring in enough income to support the families of the operators well, but not enough to repay the investment. The question remains why the kibbutzim of Hevel Eilot, while as successful as their northern neighbors in the small amounts of agriculture they attempt, do not expand these ventures.

The wage earned by Hevel Eilot farmers is high enough that one would expect the kibbutz to allocate more workers to its agricultural branches—few other enterprises bring in NIS 340,000 per worker. However, in order to generate more income from agriculture, the kibbutz must invest in preparing more land for cultivation or building hothouses on existing land. These investments, even if partially covered by the Ministry of Agriculture and Jewish National Fund, lower the profit for the operator. In addition, they require additional hired labor, an issue that will be addressed in the next section.

Finally, we must address the issue of motivation for joining the community. Most kibbutz members arrived in the Arava for social reasons including creating a new kibbutz structure (social anarchy on Samar), revitalizing non-Orthodox Judaism (Yahel, Ketura, and Lotan), and settling the Negev. For them, agriculture was a means and not an end. The

Table 18.4   Utilization of limited resources in the Arava Tichona and Hevel
Eilot (average figures during 1999–2002, NIS 2000)

	Hevel Eilot	Arava Tichona
Annual value-added (million NIS)[a]	24.0	101.5
1990s' investment (million NIS)[b]	70	281.5
Number of operators[c]	70	360
Dunam per operator	123	58
Value-added per operator (NIS)	342,857	281,944
1990s' investment per operator (NIS)	1,000,000	780,000
Annual water consumption (thousand cubic meter)[d]	16,750	25,500
Water per operator	240	70
Water per dunam	1.92	1.06
NIS value-added per cubic meter of water	1.43	3.98
Number of dunam[e]	8,611	20,767
Value-added per dunam (NIS)	2,787	4,888
1990s' investment per dunam (NIS)	8,129	13,555
Number of foreign workers[f]	250	2,520
Foreign workers per operator	3.57	7.00
Dunam per foreign worker	34	8
Foreign workers per million NIS capital	3.57	8.95
Thousand NIS value-added per foreign worker	96	40

[a] Total annual revenue minus total annual expenses, not including self-labor.
[b] From the Jewish Agency, the Jewish National Fund, and the Ministry of Agriculture.
[c] Hevel Eilot: Based on estimates by heads of the local growers associations; Arava Tichona: 90
percent of the population.
[d] Consumption in 1999 (*source*: Hevel Eilot and Arava Tichona water commissioners).
[e] Land cultivated in 1999.
[f] Hevel Eilot, based on estimates by workers in the various branches; Arava Tichona, seven
workers per family (estimate of Avi Shaham, water commissioner).

communalism of the kibbutz allows them to earn a lower salary working
in the profession of their choice and to enjoy a standard of living between
their salary and that earned in agriculture. Most, if given the choice between lowering their standard of living and giving up their profession,
would choose the former. The moshav settlers, on the other hand, came to
the Arava to establish farms and support themselves through agriculture.
Those who failed left the area. Thus natural selection has left the Arava
Tichona populated almost exclusively by successful farmers.

The kibbutz structure allows a profitable branch to cover the losses of an unprofitable one. While this could encourage "parasitism," it also allows the kibbutz to branch out in various directions, even when new enterprises are not immediately profitable. The moshav economy does not allow such diversification. A pepper farmer must put all his effort into peppers if he is to remain competitive. Diversity in the moshav economy, while clearly beneficial to the community as a whole, is a risk that no individual farmer can afford to take. This basic difference explains much of the parting of ways of the kibbutzim and moshavim of the Arava. The moshav members had no choice but to develop highly professional intensive agriculture, because their economic structure did not allow them to invest in new enterprises that did not yield immediate profits. The kibbutzim, with a variety of employment opportunities, were able to leave agriculture in the hands of the few members interested in it.

The examinations of Yahel, Samar, and Ketura show that even within the general structure of kibbutz, different communities react differently to the same objective conditions. The managers of both Yahel and Ketura claim that their communities' decision regarding field crops was based entirely on economics and not ideology, yet as partners in the same co-operative venture, they came to opposite conclusions about its viability. Four members of Yahel were employed by the enterprise, and Yahel's packing house treated the produce after harvest, providing significant additional income. Field crops were still profitable for Yahel because the kibbutz provided services for the branch. Ketura's ambivalence toward it prevented it from doing the same.

Was the "Thai Revolution" Helpful or Harmful to the Settlements of the Arava?

In the Arava Tichona a small but vibrant population has taken the resources given by public institutions to support itself through agriculture, contributing to the nation through exports. This success, however, depends entirely on a second population, which in numbers is greater than the "native" residents. Farmers stress the Thais' efficiency and professionalism, and estimate that they would need three Israelis to replace every two Thais; replacing Thais with Israelis would push the farmers' profits below a livable wage.

Technological advancements could reduce the amount of labor involved in hothouse agriculture. Yudovitch of the Ministry of Agriculture claims that the ministry encourages adopting labor-saving technology, but that the farmers are uninterested. If this were so, the same combination of attractive grants and pressure used to introduce hothouses would be applied to convince the farmers to adopt these methods. The government's lack of action in promoting technological solutions or encouraging Israeli workers in agriculture shows that this is a priority on paper only. Until the government backs up its stated policy with feasible plans to allow the continuation of agriculture in changing conditions, the farmers of the Arava Tichona have no choice but to continue employing foreign laborers.

The situation among the kibbutzim, on the other hand, is quite different. The comparison of Yahel, Samar, and Ketura shows that the weight of field crops in Samar's and Ketura's economies were equal in 2001, despite the fact that Ketura had greatly expanded its field crops in previous years. In addition, Samar did not face the same financial difficulties faced by Ketura in the 1990s. This fact implies that Ketura would not have been worse off had it never employed the foreign workers. Could it have been better off?

The high salary earned by individuals working in agricultural branches with hired workers on kibbutzim (NIS 417,000 at Yahel) represents profit from hired labor and capital. According to Kressel (1997), "the growth of the place of capital in the profits of the kibbutz . . . brings the member to see that the value of his work is not what sets his standard of living as it once did, and then he asks: 'why should I work so hard?'" Further evidence to support this view comes from research on "social loafing"—the tendency of an individual to work less when part of a group than when alone ("parasitism" in kibbutz slang). Karou and Williams (2001) found that while this tendency exists in all cultures, it does not exist in all groups: "parasitism" will be reduced if members identify strongly with the group and if they feel that their contribution is valuable. In a kibbutz that receives much of its income as rent on its assets, members may feel their contributions are not valuable to the group product and thus contribute less.

We saw that the move to expanded fields with hired workers was successful at Yahel, but failed at Ketura. While the objective conditions of the two kibbutzim were identical, the organizational culture was very different. According to Grondona (2000), moral standards that differ greatly from the social reality deter development. Yahel abandoned the ideology of self-labor with little or no regret and succeeded in agriculture based on hired laborers. Ketura agreed reluctantly to infringe on this ideology and did not profit from vegetable farming. Samar retained the ideology and abandoned vegetable farming but developed its date plantations with mechanical means to reduce labor. In all three cases, the original stated value was the same: self-labor. The economic reality was the same: small-scale vegetable farming was no longer feasible. But when the kibbutz kept its values and actions consistent with each other, whether by changing the ideology wholeheartedly or by changing the actions, the kibbutz succeeded in its enterprise. When two remained dissonant, the enterprise failed.

Bibliography

Arava Agricultural Research and Development Station. "Economic Calculations for Various Crops." 1999–2001 [unpublished, Hebrew].

Ardom Regional Enterprises. "Ardom Field Crops: Report for the Period of 01/01/2000–30/06/2001." 2001 [unpublished, Hebrew].

Barkan, Hemi, Moshav Paran. Personal Interview. December 9, 2002.

Ben-David, Yiftach, Moshav Paran. Personal Interview.

Ben-Eliyahu, Shai, Moshav Ein Yahav. Personal Interview. November 16, 2003.

The Central Arava Agricultural Committee. "Report of Agricultural Lands." Various years [unpublished, Hebrew].

———. "2001–2003 Investment Plan." 2001 [unpublished, Hebrew].

Central Arava Regional Council. Web site: www.arava.co.il.

Central Bureau for Statistics. Web site: www.cbs.gov.il.

———. *Quarterly of Agricultural Statistics, Agricultural Census.* 1976–1999.

Greenburg, Amnon, Yotvata R&D Station. Personal Interview.

Grondona, M. "A Cultural Typology of Economic Development." In *Culture Matters: How Values Shape Human Progress*, edited by L. E. Harrison and S. P. Huntington, 1st ed. New York: Basic Books, 2000.

Hevel Eilot Regional Council. Web site: www.eilot.org.il.

Hopland, Ed, Kibbutz Ketura. Personal Interview.

Karou, S. J. and K. D. Williams. "Understanding Individual Motivation in Groups: The Collective Effort Model." In *Groups at Work: Theory and Research*, edited by M. E. Turner. Mahwah, NJ: Erlbaum Associates, 2001.

Kibbutz Grofit. "Field Crops Reports 1994–1998." [unpublished, Hebrew].

Kibbutz Ketura. "Field Crops Reports 1995–1997." [unpublished, Hebrew].

———. "Economic Plan for 1996." 1996 [unpublished, Hebrew].

———. "Economic Plan for 2002." 2002 [unpublished, Hebrew].

Kibbutz Lotan. "Field Crops Reports 1998–1999." [unpublished, Hebrew].

The Kibbutz Movement. Web site: www.kibbutz.org.il.

Kibbutz Samar. "Multi-year Report 1996–2001." 2002 [unpublished, Hebrew].

Kibbutz Yahel. "Economic Plan for 1996." 1996 [unpublished, Hebrew].

———. "Field Crops Reports 1992–2000." [unpublished, Hebrew].

———. "Economic Plan for 2002." 2002 [unpublished, Hebrew].

Kressel, G. M. "Willy Incentive: Work and Careers in the Service of the Public in the Kibbutz." *Magamot* 30, no. 4 (1997): 547–77 [in Hebrew].

Kugler, Ehud, Hevel Eilot. Personal Interview.

Ministry of Agriculture and Rural Development, Agricultural Extension Services, Department of Production Economics. *Economic Calculations for Various Crops.* Various years.

Ministry of Agriculture and Rural Development, Office of the Deputy Director for Investments and Funding. *Development plans.* 1995–2001.

Shacham, Ami, Central Arava Regional Council. Personal Interview. December 9, 2002.

Slott, Bill, Kibbutz Ketura. Personal Interview.

Sperber, Matthew, Kibbutz Yahel. Personal Interview.

Ugerton, Tzvi, The Jewish Agency for Israel. Personal Interview.

Uliel, Ami, Jewish National Fund Southern District. Telephone Interview. December 3, 2003.

Yudovitch, Simha, Ministry of Agriculture. Personal Interview. September 11, 2002.

Zusman, P. *Individual Behavior and Social Choice in a Cooperative Settlement*. Jerusalem: The Magnes Press, The Hebrew University, 1998.

19

Ecology, Eco-Zionism, and the Kibbutz

Michael Livni

During the last forty years, people worldwide have become aware of environmentalism and understand that a sustainable way of life is arguably the major global challenge facing humankind in the twenty-first century.[1] The rationale for environmentalism currently is mainly utilitarian, that is, it is in our self-interest to be concerned with the environment. The argument goes that both our children and we, as we grow older, will eventually pay the price for our reckless exploitation and depletion of the resources and biodiversity of our planet. Moreover, future generations will inherit the results of our polluting the physical surroundings and the atmosphere with our waste.

The Potential of Intentional Community

Potentially, intentional communities, whether urban or rural, are an almost ideal framework for realizing the basic principles of sustainability in consumption as well as production (including services). It should come as no surprise that members' environmental awareness led many intentional communities to establish the Global Ecovillage Network (GEN) in 1996.[2] GEN enables eco-villages to learn from each other and represents the eco-village alternative to the public. GEN sees itself as promoting sustainability by means of educational programs where the eco-village framework itself serves as a model.

Examples of proactive community initiatives for furthering sustainability in consumption are meals cooked in a communal kitchen and served in a communal dining hall, community owned cars, and communal space for recreation. Community organization can facilitate the management and disposal of both organic and nonorganic wastes. A community may also be in a better position than an individual to initiate infrastructure development for alternative energy use such as solar energy. In its production of goods and services (by individuals or by the community as a whole), the community can favor initiatives compatible with the principles of sustainability. Perhaps most important, the community can set norms for and educate to sustainable consumer behavior and can serve as a pilot and model for others in its surroundings.

Initiating and maintaining a sustainable way of life assumes a world outlook in which quality of life is defined by criteria other than material consumption. If that outlook seeks to transcend a personal philosophy of life and to have an impact on society, then that outlook must express itself in an action-oriented ideology, where ideology is defined as ". . . a systematic body of concepts about human life or culture; the integrated assertions, theories and aims that constitute a sociopolitical program."[3]

Intentional communities affirm freewill and reason based on the assumption that humans have the capability of cooperating with others in order to shape their physical and sociocultural environment—whether on the basis of a religious or a humanist rationale. In so doing, intentional communities promote cooperation and reject the determinism inherent in traditional society and in the social Darwinism of neoliberal economic thinking.

It has been the fate of proactive action for sustainability to emerge at a time when the very idea of a comprehensive ideology has been discredited. Postmodernism in general, and the leading economic expression of postmodernism, neoliberalism, in particular, has rejected the legitimacy of ideology in formulating socioeconomic policy.[4]

Zionism and Eco-Zionism

Zionism was and is the modern movement for physical and cultural regeneration and redemption of the Jewish people in their ancient homeland. The establishment of the State of Israel in 1948 was a partial fulfillment of the Zionist vision and mission. An understanding of the still nascent term "eco-Zionism" requires a brief review of the Zionist idea as such. Two different but complementary processes led to the emergence of the Zionist movement. Both were the result of the impact, direct and indirect, of modernity on Judaism and each has particular implications for the idea of eco-Zionism.

Political Zionism, formally inaugurated in 1897 by the Viennese journalist Theodor Herzl (1860–1904), arose in response to the rising tide of anti-Semitism, particularly in some of the emerging European nation states. Herzl proposed the establishment of a state for the Jews so that they could be physically and economically secure, "like all the nations." Within this context, it is clear that Israel, "like all the nations," has its particular environmental problems as well as sharing responsibility for the well-being of spaceship earth as part of the family of nations.

Environmental activists in Israel, who see their activity as part of their identity as responsible citizens of the State of Israel, are comparable to the Green parties of Europe and/or the many related nongovernmental organizations (NGOs). They are part of the growing concern with the impact on the quality and viability of human life of an exploding human population, with its associated consumption, technology, and waste products. As mentioned above, their rationale emphasizes utilitarian considerations.

A second form of Zionism, labeled cultural Zionism, is associated with Achad Ha-am, the pen name of Asher Ginsburg, 1856–1927. He held that modernity posed a cultural threat to the continued relevance and existence of Judaism. In order to ensure the creative continuity of Judaism, a Jewish state in its ancient homeland would be necessary. Only then could Jewish civilization and its values express themselves in fruitful confrontation with all the challenges of the modern age. The Jewish heritage and its values would be revitalized in the process.

From a religious-cultural Zionist point of view, eco-Zionism reflects the Divine triple Covenant between God, the people of Israel, and the land of Israel. Ensuring the well-being of the land as part of a religious commitment to Divine Creation as a whole constitutes an ideological/theological basis for eco-Zionism. Eco-Zionism stemming from cultural Zionism implies a commitment to the totality of Creation with special responsibility for the Holy Land (Israel). The Midrash (Talmudic interpretations of the Bible) sees Creation as divine:

> When the Holy One, Blessed be He, created the first man, He took him to all the trees of Paradise, and told him: See my works, how handsome and fine they are, everything I have created was created for you. Make sure not to spoil and destroy my world because what you spoil, no one can repair. (Koheleth Rabbah 7:13)

This clearly is a message for all peoples, each of which is responsible for finding a way to express this universal idea and ideal through the unique prism of its particular culture.

From a cultural Zionist point of view, the State of Israel as a Jewish state must accept the obligation "to till the earth and to preserve it" (Genesis 2:15) as well as the injunction "do not destroy."[5] Viewed from this perspective, the rationale for eco-Zionism is distinct from, but not at odds with, the utilitarian rationale for eco-Zionism. Cultural Zionist intentional communities have the potential to express engagement with Creation not only by integrating sustainable practices in their daily life, but also by developing rituals and the general cultural life of the community that highlight this absolute value.

Intentional communities can integrate ecological thinking in the weekly and annual cycles of religio-cultural observance as well as in individual members' rites of passage celebrated in community. Such cultural integration is essential for maintaining community motivation necessary for implementing practical measures that can further sustainability.

Ecology, Israel and Palestine

Taken as an ecological geographic unit, Israel and the Palestinian Authority have become one of the most densely populated areas in the world. Approximately ten million people inhabit the twenty-five thousand square kilometers area between the Jordan River and the Mediterranean Sea. Over a period of sixty years, the population of Israel has increased from one to seven million—mainly (but not only) as a result of immigration. The accompanying development has led to a significant degradation of Israel's environment (Tal, 2002).

Exploitation of natural resources, water in particular, has reached an absolute limit. There is also a possibility that, in addition to population increase, global climate change may be exacerbating a process of desertification in Israel, typical of some of the world's semidesert areas.

Since the 1950s, the Israeli public has expressed concern for preserving natural habitats as embodiments of the national heritage. However, comprehensive environmental awareness came late to Israel. In 1953, kibbutz members and others established the Society for the Protection of Nature in Israel. Not until 1989, however, did the government see fit to establish the Ministry for the Protection of the Environment, which is still perceived as a "minor" ministry with a paltry budget. Nevertheless, in the past few years, environmental concerns are receiving greater attention. Significantly, at the Copenhagen climate summit in December 2009, President Shimon Peres committed Israel to a 20% reduction in carbon emissions by 2020. In fact, the government is committed to only 10%.

Kibbutzim and Ecology

Kibbutzim often find themselves on the front line of ecological controversy. Real estate developers prize their land, particularly the land of kibbutzim in the center of the country. The kibbutzim are de facto guardians of green areas but agricultural utilization of land is not always compatible with sustainability. As for industry, kibbutz industries have on occasion been faulted for industrial pollution. An awareness of the interface between the social and the ecological has begun to express itself only recently on the Israeli political scene.[6] For the first time, the national elections of 2009 featured a cultural Zionist green party. It failed to recruit the minimum number of votes required for representation in the Israeli parliament.

In the first seventy-five years of the twentieth century, kibbutzim emerged as a network of intentional communities, the largest communal movement in the world. The kibbutz movement must be understood within the context of Zionism, with the kibbutzim seeing themselves as a synthesis of political and cultural Zionism. As a settlement movement, they served political and settlement purposes by pioneering agriculture and settling remote areas. They did so within the framework of intentional communities attempting to realize the value of social justice as expressed in the principle of equal worth of all members—an expression of their particular cultural Zionism. They saw themselves as having a mission and were perceived as such in the surrounding society.

Henry Near describes the kibbutzim as ". . . an intentional society created in the light of an ideal . . . and embodying that ideal."[7] In so doing, the kibbutzim played a significant role in shaping the dominant Israeli ethos before 1948 and in the generation after the establishment of the state. In the 1970s, however, a combination of factors led to the loss of ideology and "intention" in the kibbutzim. The ousting of the Labor government in the Israeli elections of 1977 was a formative event in the history of Israel as well as the kibbutz movement. The wave of "end of ideology" postmodernism in the West and the attendant apotheosis of the individual swept Israel—including a majority of the kibbutzim. It was precisely during this period that "green" movements and causes emerged as a political force in the Western world. The ideological disarray and focus on ideological and economic survival were not conducive to kibbutzim adopting new perspectives and redefining their mission. The marginal attention of the kibbutzim to ecological questions reflects this situation.

The kibbutz decline and the emerging worldwide ecological consciousness were out of synch. Perhaps that is why only one kibbutz, Kibbutz Lotan (see below), is affiliated with GEN. The defining feature of the ideological crisis is the loss of vision together with the loss of belief in shlichut (mission). Martin Buber has described the decisive role of the belief in infinite ideals, "an eternal center," as a focus for intentional community.

Buber wrote: ". . . the real essence of community is to be found in the fact—manifest or otherwise—that it has a center. The real beginning of a community is when its members have a common relation to the center overriding all other relations . . ."[8]

At present, a minority of kibbutzim are collective, the majority are not. However, GEN has demonstrated that the economic paradigm is secondary to the intentional aspect of the community to which members commit themselves. Most of the eco-villages affiliated with GEN are not collective. However, they do have a Buberian "center."

Currently, even those kibbutzim that maintain a collective framework are no longer intentional communities. They no longer have a vision with an action program to create an impact on the surrounding society. As a group, only the urban kibbutzim are currently intentional communities (see below) that have set themselves tasks for assisting the surrounding society.

The Case of Kibbutz Lotan

In 1983 Israeli and American graduates of the Reform Movement in Judaism founded Kibbutz Lotan in Israel's Southern Arava desert. Among Israel's 275 kibbutzim, it is unique in its formal eco-Zionist commitment. Lotan has remained a small (fifty-five adult members) collective and intentional community. From its founding, Lotan has seen its intentional communal commitment linked to cultural Zionist pioneering. In the mid-1990s, a handful of determined members succeeded in integrating the challenge of ecological sustainability as a part of Lotan's social and Zionist vision. This commitment became part of a comprehensive mission statement.[9] That statement, formulated in 1997 as a response to an internal crisis, includes a religio-cultural approach to integrating ecology within a Jewish-Zionist rationale. The collective and liberal religious identities of Lotan were instrumental factors in responding to the crisis and integrating ecology into the Lotan vision. Two additional factors heightening ecological awareness were Lotan's geographic location within a highly fragile desert ecosystem and its position on the global flight path of birds migrating between Africa and Europe.[10] These form the background for the ecology "plank" in Lotan's mission statement:

Ecology: We strive to fulfill the Biblical ideal, 'to till the earth and preserve it' (Genesis 2:15) in our home, our region, our country and the world. We are working to create ways to live in harmony with our desert environment.

In following the path of eco-Zionism, Kibbutz Lotan has begun to demonstrate the potential of an intentional community committed to sustainability, as well as its challenges in the contemporary real world of Israel. Lotan has emphasized waste management. It composts organic wastes, as well as reusing and recycling many solid wastes. A subsurface constructed wetland for Lotan's sewage, funded by the Jewish National Fund, has become partially operational, and a Center for Creative Ecology has been established. The Center has pioneered alternative building and maintains an organic garden demonstration center. An eco-campus neighborhood of 650 sq. m. has been built using techniques of natural building (straw bales and earth plaster on a galvanized pipe geodesic dome framework). A salient achievement has been that Kibbutz Lotan succeeded in getting the eco-campus licensed for residential purposes.[11]

The eco-campus houses ecological volunteers and training programs such as the Green Apprenticeship. These programs incorporate both practical ecological techniques as well as principles of eco-village design formulated by GEN. So far, financial constraints have limited the utilization of solar energy (e.g., solar panels) to replace electricity generated by fossil fuels. The kibbutz is dependent on private donations to its registered nonprofit society, Amutat Tzell Hatamar, for developing its ecological projects.

Lotan is the exception that demonstrates the unrealized potential of the kibbutzim. It demonstrates that the rationale for eco-Zionism lies both in political and cultural Zionism. There is a particular awareness among Lotan eco-activists that the ecological challenge is regional. Lotan has been actively involved in ecological outreach to minority groups in Israel because sustainability should be a common concern to all citizens of the state—Jewish and Arab. When politically feasible, this outreach has also included Jordan and the Palestinian Authority.[12]

In 2001, the Ministry for the Environment bestowed an award on Kibbutz Lotan for outstanding volunteer work for the ecology of Israel. In 2006 Lotan received the annual award for eco-village excellence from the European region of the GEN. Kibbutz Lotan is the lone Israeli presence in GEN—a factor of significance for the image of Israel and Zionism in the entire network.

Current Status: Ecology and the Kibbutz

It is doubtful that the kibbutz movement can initiate eco-Zionist activity on a national level similar to Kibbutz Lotan's initiatives. In particular, it is doubtful if the kibbutz movement can project eco-Zionism as an expression of a cultural Zionist vision. An attempt in the mid-1990s to establish a Green Kibbutz Organization to set ecological standards for the kibbutzim foundered. After the implosion of the kibbutz as a movement, there was no way to fund activists for such a national program.

Indeed, the term "kibbutz movement" has become a misnomer. What exists is an umbrella organization numbering some 275 kibbutz communities divided into three different types of kibbutzim as defined by Cooperative Societies Ordinance (CSO), revised in 2005.

1. The collective kibbutzim—currently some 25% of the total.
2. "New" kibbutzim—essentially privatized or in the process of becoming privatized.
3. Urban kibbutzim—a development of the last two decades. Ironically, only the urban kibbutzim are defined as intentional communities in the CSO. In my opinion, the educational orientation and local activism of most urban kibbutzim will lead many of them to become involved in ecological endeavor. Whether they will view this in a cultural Zionist context is an open question.

The Role of Kibbutzim in Regional Initiatives

In general, a degree of partial kibbutz involvement in promoting sustainability has recently evolved—not necessarily with a formally stated eco-Zionist rationale.

In the Chevel Eilot regional council area (Southern Arava), two of Kibbutz Lotan's neighbors—Kibbutz Ketura and Kibbutz Neot Smadar— have a defined ecological commitment. Kibbutz Ketura has established the Arava Institute for Environmental Studies (AIES). AIES is academic and geared to recruiting students from all over the world—including Arab countries where possible. This precludes it from making the institute a formal venue for eco-Zionist ideology although its founders were personally motivated by a cultural Zionist eco-Zionism. Ketura is also a founding partner in the Arava Power Company which aims to supply green (solar) power to the region on a commercial basis.

Kibbutz Neot Smadar practices organic agriculture, recycles, has an operational constructed wetland, and is committed to living in harmony with its surrounding desert ecosystem. However its core concerns, inspired by the ideas of Jiddu Krishnamurti, focus on community togetherness for the purpose of examining one's personal existence in the light of interpersonal relations and relationships to the environment. Neot Smadar's approach to ecology is based on absolute values, but their source lies outside the cultural Zionist enterprise.

Kibbutz Sde Eliyahu, an Orthodox religious-Zionist kibbutz, in the Beit-Shan valley bases a major economic branch, organic agriculture, on a cultural Zionist rationale similar to that of Kibbutz Lotan. Indeed, it is possible that Sde Eliyahu will evolve a comprehensive eco-Zionist commitment based on an Orthodox religious rationale.

Perhaps the two most promising venues for grassroots eco-Zionist initiatives involving kibbutzim within the current Israeli reality are via the regional councils and the regional schools. The regional councils have jurisdiction over land use and waste disposal in their regions. Many regional councils now have ecological units. With the support of its member communities, the councils can further ecologically proactive policy. In the two most prominent examples, the Chevel Eilot and Megiddo Regional Councils, local kibbutz support and leadership are decisive. In the case of regional kibbutz schools, the initiative of local educators is significant and is often linked to regional council initiatives.

Together with the city of Eilat, the Chevel Eilot Council has set a goal of at least 50% renewable energy by the year 2020. In 2008 its outstanding ecological unit was instrumental in initiating annual international conferences on alternative energy in Eilat. The Council also recruited the Jewish National Fund and the European Union to further the constructed wetlands of Lotan and Neot Smadar.

The Megiddo Regional Council has initiated a biosphere for the Ramat Menashe region Southeast of Haifa. Biospheres are UNESCO monitored plans to create balanced relationships between humans and the environment in a given region. Biospheres will impact on the environmental behavior of all the settlements and will connect the area's ecological endeavor to an international framework.

For eco-Zionism to become a significant factor in the kibbutzim, it will have to be adopted as an ideology and a political program with national and international ramifications. On a national level eco-Zionism would parallel the former function of the kibbutz as an expression of socialist Zionism. International links with bodies such as the GEN and UNESCO would echo the past significance of the kibbutz in the socialist and communal movement worldwide. Eco-Zionism on the kibbutz would also reflect the ecological mandate—think globally, act locally. Eco-Zionism could become a unifying focus of meaning for those kibbutzim viewing themselves as intentional communities with a particular vision expressing one aspect of what a Jewish state should be.

Notes

1. A detailed review and discussion of the development of ecological awareness is beyond the scope of this essay. Suffice it to say that three thinkers have catalyzed this process: Rachel Carson, *Silent Spring* (1962), John Lovelock, *Gaia: A New Look at Life on Earth* (1979), and Paul Harrison, *The Third Revolution: Population, Environment and a Sustainable World* (1992).
2. See gen.ecovillage.org (Google: Global Ecovillage Network).
3. "Ideology," Merriam–Webster College Dictionary. 10th ed., 2002, p. 574.
4. A discussion on the roots of the postmodern rejection of ideology is beyond the scope of this chapter. At this time (2009), it remains to be seen whether the current economic crisis engendered by unbridled neoliberalism will impact on postmodernity. See Michael Livni, "Intentional Community, Modernity, Post-Modernity and Globalization: Challenges and Prospects," 2007 (online at www.michael-livni.org) for a more detailed discussion of the implications of postmodernity for movements of intentional community including eco-villages.
5. The injunction "do not destroy" is derived from the Biblical verse prohibiting the destruction of fruit trees while besieging a city (Deuteronomy 20:19–20). See Eilon Schwartz, "Do Not Destroy—Variant Readings of the Famous Verse," jhom.com/topics/trees/bal_tashkhit.htm. Google: "Eilon Schwartz–Do Not Destroy."
6. Murray Bookchin (2001 in Bookchin 2007) has dealt with the interface between the ecological and the social.
7. Henry Near, *The Kibbutz Movement—A History*, 1997, p. 325.
8. Martin Buber, *Paths in Utopia*, 1945 [1958], p. 135.
9. The full mission statement as well as additional information on Kibbutz Lotan can be found on its Web site. www.kibbutzlotan.com.
10. Michael Livni, "In Our Community—Ecology Is for the Birds," 2009, pp. 40–41.
11. Michael Livni, "Battling the Bureaucracy in Israel," 2008, pp. 54–58.
12. Michael Livni, et al., "Building Bridges of Clay, Mud and Straw—Jews and Arabs Learn Natural Building in the Desert," 2006, pp. 42–45.

Bibliography

Bookchin, M. *Social Ecology and Communalism*, edited by E. Eikland. Oakland: AK Press, 2007.

Buber, M. *Paths in Utopia*. New York: Macmillan-Beacon Paperbacks, 1945 [1958].

Carson, R. *The Silent Spring*. Boston: Houghton-Mifflin, 1962.

Global Ecovillage Network. gen.ecovillage.org or via Google, Global Ecovillage Network.

Harrison, P. *The Third Revolution: Population, Environment and a Sustainable World*. London: Penguin, 1992.

Ideology. *Merriam–Webster College Dictionary*. 10th ed. Springfield, MA: Merriam-Webster Inc., 2002.

Kibbutz Lotan. www.kibbutzlotan.com.

Livni, M. "Intentional Community, Modernity, Post-modernity and Globalization: Challenges and Prospects." *Ninth International Communal Studies Association Conference*. Damanhur, Italy, 2007. Online www.michael-livni.org.

————. "Battling the Bureaucracy in Israel." *Communities—Journal of Cooperative Living*, Summer, no. 139 (2008): 54–58.

————. "In Our Community—Ecology Is for the Birds." *Communities Journal of Cooperative Living*, Summer, no. 143 (2009): 40–41.

Livni, M., A. Cicelsky, and M. Naveh. "Building Bridges of Clay, Mud and Straw—Jews and Arabs Learn Natural Building in the Desert." *Communities—Journal of Cooperative Living*, Summer, no. 131 (2006): 42–45.

Lovelock, J. *Gaia: A New Look at Life on Earth*. Oxford and New York: Oxford University Press, 1979.

Near, H. *The Kibbutz Movement—A History*, Vol. 2. London and Portland, Oregon: Littman Library of Jewish Civilization, 1997.

Schwartz, E. "Do Not Destroy—Variant Readings of the Famous Verse." jhom.com/topics/trees/bal_tashkit.htm or via Google, "Eilon Schwartz—Do Not Destroy."

Tal, A. *Pollution in a Promised Land: An Environmental History of Israel*. Berkeley: University of California Press, 2002.

20

The New Communal Groups in Israel: Urban Kibbutzim and Groups of Youth Movement Graduates

Yuval Dror

Introduction

Communal groups scattered throughout Israel are a phenomenon that has emerged within the last thirty years. On the whole these groups are an outgrowth of the kibbutz movement, and it should come as no surprise that they have preserved their ties with that movement. At the same time these groups represent an innovative and independent development, consisting of various forms of communal living that are different from both the classic and the new privatized kibbutzim. The groups' members (about fifteen hundred to two thousand) earn their livelihood mostly through educational community activity, not through agriculture or industry, and they have settled mainly in urban development areas unlike kibbutzim.

A group of fourteen scholars from Tel Aviv, Haifa, and Ben-Gurion Universities working at Yad Tabenkin studied the new Israeli communal groups from 2002 to 2008. Their research questions were based on developmental, historical–sociological, and comparative approaches to the study of "intentional communes." They examined social movements, youth movements, and the kibbutz; and development areas in Israeli society. The researchers' goal was to identify the aims, mechanisms, and products in the internal and external life of the communal groups. They asked about types of ideological, social, and economic internal and external partnerships. Other topics included education within the groups as well as their educational community external activities. The political and public activities of these new communal groups in the development areas and in Israeli society in general were of interest. And finally, the team hoped to understand these new communal groups according to the classical models of kibbutz research. This chapter offers a basic description of the new Israeli communal groups, information about their historical and biographical backgrounds, and some answers to the research questions mentioned above. Most of the new communal groups can be divided into *urban kibbutzim* and *groups of youth movement graduates* connected to educational kibbutzim.

The first urban kibbutz was established in Jerusalem in 1979. Today there are four urban kibbutzim in Israel: Reshit (Kiryat-Menahem, Jerusalem, founded in 1979); Tamuz (Beit Shemesh, founded in 1987); Migvan (Sderot, founded in 1987); Beit Israel (Gilo, Jerusalem, founded in 1992). Each numbers dozens of members, living on various levels of communality, while additional families and single people participate in their educational and other community work without becoming members of the kibbutz. In Migdal Haemek, a northern development town to the west of Nazareth and Afula, there are four communes of the *Movement of Groups by Choice*, established by kibbutz graduates, the first having been founded in 1998. Groups by Choice is a voluntary movement of kibbutz-born young people, founded in the 1980s within the framework of the Takam youth section of the Movement of Working and Learning Youth. In 1989, this section was disbanded and the Movement of Groups by Choice remained. At the beginning of the twenty-first century, this group began to merge with the Mahanot Haolim Movement. Each of these communes has about ten members. Currently they are considering the establishment of a new urban kibbutz with three additional communal groups from the *Movement of Groups by Choice* in Upper Nazareth. In Migdal Haemek, there is also an additional group, graduates of the Habonim-Dror Movement, that cooperates with the others.

Groups of Youth Movement Graduates represent a new stage in the development of pioneer youth movements. The first one, belonging to the Movement of Working and Learning Youth, was founded in 1981 as a new form of the "preceding year of service" (i.e., the year before army service) and was institutionalized in the 1980s. This process of creating small groups before army service intensified in the wake of the crisis in the kibbutz movements, followed by the crisis in the Nahal army groups (Noar Halutzi Lohem, i.e., Fighting Pioneer Youth). They also benefited from the wake of changes in youth culture, manifested in the lengthening of the period of adolescence. The Movement of Working and Learning

Youth (1993–1994), followed by Mahanot Haolim (1997–1998) and finally Hashomer Hatzair (2003–2004), prolonged the period when young people were under the aegis of the youth movements and established the graduates' movements—all of them after protracted discussions lasting many years. The discussions and implementation were influenced by their sister movements in the Diaspora—Habonim, Dror, and Hashomer Hatzair—in all of which the graduates, mostly students, played a decisive role in the youth movement leadership. Today the graduates' movements number many hundreds of young people from army age to forty years old, living in dozens of communal groups: The Movement of Working and Learning Youth has sixteen training farms for those eighteen to nineteen years old (between completion of high school and the start of army service). In the Mahanot Haolim, there are six such training farms. In Hashomer Hatzair, the old model of core groups (Shalat Mukdam, early unpaid service) in kibbutzim still persists.

The kibbutzim in the post-army age-group are educational entities, serving as an ideological center for their youth movements. Their members are active in their immediate and distant surroundings in educational and community spheres. Examples are Ravid in Lower Galilee (the first educational kibbutz, founded in 1994), Eshbal in Western Galilee, and Hanaton in lower Galilee—three educational kibbutzim connected to the Movement of Working and Learning Youth. In addition, Na'aran of Mahanot Haolim in the Jordan Valley (re-established in 1999) and Peleh in Upper Galilee (2003) belong to Hashomer Hatzair. These educational kibbutzim are located in the periphery of the country and were before unsuccessful as classical agricultural-industrial kibbutzim. An additional (urban) educational kibbutz of the Mahanot Haolim Movement has emerged in Migdal Haemek. Each of these educational kibbutzim has links with the *communes,* communal groups of army graduates in various development areas throughout the country—over 300 graduates of the Movement of Working and Learning Youth in twenty-two groups work in development areas in Jerusalem, Tel Aviv, Rishon Letzion, Ramle, Haifa, Natania, Afula, Ashdod, and Beersheva. Some twenty graduates of Mahanot Haolim have formed four groups—three in Jerusalem (in one of them, on the French Hill, another kibbutz of that movement is in preparation) and one in the Haifa suburbs. One group of eight graduates of Hashomer Hatzair has created a commune in Jaffa and three communes of the Movement of Groups by Choice in Upper Nazareth have formed with thirty-eight graduates of that movement. Other independent communal groups have been active under the aegis of various bodies, such as the Jewish National Fund. Examples are the educational community group in Kiryat Shalom and the Shapira neighborhood in south Tel Aviv, a commune linked to the Bina Center in Efal.

Historical-Biographical Background of the Communal Groups and Their Members

In the 1970s, both internal and external factors led to the establishment of urban kibbutzim and to changes in the type of commitment the youth movements perceived as their goal. That period was characterized by crises within the youth movements themselves (both of kibbutz-born and city-born members), within the kibbutz movements in general, and Israeli society as a whole. In those days, the mutual relations between the youth movements and the kibbutz movements began to decline. As the "traditional" kibbutz education became less prominent with changes in the children's sleeping arrangements, the regional kibbutz schools became progressively more similar to those in the surrounding society, and increasing numbers of kibbutz-born youth left the kibbutz. In the wake of the political upheaval in 1977, kibbutzim and the kibbutz movement backing them lost their political clout and the governmental authorities' financial support. The economic-social crisis reached a climax in the mid-1980s, sparking the process of privatization, culminating later in differential salaries in many kibbutzim. This process reduced the involvement of kibbutzim in its own pioneer youth movements considerably and led to the establishment of the Public Committee for the Classification of Kibbutz (2002/2003, chaired by Professor Ben Rafael), aimed at adapting the legal and judiciary definitions of the kibbutz to the changing reality. The Public Committee differentiated three prototypes of kibbutzim: (a) a *communal* kibbutz, preserving a high level of communal ownership; (b) a *changing* kibbutz, undergoing privatization, while preserving certain aspects of mutual responsibility and communal ownership of kibbutz property; and (c) an *urban* kibbutz, a community living a communal life in a town or city.

The change processes also reflected changes in values and in kibbutz movement ideology.

Alongside these processes, changes occurred in the type of goals to which kibbutz youth felt committed. In the 1970s, a new movement of kibbutz-born youth gradually took shape within the Movement of Working and Learning Youth, which called itself "Groups by Choice," and exerted an influence on all the pioneering youth movements, in and outside the kibbutz. The kibbutz crises affected the members of the urban youth movements as early as the 1970s, and in particular in the 1980s and early 1990s. During their "preceding year of service", kibbutz youngsters tended to take on educational community tasks not connected to the youth movements, and the number of post-army-service kibbutz emissaries working in the youth movements rapidly declined. The changing kibbutz, plagued by crises, ceased to attract urban youth in search of worthy goals, leading to a sharp drop in the number of youth movement members, graduates that served together as "Nahal" soldiers (branch of the Israeli army) that aimed to join the kibbutzim, and above all of those choosing kibbutz life. This reduced still further the number of kibbutz members active in the youth movements and the financial support they received, since the kibbutzim realized they did not benefit from this expenditure and no longer felt committed to assist them, creating a vicious circle. Until the early 1990s, two other financial sources were gradually reduced—the contributions by the Histadrut (General Federation of Labor) and the Ministry of Education.

During recent decades, postmodern and post-Zionist discourse in Israeli society has gained momentum, as part of social-cultural tendencies worldwide. This approach questions every "truth" and emphasizes individualist values and consumerist hedonism as opposed to collectivism. In the wake of the waning of the great "ideologies," searching for meaning and a meaningful way of life have become prevalent among Israelis, in particular among young people. These concerns are manifested in the trend of engaging in long-term travel abroad and the flourishing of "spiritual" enlightenment organizations. Another worldwide cultural and social change is the lengthening of the period of "youth," the appearance of a new intermediate stage in life called "young adulthood," as part of the process of growing up. It lasts at least several years, sometimes until the early thirties. On the one hand, these are adults, living an independent life; on the other hand, they tend to postpone crucial decisions till their thirties—it is a moratorium, marked by avoidance of accepting full responsibility mainly in their professional and familial life. Besides this general background, the members of these communal groups share certain biographical characteristics. Many of them grew up in a kibbutz or spent at least a few years there. Many of them considered the youth movement as their natural home; the experience was meaningful to them and made an impact on their life. The factor most significant to them was their year of social service prior to their military service, for three main reasons. This pre-military year enabled them to experience intimate life in a close-knit group, usually accompanied by study of various Jewish–Zionist and social texts. They assumed leadership roles as representatives of the youth movement. The military units in which most of them served together (men and women separately) enabled them to remain in close contact and to continue to foster their sense of group cohesion and the collectivist ethos during their military service as well.

The research conclusions reflect the entire "Communal Groups" research program. We found that:

- The ideological social-economic partnership of the members of the groups is anchored in their kibbutz-youth movement background, their preceding year of service, and their unique military service track. Their shared aims distinguish them from the surrounding Israeli society owing to the socialist-communal ethos they ascribe to. Communal group members believe in the need for greater social justice and equality, both within the groups and for the sake of the weaker strata in Israeli society.
- The dialog as a way of life is also manifested in their shared ideological discussions: The groups hold weekly study sessions of Jewish–Zionist and social-economic texts and try to implement ideas derived from them in their own lives. All decisions are made by consensus, thereby displaying the antithesis of today's "changing kibbutz" type.
- While the internal ideological partnership is sound, their external ideological solidarity is only partial. Among those belonging to the graduates' movements, the connection between the communes and the 'educational kibbutzim' is relatively close. But the urban kibbutzim benefit from each other's experience only from a distance, and each preserves its unique coloring. The "circle of groups," an unsubstantial overarching framework, hardly ever gets together and does not include the Movement of Working and Learning Youth, the largest movement among the graduates' movements. The urban groups carry on an ideological dialogue with their surroundings, mainly regarding Judaism and the organization of cultural, educational, and local community activities. Their internal ideological and social partnership, however, distances them from their environment.
- In the graduates' movements of the youth movements, the model of a "kibbutz of (intertwined) groups" is prevalent, namely groups composed of subgroups, living according to various levels of social and economic partnership. This type of community also exists among urban kibbutzim, since there are families and individuals living in their environment and physically close to them, who participate only in their educational community tasks and activities, but not in their collective economic arrangements.
- In the various graduates' youth movements, economic partnership is nearly universal, but their members admit that money is available from external sources such as their parents. According to T. Miller (1999), a

researcher of the American Communes, the urban kibbutzim Migvan and Tamuz also permit this type of "modern" partnership alongside total sharing of the resources. The members' families help "from the outside" in the purchase of apartments and in payment for studies or travel abroad, but there actually are no great differences in the members' standard of living. The members of these new urban kibbutzim, living on their salaries and subsistence allowance, do not create the technocratic hierarchy with wide economic disparity and ongoing decrease in partnership and equality, developing in the old changing kibbutzim.

- Education within the communal groups differs greatly from the traditional kibbutz type. In the urban kibbutzim, there are a large number of children, compared to that in the graduates' movements (where there are, as yet, few families). From early childhood, the children participate in both formal and nonformal educational frameworks, according to the parents' and the children's own choice. However, informal education on the lawns and in the open spaces that these groups share is intensive and multiage. The choice available to the parents and their children represents the antithesis of education in the traditional kibbutz, as though flying in its face. The parents perceive themselves as "a movement of educators," but precisely because they have chosen to participate in "a movement for life," they do not consider their children as obliged to follow in their footsteps.

- The external educational community activities are similar in all the communal groups, though not equally intensive. They are anchored in social values, their direct and indirect messages are political-critical and social-economic, and the frameworks and methods employed are nonformal, run under the aegis of associations of "The Third Sector (nongovernmental/nonprofit organizations)". Some of the nonformal activities take place within formal educational institutions. Members of the groups are gradually arriving at the conclusion that unless they become integrated into the regular education system, they will not be able to make a living. For this reason they tend to undertake academic studies alongside their educational work. Most of the members of the movements of graduates convert their left-wing criticism of Israeli society into educational activity within their surrounding communities.

- Internal "movement" activity is significant for all the groups, but as mentioned above, varies in its intensity. The kibbutz movement assists the movement of graduates, but only on a technical level. Some of the urban and educational kibbutzim belong to the kibbutz movement formally, but their relations with it were significant mainly during the first stages of their establishment. However, the kibbutz movement and the communal groups perceive themselves as passing on the pioneering spirit of the early settlements and of the former communal kibbutz way of life. The groups add to it their protest against the current gradual privatization of the kibbutzim.

- Political activity by members of the groups is rare and takes place on a personal basis only, mainly in the urban kibbutzim. Even there, the

members avoid displaying their collective identification with ideologically analogous bodies to ensure maintaining good relations with their
neighbors in the urban development areas. On the other hand, they do
participate in public activity by means of a journal and an association,
led mainly by members of Tamuz, and also via other national institutions, promoting social justice and strengthening Jewish identity. Political education may seep through during educational and community
activities. It is even less obvious in the project, which guides teachers of
social studies (run by Kibbutz Tamuz). No study has so far been carried
out to examine how the environment perceives the communal groups,
but it appears—judging by the impressions mentioned by researchers,
quoting statements by the groups' members—that the situation has
greatly improved in this respect. Criticism by the surrounding population has declined, because the groups' members continue to live in the
area, unlike those doing social service for one year or showing up in
anticipation of elections.

- Personal self-actualization and academic studies are similar and different in a sense in urban kibbutzim and graduate groups. Group members
  in all the different types of groups have personal altruistic motives
  that are evident in their choice of studies. The members' reference and
  identification group is not merely the one within which they live, but
  also the group of the same age with the same background living elsewhere, including those who have left the graduates' groups and urban
  kibbutzim. In urban kibbutzim, studies and personal development are
  a high priority, so much so that some members study and accept jobs
  unrelated to education or the surrounding community. In these kibbutzim, and in particular in Migvan and Tamuz, self-actualization, on
  the one hand, and personal commitment to the group's commitment,
  on the other hand, are considered equally important and worthy. In the
  more recently established graduates' movements, the individual's needs
  are considered secondary to those of the group, and personal aspirations and sometimes even family life are postponed, since they do not
  fit in with definition of "personal commitment" as perceived by youth
  movements.

- In urban kibbutzim, academic studies are legitimate and the whole
  group may join in to enable a member to study. The studies usually
  undertaken by members of the graduates' groups take place within
  Labor and Kibbutz Movement institutions providing academic teach-
  er education and training for community work. These include Beit
  Berl and the Tel Aviv and Oranim Kibbutz Academic Colleges. In
  urban groups, academic study is considered as enriching the group's
  activities as a whole, in addition to the weekly study sessions. In the
  graduates' groups, the collective academic tracks complement the
  weekly group study and are considered "a must" not to be frowned on,
  owing to the existential need to function within the institutionalized
  daily formal frameworks, as well as cope with pressure by parents
  and their own age-group.

- Almost all the studies of the project, qualitative and historical by their nature, did not reveal the feminist/gender aspects as crucial issues in the communal groups and therefore they were not researched from this angle. Equality between men and women is self understood in the educational and community activities of the groups of youth movement graduates as well as in their communal life. Orly Ganany (2007) studied "The boundaries of the private and public spheres of the home in an urban kibbutz" from the communal and gender points of view, taking into consideration the traditional identification of the first sphere with women and the second with men. She found that this distinction in the urban kibbutz is not so clearly defined. The perceptions of the personal and public realms in the urban kibbutz are influenced by the gender structure of the rural kibbutz, but at the same time its critical examination can be clearly seen in the allocation of gender roles: The women in the urban kibbutz are dominant figures in the small and intimate community; they are active subjects in all the familial and communal subsystems, equal to the men who are ideological and practical partners in everyday life both in the private and the public spheres. These active and equal gender roles and the blurring between the private and the public characterize the groups of youth movement graduates as can be learned from their studies.

In conclusion, the communal groups can be studied in framework of kibbutz research. According to Pitzer (1989) and Oved (1988), the groups feel they have arrived at the right "azimuth" in their goals, but have only started out on their journey. The transformational model proposed by Talmon (1972) and Cohen (1988 [1976]) (using the terms "bund," "commune," and "association") warrants using "bund" regarding all these groups, including the urban kibbutzim that have existed for more than twenty years. This is because they insist on remaining a group of no more than a few dozen members and their meticulous selection of new members. At this stage, if the various communal groups preserve a balance between external and internal considerations, they will not lose their vitality—according to Oved (1988) and Kanter (1972)—in particular since all of them comprise only a single generation.

Although the communal groups are an outgrowth of the kibbutz movement, they vary widely. Even their division into urban kibbutzim and communities created by graduates of youth movements is vague, since both emerge from the globalization processes, from a new "young adults" stage, and from revitalization of civil society during the post-modern era. These features justify perceiving them as a case of "total revolution," a completely different mode of kibbutz life, according to Eliezer Ben-Rafael (1997). To summarize, they are education-community centered, not agricultural or industrial; they are intimate manifestations of the "bund" type, comprising a few dozen partners, not a large community of hundreds of people; they are communal (in a "modern" way that permits the use of external resources), but not privatized in a way that flaunts the original principles that harken to the kibbutz ethos; they are based on personal autonomy and choice with respect to ways of self-actualization and advancement, less on collective needs and systemic and individual constraints; they are committed to community values as a whole, with communality and commitment complementing each other; they actually live in urban development areas, and do not turn into patronizing external sponsors for specific periods; and they are a society eager to learn together on a weekly basis, not only a community that enables individuals to study.

Time will tell if these communal groups will persist on a long-term basis. We do not yet know if they will become a source of inspiration, as did the kibbutz movement in its great influence on Israeli society during the period of the "yishuv" and the first decades after the establishment of the State of Israel. "The kibbutz genes" of the members of the communal groups, whether stemming from nature or nurture, are the primary factors producing this new and truly revolutionary version of kibbutz life. In a complementary fashion, we can expect that this kibbutz-born revolution will have an impact on "the old kibbutz" from which it grew.

Bibliography

Ben-Rafael, E. *Crisis and Transformation: The Kibbutz at Century's End*. Albany, NY: State University of New York Press, 1997.

Cohen, E. "The Structural Transformation of the Kibbutz." In *Personal and Social Education: Choices and Challenges,* edited by G. K. Zollschan, A. Hargreaves, E. Baglin, P. Henderson, P. Leeson, and T. Tossell. Oxford: Blackwell, 1988 [1976].

Ganany, O. *The Boundaries of the Private and Public Spheres of the Home in an Urban Kibbutz*. MA thesis. Tel Aviv: Tel Aviv University, 2007.

Kanter, R. M. *Commitment and Community: Communes and Utopias in Sociological Perspective*. Cambridge, MA: Harvard University Press, 1972.

Miller, T. *The 60s Communes: Hippies and Beyond*. New York: Syracuse University Press, 1999.

Oved, Y. *Two Hundred Years of American Communes*. New Brunswick, NJ: Transaction Books, 1988.

Pitzer, D. E. Developing Communalism: An Alternative Approach to Communal Studies. In *Utopian Thought and Communal Experience*, edited by D. Hardy and L. Davidson, 68–76. Geography and Planning Paper, No. 24. Middlesex Polytechnic, 1989.

Talmon, Y. *Family and Community in the Kibbutz*. Cambridge, MA and London, UK: Harvard University Press, 1972.

Contributors

Irit Amit-Cohen is a senior lecturer and head of the MA program, "Preservation and Development of Cultural Heritage," Bar Ilan University, Department of Geography and Environment. Among her publications are "Cultural Heritage Landscapes in the Kibbutz: Values, Assets and Development" [*Horizons in Geography* 66 (2006): 154–75 (Hebrew)] and "Cultural Heritage and Cultural Landscapes: Implications for the Planning and Preservation of Rural Landscapes, the Case of the Kibbutz in Israel" [in Tony Sorensen, ed. *Progress in Sustainable Rural Development*, 90–98. Cairns, Australia: Cairns University Press, 2007].

Yasmin Asaf was born, raised in, and continues to be a member of a kibbutz. She is a graduate of the Department of Social Work, The University of Haifa. Presently she is working as an account manager for foreign customers in one of the biggest packaging companies in Israel. As a kibbutz member, Yasmin continues to be involved with and to care for the changing community.

Eliezer Ben-Rafael was a member of Kibbutz Hanita for about twenty years. In 1974, he earned his Ph.D. in sociology from the Hebrew University of Jerusalem. Currently, Ben-Rafael is a professor emeritus of sociology at Tel-Aviv University. He is past president of the International Institute of Sociology. His recent works include *Jewish Identities* (2001) and *Is Israel One?* (2005). His edited works include *Transnationalism: The Advent of a New (Dis)order* (2009), *Comparing Modernities* (2005), *Sociology and Ideology* (2003), and *Identity, Culture and Globalization* (2001).

Igal Charney is a senior lecturer, Department of Geography and Environmental Studies, The University of Haifa. His areas of interest are urban geography and urban planning. He has published on office and real estate development and on the politics of tall buildings development in various journals, including *International Journal of Urban and Regional*

Research; Urban Geography, Environment and Planning, A Journal of Urban Affairs; Geoforu; Area; and Canadian Geographer.

Hadas Doron is a lecturer of social work at the Academic College of Tel-Hai. Among her publications are "Spousal Violence among Immigrants from the Former Soviet Union," *Journal of Family Violence.* Springeronline.com (with G. Markoviztky and M. Sarid, 2007), "Contagious love—The Couple Relationships of AIDS Carriers." *The Open Aids Journal* 2, 58–67 (with Teichner, N., A. Grey, and Y. Goldstein, 2008), and "Birth Order, Traits and Emotions in the Sibling System as Predictive Factors of Couple Relationships." *The Open Family Journal* 2 (2009): 23–30.

Israel (Issi) Doron is a senior lecturer at the Faculty of Welfare and Health Sciences, The University of Haifa. Dr. Doron specializes in elder law, social policy and aging, and seniors' rights. He is the editor of *Theories on Law and Aging: The Jurisprudence of Elder Law* (Springer, 2008) and the author of numerous articles in international journals. He is active in various nongovernmental organizations, and one of the founders of the Israeli NGO, *The Law in the Service of the Elderly.*

Yuval Dror is a professor and head of the School of Education, Tel-Aviv University. Formerly he was the director of Oranim, The School of Education of the Kibbutz Movement, and The University of Haifa. His areas of specialization are the history of Zionist education and educational policy in Israel. His numerous publications include journal articles and book chapters, four edited books and 'special issues' on kibbutz education, and six solo-authored books, among them *The History of Kibbutz Education: Practice into Theory* (2001) and *Communal Groups in Israel* (2008). Between 1970 and 2001, Yuval Dror was a member of Kibbutz Hamadia. Since 2001 he has been a member of the "community neighborhood" of Kibbutz Kfar-Ruppin.

Sylvie Fogiel-Bijaoui is a professor of political sociology at the College of Management, Rishon LeZion, where she also heads the MA program in family studies. She received her Ph.D. in 1981 from Paris X-Nanterre University and the *École des hautes études en sciences sociales* in Paris. Among her most recent publications is the edited volume: *Old Dreams, New Horizons: Kibbutz Women Revisited* (Hebrew; Ramat Efal: Yad Tabenkin, 2009) and *Democracy and Feminism: Gender, Citizenship, and Human Rights* (Hebrew).

Alon Gan is the head of the history department at the Kibbutzim College of Education, Technology, and the Arts, and lecturer at Tel Aviv University. His research deals with Israeli society from the inception of the Zionist enterprise to this day. His Ph.D. dissertation examines the processes undergone by the kibbutz movement and Israeli society in the wake of the Six-Day War.

Zeev Greenberg is a geographer specializing in economic and social geography, as well as education. His latest research focuses on development processes in peripheral regions, local empowerment, immigration and social processes in communities absorbing immigrants, as well as entrepreneurship and change in rural communities. Dr. Greenberg is the dean of students at Tel Hai College and a lecturer in its Department of Multidisciplinary Studies.

Eldad Kedem holds a teaching position at The Open University of Israel. His areas of research include Israeli cinema, postcolonialism, film theory, new German cinema, and contemporary American cinema. Dr. Kedem has published articles on Israeli cinema, the kibbutz on screen, and the cinema of the German director Wim Wenders. He is a former member of Ma'agan, a kibbutz in the Jordan Valley.

Shula Keshet, a member of Kibbutz Givat Brenner, is a senior lecturer in the Graduate Faculty of the Kibbutzim College of Education, Technology and the Arts in Tel-Aviv. Her areas of research include kibbutz literature and kibbutz culture. Previous publications include "Underground Soul, Ideological Literature: The Case of the Early Kibbutz Novel," Tel-Aviv University–Hakibbutz Hameuchad, 1995 (Hebrew); "The Story of Bithania: Origin and Literary Transformations," Hakibbutz Hameuchad, 2009 (Hebrew).

Amia Lieblich, a professor of psychology at The Hebrew University, Jerusalem, and The Academic College of Tel Aviv-Jaffo, is not a kibbutz member. Her previous work on the kibbutz includes *Kibbutz Makom* (Hebrew, English, and Japanese), *Gilgulo shel Makom* (*Gilgal—A kibbutz in a process of change*) (Hebrew) , and *Yaldei Kfar Etzion* (*The Children of Kfar Etzion*) (Hebrew).

Michael Livni, a member of Kibbutz Lotan, received his MD from the University of British Columbia in 1959. He is the chairperson of Tzell Hatamar, an NGO for ecological projects in Kibbutz Lotan. His publications include *Reform Zionism-An Educator's Perspective* (Gefen, New York, and Jerusalem, 1999); *The Reform Option: A Different Zionism* (Hebrew) (Kibbutz Lotan, 2002); "Case Study: Kibbutz Lotan-Eco Zionism and Kibbutz" (ICSA, Amana, Iowa, 2004); "Intentional Community, Modernity, Post-Modernity and Globalization: Challenges and Prospects" (ICSA. Damanhur 2007). Other publications can be found on his website www.michael-livni.org.

Iris Milner is a senior lecturer in the literature department at Tel Aviv University, specializing in the study of modern Hebrew literature in the context of the Israeli social, cultural, and political milieus. She has written extensively on the role of literature in mediating changes in collective memories, particularly with regard to the trauma of the Holocaust. Her 2003 book, *Kiray avar-biographyah, zehut vezikaron besiporet hador hasheni (Past Present: Biography, Identity and Memory in Second Generation Literature)*, is a study of the representation in Hebrew prose of the second generation of the Holocaust. Her 2008 book *Ha-narativim shel sifrut ha-Shoah (Narratives of Holocaust Literature)* investigates major themes and modes of representation in a multilingual corpus of Holocaust literature.

Ranen Omer-Sherman is a professor of English and Jewish studies at the University of Miami and the author of two books, *Diaspora and Zionism in Jewish American Literature* (University Press of New England, 2002) and *Israel in Exile: Jewish Writing and the Desert* (University of Illinois, 2006), as well as coeditor of *The Jewish Graphic Novel: Critical Approaches* (Rutgers University Press, 2008) and the forthcoming *War and Narrative in Israeli Society and Culture*. Previously, he was a desert guide and founding member of Kibbutz Yahel in the Arava.

Yaacov Oved is a professor (emeritus), Department of History, Tel-Aviv University, head of the Department of Communal Studies at Yad Tabenkin, and cofounder of "The International Communal Studies Association" and its executive director (1985–2004). Prof. Oved was a founding member of Kibbutz Palmachim (established in 1949). He is the author of *Two Hundred Years of American Communes* (Transaction, 1988, second edition, 1993), *The Witness of the Brothers—A History of the Bruderhof* (Transaction, 1996), *Communes and Intentional Communities in the Second Half of the 20th Century* (Hebrew: Ramat Efal: Yad Tabenkin, 2009).

Gilad Padva is a scholar of Israeli cinema, media, and culture and a gender scholar. He teaches at Tel Aviv University and Beit Berl Academic College. Dr. Padva publishes extensively in the academic journals, *Cinema Journal, Feminist Media Studies, Journal of Communication Inquiry, Communication and Critical/Cultural Studies, Social Semiotics,* and *Sexualities*. He has also published chapters in edited collections and entries in international encyclopedias.

Michal Palgi, a professor of organizational sociology and kibbutz member, is the chair of the graduate program in Organizational Development and Consulting at the Emek Yezreel College in Israel and a senior researcher at the Institute for Research of the Kibbutz and the Cooperative Idea at The University of Haifa. She is the president of the International Communal Studies Association and former president of the International Sociological Association Research Committee on Participation, Organizational Democracy and Self-Management. Her areas of research and activity are kibbutz society, organizational democracy, organizational change, gender-based inequality, and social justice and community development, on which she has published extensively. Prof. Palgi is the coeditor of the *Journal for Rural Cooperation* and a member of Kibbutz Nir-David.

Alon Pauker, a member of Kibbutz Beeri, is the head of a special B.Ed. program at Beit Berl College for graduates of youth movements in Israel. He is also a researcher at Yad Ya'ari—Hashomer Hatzair Institute for Research and Documentation in Givat-Haviva and a lecturer in history at Seminar Hakibbutzim and Beit Berl colleges. His Ph.D. thesis is *The Self-Imagery of the Different Kibbutz Movements vis-à-vis the State of Israel, 1948–1958: A Comparative Analysis* (2006). Other publications in press are "When the pioneering kibbutz encountered the elitist state—A self image issue" (Hebrew) and "The kibbutz and the Israeli political elite in the current generation" (with Sigal Ben-Rafael Galanti) (Hebrew).

Avraham Pavin, a member of Kibbutz Ginegar, is a sociologist and senior researcher at the Institute for the Study of the Kibbutz and the Cooperative Idea at The University of Haifa and formerly a researcher at Yad-Tabenkin, Research Institute of the United Kibbutz Movement. His numerous publications include *The Kibbutz Movement—Facts and Figures* (Ramat Efal: Yad Tabenkin, Yearbook, Hebrew), *Community Resilience: Social Capital in the Kibbutz* (Ramat Efal: Yad Tabenkin, 2006, Hebrew), and "Looking at a Society of Equals through a Stratified Prisma," *Psychosozial* 87 (2002): 57–74 (German).

Shulamit Reinharz holds the Jacob Potofsky professorship in sociology at Brandeis University, where she established the Hadassah-Brandeis Institute for the study of Jews and gender. Her publications consist of numerous articles and chapters. Her eleven books include one on Manya Wilbushewitz Shohat (Hebrew, Yad Ben Zvi, with Jehuda Reinharz and Motti Golani). Her most recent book, *Observing the Observer: Exploring Our Selves in Field Research* (Oxford University Press, 2010) focuses on aging on a kibbutz. With kibbutz member and lecturer Esther Carmel Hakim (Ramat Hashofet), Reinharz has developed a website (Hebrew) entitled *Putting Women on the Map* that indicates towns in Israel named for women and explains who these women are. She has also worked with Kibbutz Mishmar Ha'emek to convert the small cottage (*tsrif*) of Irma Lindheim into a permanent historic site.

Marjorie Strom made aliyah from the United States in 1987. She received her BA from Cornell University and her M.Sc. in agricultural economics from the Faculty of Agriculture of the Hebrew University of Jerusalem. Marjorie was a member of Kibbutz Lotan for ten years and has been a member of Kibbutz Samar since 1997. A scientific editor for the Arava Institute for Environmental Studies, she is married and has three children.

Menachem Topel, member of Kibbutz Mefalsim, is a senior lecturer at the Ashkelon Academic College, senior lecturer at Sapir Academic College, and head of the Social Studies Department at Yad Tabenkin, the Institute for Research on the Kibbutz. His latest studies, some of which are published as book chapters, are focused on kibbutz transformation. His most recent publications are two books in Hebrew: *The New Managers—The Kibbutz Changes Its Ways* and *The Kibbutz on Paths Apart* (with Eliezer Ben-Rafael).

Index

Note: Page numbers in *italics* denote figures or tables.